Springer Series in Agent Technology

Series Editors: T. Ishida   N. Jennings   K. Sycara

Raymond S.T. Lee

Fuzzy-Neuro Approach to Agent Applications

From the AI Perspective to Modern Ontology

With 126 Figures

 Springer

Author

Dr. Raymond S.T. Lee
Hong Kong Polytechnic University
Department of Computing
Hung Hom, Kowloon
Hong Kong/PR China

csstlee@comp.polyu.edu.hk

Series Editors

Professor Toru Ishida
Dept. of Social Informatics
Kyoto University
Yoshida-Honmachi
Kyoto 606-8501, Japan

ishida@i.kyoto-u.ac.jp

Professor Nicholas R. Jennings
Intelligence, Agents Multimedia Group
School of Electronics & Computer Science
University of Southampton
Highfield, Southampton, SO17 1BJ, UK

nrj@ecs.soton.ac.uk

Professor Katia Sycara
The Robotics Institute
Carnegie Mellon University
5000 Forbes Ave., DH 3315
Pittsburgh, PA 15213, USA

katia@cs.cmu.edu

Library of Congress Control Number: 2005935328

ACM Computing Classification (1998): I.2.11, C2.4, F.1, I.2, F4.1, H.5, K.4.4

ISBN-10 3-540-21203-5 Springer Berlin Heidelberg New York
ISBN-13 978-3-540-21203-4 Springer Berlin Heidelberg New York

Springer is a part of Springer Science+Business Media

springeronline.com

© Springer-Verlag Berlin Heidelberg 2006
Printed in Germany

Typeset by the authors using a Springer TEX macro package
Production: LE-TEX Jelonek, Schmidt & Vöckler GbR, Leipzig
Cover design: KünkelLopka Werbeagentur, Heidelberg

Printed on acid-free paper   45/3142/YL - 5 4 3 2 1 0

"Thinking" is the way we ascertain our existence.

"Intuition" is the way we show our differences with Machines.

Raymond Lee, Spring 2004

This book is dedicated to UNICEF and the royalty will be wholly
donated by the author to UNICEF for the
purpose of assisting children
living in poverty to acquire their innate rights for
knowledge and education

*I now want to know all things under the sun, and the moon, too. For
all things are beautiful in themselves, and become more beautiful
when known to man. Knowledge is Life with wings.*

Beloved Prophet, Kahlil Gibran

Preface

"Anything happens must have its own reason". Although I cannot really recall exactly when I heard of this statement for the first time, it is always in my mind and in fact it has been one of the motivations for me to carry out research and study. When I asked myself again about the purpose of writing this book at the time of writing this preface, several "add-on" reasons that had never occurred to me at the start of writing this book in the spring of 2003 surprisingly came up.

Back then, when I was preparing the progress report for the iJADE (2.0) project, a "fuzzy" idea of whether it was feasible to write a book on intelligent agents came to my mind. This book not only would discuss and deal with the theory but also the "spin-off" applications from the iJADE project, including: the iJADE WeatherMan, the iJADE Stock Advisor, the iJADE Surveillant and the latest works on iJADE Negotiator. The fact that I had to launch the iJADE development kit officially over the Web in the summer of 2003 (http://www.ijadk.org) and to arrange courses and seminars to teach and train our undergraduate students to make use of this toolkit further supported the idea and the future use of this book. Hence, the "archetype" of this book emerged.

Different from my previous two books, I started the writing of this book from the second part, the applications of agent technology, instead of writing first the theoretical part. In the course of writing this book I had seriously considered starting with the theoretical concepts of agent technology but I had failed to convince myself of the depth of the concepts that should be discussed in the book. However, after I had started my phase III iJADE project – the Cogito iJADE in the summer of 2003 – such "struggling" had settled down.

The Cogito iJADE project was designed to explore and tackle the "ultimate" problem of agent technology – the ontology of intelligent agents – and focus on the design and construction of highly autonomous, adaptive, self-knowledge ontological agents, and to explore the feasibility of building self-aware agents. This topic is really fascinating in the sense that it not only involves computer science but is also a cross-disciplinary topic involving cognitive science, human psychology, philosophy and metaphysics. In fact, ontology itself is one of the major topics in modern philosophy.

After writing Chaps. 5–9 in July 2003, I immediately started to plan for the integration of Modern Ontology and Ontological Agents as discussed in Chap. 11 of this book. My research into ontology which had started in the mid-2001 had caused a substantial change in my views of AI. In the couple of years of literature reviews and research on ontology, I had the opportunity to "refresh" and "trigger" my thoughts and knowledge on philosophy and epistemology, subjects I had studied in college about 10 years ago. I have to acknowledge that the great thoughts from all the distinguished philosophers – including Plato, Aristotle, Berkeley, Hume, Descartes, Kant, Russell and Wittgenstein – had given me fresh inspiration and new ideas that helped me to consolidate the concepts and theories of AI and human intelligence and to form a solid foundation for the theories of intelligent agents and their ontological aspects.

Different from most of the other contemporary books on agent technologies, ranging from discussions on mobile agents to elaborations of multi-agent systems, this book is totally focused on the theory, the design and implementation of intelligent agents and their corresponding systems. One important feature of this book is that I provide a "structural" discussion on all critical theoretical bases for the understanding of intelligent agents. This book begins with a discussion of the theories of human intelligence and is followed by an overview of research on artificial intelligence and the theories for the development of intelligent agents and agent-based systems. The fact is I strongly believe that AI (including agent technologies) should be closely related to the exploration of the human mind and intelligence, which is in turn a highly complex and critical topic, not only related to computer science but also to cognitive science, neurophysiology, psychology, neuroscience, mathematical science and philosophy. As you will see in the book, my philosophical beliefs and ideas on human knowledge, intelligence and ontology have been strongly influenced by Kant and Russell – the two most influential philosophers in the history of mankind. Also, my religious belief in Zen Buddhism gives me a great deal of inspiration.

As one will see in Chaps. 2 and 3, most of the critical theories of AI and agent technologies are strongly related to the research and study in these disciplines, especially in the topics that relate to the fundamental concepts of AI and the latest development of intelligent agents, ontological agents. Generally speaking, all these basic theories and researches on ontological agents basically originate from the philosophical study of ontology and epistemology. As a matter of fact, my Unification Theory of Senses and Experiences and the fundamental idea of the Cognitron Theory were also inspired by the great thoughts of those distinguished philosophers and ontologists.

Last but not least, one of the major purposes of writing this book was to provoke my belief that current AI (and agent technologies) should not be limited to research and development in computer science but rather should involve an "alliance" across many different disciplines and faculties. I strongly believe that the contributions in this area should not only benefit academia and industry but also the wider community and all mankind in future! I hope that this *tiny book* can trigger more *great thoughts* on the exploration of human and machine intelligence.

Acknowledgments

I took over a year to write and finish this book and would like to express my thanks to the following people for their support and assistance.

To my wife Iris for her patience, encouragement and understanding, especially during my days and nights working on the book writing in the past year.

To Ms. Ingeborg Mayer, Springer Associate Editor, for her support and encouraging comments and advice.

To Mr. Martin Kyle of the Department of Computing, Hong Kong Polytechnic University for his patience and help in proofreading this book.

To Mr. Herman Ho, my father-in-law, for his support and patience in proofreading the book.

To Alex, Gary, Tony and Toby, my lovely research students, for their help and assistance in the development of iJADK and all the online tutorials.

To the Department of Computing, Hong Kong Polytechnic University for providing support, RCG grants for the iJADE Surveillant project (B-Q569) and the CORN project (G-T850) and Department Research Grants for the iJADE project (Z042); and for the provision of an excellent environment and facilities for conducting the experimental tests and system evaluations.

Last but not least, to all my colleagues in the iJADE development team, including Dr. James Liu, Prof. Keith Chan, Dr. Hareton Leung and Dr. Jane You, for their fruitful academic advice and stimulating discussions.

I am certain that without all the above supports and assistance, the publication of this book would not have been successful.

Spring 2004   Raymond Lee
Hong Kong Polytechnic University

Contents

1 Introduction

There is no rational life, therefore, without intelligence, and things are good only in so far as they assist men to enjoy that life of the mind which is determined by intelligence. Those things alone, on the other hand, we call evil which hinder man from perfecting his reason and enjoying a rational life.

Baruch Spinoza

1.1 The Coming of the Age of Intelligent Agents

Imagine one day you (Jack) arrive at work, switch on your computer and hear a pleasant voice from your personal assistant, Janet:

Janet: *Good morning sir, can you look at the web camera and let me have a check for authentication, please?*

Jack: *Of course (glimpses at the web cam with a smiling face).*
(After a couple of seconds ...)

Janet: *Hi, Jack! Good morning to you. You look terrific today. What makes you so happy?*

Jack: *My best friend George and his family will come to stay with us for a week. I was thinking of where to take them for dinner when they arrive. Do you have any suggestions?*

Janet: *Sure, let me think .... Maybe you can try Ichikawa, the Japanese restaurant not far from our office. Some other PAs told me that they serve excellent food. What do you think?*

Jack: *Sounds good, could you book a table for five at 7:00 pm? By the way, is there anything urgent to handle today?*

Janet: Nothing particularly urgent. But you will have a weekly morning briefing with all marketing staff at 10 am in Conference Room 1. I sent voice reminders to them five minutes ago. Also, there will be two meetings in the afternoon, all the related information can be found in your e-tray.

Jack: That's good. How about the deal with our supplier, B&L?

Janet: According to the baselines you gave me yesterday, I had a long negotiation with Tom – their representative agent – for over half an hour. They are seriously considering our counter-offer, and I think the deal is close to completion. Tom will call me later today. By the way, a non-smoking table has been reserved for dinner tonight. A non-smoking table – is that right? Also, the weather may change later today due to a rainstorm approaching Hong Kong, please remember to take an umbrella.

Jack: Thanks Janet. You're great. Let's talk about the strategy for another deal with Jackson International for the afternoon meeting. Do you have any suggestions?

Janet: Let me think ...

Of course, Janet is not a human being, but rather a PA intelligent agent. All of the above events seem to be science fiction, but, technically, they are not. Agent technology (a spin-off of AI technology) seeks to provide all kinds of assistance, not only for business, but also in our daily lives as well.

Starting from the mid-1990s, scientists have tried to build intelligent software objects or devices (what we call *intelligent agents*) that can mimic human intellectual behavior for the purposes of problem solving, scheduling, data mining and generally assisting humans in all of their activities. In the past few years, the developers of agents have implemented various agent systems (Murch and Johnson, 1998), ranging from Auction-Bot for e-auction to our own iJADE Web Miner for intelligent web mining.

However, most of the textbooks and technical references in this field are either too technical and focused only on the technical implementation of agent technology (Bigus 2001) (i.e., without detailed discussions and elaborations of the core AI technologies being adopted in the field of intelligent agents), or are too "application-oriented", i.e., they are focused too much on the introduction of different kinds of contemporary agent-based systems, and lack complete explanations and discussions of the design and implementation of intelligent agents. Other research-oriented textbooks and references (Weiss 2000; Jain et al. 2002) do provide details on the design and implementation of contemporary agent-based systems and applications; however, the lack of descriptions of the basic concepts and theory of intelligent agents defeats the research students and college students who would like to learn this new and interesting technology from scratch.

Some classical AI books, such as the remarkable book written by Russell and Norvig (Russell and Norvig 2003), do provide some introductory discussion on agent technology, but these AI books are mainly focused on the description of the classical AI technology (what we call "macroscopic AI"), including predicate logics, logical reasoning, expert systems, rule-based and frame-based AI systems, and so on. However, the main "theme" AI techniques (the so-called *microscopic AI*) such as artificial neural networks, genetic algorithms, fuzzy logics and other advance techniques, such as chaos theory, are never touched upon, let alone the descriptions of the basic concepts and architectures of intelligent agents (both the conceptual and implementation models) and the contemporary R&D of agent-based systems.

In the above scenario agent Janet demonstrates the typical *intellectual activities* that an intelligent agent (IA) might possess, and such intellectual activities include: natural language processing (NLP) skills, negotiation skills, forecasting skills, planning & scheduling skills, and data-mining and knowledge acquisition skills (from her "memory" and "experience"). Of course, "high-level" intelligent agents also possess the skills of adaptive learning and decision making.

As one can see in the above example, most of the so-called *intellectual activities* of the intelligent agents involve highly uncertain (so-called *fuzzy*) and sometime even *chaotic* reasoning and decision making. Typical examples can be found in multi-agent negotiations, severe weather (such as rainstorm) prediction, active vision and invariant face recognition (for automatic user authentication), etc. These can be tackled by applying fuzzy-neuro machine learning and reasoning techniques – one of the feverish topics in contemporary AI, and also one of the main focuses of this book.

Most AI books on intelligent agents are focused mainly on the design and implementation of agent applications, but the fundamental theory, definition and classification of intelligent agents are seldom touched upon. The development and fundamental theory of intelligent agents are closely related to AI, and the human exploration and interpretation of intelligence is a cross-discipline topic involving neuroscience, neurophysiology, cognitive science and even modern philosophy. Moreover, the latest research and development in intelligent agents – the design and implementation of ontological agents (OAs) – is itself a typical topic in the field of modern ontology, one of the major branches of modern philosophy and epistemology. All of these *"critical masses"* of agent technology are also covered in this book.

The main objectives of this book are:

1. To provide complete and detailed interpretations and explanations of the concepts and theories of intelligent agents, AI and the search (and research) for human intelligence in terms of computer science, cognitive science, neuroscience, neurophysiology and philosophy.
2. To provide a complete discussion on the design and development models of intelligent agents, and the major requirements and main features of intelligent agents.
3. To discuss different types of agent-based systems.
4. To discuss the major and contemporary AI techniques for the design and implementation of intelligent agents.
5. To provide technical details for the design and implementation of intelligent agents and agent-based systems using iJADK.
6. To discuss the latest research and development of intelligent agents, including the adoption of modern ontology and the concepts, design and implementation of ontology agents.

1.2 The Structure of This Book

For ease of reading, understanding and concept development, the book is organized into two main sections, namely:

Part I: Intelligent Agents – Concepts and Theories

Part II: Applications of Intelligent Agents Using iJADK

Part I is the introductory section, which focuses on the basic concepts and theories of intelligent agents. It discusses the major requirements and main features of an intelligent agent, and contrasts the differences between intelligent agents and other related technologies such as multi-agents, mobile-agents and distributed computing. It also discusses the major and contemporary AI techniques for the design and construction of intelligent agents, especially the fuzzy-neuro and chaotic-neuro AI techniques for agent development.

Part II focuses on the design and implementation of intelligent agents using the iJADK agent development kit. For ease of illustration in the book, the author has chosen five of his latest iJADE applications: iJADE Shopper, iJADE WeatherMan, iJADE Stock Advisor, iJADE Surveillant and iJADE Negotiator. At the end of this part, the author also discusses the latest research in agent technology – the design and development of ontology agents – a fascinating topic originated from modern ontology, a topic which has drawn the interest of scientists, philosophers and scholars for centuries. In order to provide readers with an in-depth introductory knowledge about this interesting doctrine, this part begins with the history and overview of ontology, especially the philosophical views and ideas from classical philosophy to modern ontology. It discusses the contemporary works and standards of ontology agents and the agent platforms being developed in recent years, and the future development of intelligent agents and related research works to be undertaken.

It is anticipated that this book will not only provide a complete reference and textbook of intelligent agents, but will also serve as a technical and implementation guidebook for the design and implementation of agent-based systems, as well as vital literature for ongoing research in this field.

1.3 Outline of Each Chapter

Chapter 1: Introduction

This is an introductory chapter of the book which gives a general overview of intelligent agents. This chapter gives a brief overview of the organization of the book, the main focus of each section and a roadmap of reading for different categories of readers.

Part I: Intelligent Agents – Concepts and Theories
Chapter 2: The Search for Human Intelligence

This chapter gives an in-depth discussion on the "source" of artificial intelligence (AI) and intelligent agents (IAs), i.e., human intelligence, a foundation research topic which has been developed for over thousands of years, starting with the Age of the Ancient Greeks, and developed by distinguished philosophers including Plato, Aristotle, Descartes, Kant, etc. In this chapter, the author presents a thorough, cross-discipline exploration of this fascinating topic, ranging from the key philosophical schools of thought of human knowledge and intelligence to the contemporary theories and studies on human intelligence in the areas of psychology, cognitive psychology, neuroscience and neurophysiology.

The author also presents his latest theory on intelligence and knowledge – the Unification Theory of Senses and Experience – which provides the foundation works of the latest research on modern ontology and ontological agents.

Chapter 3: From AI to IA – The Emergence of Agent Technology

In the first part of this chapter, the author gives an overview of artificial intelligence (AI) and also presents the contemporary AI architecture and discusses the latest research and applications of AI. In the second part of this chapter, the author gives in-depth information on agent technologies. Firstly, the author gives a general definition of intelligent agents, as well as the basic concepts and requirements. Secondly, the author presents the main features and characteristics of intelligent agents. Thirdly, the author discusses the conceptual models for the design and development of agent-based systems. Lastly, the author introduces contemporary agent-based systems, both commercial applications and the latest research and development.

Chapter 4: AI Techniques for Agents Construction

This chapter focuses on the major AI techniques being adopted in the construction of intelligent agents and agent-based systems. It serves as an extension of Chap. 3 for the discussion of key AI modules for the design and construction of contemporary intelligent agents – the Fuzzy-Neuro Intelligent Module. In this chapter, the author presents the detailed AI components of this module, including artificial neural networks, fuzzy logics, genetic algorithms and the contemporary works on chaos theory. The author illustrates how these contemporary AI techniques can be integrated to solve complex AI problems. In particular, besides the fuzzy-neuro intelligent agents discussed in Part II of this book, the author also presents his latest research on the chaotic neural network in this chapter, and discusses how it can be used to simulate human visual intelligence behavior, which forms the foundation work for the latest research on modern ontology and ontology agents.

Part II: Applications of Intelligent Agents Using iJADK

Chapter 5: The Design and Implementation of Intelligent Agent-Based Systems Using iJADK

This chapter focuses on the design and implementation of agent-based systems using iJADK. Firstly, the author gives a general overview of the iJADE framework and some background information. Secondly, the author presents and discusses the iJADE Model (version 2.0), its architecture and the functions of different logical layers. This is followed by the description of the different functional modules in the conscious layer (intelligent layer) of the model, which is summarized in a discussion of the latest developments in and implementations of the iJADE applications.

Chapter 6: iJADE WShopper – Intelligent Mobile Shopping Based on Fuzzy-neuro Shopping Agents

This chapter focuses on the design and implementation of a fuzzy logic-based shopping agent system – iJADE Shopper – which provides intelligent agent-based shopping over Wireless Internet.

In particular, this chapter discusses:
- The design and implementation of iJADE WShopper.
- The system architecture of iJADE WShopper.
- The AI technique being adopted in this agent application (fuzzy-neuro technique).
- The implementation details.
- The experimental results and analysis.
- The latest research and development.

Chapter 7: iJADE WeatherMan – A Weather Forecasting Agent Using Fuzzy Neural Network Models

This chapter focuses on the design and implementation of a fuzzy-neuro based weather forecasting agent, iJADE WeatherMan, which provides an intelligent agent-based weather prediction capability over multiple locations.

In particular, this chapter discusses:
- The major considerations and background on weather prediction, as well as the major obstacles and challenges.
- The design and implementation of iJADE WeatherMan.
- The system architecture of iJADE WeatherMan.
- The AI techniques being adopted in this agent application (fuzzy-neuro – the integration of fuzzy logics with feedforward backpropagation neural networks [FFBPN]).
- The implementation details.
- The experimental results and analysis.
- The latest research and development.

Chapter 8: iJADE Stock Advisor – An Intelligent Agent-Based Stock Prediction System Using Hybrid RBF Recurrent Networks

This chapter focuses on the design and implementation of an intelligent agent-based stock prediction and advisory system based on the hybrid RBF recurrent network (HRBFN) for stock prediction.

   In particular, this chapter discusses:
– The major considerations and background on stock prediction, as well as the major obstacles and challenges.
– The design and implementation of iJADE Stock Advisor.
– The system architecture of iJADE Stock Advisor.
– The AI techniques being adopted in this agent application (HRBFN).
– The implementation details.
– The experimental results and analysis.
– The latest research and development.

Chapter 9: iJADE Surveillant – A Multi-resolution Neural-oscillatory Agent-Based Surveillance System

This chapter focuses on the design and implementation of a fully automatic and multi-resolution agent-based surveillance system – iJADE Surveillance – based on an innovative neuro-oscillatory model for automatic scene segmentation and object recognition. In fact, it is one of the author's latest works for adopting agent technologies for commercial use.

   In particular, this chapter discusses:
– The major considerations and background on the automatic surveillance system, the major obstacles and challenges.
– The design and implementation of iJADE Surveillant.
– The system architecture of iJADE Surveillant.
– The AI techniques being adopted in this agent application.
– The implementation details.
– The experimental results and analysis.
– The latest research and development.

Chapter 10: iJADE Negotiator – An Intelligent Fuzzy Agent-Based Negotiation System for Internet Shopping

This chapter focuses on the design and implementation of intelligent agent-based negotiation agents for Internet shopping. This chapter: (1) presents an innovative negotiation protocol with a data exchange which is not troublesome to set up beforehand and supports highly dynamic and flexible changes in negotiation attributes; (2) integrates fuzzy logic to compute the utility function and apply the most appropriate strategies to maximize profits; and (3) shows the learning ability and cooperation between negotiator agents.

In particular, this chapter discusses:

- The major considerations and background of the contemporary negotiation strategies and systems.
- The design and implementation of iJADE Negotiator.
- The system architecture of iJADE Negotiator.
- The implementation details.
- The experimental results and analysis.
- The latest research and development.

Chapter 11: Future Agent Technologies – Modern Ontology and Ontological Agent Technology (OAT)

This chapter focuses on the latest and future research on intelligent agents – modern ontology and ontology agents. Basically, this chapter is divided into three main sections. Section 11.1 begins with a general introduction of ontology, including the definition of ontology, the history of ontology, the main concerns in modern ontology, the major relationship issues and differences between ontology and epistemology, and how it is related to contemporary AI and agent technology. This section also focuses on the introduction and summarization of the critical thoughts and theories of ontology investigated by major distinguished philosophers and scholars, including Plato, Aristotle, Kant and Russell.

Section 11.2 focuses on modern ontology and how it impacts modern AI and agent technologies. The questions addressed include: What is conceptualism? What are the major differences between conceptualism and other major ontological theories? What are the major features of conceptualization theory? How can modern ontology be adopted into contemporary AI and agent technologies?

Section 11.3 discusses the latest and future R&D of the iJADE system, which includes the design and development of a self-aware, adaptive and ontological agent platform – Cogito iJADE. First of all, it gives a brief overview of the main ontological concept and theory of Cogito iJADE – the "Cognitron Map" – and discusses its basic mechanisms for ontology learning and knowledge updating. At the end of this chapter, the author gives a general summarization of the future development of Cogito iJADE and its Cogito Agents.

1.4 Readers of This Book

This book has a multi-disciplinary focus, targeting a range of reader/student categories including:
- Computer science students who are taking intelligent agent and related courses. This book will serve as their main textbook and reference.
- Research students and research personnel working in the field of AI, intelligent agents and related disciplines. This book will serve as their major technical reference. The advanced topics "Modern Ontology and Ontology Agents" can also serve as literature reviews on the latest developments in agent technology.
- Agent developers and scientists who are using iJADK as their agent development toolkit. In fact, this book will also serve as a technical reference for those wishing to develop intelligent agent-based systems using iJADK. The intelligent agent-based systems discussed in this book were developed using the author's intelligent agent toolkit, iJADK (intelligent Java agent-based development kit) version 2.0 (which can be downloaded free of charge from the iJADK official site http://www.iJADK.org).

1.5 Concluding Remarks

Before ending this introductory chapter, I would like to make one important observation: In the old days we often heard that intelligence (and hence AI) is the investigation and study of the "rational thinking" of human beings. However, the author believes differently, and, in addition to Spinoza's quotation at the beginning this chapter, the author believes that:

The most precious of human intelligence is not only its rational and logical thinking, but rather its irrational, and sometimes "fuzzy" or even "chaotic" reasoning, thinking and decision making. I think the beauty of nature is not only its state of "balance," "harmony" and "completeness" – the state of Prägnanz – but rather it is the "art" and our "act" of handling highly chaotic, fuzzy and even uncertain situations to seek for harmony from the nature of fuzziness and incompleteness.

It is exactly what we (AI workers) should think about for the development of intelligent agents in this millennium.

Part I – **Concepts and Theories**

2 The Search for Human Intelligence

One day, however, I heard someone reading from a book he said was by Anaxagoras, according to which it is, in fact, intelligence that orders and is the reason for everything. Now this was a reason that pleased me; it seemed to me, somehow, to be a good thing that intelligence should be the reason for everything. And I thought that, if that's the case, then intelligence in ordering all things must order them and place each individual thing in the best way possible; so if anyone wanted to find out the reason why each thing comes to be and perishes or exists, this is what he must find out about it: how is the best for that thing to exist, or to act or be acted upon in any way? On this theory, then, a person should consider nothing else, whether in regard to himself or anything else, but the best, the highest good; though the same person must also know the worst, as they are objects of the same knowledge. Reckoning thus, I was pleased to think I'd found, in Anaxagoras, an instructor in the reason for things to suit my own intelligence.

Phaedo (97c-d,) Plato

Artificial Intelligence – AI has been explored by humans for centuries. It not only relates to the field of computer science, but it also relates closely to other disciplines such as psychology, epistemology, neuroscience, neurobiology, neurophysiology, physics and philosophy.

Human Intelligence – The philosophical foundations of AI have been developed for over thousands of years, starting with the Age of the Ancient Greeks by remarkable philosophers such as Plato and Aristotle. In this chapter, we have a cross-disciplinary overview of human intelligence, ranging from the key philosophical thoughts on human intelligence (and knowledge) to the contemporary theories and explorations of human intelligence in the areas of psychology, neurophysiology and neuroscience. The author will also introduce his theory of the MIND Model and the Unification Theory of Senses and Experiences for the exploration of human knowledge and intelligence in the disciplines of philosophy, psychology, cognitive science, neuroscience and neurophysiology.

2.1 What Is Intelligence?

Before we start to explore the territory of artificial intelligence, it is natural and critical for us to have a clear picture and understanding of the following fundamental issues about intelligence:

- What is intelligence?
- What are the main schools of thought and approaches for the study of intelligence?
- How can we interpret and measure intelligence?
- How does our brain work to "facilitate" intelligence?

In fact, to answer even the first question is not an easy task. "Intelligence" (or more precisely the exploration of *human intelligence*) is an important topic, which has different focuses and definitions in different disciplines ranging from general psychology, cognitive psychology to philosophy and epistemology. Amongst the most "representative" and world-wide accepted definitions of human intelligence should be the statement condensed by Gottfredson (1997) that appeared in the editorial of the journal *Intelligence* in 1997 and was signed by 52 distinguished researchers of that century:

Intelligence is a very general mental capability that, among other things, involves the ability to reason, plan, solve problems, think abstractly, comprehend complex ideas, learn quickly and learn from experience. It is not merely book learning, a narrow academic skill, or test taking smarts.

Rather, it reflects a broader and deeper capability for comprehending our surroundings – "catching on", "making sense" of things, or "figuring out" what to do ...

Gottfredson, 1997

From the above definition, it is clear that *intelligence* (or more precisely *human intelligence*) is a highly complex psychological, cognitive and mental activity (and capability) that cannot be evaluated directly by any simple means and tests.

Consider the so-called idiot savants (Smith and Tsimpli 1995). Despite below average general intelligence, all have outstanding (and almost *unbelievable*) talent in specific areas – for example, extraordinary memory capability in numbers and images (e.g., human faces), *automatic* conversion of specific dates in a century into days of the week (with incredible speed), and even instant decryption powers given complex ciphers. It does not appear as if these people need to acquire any prerequisite knowledge and expertise in order to achieve such outstanding performances. However, whether we should call them *intelligent* is subject to debate.

So modern psychology chooses to believe that *intelligence* should be determined and evaluated in term of the mental abilities and capabilities in various aspects including verbal, perceptual, memory capability and manipulation speed. A typical example can be found in the Wechsler Adult Intelligence Scale version III (WASIS-III) test, which involves the evaluation of General Human Intelligence (the so-called g value) in terms of the following aspects (Wechsler 1997):
- Verbal comprehension
- Perceptual organization
- Working memory
- Processing speed

Figure 2.1 depicts the block diagram for the WASIS-III test.

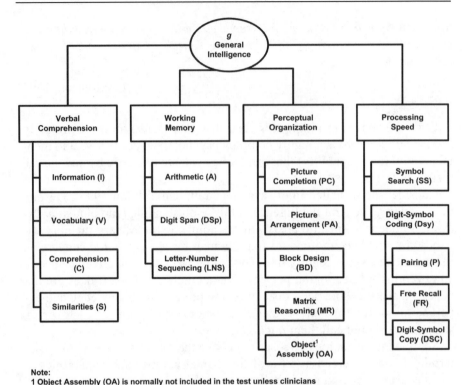

Note:
1 Object Assembly (OA) is normally not included in the test unless clinicians
choose to substitute it for a spoiled performance subset for the subject ages
between 16 to 74.

Fig. 2.1. Block Diagram of the WASIS-III Test (Wechsler 1997)

In the following sections, we will take a look at how different disciplines try to interpret intelligence, and how to understand and seek the solution to the mystery of *human intelligence – the search for human intelligence.*

2.2 The Philosophical View on Intelligence

2.2.1 Introduction – The Search for Intelligence and Ultimate Knowledge

From the beginning of civilization, philosophers have tried their best to have a better understanding of the world and ourselves. They have tried to explore all those fundamental, critical, and yet difficult to answer (and even to comprehend) problems, including the nature of existence, the truth of sensations (and perception), the philosophy of the mind and science, and so on. However, the issue of *intelligence* (or *human intelligence*) cannot be found directly in the major philosophical literature. One plausible explanation is that intelligence itself is not a unitary phenomenon and mental activity, but is rather the complex integration of various *mental components* (such as Howard Gardner's beliefs in multiple intelligence) (Gardner 1983). In other words, although we can hardly find any in-depth interpretation of intelligence from the philosophical point of view, the major components of intelligence – knowledge, self-consciousness, epistemology and the philosophy of the mind – are all fundamental topics in philosophical territory.

In this section, we will explore the most critical component of intelligence – knowledge – and explore how philosophers address this problem.

2.2.2 The Traditional Philosophical View of Knowledge – Belief, Truth and Justification

In our daily lives, we all (consciously) believe that we *know* some things, but don't know some other things. We believe *knowledge* should be something (or some facts and ideas) that can be explained or identified clearly by ourselves. In fact, starting from the Ancient Greek philosophers, there was already a clear definition of knowledge. Plato, in his remarkable work *Thaetetus,* described *knowledge* as "*justified true belief,*" which means something (it can be notions, ideas, facts and subjects) that has sufficient reason(s) to assert that it is truth.

Under this definition, there are basically three kinds of knowledge:
- Belief
- Truth
- Justification

Belief

Belief describes the way we perceive, understand and interpret our (individual) world of experience. It is also the way we *shape* our world of perception and existence. From the philosophical point of view, our world of experience is a totally *private matter* to each individual. More importantly, philosophers have told us that all the existence of so-called *external objects and matters* that appear in our world of experience is solely dependent on our own belief (Connor and Robb 2003). To a certain extent, what we can barely be sure about might be our own existence, as Descartes said in his remarkable work *Meditation* (Clarke 1998) with the phrase *Cogito,* *ergo sum* (I think, therefore I am). In fact, some philosophers query solely on this statement (Sartre 1965).

Truth

Truth is the *accurate* description of our world of experience. It *appears* when *belief* can *faithfully* describe the true appearance and nature of matter, such that we can believe it to be *real*. In other words, a particular matter is claimed to be an *untruth* (*falsity*) when belief cannot accurately describe the true appearance or the nature of that particular matter. This definition of *truth* (and *falsity*) is widely accepted in the various doctrines of philosophy, and the only difference is the standard to define what is truth (and what is falsity), and how to interpret *the accuracy used to describe the world of experience*.

There are basically three prevailing theories of truth: (1) the Correspondence Theory of Truth; (2) the Coherence Theory of Truth; and (3) the Pragmatic Theory of Truth. The Correspondence Theory focuses on the relation (and association) between the truth of the subject matter (which can be a proposition, a belief or a judgment) and that which makes it true (which can be a fact, a state of affairs or events). For idealists who refuse the independent existence of matters (and notions), they choose to believe that truth is the coherence between beliefs – the Coherence Theory of Truth. For example, the belief that *"walls must exist in a room"* is truth according to the Coherence Theory, mainly due to the fact that this belief is consistent (and coherent) to what you have seen, what you touch and what you remember in all your past experiences, without any conflicts. The Pragmatic Theory of Truth maintains that the truth of any beliefs, facts and notions are mainly due to their pragmatism (i.e., their practical values). The main logic behind this theory is rather straightforward: we believe something to be truth only when that belief has its own practical value(s) for us to achieve our target, or the thing we want. For instance, we believe the existence of *"electricity"* as a truth notion mainly because we can "see" the effect of electricity in driving a fan, lighting lights or showing pictures on the television.

Justification

Even if we have a particular belief, or we have to ascertain that belief to be truth, the situation is not sufficient for us to gain knowledge. The reason is, we still need another critical component – *justification* of the belief to be truth. In fact, the reason behind this is quite obvious: one always needs an effective method to justify his/her belief to be truth or falsity. In other words, *justification* is the tool and reason to prove (or disprove) one's belief and notion. Let's take a look at our daily lives: Every day we use most of our time (and try very hard indeed) to ascertain our beliefs, notions and judgments to be truth (which we called *knowledge*), and indeed we need to find the evidence(s) to justify that these beliefs (and notions) are truths. For instance, if one can tell tomorrow's weather only by simple guesswork and luckily it happens to be truth, we cannot still say that this "prediction" for the day after is truth as well, mainly because we do not have good reason to *justify* this belief to be truth. However, if one has sufficient *knowledge* (e.g., the prediction is done by a meteorologist with sufficient information and prediction algorithms) we will then have a good reason to ascertain that prediction (and belief) to be truth. In other words, *knowledge* is both the condition and the reason for one to make a truth judgment, and justification is the tool (and channel) to prove a particular belief to be truth.

For a thorough overview of the traditional beliefs on the components of knowledge, please refer to the remarkable works by Doren (1991) and Audi (1998).

2.2.3 Rational Versus Empirical View of Knowledge

Rationalism and empiricism – the two major historic controversies in philosophy – hold totally different views on the interpretation of knowledge. In this section, we take a look at their controversial views of knowledge, and how these theories affect the philosophical view of knowledge in history.

Rationalism

The most remarkable rationalists in history, including Rene Descartes (1596–1650), Benedictus de Spinoza (1632–1677) and Gottfried Wilhelm Leibniz (1646–1716), maintained that knowledge must be absolutely ascertained, and this knowledge must come with sufficient rationale (of fundamental reasons). They also believed that *deductive argument* is the most critical method to attain "truth" knowledge. Typical examples are the mathematical proofs of new theories in geometrical mathematics. Under these theories, generally speaking, all knowledge can be deducted by some basic knowledge (and beliefs). But the question is: How can we prove (and deduce) the truth of the most basic knowledge, beliefs and principles? It is clear that all these logical principles are just "*made known*" to us and cannot themselves be proven by experience, as all possible proofs must presuppose them. So, in addition to what we know by experience, rationalists also believe in the existence of *innate notions* and *innate principles*, which are known to exist independently from experience. Under this point of view, rationalists are "smart enough" to avoid this paradox and simply admit the truth of the existence of these innate principles and beliefs.

This theory seems to be *"reasonable enough"* to explain the attainment of knowledge, but it leaves one final (and the most fundamental) problem: Where did these are *innate* notions and principles come from? Rationalists like Descartes and Leibniz had no choice but to maintain that these basic principles and ideas are *innate* in the sense that they are all borne in *every* mind when we were born – as the rationalists claimed *"they are part of our spirit."* One interesting question: Does it mean that we can *manipulate* these principles and ideas *automatically* after we are born? From the rationalist point of view, the existence of these innate ideas and principles does not mean that they can be *used* by us automatically, as they must be *triggered* and *activated* by some external stimuli (e.g., our five senses).

Empiricism

Distinguished empiricists, including John Locke (1632–1704), George Berkeley (1685–1753) and David Hume (1711–1776), maintained that sources of knowledge are derived from either: (1) sense perception; (2) inner perception; or (3) experience. As opposed to rationalists, empiricists do not believe in the existence of innate knowledge and principles. They believe that our spiritual mind originates from a *"blank tablet"* (Berkeley 1710; Locke 1690; Hume 1739), and all our knowledge and experience are just "traces of notion" due to the senses and perceptions.

This theory not only affects the understanding of the source of all our ideas and notions, it also explains the way we attain new knowledge. Locke in *An Essay Concerning Human Understanding (1690)* maintained that the coherence between our inner perception and outside matters (that exist independently) *triggers us* to attain the truth of beliefs and knowledge. Berkeley (1710) denied the *truth existence* of any matters upon (and outside) our beliefs; however, he still believed that we can still learn and attain these *outside* beliefs (facts and notions). Hume in his *An Enquiry Concerning Human Understanding (1739)*, even queried the truth of the knowledge, and believed that we had no way to perceive and recognize any truth of beliefs and notions!

Nevertheless, empiricists do not deny that we have the ability to prove and justify the ideas and notions we have. For example, we can still process the proof of mathematical knowledge, and we can even generate some new knowledge of them. However, these ideas (and notions) must *truly correspond* to their appearances in the outside world if they are to lead us to produce new knowledge. That is the main reason why empiricists so insisted on the fact that all ideas must come from senses and perceptions (or the *reflections* of these notions from the *outside world*).

The Search for Priori Knowledge

Priori knowledge is a kind of knowledge which does not (and in fact cannot) rely on sense perception to justify its truth and existence. In other words, we need another *"channel"* (of understanding and perception) to attain this kind of knowledge. In fact, there are many cases of priori knowledge that are being attained and used by us in our daily lives. The most critical example of priori knowledge is our knowledge of basic mathematics. For example, the *knowledge* of *"one plus two is three"* does not come from our sense perception, even though we have seen the instance of *"one object adding to two other objects will become three objects,"* and the notion (and knowledge) of *"one plus two is three"* will still be truth. But the problem is twofold: (1) How can we know (and learn) priori knowledge, if it cannot be derived and deduced by any substances and notions? And (2) Can priori knowledge give us a better understanding of the truth of our world of perception?

Rationalism and empiricism hold totally different views and interpretations of priori knowledge. Rationalists believe that all our knowledge ultimately came (and originated) from priori knowledge. They maintain that we make use of the so-called *"light of reason"* or *"rational intuition"* to understand and attain these knowledge. Empiricists, on the other hand, insist that all our knowledge can be attained by deduction and derivation, and even priori knowledge like basic arithmetic and geometrical mathematics cannot "escape" from this territory. They believe that no matter how *abstract* the idea (and knowledge) is, it must be justified and must correspond to the sense perception before we claim that it is truth knowledge. However, even if it is true, the empiricists still cannot explain how we can attain the (universal) truth of this priori knowledge if this knowledge just comes from the sense perception from our world of experience (McInerney 1990).

In the next section, we will investigate how Kant addressed this question in his remarkable work *Critique of Pure Reason (1781)* using a so-called "colored-spectacles" analog.

2.2.4 Kant's Critique of Pure Reason and the Theory of Knowledge

Immanuel Kant (1724–1804) is celebrated the most influential and important philosopher in modern philosophy. In his most remarkable work *The Critique of Pure Reason*, he tried to explore the *"limits of knowledge"* and stated an important claim that:

The limits of knowledge therefore coincide with the limits of experience: what can be known is what can be experienced, and what cannot be experienced cannot be known...

Critique of Pure Reason, Immanuel Kant, 1781

In fact, it is quite impossible to present all the related works and beliefs of Kant in the territory of *knowledge* in this tiny section. But it is critical for us to have a general overview of the great work of Kant's structure of the Critique of Pure Reason, his ideas on priori knowledge, which are all *critical masses* for one to start the study of knowledge and the source of intelligence.

Kant's Critique of Pure Reason

Kant did not strictly follow that Newtonian science provides a complete *"solution"* of reality. Rather, he believed in Leibnizian rationalism that "Natural science is not self-sufficient to explain everything, but requires metaphysics as support. Metaphysics, in turn provides necessary evidences to explain the knowledge of nature." He proposed that cognition is categorized into two main aspects: sensibility and intellect. Sensibility includes all the *sensible objects* of the world in space and time; and it is being nothing but subjective forms of sensibility. Intellect includes all nonsensible, intelligible objects. Kant also split *intellect* into two separate powers: *understanding* and *reasoning*. Under this theory, *reason* is competent to know things lying within the bounds of our sense of experience, but not to know anything lying "outside" them (Gardner 1999).

In Kant's *Critique of Pure Reason*, *critique* does not simply mean the denial and the disproof of all events, but rather it means a critical reasoning (and enquiry), its result can be positive or negative. *Pure* is a technical term defined by Kant as "not containing anything derived from our sense of experience"; in fact, it is an important and fundamental concept in his exploration of priori knowledge. *Reason* is another technical term defined by Kant as "conceptual elements in cognition which we bring to experience and also which are not derived from it" – in other words, it means the *priori* concepts and notions. So, the *Critique for Pure Reason* should be interpreted as the critical enquiry (and reasoning) according to one's mental knowledge to know anything by employing our reason in isolation, in particular, without *interference* from our sense of experience (Gardner 1999).

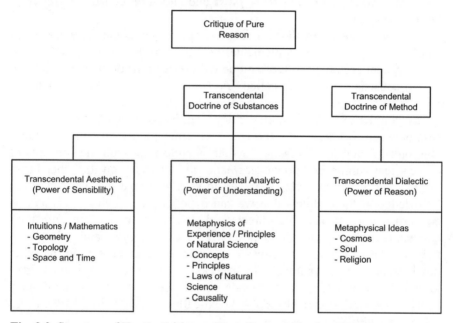

Fig. 2.2. Structure of Kant's Critique of Pure Reason (Gardner 1999)

In summary, the structure of Kant's Critique of Pure Reason consists of three main divisions: transcendental aesthetic, transcendental analytic, and transcendental dialectic (Fig. 2.2). Each corresponds to a different cognitive power or faculty, and a different area of presumptive knowledge, as clearly concluded by Gardner (1999):

Aesthetic – concerned with what Kant in his dissertation called the "power of sensibility," and with mathematics, inclusive of geometry. It also involves all those fundamental *pre-scientific* propositions about space and time.

Analytic – concerned with the power of understanding, the metaphysics of experience and natural science.

Dialectic – concerned with the power of reason (a narrow sense of reason), and with the transcendent metaphysics, which is further divided into three doctrines: rational psychology (the metaphysics of the soul); rational cosmology (the metaphysics of the world); and rational theology (the metaphysics of God).

These three major doctrines are grouped together as the *Transcendental Doctrine of Elements* as each doctrine is concerned with an "*element*" of cognition. *Aesthetic* constitutes the *intuitions*; *analytic* constitutes the *concepts and their associated principles*; and *dialectic* constitutes *ideas* (a kind of concept).

The other major (but shorter) division of doctrine is the *Transcendental Doctrine of Method* – a supplementary doctrine of the epistemological and metaphysical argument of the critique with reflections on its methodology. It also consists of a section called *The Canon of Pure Reason*, which is a pointer towards the rest of Kant's critical system.

In a simpler organization, the Critique can be conceptualized as the division between *Aesthetic and Analytic* – which is concerned with the knowable objects, and the *Dialectic* – which is concerned with the concepts of objects that cannot be known. *Aesthetic and Analytic*, on the other hand, are positive in nature, which is used to seek to prove that we can attain knowledge of those things that we can experience, for which *Aesthetic* is concerned with all sensible objects and *Analytic* is concerned with their conceptual aspects, including the concepts of *substance* and *causality* – they are the so-called *Metaphysics of Experience*. *Dialectic*, on the other hand, is negative in nature, which seeks to prove that we cannot have knowledge of anything at all outside experience. It denies any legitimacy to the other kind of metaphysics – the so-called *Transcendent Metaphysics* (Gardner 1999; Kant 1781).

Kant's *Critique of Pure Reason* not only provides a clear and structural framework for us in metaphysics; it also provides us with a clear picture and direction to explore the truth of knowledge and the exploration of ultimate intelligence.

Kant's Theory of Priori Knowledge

One of the major contributions of Kant was his interpretation of priori knowledge. He maintained that we (humans) have the capability to attain priori knowledge and to ascertain the (universal) truth of this ultimate knowledge, even applied to the physical world. Kant's interpretation of *priori knowledge* is our *mindful explanation* of the substances (things, facts, notions and ideas) that *appear* in the *outside world*. His major breakthrough is that he believed that during our mental process (e.g., thinking and perception), we *automatically* manipulate all the fundamental entities including space, time, logics, numbers, and substances (of matters) together with *causation* to achieve our goal.

From a layperson's point of view, this idea is quite *weird* as we normally believe that we are all living and exist in the universe (*outside* environment) of *space* and *time*, which exists independently from our own existence. Kant even stressed that all these substances (space, time, etc.) are only *features* and *reflections* of our mind, rather than something existing independently. These substances seem to exist independently only because we make use of them to perceive the *outside world*. Kant used the "*colored-spectacles*" paradox to illustrate his idea: When we wear *colored-spectacles* (say red in color) to view the world, all the matter and substances appearing in the world will turn red in color. Does it mean all the substances and matters in the world are *red* in color? Of course, we know it is not the truth. The only reason for us to have this wrong *perception* is because we are wearing a pair of "colored-spectacles" to view the world. A more in-depth interpretation of this analogy is: The reason why the appearance (i.e., color in this case) of all the substances we see through these spectacles are so *coherent* (although this might be false) is that we "*make use*" of these spectacles to view the world. Based on this simple analogy, Kant told us that we are all living in a *physical world* with our *self-created space*, *time*, and *causation* frames of reference. So all the substances and matter appearing in our perception (sense and mental activities) cannot escape but just *nicely follow* and *cohere* with these preset models.

Based on this innovative theory, Kant, in his *Critique of Pure Reason,* gave a very good explanation of "*How priori knowledge can be accepted universally in all instances that happen in the physical world*" – a question that had puzzled philosophers for years! His explanation is that if we take Euclidean geometry as an example of priori knowledge, if we can prove that the summation of the three internal angles within a triangle is 180 degrees, then we can make a claim that all the triangles appearing in the universe should have this property. Kant maintained that geometry is the most typical case where we *manipulate* our mind on the concepts and ideas of the space domain. He stressed that we can accurately handle the space of geometry mainly because it is part of our mind. Under Kant's "*spectacles*" analogy, we are all "*wearing*" the "*spatial-spectacle*" to perceive and comprehend the world of geometry. So all the truth knowledge we attain through this "*spatial-spectacle*" must be *universal* truth and coherence.

In fact, Kant's breakthrough idea on the priori knowledge had an influential impact on the study of metaphysics, epistemology and modern ontology. It is also the cornerstone for the philosophical development of the Unification Theory (Lee 2004b).

For a thorough overview of Kant's philosophical work on the *Critique of Pure Reason*, please see the remarkable translations (with author's interpretations) from Politis and Gardner (1999). For other selected writings of Kant, such as *Critique Reason, Critique of Judgment* and *Fundamental Principles of the Metaphysics of Morals,* Wood's work (Wood 2001) is a perfect place to start.

2.2.5 Russell's View of Knowledge

Bertrand Russell (1872–1970) – one of the greatest philosophers of the twentieth century – did a great deal of work on the exploration of truth and the origin of knowledge. In his work *The Problems of Philosophy* (Russell 1912), he declared that there are two kinds of knowledge: the *Knowledge of Things* and the *Knowledge of Truths.* The *Knowledge of Things* represents the truth appearance of the so-called *physical* substances, which is *spatial* but *temporal* in nature, whereas the *Knowledge of Truths* represents the truth of the so-called *abstract ideas*, what Russell called *notions*, which is in turn *nonspatial* but *atemporal* in nature.

Russell further categorized the *Knowledge of Things* into two main types: (1) *Knowledge by Acquaintance*, and (2) *Knowledge by Description*. *Knowledge by Acquaintance* represents all the substances that we perceive *directly* without any intermediary process of inference or knowledge of truths. *Knowledge by Description*, on the other hand, cannot be directly acquired solely through our senses, but rather it needs some "*add-on*" descriptions and knowledge for declaration. For example, for the desk in front of us, the color of the desk is something (knowledge) that can be directly acquired by acquaintance (in this case, through our senses). However, recognizing that the desk in front of us as is "*really a desk*" requires add-on descriptions and conditions of knowledge (for example, a desk should have a table top, four legs, etc.).

Owing to the different sources of origins, every single concept and knowledge in our world of perception has its own nature, persistence and characteristics. According to his view of knowledge, Russell further divided the nature of the generation of knowledge into two main categories: (1) *derived knowledge*, knowledge that comes from either deduction or induction from other *primitive knowledge*; and (2) *intuitive knowledge*, knowledge that is *innate* with our existence, the so-called *priori knowledge* in Kant's view.

Russell's views had tremendous influence in the contemporary philosophy, and he also had an impact on other disciplines, including psychology of human intelligence and modern ontology. For the implications for the psychology of human intelligence and knowledge interpretation, in the next section we briefly go through the "*Cognitive-Scientific View on Intel-*

ligence", and in Chap. 11 we look at modern ontology and the future of intelligent agents.

2.2.6 Krishnamurti's *The Awakening of Intelligence* – Thought Versus Intelligence

In the final section on selected works on the philosophical study of knowledge (and hence intelligence), the author would like to elaborate on the philosophical ideas of J. Krishnamurti (1895–1986) – a world-renowned philosopher who dedicated over 50 years to critical philosophical topics, including: fear, conflicts, religious experiences, self-knowledge, and, most importantly, intelligence. In this section, the author will extract the key philosophical ideas of intelligence from one of Krishnamurti's remarkable works, *The Awakening of Intelligence* (Krishnamurti 1973).

Unlike most people who think that *intelligence* is a kind of (high-level) *mental activity*, Krishnamurti maintained that *thought* is of the order of *time*, while *intelligence* is of a totally different order, one *independent of time*. Instead of saying that thought is a kind of mental activity of intelligence, Krishnamurti stressed that thought should rather function as the "*pointer*" to intelligence. He also believed that thought (not intelligence) dominates the world, while intelligence has very little place here. For the exploration of the source of intelligence, Krishnamurti added that thought, matter and intelligence have the same source – *energy*. However, thought is confused, polluted and fragments itself, while intelligence is *bright* and *clear* – without any *contamination*.

Remarks on Krishnamurti's Theory of Thought and Intelligence

Krishnamurti actually gave an interesting description and interpretation of intelligence. His theory on *Thought Versus Intelligence* is quite close to the Buddhist theory of *Buddhata* (meaning *Enlightenment*). In Buddhism's point of view, our *truth intelligence* is something that is possessed by every human being, it is *pure* and *uncontaminated* (by our mind). Very few people in history have so far achieved *enlightenment* and rediscovered the *ultimate intelligence* because our minds are always covered (and deceived) by the so-called *Three Ailments*: Lobha, lust; Dosa, anger; and Moha, ignorance (Prajnaparamita Hrdaya Sutra).

As Krishnamurti stated in his work:

"What I am trying to convey is that the desire for this intelligence, through time, has created this image of God. And through the image of God, Jesus,

Krishna, or whatever it is, by having faith in that – which is still the movement of thought – one hopes that there will be harmony in one's life."

"On Intelligence", *The Awakening of Intelligence*, J. Krishnamurti

2.2.7 Lee's Theory on Knowledge and Intelligence – The Unification Theory of Senses and Experiences

Inspiration from Kant's Theory

If Kant's theory in the *Critique of Pure Reason* says that we are all living in the perceived world, in the sense that all our sensory perceptions and thoughts are *confined* and *filtered* by our own "*colored-spectacles*" of the *space-time relationship*, we can make a claim one step further by saying that:

"All our senses and experiences, together with thoughts and memories, are of the same nature "stored" in our mind. The only reason that we "feel" that each of them is of a different nature and of different characteristics is mainly because our mind always "wants" to make them unique such that we will believe that they are all "truth" substance perceived from reality."

Unification Theory of Senses and Experiences, Raymond Lee

Although this seems a bit "bizarre", one will find that this Unification Theory can provide a simple solution to some key psychological paradoxes and problems in visual intelligence and mental activities, as discussed in the next section, Lee's Unification Theory of Senses and Experiences (Unification Theory for short), where the cornerstone of the Unification Theory – the MIND Model for the interpretation and structure of knowledge – will also be discussed.

Lee's Unification Theory of Senses and Experiences – The Framework of Intelligence

As an extension and integration of the contemporary beliefs on intelligence and knowledge from various disciplines, including philosophy, cognitive psychology, neuroscience and AI, the author proposed a new model and theory of intelligence called the *Unification Theory of Senses and Experience* (Lee 2004b) in early 2004. The main focus and objective of this theory is to tackle three basic problems: (1) in view of the paradox and observations existing in the exploration truth of knowledge, matter and notions (as stressed by Kant, Russell and other distinguished philosophers), the Unification Theory tries to propose a possible solution to interpret all these major issues; (2) by integrating and extending the philosophical thoughts of Kant, Russell, Krishnamurti and other remarkable philosophers, the Unification Theory tries to propose a new interpretation of intelligence; and (3) with the adoption of the current findings and research on neuroscience and neurophysiology on the exploration of the relationship between neuronal activities and knowledge, memories and perception processes – especially in the area of the chaotic behavior of brain waves – the Unification Theory tries to provide a physical meaning, and, more importantly, a neurodynamics interpretation of knowledge, mind and intelligence, something that has puzzled neuroscientists and philosophers. More importantly, as presented in Chap. 11, Modern Ontology, the author introduces the latest works on the implementation of ontology-based and self-aware intelligent agents and robot systems.

The core of the author's *Unification Theory of Senses and Experiences* is the Framework of Intelligence, as shown in Fig. 2.3.

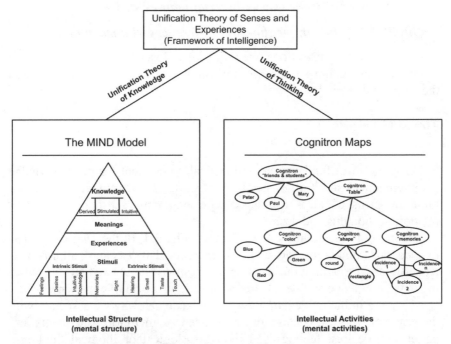

Fig. 2.3. The Framework of Intelligence – Unification Theory of Senses and Experiences (Lee 2004b)

Based on this theory, *Intelligence* is interpreted not only as the collection of our mental activities, as mentioned by the cognitive scientists, nor only as the high-level *"mystery"* of existence, as maintained by Krishnamurti's theory of Intelligence, but, in fact, *intelligence* is the integration of: (1) the *intellectual structure*, which describes the so-called *mental structure* (or what we called *knowledge* in layperson's terms); and (2) the *intellectual activities*, which describes the so-called *mental activities* (or what we call *thoughts* in layperson's terms).

What the Unification Theory would like to point out is that:

Intelligence is not equivalent to *thinking*; however, it needs *thinking* to show its *existence*. Without *thinking*, *intelligence* is just like *"a machine without operations."*

Intelligence is not equivalent to *knowledge*; however, it needs *knowledge* to make it *self-sufficient*. Without *knowledge*, *intelligence* is just like *"a machine without power."*

As the author mentioned at the beginning of the book:

"Thinking" is the way we ascertain our existence.

"Intuition" is the way we show our differences with machines.

In the next two subsections, we will take a closer look into the two core modules of the author's Framework of Intelligence – the *MIND Model* and the *Cognitron Map*.

The MIND Model

Belief is the most fundamental and critical component for our knowledge (of intelligence) and it originates from all sorts of matters that come to our mind in terms of ideas (notions), representations, sensations, feelings, memories, thoughts and desires.

According to the author's *MIND Model* (Fig. 2.4) of the *Theory of Intelligence*, our mind is just like a *"meat machine"* that *"crushes"* all this matter restlessly throughout our lives, taking responses and reactions, or building new knowledge and beliefs to *"reshape"* our world of experience.

As shown in the model, *stimulus* is the basic gateway we associate with the physical world. It consists of the five senses, memories (the mental experiences), desires, feelings and thoughts (logical or illogical thinking). These stimuli are collectively captured and stored in our mind as *experiences*. These experiences, either intentionally or unintentionally (via our mind), are *"labeled"* with the corresponding *"meanings."* Through training and learning, either consciously or unconsciously, *"knowledge"* is generated from all these *"meanings"* of facts and events. In fact, sometimes knowledge can be directly generated from experiences.

This is in contrast to the empiricists such as Berkeley, Locke and Hume who believed that all our knowledge must be derived from experience (Berkeley 1710; Locke 1959; Hume 1975), and the rationalists such as Descartes and Leibniz who maintained that in addition to the knowledge which came from our experiences, there exist some *innate ideas* or *innate principles* which we believe should be independent from experience (Clarke 1998; Leibniz 1982).

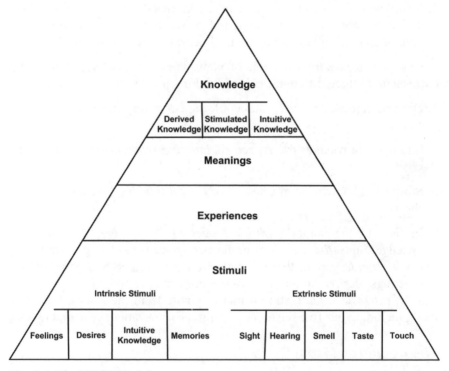

Fig. 2.4. The MIND Model

It might be too hard for us to believe that either all our knowledge must be derived from experience or there exists *innate knowledge* (and intelligence) that is born with us. The author rather chooses to agree with Russell's philosophical theory (Russell 1912) and maintains that there might be some *priori knowledge* that provides other possible *sources of knowledge* (and intelligence).

As an extension to Russell's theory of knowledge, and inspired by the author's work on the chaotic neural oscillatory system on visual intelligence in the author's *MIND Model*, the *knowledge level* consists of three kinds of knowledge:

1. *Derived Knowledge* – knowledge that is derived from senses and experience using induction, deduction and association (as mentioned in Russell's work).

2. *Intuitive Knowledge* – the *priori knowledge*, which does *not* originate from any other sources of substances and notions.

3. *Stimulated Knowledge* – this kind of knowledge comes neither from derivation nor innate capability, but rather comes from stimulation (a kind of chaotic and highly dynamical neural attraction and oscillation).

From the psychological point of view, these categories of knowledge correspond to three different kinds of thinking processes:

1. Derived knowledge, the source of *logical thinking* (or *thinking*, for short).

2. Intuitive knowledge, the source of *intuitive thinking* (or *intuition*, for short).

3. Stimulated knowledge, the source of *lateral thinking* (or *inspiration*, for short).

In fact, in the author's *MIND Model of Knowledge*, the *source* of knowledge – the *stimulus* – can be further divided into two categories: (1) *intrinsic stimuli*, stimuli that originate from one's mind and body, including feelings, desires, intuitive knowledge, memories and past experiences; and (2) *extrinsic stimuli*, stimuli that originate from the *external* environment, including our five senses (i.e., sight, hearing, smell, taste and touch).

The Cognitron Maps

Unlike the author's *MIND Model* – which focuses on the structure of *intelligence* – the *Cognitron Map* focuses on the *intellectual activities* of our mind – the so-called *thinking* in our daily experiences.

Based on the *Unification Theory of Knowledge*, all our senses and experiences, although different in *appearance*, are of the same *nature* when stored in our mind. So one might ask what kind of *nature* (of existence) are they? How do they operate in mental thinking processes?

The *Unification Theory of Thinking* provides an innovative solution – *Cognitrons* and *Cognitron Maps*. Cognitrons – according to Lee's *Unification Theory* (Lee 2004b) – are the *"basic functional units"* stored in our mind that represent each single notion and idea, sense and experience (memory), feeling and desire, etc. Since they are all of different natures; they are not organized in the form of a hierarchy tree, but rather organized *dynamically* during our daily mental processes, including thinking (nonintuitive), perception, intuitive thinking, learning, etc.

Figure 2.5 uses a simple Cognitron Map for the notion *"Table"* to illustrate the idea of *Cognitron Theory*.

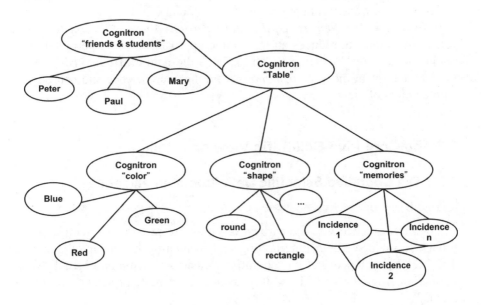

Fig. 2.5. The Cognitron Map for the concept "Table"

In Fig. 2.5, the notion *"Table"* is depicted as a *"node"* (what the author calls a *cognitron*), *"surrounded"* by all the concepts, ideas, colors, shapes and memories *"relating"* to this cognitron. For example, in your mind, when you *think* about the notion *"Table,"* you might *think* that a table should have a table top with four legs. You may also *think* about a table of a particular size or shape. More interestingly, you might *think* about some memories *"relating"* to a table, or even some familiar *faces* or even *feelings "relating"* to it (for example, the pain of getting hurt by a broken table at the age of six!).

One interesting thing is that all the concepts, memories, sizes, colors, faces and feelings are not related in any *orderly relationship* (e.g., master-and-slave). Also, they are not related in any *rigid manner*. For example, at one time when you see a man, you might think about some unpleasant feelings and memories, but when you see him again, say one year later, your mind might *"trigger"* you to have some pleasant feelings and wonderful memories! That's the wonder of the *dynamic* nature of *Cognitron Theory*.

One might wonder if *cognitrons* (and *cognitron maps*) really exist in our mind and what kind of existence they have from the neuroscience and neurophysiology point of view. And, more importantly, how can these "thinking" processes work from the neurodynamics point of view?

In Sect. 2.4, *The Neuroscientific and Neurophysiology View on Intelligence,* the author introduces an innovative approach for the interpretation of the *Unification Theory* and also explains the nature of *cognitrons* and the interactions of the *cognitron maps* from the neuroscience and neurodynamic points of view.

2.3 The Cognitive-Scientific View on Intelligence

2.3.1 The Cognitive-Scientific Definition of Intelligence

Cognitive science was the earliest discipline to provide a scientific approach to understanding, interpreting and evaluating human intelligence. The MIT Encyclopedia of the Cognitive Sciences (Wilson and Keil 1999) defines *intelligence* as "The ability to adapt, shape, and select environments."

Throughout recent centuries there have been numerous schools of thought on the understanding and interpretation of human intelligence. The first systematic and notable approach to understanding intelligence was the *Psychological Approach* proposed by Sir Francis Galton in 1883 based on the typical psychological skills such as the JND (Just Noticeable Difference) approach for the evaluation of human intelligence. This kind of approach has also prevailed in experimental psychology (e.g., perceptual psychology) for the evaluation of human perception (e.g., determining the furthest distance at which a human subject can differentiate between two neighboring spotlights, or the minimum weight difference between two objects that can be determined by a human subject, etc.; Gordon 1991).

Binet and Simon (1916) interpreted intelligence as the Complex Judgmental Abilities (CJA), which consisted of three core cognitive abilities:

1. Directional Ability – focuses on the achievement of tasks and how these tasks are achieved.
2. Adaptable Ability – focuses on the modification and monitoring of the strategies during the task achievement.
3. Controllable and Regulation Ability – focuses on the adjustment and control of one's decision making and final judgment.

2.3.2 Spearman's Model of the Nature of Intelligence

Charles Spearman (1923) – who was at the frontier of modern cognitive psychology – in his remarkable work *The Nature of Intelligence and the Principles of Cognition* conceptualized intelligence into three main mental activities: the *apprehension of experience*, the *eduction of relations*, and the *eduction of correlates*.

Based on his theory, experience itself cannot be apprehended without the intervention of certain constructive *assimilations* (an important mental process in cognitive psychology). And also the *eductions of relations* are believed to be genuine operations. The *eductions of correlates* are the presentations of certain characters together with some particular mental relations that tend to evoke immediately the knowing of some correlative characters (Spearman 1923).

Spearman was also one of the pioneers in making use of factor analysis – a kind of statistical technique used to evaluate one's intelligence ability – and he also proposed the "*g*" factor ("*g*" meaning "general") and defined all the essential factors that are related to our so-called *general intelligence*.

2.3.3 Piaget's Psychology of Intelligence

Jean Piaget (1896–1980), the founder of child psychology and developmental psychology, in his celebrated work *The Psychology of Intelligence* (Piaget 1950) tried to give multiple viewpoints of intelligence in terms of:

1. Biological Adaptation – in which *intelligence* appears as one of the activities of the organism, while the objects to which it adapts itself will constitute a particular sector of the surrounding environment.

2. Psychological Nature of Logical Operations – the so-called *Thought Psychology*, which describes *intelligence* as logical mental operations.

3. Gestalt Theory of Intelligence – based on this theory, mental systems (and human intelligence) do not appear and establish themselves as in-

dividual and isolated (mental) elements, but rather they are usually organized with *meaningful configurations* or some complex structures. Typical examples can be found in the Rubin's Vase Phenomenon and the Phi Phenomenon (Kohler 1947).

Besides providing a thorough explanation and interpretation of intelligence, in this book Piaget also described how these schools of thought were related to the development of intelligence in child psychology, and the determination of the *mental age*.

2.3.4 Major Approaches to Intelligence – from Psychometric Approaches to the Latest Studies

In terms of the approach to the evaluation of human intelligence, the early twentieth century was mainly dominated by the *Psychometric Approach,* which focused on the measurement of the individual differences (the "*quantities*") in the intelligence abilities, rather than the cognitive processing powers (the "*qualities*"). A substantial change in approach happened in the early 1970s: W.F. Estes (1970) proposed the *Cognitive-Correlates Approach* to intelligence, and started to evaluate intelligence by calculating the correlation factors between the parameters of the rates of information processing for particular tasks, such as the letter-memorization task, and the scores on conventional psychometric tests. In fact, this intelligence evaluation approach is still being used today.

The latest studies on the cognitive-scientific approach to intelligence include the *Cognitive-Components Approach* proposed by R.J. Sternberg (1977). In his distinguished work *Intelligence, Information Processing, and Analogical Reasoning: The Componential Analysis of Human Abilities*, Sternberg proposed that *intelligence* can be interpreted as the information-processing components with underlying complex-reasoning and problem-solving tasks such as analogies, syllogisms, verbal comprehension, decoding of nonverbal cues and the prediction of future outcomes (Sternberg 1977; Wilson and Keil 1999).

In 1985, R.J. Sternberg further extended his work on human intelligence and proposed the *Triarchic Theory of Human Intelligence* (Sternberg 1985). The *Triarchic Theory* provides an integrative way to consider the relationships between intelligence and:

1. the internal world of the individual and the corresponding mental activities underlying intelligent behaviors;

2. the experience and the mediating role of one's life between the internal and external worlds of experience; and

3. the external world of the individual making use of all sorts of mental activities in daily life to adapt to the environment.

2.3.5 Gardner's Theory on Multiple Intelligence

Howard Gardner, another major cognitive psychologist in the twentieth century, proposed an innovative view of the understanding of human intelligence – the MI (Multiple Intelligence). In his remarkable work *Frame of Mind: The Theory of Multiple Intelligence* (Gardner 1983), he queried the unitary nature of human intelligence and proposed that *intelligence* should be interpreted as the integration of eight different aspects: linguistic intelligence, musical intelligence, logical-mathematical intelligence, spatial intelligence, bodily-kinesthetic intelligence, interpersonal intelligence, intrapersonal intelligence, and naturalistic intelligence. More importantly, Gardner believed that each of these intelligence components is somehow independent of the others.

One major difference between *MI theory* and the "*mainstream*" cognitive development theory of human intelligence (as proposed by Piaget and his followers) is that in traditional Piaget cognitive theory the development of human intelligence (e.g., child intelligence) is essentially the result of the child's spontaneous tendencies to learn about the external world, in which the environment only plays a very minor role in the cognitive process. However, MI theory believes that for the progressive and productive change of human intelligence specific environmental forces must be systematically presented and sustained over time. In other words, the role of education is not to wait passively for the cognitive actions of the learner to take place, but rather it is to promote a variety of environmental conditions to trigger, facilitate and enable the mental development processes in these diverse intellect domains (Gardner 1983, 1993).

These innovative ideas of the contemporary *cognitive-psychology theory of intelligence* trigger a popularity and interest in the understanding and exploration of intelligence not only among cognitive scientists but also among laypeople – it's one of the hottest *popular science* topics in the new millennium.

For a detailed discussion of the cognitive scientific views of intelligence, please refer to the remarkable books written by Sternberg (1990) and Gardner (1987); both provide in-depth explorations of human intelligence in terms of cognitive science.

2.3.6 Lee's Unification Theory of Senses and Experiences – The Psychological Interpretation

Implications of Russell's Paradox on the Reality of Matters on Gestalt Psychology

Russell (1912), in his distinguished work *The Problems of Philosophy*, brought a very interesting and important philosophical challenge to our attention with "*What is reality?*" He started his argument with the visual perception of a desk in front of him, saying that what we perceive in our world of physical objects (of matter) in our daily life is not the *real nature* of the objects, but is rather just the *appearance* of their existence (if they really exist!?) subject to our perception. Following this stream of observations, he came up with two questions: (1) Is there a matter of such things? (2) If so, what is its nature?

Russell's observations on visual perception have critical implications not only for the area of metaphysics but also on the doctrines of visual psychology, neuroscience and the study of ontology.

In the next section, we will focus on the impact and interpretation of Gestalt psychology, which leads to the study of the nature (and the truth) of our senses of experiences – the core idea of the *Unification Theory of Senses and Experiences*. In Chap. 11 we will revisit Russell's theory and start to investigate the interpretations on modern ontology.

Gestalt Psychology on Visual Intelligence

From the psychological point of view, what Russell observed from the visual perception of the table is closely related to the *Gestalt Theory of Perception* relating to the constancy theory of object perception. A classical and well-known visual psychology theory proposed by Ehrenfels in 1890 was further developed and elaborated by Wertheimer (1912), Kohler (1947) and other Gestaltists in the early twentieth century.

Recent developments include the work of Beck in 1966 on Gestalt grouping by similarity, and Kaniza in 1979 on his remarkable Kaniza Cubes, used to illustrate the difference between thinking and seeing Gestalt Theory. Other works included Restle's *Coding Theory of Perception and Motion Configuration* (Restle 1979) and Shepard's work on his remarkable discovery of *Apparent Motion* (Shepard 1984).

From the Gestaltian point of view, our perceived world is a world of completeness, coherence and wholeness, the so-called *Prägnanz* (Gordon 1991), and we are all *born* with that *precious capability*.

One of the most critical phenomena of Gestalt Theory is the constancy of visual perception of all physical objects (e.g., shape, color) in the sense that although our perception stimuli (e.g., shape, color) of an object are different under different perspectives (e.g., location, visual position, illumination), our perception of that object will remain the same (i.e., constancy).

Using the same example (the "table") for illustration, simple geometry and visual biology tell us that the projection for the shape of the rectangular table onto our retina will be different from different viewing perspectives; however, our visual perception of the table will "*tell*" us that it is still the *same* rectangular table. On the other hand, fundamental optic theory tells us that the color of an object is due to the reflection of light from the object into our eyes, which varies according to the intensity and color of the illumination. However, *common sense* tells us that our perceived color of the table will not be changed subject to illumination. These evidences are collectively called the *Constancy Phenomena of Gestalt Perception* in color and shape.

Gestalt Theory (and the related Gestalt Perception) is not a new human "*discovery*," but rather is a "*rediscovery*" about the way humans perceive our *World of Experiences*. It is not difficult to imagine that there is a very close relationship between Russell's findings on "*Appearance vs. Reality*" and *Gestalt Theory*. So what is the relationship between the two? Did Gestalt Theory answer Russell's findings? If not, what is it?

The Critique of Gestalt Psychology Based on Russell's Theory

Remember that Gestalt Theory was just a way to *describe* the common visual perception phenomena that we encounter in our daily lives – although innovative, it surely cannot *explain* how it happens. In other words, we can only say that Gestalt Theory provides a "*true*" evidence to support Russell's findings, but it cannot help us to explain why it happens.

Russell's findings on the "*appearance vs. reality*" of visual objects gives us valuable insights into visual psychology: If what we perceive for every physical object is not "*real*" – only the "*appearance*" induced by the *sense data* through our sense organs (e.g., eyes, ears) – then Gestalt Theory tells us that we maintain constancy for all these "*unreal*" perceptions. It comes up with two possibilities.

Although what we perceive through our sense organs is "unreal" sense data, we can somehow automatically "*associate*" these with the "*real (coherence) nature*" of the object in our mind. That can explain why even though the sense data are varied we can still maintain the state of coherence.

For every physical object we perceive (by whatever means, e.g., through vision, touch, smell, etc.), we will associate it with something what the author calls "*concept*" in our mind. The "*concept*" might not be the "*reality*," but it is a useful "*link*" for us to associate all the different perceptions (e.g. the sense data) of the same physical object as one single "*point*" in our mind such that we can still maintain the same state of *coherence* with various perceptions.

Possibility (1) itself is a vital philosophical and religious problem. For example, Buddhism tells us that our perceived world is unreal (what Buddhists call *Sunyata* in the *Heart Sutra* (Prajnaparamita Hrdaya Sutra); it is not empty, but *ordinary* people like us just perceive the unreal nature (called *Rupa* in the *Diamond Sutra* [Vajracchedika Prajnaparamita]), and only *enlightened* people with sufficient *Buddhata* can perceive the reality. Other religions, such as Taoism, have a similar philosophy, but they are a little different in their interpretations and theories. Some distinguished philosophers such as Aristotle, Kant and Descartes had similar theories (of course in nonreligious interpretations), but an in-depth discussion is not within the scope of this book.

From a layperson's point of view, possibility (2) may be a bit easier to comprehend. The main reason behind it is: If all our perceptions of the object are unreal, how can we "*know*" the reality of that object, such that we can associate all the related perceptions about it mentally? Why not just make it simple to accept the second possibility by saying that we really do not know the reality; all we know (and store in our mind) is merely the "*concept*" of that object, and we use it as a "*tag*" or "*link*" to associate all these "*unreal*" perceptions about that object to a single "*point*" in our mind in order to make us "*feel easy*", or in order to achieve the state of *Prägnanz* in the psychological point of view.

If we accept the second possibility, there will be some subsequent questions that we need to tackle: If the "*concept*" is not the reality of the object, what is it? In what form of existence is that "*concept*" in our mind? And, more importantly, how can this matter "*concept*" be associated with all other perception elements and provide our *mental world of coherence* as described in Gestalt Theory?

The Unification Theory of Senses and Experiences – A Possible Psychological Solution

From a skeptical point of view, it seems that the question *"What is a concept?"* is as difficult to answer as the philosophical question *"What is matter?"* brought up by Russell (Russell 1912). However, it is not the case. *"What is matter?"* is a more elementary and philosophical question which involves even the existence of *matter*! As Russell mentioned in his remarkable work *The Problem of Philosophy*, the existence of sense data does not imply the existence of matter itself, simply because what we perceive is the sense data but not the matter itself! So what we can do, at best, is agree with our own existence – as Descartes said in his remarkable work *Meditation* (Clarke 1998): *Cogito, ergo sum (I think, therefore I am)* – such that we can deduce the existence of the sense data that "interact" with our sense organs, or we just deny our existence altogether with the existence of the sense data!

Generally speaking, the question *"What is a concept?"* is a *bit* easier to tackle. The reason behind this is threefold: Firstly, it involves only the *continent* of psychology, which is a bit easier to *control*. Secondly, we do not need to puzzle over whether the matter *"concept"* really exists or not (because our argument is based on the proposition that we accept the second possibility and the existence of a *"concept"* is not a point of argument at all!). Thirdly, the most important reason is that a *"concept"* is just a *"sign,"* a *"symbol,"* or maybe a *"tag"* to link all the subsequence sense data that are related to a particular object. As described in the author's recent work on the Unification Theory of Senses and Experiences:

These sense data may be sound elements, image fragments, even "feelings" or "impressions" about that object. The importance is not "What is a concept?" but rather "How can these sense data associate with this "concept" element – the process of memory storage?" And also, "How can we return this information back to our conscious mind – the process of memory recalling?"

For a further illustration of what a *"concept"* is in the author's Unification Theory, we can make use of a simple analogy on a relational database. In classical Relational Database Theory, information is stored as records of elements in 2-dimensional storage areas called *tables*, and a *database* is simply a collection of all these *tables*. The most critical part of Relational Database Theory is that these tables are *"related"* by some elements called *"index fields."* The importance of these *index fields* is that they are used to *"link up"* all the so-called *related tables* together in a logical manner such that useful information can be effectively "*extracted out*" across different tables through these "*linkages*" (using database operations, so-called "*queries*"). By adopting this simple analogy, "*concepts*" are just these "*tiny linkages*" that link up all the related sense data about a particular object. The importance is not the *nature* of these "*linkages*" but rather how can we define the linkages (i.e., the memory storage)? And, how can we perform the queries (i.e., memory recalling)?

These are major questions in the areas of cognitive science, neuroscience and artificial intelligence which also act as the building blocks for the development of agent intelligence as discussed in Chap. 3.

The Psychological Interpretation of the Three Kinds of Knowledge and Thinking Models in the Unification Theory

In Sect. 2.2.6 the author introduced *Lee's MIND Model* together with an illustration of the three kinds of knowledge: *derived knowledge, intuitive knowledge* and *stimulated knowledge*. From the psychological point of view, the difference between *derived knowledge* and *intuitive knowledge* is quite obvious and many distinguished philosophers and psychologists have provided numerous explanations and interpretations on it. So, what is the difference between *stimulated knowledge* and the other two? From the *mental* (thinking) point of view, it seems that *lateral thinking* (corresponding to *stimulated knowledge*) is quite similar to *logical thinking* (corresponding to *derived knowledge*) in the sense that both have to relate something (e.g., notions, subjects, substances) in order to *generate* new knowledge; however, it is also similar to *intuitive thinking* (corresponding to *intuitive knowledge*) in the sense that these kinds of thinking are highly "*unstable*" and "*illogical.*" So how can we interpret *lateral thinking* as compared with the other two?

Lateral thinking seems to be quite similar to logical thinking which must need *something* for *correlation*; the correlation of notions (facts) to generate *stimulated knowledge* (via lateral thinking) must not be derivable by induction, deduction or association, but rather they are only related by stimulation (which is believed to be a kind of *chaotic neural attraction process*). On the other hand, lateral thinking seems to be quite similar to intuitive thinking which is highly *unstable* and *illogical* while lateral thinking must need an object(s) to simulate its *stimulated knowledge*, and intuition does not need any object to *trigger* new knowledge.

One interesting fact is that in Chinese the phrase "思想" (meaning *thinking*) consists of two characters in which "思" corresponds to thinking without any *object* for correlation while "想" corresponds to thinking with *something* for correlation. Furthermore, the character "想" can be further decomposed into two *primitive* characters: "心" means *mind,* while the character "相" means *something.* Similarly, the character "思" can also be decomposed into two *primitive* words: "心" means *mind,* while the character "田" means *field.* In fact the phrase "心田" in Tibetan Buddhism means *Spiritual Mind,* which is believed to be clear and pure, without any contamination from the physical world (which is quite similar to Krishnamurti's theory of *intelligence).*

A New Psychological Interpretation of Our Five Senses Based on the Unification Theory

A traditional belief of our senses is that the stimulus from vision is quite different from other senses of stimulus in which all other stimuli are normally in *temporal* form while the vision sense (e.g., a vision scene) is in *static* form (Gordon 1991).

Based on the author's *Unification Theory,* the five senses, although different in *appearance,* share the same *nature.* The vision stimulus seems to be static, but in fact this is *not* the case. The latest research in active vision has revealed that vision stimuli (e.g., from vision scenes) appear as EM waves reflected from vision objects which are intercepted by our neurons in the vision organ in terms of neural oscillations (Freeman 2001).

From the psychological point of view, when we look at a vision scene, we continue to receive the visual stimulus in temporal sequences. Every *snapshot* of the visual scene may not be the same, but *appears* to be, only because of the visual constancy effect of *Gestalt psychology*!

The stimuli of all these *five senses* (maybe six if we include consciousness as the sixth sense, as in Buddhist theory) are only different in the *appearance* of the stimuli, but their *nature* − more precisely the *experiences* being stored (captured) in our mind − are of the same nature. That means that all these experiences (what the author calls the *processed stimuli*) are *unified* and *stored, captured* and *interpreted* in our mind as *meanings* and *knowledge* (from the AI point of view) − the so-called *Unification Theory of Senses and Experiences* (Lee 2004a, 2004b).

There are several common but classical experiences that we can share for illustration:

(a) For some distant experiences, for example some unpleasant experiences in primary school life, it is difficult to tell whether it is an actual experience, a distant dream or even an *imagined event in the past*! The reason behind this is because our experiences of the senses of consciousness, vision and feeling in the distant past are *mixed together* to determine which is the *true* source!

(b) When we see someone with whom we are familiar, we can normally recall his or her name and other details right away. Under this *Unification Theory*, all the experiences (with sources from the various senses of experience) are consolidated together in our mind such that we can achieve that kind of prompt recall!

In fact, example (a) comes with some interesting implications.

If this memory recall mechanism is true, how can we explain the following scenarios?

Each experience with your friend might "*contain*" some other *objects* (it may be some other events, some other people, etc.). Why does the mind store that *experience* under the "*codename*" of your friend and not under any other? Or is it like a database system, thus making a "*link*" or even a "*copy*" in another memory area?

Sometimes, you meet a person in the street and "*feel*" you know him but you just cannot recall his name (and some other details). But what is the mechanism behind this in terms of the *Unification Theory of Senses of Experiences*?

Observation (a) discloses a very interesting fact, which can be explained by *Gestalt psychology*. One important feature of *Gestalt psychology* is the idea of *Prägnanz*, in which our minds are good at *discovery* and *intensification* of the characteristics of the perceived objects and events. If we apply this concept in (a), we can use the following interpretation: In our daily experiences with other people and objects, our minds will *automatically recall* the major characteristics of each of these events, "*label them*" and *store them* in our memory. When we think of someone, some *special* events "*focused on*" that person will come to our mind first, and these experiences are what the author calls the *characteristics* related to that person in your mind. But it does not meant that other *unrelated* or *less important* experiences related to that person cannot be recalled, it might take a bit more time to *recall* them because it needs what we call *lateral thinking* to dig out these memories!

There are two possible explanations of observation (b):

1. Experiences are in fact memories in our mind, which are volatile in nature. If we have not recalled that person for a long time, related experiences with that person will *fade out* in a *decay* manner in our mind like some other experiences in our memory, as the author mentioned: "... the progressive decay nature of memory which resulted in the chaotic dissociation of memory fragments in the unification theory" (Lee 2004c).

2. If that person has only been met in a "*causal*" manner, all the experiences related to this person are not event stored in your STM (short-term memory) or your LTM (long-term memory), so naturally it is difficult for you to recall the details of this person! But why have we the "*feel-*

ing" of knowing this person? The answer might be because human vision experiences are the most "*impressive*" elements as compared with the other senses. We always "*float around*" all sorts of visual images in our mind! It doesn't mean that they are all *meaningful* memory experiences! They can even be imagined experiences!

The next section will talk about the latest findings and developments in these areas and the latest findings and research on chaotic neural oscillatory systems, which might provide a viable solution to answer these questions.

2.4 The Neuroscience and Neurophysiology View on Intelligence

In the previous three sections, we explored the interpretations and theories of human intelligence in terms of philosophy, cognitive science and psychology. The author also proposed his own ideas and theories of intelligence. It seems that we have only addressed some of the questions relating to the *mystery of intelligence* as stated at the beginning of this chapter:

- What is *intelligence*?
- What are the main schools of thought on and approaches to the study of *intelligence*?
- How can we interpret and measure *intelligence*?
- How does our brain work to *facilitate intelligence*?

So far we have addressed the first three questions, but not touched on the last question at all. Although the *Unification Theory and the Cognitron Model* discussed in the previous sections have some insights that address the third question about *intelligence* (i.e. How can we interpret and measure *intelligence*?), we still have not explained how our mind (and brain) operates to *exemplify Intelligence*. Here the author deliberately replaces *facilitate* with *exemplify* mainly because, based on the Framework of Intelligence discussed in the previous section, intelligence is *not* a physical *substance* or just an abstract notion for our mind to *facilitate*, but rather it is an overall *quality* through which we attain knowledge and mental activities (so-called *thinking*). So it should be a kind of *exemplification* rather than *facilitation*.

In this section, we study how our brain (mind) works for intellectual activities (thinking and knowledge achievement) from the neuroscience and neurophysiological point of view. The author also explores how the *cognitron* works (in the neurodynamics point of view) to achieve these mental activities.

2.4.1 The Major Challenges of Mind Science – The Exploration of the Mind from the Neuroscience Perspective

The 1990s can be called the age of *mind science*. In the past 15 years, the field of neuroscience and neurophysiology has achieved promising results in the exploration of functionality and mental activities – the so-called *mind science*. These studies have not only triggered the interest of neuro-biologists and neurophysiologists, but also provided tremendous new ideas and directions for the research and development of the AI scientists working in the areas of artificial neural networks (or neural networks in short) and neural oscillatory theory.

In summary, the major topics (and challenges) in *mind science* include the following problems:
– How does the brain work?
– How do the numerous (over billions) neurons in our brain operate in order to bring out our thoughts, feelings, ideas and emotions?
– How do the neurons operate and organize in order for us to process *external* information into knowledge, to learn new things and ideas?
– How do the neurons operate in order for us to recall our memories, to recognize a familiar face and to segment the figure objects from a clutter and noisy background?
– How do the neurons (and the neural networks) bring to us the *high-level* cognitive powers, including lateral thinking, intuitive thinking and self-awareness?

In this section, we will explore the development of this *mind science* and will take a look at how far we are from solving these *ultimate* challenges of *mind science*.

2.4.2 A Brief History – The Search for Intelligence in Neuroscience

The latest neurophysiology tells us that our brains consist of over 10^{11} neurons. How these neurons organize is in itself a highly complex problem, let alone the study of how can these neurons work together to perform functions in the layperson's point of view!

The first scientist to work in this area of *brain science* (the architecture and neurofunction of the brain) was an Italian physician Camilo Golgi (1843–1926) who invented the *stain method* to investigate the neural activities in the brain. By using silver salts to stain the meninges, he surprisingly discovered that only some portions of the cells in the brain changed into black, while most of the other parts remained unstained. Based on this discovery, Golgi proposed that the brain was made up of *syncytium* – a sponge-like structure. Of course, as we know now these stained *tissues* are the neuron cells (neurons) that are *activated* by the staining operation instead of by sponge-like tissue. Nevertheless, Golgi's discovery provided a critical breakthrough in the understanding of the structure of the brain.

Based on Golgi's staining method, a Spanish neuroanatomist Santiago Ramon y Cajal proposed an innovative idea: that these staining tissues were not sponge-like elements, but rather the collections of the brain cells known as *neurons*, which were *interlinked* together to form a complex units – so-called *neural networks* (Fig. 2.6).

As shown in Fig. 2.6, each neural cell (neuron) consists of: (1) a nucleus, the central body of the neurons, which is embedded in cytoplasm; (2) an axon, the prolonged filament which branches from its neuron extensively for *connections* to another neurons; (3) dendrites, tree-like structures which branch from the neuron, acting like *sensors* to intercept *stimuli* from the other neurons; (4) synapses, the axon tips (junctions) that make contact with other neurons by attaching to the dendrites of these *neighboring* neurons. In fact, there are over 1000 synapses on the dendritic tree of each neuron, and current neurophysiology believes that the reason for these *tree-like* structures is to maximize the number of contact points between one neuron and its neighboring neurons in order to facilitate effective information transmissions.

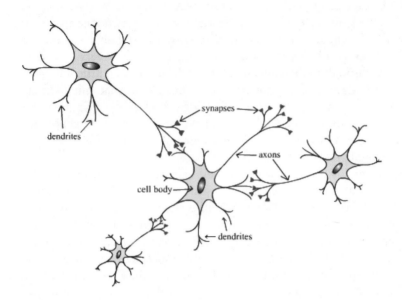

Fig. 2.6. Neural networks

The early twentieth century was really the *Golden Age of Psychology*, especially in the area of analytical psychology and neuropsychology. Sigmund Freud (1856–1939), one of the most remarkable and influential psychologists of his time, proposed that the interconnecting networks of neurons could possibly explain the difference between a (mentally) normal person and a person with a mental disorder. Most psychologists believe that Freudian's Psychoanalytic Theory can be traced back to his original concepts and understanding during the time when he was working in the field of neurophysiology, investigating the *flow of energy* in the brain's neural networks.

For instance, one of the most fascinating ideas proposed by Freud was his neurophysiology theory of dream, in which Freud proposed that the phenomena of dreams involved the unconscious neural activities that resulted from the energy-release process that *accumulated* in our daytime, conscious mental activities (Strachey 1976). Over half a century later, neurophysiologists discovered the phenomena of the *membrane potential*, the synaptic transmission of neural impulses between neurons and the release of chemical substances across synapses!

The 1940–1950s can be called the *First Golden Age of Neural Networks* and the *Birth of Computing Technology*. In earlier decades, almost all neuroscientists believed that the sole purpose of the neurons (and their neural networks) was to process *energy*. However, the neurophysiologist Warren McCulloch and the mathematician Walter Pitts in 1943 published an influential paper in the *Bulletin of Mathematical Biophysics*, namely "A logical calculus of the ideas immanent in nervous activity" (McCulloch and Pitts 1943). Instead of an *Energy Theory* to explain neural activities in the brain, they proposed that the main function of neural activities was to process *information*. They maintained that the functions of the neurons were just like "*logical switches*." In this influential paper, they also demonstrated how their proposed neural networks could be used to perform basic logical operations such as AND, OR and NOT operations.

Actually, this finding not only provided a major breakthrough in the field of neurophysiology, but also provided a solid foundation for the future development of digital computing technology. Although we now know that the property of the neurons (in our brains) is quite different from that of logical switches such as transistors and silicon chips in computers, neurons are rather like nonlinear (sometimes *chaotic*) *integrate-and-fire* operators for the transmission and storage of information (Freeman 2001). McCulloch and Pitts's contributions impacted on the development of AI with the start of the *First Golden Age of Artificial Neural Networks*. In Chap. 4, AI Techniques for Agent Construction, the author gives an in-depth discussion on the research and latest developments in *artificial neural networks*.

2.4.3 Contemporary Research in Mind Science – From Neural Oscillators to the "Chaos in the Brain"

The latest research into neuroscience and neurophysiology has revealed that our major senses of perception, including vision and olfaction, work very much in a spatiotemporal manner rather than simply in a spatial manner in terms of pattern representation, processing and cognition (Freeman 2001; Haken 1996). As described in the celebrated *correlation theory* developed by von der Malsburg and his colleagues (Malsburg 1981), which was subsequently condensed into the DLA (dynamic link architecture) for memory association (Malsburg 1985), all visual systems for pattern association and recognition are achieved through a temporal correlation between neurons in the brain. In fact, this *spatial-temporal memory coding theory* has gained a considerable amount of support from the findings of various physiological experiments. The experiments have included examinations of the visual cortical areas of the cat and of the nonlinear dynamics of the olfactory system where the system encodes and processes the stimulus (e.g., odor, visual image, etc.) by altering its neural dynamics in an oscillatory manner rather than by presenting the neural dynamics in a state pattern (Engel et al. 1991; Freeman 1979; Gary et al. 1989).

The latest developments and studies based on this *correlation theory* include work on coupled neural oscillators for sensory segmentation (Malsburg and Buhmann 1992), face and hand gesture recognition (Lee 2002; Triesch and Malsburg 1996, 2001; Wiskott et al. 1997) and composite neural oscillators for complex scene analysis and surveillance systems (Lee 2003; Lee and Liu 2002).

Moreover, regarding these spatiotemporal neuron coding information processing systems (Ishii et al. 1996; Yao and Freeman 1990), the latest research on brain science and neurophysiology has reported that *deterministic chaotic patterns* were found in these nonlinear dynamic systems. They include chaotic EEG patterns found in the olfactory system (Freeman 1987), chaotic oscillations and bifurcations in the giant axons of squid (Aihara and Matsumoto 1986, 1987), chaotic neurons found in the pyloric central pattern generator (CPG) of the California spiny lobster (Falcke et al. 2000; Huerta et al. 2001), and various chaotic phenomena in brain functions (Freeman 1992, 2000; Haken 1996; Lehnertz et al. 2000), such as the chaotic ECoG (cortical EEG) in the human brain (Menon et al. 1996) and the chaotic dynamics of the EEG during the perception of $1/f$ music (Jeong et al. 1998). Prof. W.J. Freeman, in his remarkable work on brain science *How Brains Make up Their Minds* (Freeman 2001), concluded that:

"Many other parts of the brain have chaotic attractors and multiple wings, and the stability of their EEGs shows that they are exceedingly robust. Chaotic dynamics provide a basal state with ideal properties ... Chaos generates the disorder needed for creating new trial-and-error learning, and for creating a new basin in assimilating new stimuli."

Freeman, 2001

According to this challenging theory of neuroscience, researchers have proposed various chaotic neural models to simulate these chaotic neural phenomena (Chen and Aihara 1995; Falcke et al. 2000; Hoshino et al. 2003; Minai and Anand 1998; Wang 1991, 1992). However, most of the chaotic neural models based on the seminal models of Hodgkin and Huxley (Fukai et al. 2000a, 2000b; Hodgkin and Huxley 1952) or Wilson and Cowan (Wilson and Cowan 1972) are either too complicated to be adopted in artificial neural networks or too simplified to reproduce satisfactory chaotic phenomena (Aihara and Matsumoto 1987; Aihara 1997; Chen and Aihara 1997; Minai and Anand 1998; Tsuda 1992; Varona et al. 2001).

As an extension of the author's previous work on the EGDLM (Elastic Graph Dynamic Link Model) and on the composite neural oscillator (Lee and Liu 2003) for vision object recognition, and inspired by the work of Aihara et al. on chaotic neural networks (Adachi and Aihara 1997; Aihara and Matsumoto 1986, 1987) and of Wang on the Wang oscillator (Wang 1991, 1992), the author proposed a new transient chaotic oscillator – namely, the *Lee oscillator* (Lee 2004c) to provide a chaotic-based, temporal neural coding and information processing model, which serves as the cornerstone for his theoretical work *Cognitron Theory and the Unification Theory of Senses and Experiences* (Lee 2004a, 2004b).

The theory of *brain chaos* has begun to gain significant support from researchers in various fields including neuroscience, neurophysiology, neurobiology and AI. It is anticipated that we will have more exciting and promising evidence and theories in the near future.

2.4.4 The Neuroscientific and Neurophysiological Implications of the Unification Theory of Senses and Experiences

In the previous sections, we discussed the interpretation of *Lee's Unification Theory of Senses and Experiences* in terms of its philosophical and cognitive psychological aspects. So, how about its interpretation in doctrines of neuroscience and neurophysiology? Are there any physical interpretations and evidences for the Unification Theory in terms of neural dynamics and/or neurophysiological behaviors?

The answer is … Yes!

One concrete evidence is the *neuroplasticity phenomenon* found in the brain. According to neurophysiological research in the past 15 years, it was found that in the brains of people who read *Braille* the cortical areas devoted to processing sensory information from the tip of the right index finger are larger than the corresponding areas for the left index finger. Surprisingly, neurophysiologists found that for people who had limbs amputated, the cortical areas used to carry out the processing of the sensory information from those amputated limbs shrank a period of time after the operations (Spitzer 1999). Similar evidences for the senses of hearing, touch and sight were found in the past 15 years (Merzenich et al. 1988; Merzenich and Sameshima 1993; Allard et al. 1991; Jenkins et al. 1990). Such *self-adaptive* behavior of the cortical tissues of the brain which are subjected to changes in *sensory requirement* is known as *neuroplasticity*. Although most neurophysiologists now agree on the existence of *neuroplasticity*, they are still puzzled as to how our brain tissues can provide such a highly adaptive capacity, as we all agree that different portions (areas) of our brain cortex are specifically related to different sensory, emotional and mental functions.

The other *"mystery"* evidence is the phenomena of the *phantom limb*, i.e., after the amputation of a leg, a patient will still *feel* the existence of the leg. For instance, they will still feel *pain* and *itching* for the *"leg"* and feel the *position* of the leg during walking and moving (Jensen and Rasmussen 1989). Instead of just a psychological problem, are there any other possible reasons? Increasing numbers of neurophysiologists choose to believe that instead of just a psychological problem, these *phantom phenomena* might be due to the fact that the stump has *"taken over"* the sensation job of the original limb after the amputation operations (Cronholm 1951; Jensen and Rasmussen 1989; Spitzer 1999). But, again, how does that happen?

An even more fascinating evidence of brain plasticity is the *"See with your tongue"* experiment led by Prof. Paul Bach-y-Rita and his researchers of the University of Wisconsin at Madison (Sampaio et al. 2001). In the experiment, the subject was blindfolded by sitting in a room surrounded by black curtains. All the senses of experience could only come from the sense of *touch* from the tongue, which was filled with electrodes; these electrodes were connected to a long stripped wire, which was in turn attached to a small video camera worn over the hand of the subject. In one of the experiments, the subject was told that a ball would be rolled in front of him or her. With the sense of sight being *blinded*, the subjects could *use* their sense of touch (from their tongues) to *"see"* (or to *"feel"*) the approaching ball. Surprisingly, when the ball was approaching in front of the subject, the subject felt a tingling that passed over his or her tongue, and finally he or she could catch the ball.

Bach-y-Rita believed that our sense organs have an astonishing *neuroplasticity capacity* in the sense that if one of them is damaged, the others will try to *serve* their functions. In this experiment, he concluded that it is not our eyes that see things, but rather it is our mind! However, it is still an open question as to how our mind works in order to perform these *extraordinary* functions.

The most fascinating result of this experiment is that it seems that our sense organs can *exchange* their sensing functions if one is *disabled*. Again, how does it work?

In the previous sections we discussed the main theory of the *Lee's Unification Theory of Senses and Experiences*. Based on this innovative theory, all the senses and experiences, including our thoughts, feelings, emotions, desires, memories and experiences exist (and are stored) in our mind with the same nature of existence. So, if this is true, all the above problems can be solved automatically.

The reasons behind this are:

1. For the *Neuroplasticity phenomenon*, the central problem is the conflict that our *traditional* belief of a *fixed* cortex structure does not allow us to have a highly dynamic and adaptive brain cortex. So if the *Unification Theory* is true, this problem should not exist anymore because if all our senses and experiences are stored in our mind with nature, it is not a problem that our brain can *"relocate"* one part of the cortex to store and process other senses or experiences.

2. Following the same logic, the phenomenon of the *phantom limb* can also be explained. According to the *Unification Theory*, the sense of *touch* (which is an *extrinsic sensation* as defined in the *Unification Theory*) of the patient's leg after amputation is *"replaced"* by the sense of *feelings* (which is a kind of intrinsic mental activity) after the operation. And, more importantly, the reason why the patients still *"feel"* the existence of their leg is mainly because of the *knowledge* (other than the actual sensation of touch) that comes from the previous *experiences* – which are also *unified* with the other sensations and stored in our mind!

3. According to the previous explanations, the interesting phenomenon of the *exchange of senses* is not a problem at all, mainly because if our senses and experiences are unified, stored and processed by our brain as a whole, the exchange of senses will not be an impossible situation. Of course, it takes time for our mind to make some "tuning"!

In Chap. 4, the author presents his latest work on the design and implementation of *Lee oscillators* (and the corresponding *Lee associators*) (Lee 2004c) – a chaotic neural oscillatory model that might provide a feasible solution to illustrate how our brain (neurons) works to provide such a highly dynamic (and even chaotic) mode of operation. In the experiment, the author illustrates how these chaotic neural oscillators can be used to stimulate the human *Progress Memory Recalling Scheme (PMRS)*.

2.4.5 Summary

In this section we have explored the neuroscientific and neurophysiology approaches of mind and intelligence. In fact, one may wonder that the major challenge in the neuroscientific exploration of mind science is mainly focused on the study and investigation of the neural structure and the corresponding neural activities during mental operations. The answer is "Yes" and "No". "Yes" in the sense that the study of the neural activities (especially now as scientists start to focus on *chaotic neural activities* in brain science) is one of the major trends of development, but "No" in the sense that it should not be the *ultimate challenge*. The ultimate challenge should rather be finding out how the brain *encodes* and *represents* external and internal stimuli – including feelings, desires, memories, and our five senses, etc. – and this is still an open-ended question for us to further explore in the future.

Below the author presents his Unification Theory and explains how the *Cognitrons* (and *Cognitron Map*) work in the neuroscience point of view.

In the section *Chaos Theory and Chaotic Neural Networks* of Chap. 4, the author presents his latest scientific work on a chaotic neural oscillator – *Lee oscillator* – for progressive memory recall and recognition. Moreover, in Chap. 11 the author presents his latest work on ontological agents and illustrates how *Cognitron Theory* can be adopted for the design and implementation of self-awareness agents – the *Cogito iJADE Project*.

2.5 Concluding Remarks

In this chapter, the author presents an overview of intelligence as seen in various disciplines, including philosophy, psychology, cognitive science, neuroscience and neurophysiology. The main reason behind this is that *intelligence* is no longer – and should not be – the "*gift*" or "*asset*" of any particular discipline to study and explore, it needs cooperation from different fields to understand it, explore it and test for it. The author believes that:

Philosophy gives us the philosophical interpretation of "intelligence" and shows us the way to understand "intelligence."

Cognitive Science gives us the mental interpretation of "intelligence" and shows us the way our minds behave to achieve "intelligence."

Neurophysiology gives us the neural interpretation of "intelligence" and shows us the neural activities through which "intelligence" works.

In the opening dialogue of this chapter, Plato's belief was that intelligence was something *supreme*, something which gave the *reason* for everything, and something that would show us the *best way* to view all the things in the world. The author would like to add: "*Intelligence is a gift to us. It is precious and it has the capacity to direct us to the truth of reality.*"

One may wonder: "*How far are we from the ultimate solution in the understanding of intelligence – the truth?*" My answer: "*We don't know. The fact is the more we know about intelligence, the more we believe we don't know about it.*" However, the author always believes that an optimistic and open mind is our *key* to unlocking this door!

3 From AI to IA – The Emergence of Agent Technology

Robots – The *exemplification* of Intelligent Machines

Intelligent Agents – The *exemplification* of Human Intelligence

Raymond Lee, 2004

Starting with the Dartmouth Meeting in 1956, artificial intelligence (AI) – the exploration, design, and implementation of human intelligence – was no longer a fantasy idea or science fiction, but rather a new discipline of scientific research. Over the past 50 years, scientists from all over the world have *nourished* this piece of "Intelligent Land" with their wisdom, thoughts, and innovative ideas. In addition to the design and implementation of robots to model the behavioral activities of humans, contemporary AI scientists started to focus on the implementation of devices (including both software and hardware devices and systems) that mimic human intellectual behavior and computational intelligence – namely, *intelligent agents* (or *agents* for short).

This chapter firstly presents a brief overview of the birth and development of AI and discusses its major achievements and obstacles. The chapter also presents AI architecture and discusses the contemporary applications of AI. The second part of the chapter presents the *intelligent agent* (IA) *model*, as well as its general definition and contemporary development, and concludes with a discussion of the future research and development in IA technology.

3.1 What Is AI?

AI is a fantastic term for most of us, not just in the discipline of computer science, but also in other disciplines including neuroscience, psychology, and philosophy. Although there is no *official* definition of AI, the definitions from *Webster's Dictionary* and the American Association for Artificial Intelligence (AAAI) might be a good place to start:

The capacity of computers or programs to operate in ways to mimic human thought processes, such as reasoning and learning

Webster's New College Dictionary

The scientific understanding of the mechanisms underlying thought and intelligent behavior and their embodiment in machines

AAAI

Stuart Russell and Peter Norvig, in their remarkable work *Artificial Intelligence: A Modern Approach* (Russell and Norvig 2003), provided a complete survey of the contemporary definition of AI in four major categories:
– Systems that think like humans.
– Systems that think rationally.
– Systems that act like humans.
– Systems that act rationally.

It seems that the variety for the definition of AI is mainly due to two aspects: (1) the different focuses of AI functionality, and (2) the different interpretations of intelligence. For (1), there are two controversial focuses on AI: the *behavioral approach* – that is, to *act* like humans – and the *cognitive approach* – that is, to *think* like humans. For (2), most AI books and literature that focus on the *cognitive approach* attempt to interpret AI as the "mimics of the human rational thinking processes" (Russell and Norvig 2003). The reason behind this is that they interpret *intelligence* as the *rational mind* of mental processes. However, is that really the case? Put simply: Are we humans (who are supposed to be *intelligent*) "always" a rational species, in all our acts and mental processes?

The answer is simply "no." In fact, we are always doing things, selecting choices, and making decisions in a rather *irrational* (so-called *fuzzy* and sometimes even *chaotic*) way such that even we do not understand the rationale. It is believed that this kind of fuzzy act and decision making might be our "precious assets" for us to claim to be *intelligent*.

As we discussed in Chap. 2, in the author's view, *intelligence* is the overall capacity for humans to attain, to build, and to develop *knowledge*, and at the same time to manipulate this *knowledge* (i.e., our *thinking processes*). *Thinking* can be categorized as intellectual processes that consist of three main categories: (1) *logical thinking* (from derived knowledge); (2) *lateral thinking* (from stimulated knowledge); and (3) *intuitive thinking* (from intuition). Also, owing to the changes and diversifications in the design and implementation of AI (and AI systems), AI should cover both the mimicking of *acts* and the *thoughts* of humans.

So in this book, AI is defined AI as:

The exemplification of human intellectual thoughts, acts, and behaviors for the design and implementation of intelligent systems, software objects, and robotic systems.

3.2 A Brief History of AI

3.2.1 The Dartmouth Meeting (1956) – The Birth of AI

Since we have already been on a "fantastic journey" involving the definitions, meanings, and interpretations of *human intelligence* (or *intelligence* in short) in Chap. 2, our starting point for the discussion of the history and development of AI will be rather smooth and straightforward – that is, the Dartmouth Meeting on AI in 1956.

In the summer of 1956, a group of young scientists working in the fields of logic and mathematics gathered at the campus of Dartmouth College in Hanover for a meeting "To confer about the possibilities of producing computer programs that could 'behave' or 'think' intelligently." Furthermore, as they had declared in their application to the Rockefeller Foundation: "The study is to proceed on the basis of the conjecture that every aspect of learning or any other feature of intelligence can in principle be so precisely described that a machine can be made to simulate it" (Gardner 1987; McCorduck 1979).

At this meeting, the four young scientists from different disciplines who started the development of the new field of AI were: John McCarthy, a mathematician from Dartmouth who eventually became the founder and the first director of the AI Labs at both MIT and Stanford University (1963) and was also the one who coined the term "Artificial Intelligence (AI)"; Marvin Minsky, both a mathematician and a neurologist from Harvard who also eventually became the director of the AI Lab at MIT; and Allen Newell and Herbert Simon from Carnegie Tech (now Carnegie Mellon College, CMU). Other researchers present included Trenchard More from Princeton, Arthur Samuel from IBM, and Ray Solomonoff and Oliver Selfridge from MIT.

At this summer meeting, these scholars presented their latest research, exchanged their ideas and thoughts for the possibilities of developing machines that could mimic human acts and thinking, and also discussed the chances of future collaboration. For instance, Samuel presented his work on a chess-playing program; Newell and Simon presented their work, the so-called *Logic Theorist* (LT), a program which was designed to solve theorems in logic; while Minsky presented his work on using computers to prove Euclidean theorems (McCorduck 1979; Gardner 1987).

Although this meeting did not come up with any concrete ideas or breakthroughs, it was still a "symbolic" event for the birth of modern AI. As a matter of fact, the meeting had a great impact on the research development of AI over the world, which was dominated by the major AI centers at MIT, Stanford, CMU, and IBM from the 1960s onwards. All the major participants at this meeting eventually became key figures in the history of AI.

3.2.2 The Turing Test – A Prelude of AI

Long before the Dartmouth meeting, research and studies had already been undertaken on the design and modeling of so-called *intelligent machines*. The most important and influential of these was the renowned Turing Test of artificial intelligence, named after the computer pioneer Alan Turing. After finishing his remarkable work on the study of the *Turing Machine* (Turing 1936), which became one of the foundational works on the algorithmic analysis of complex systems and problems, Turing started to focus on the possibility of building intelligent machines and on theoretical research investigating the relationship between and differentiation of *machine thoughts* and *human thoughts* – the Turing Test.

In the test, the interrogator (who is of course a human) is confined in a room equipped with a keyboard and a monitor. This room is connected to two other rooms, in one of which is a human who speaks the same language as the interrogator and in the other is the computer program under test. The test is straightforward. Given a fixed period of time, say 10 minutes, the interrogator can ask any questions he or she likes, and the subjects in both rooms *must* give answers. So by judging the answers given by these two subjects, the interrogator (at the end of the test) has to determine which answers are from the human, and which answers are from the machine.

Starting with the first Turing Test in 1950, some scientists anticipated that the computer would finally "win" the game by the year 2000. In fact, this test still continues: no one dares to say that his or her machine can pass the test totally without any problems!

Although there are certain criticisms that these tests cannot "faithfully" report the intelligence of the machine, it is maintained that Turing Tests can only reflect the NLP (Natural Language Processing) ability of the machine – which is believed to be one of the major aspects of AI. However, the author shares the views of Turing (Boden 1990) and believes that natural language is not only a means of communication between us, but also a vital and highly intellectual activity which in turn reflects the "overall intelligence" of the subject under test.

3.2.3 Strong Versus Weak AI

In the decades following the birth of AI at the Dartmouth meeting, there were debates on the general definitions and the so-called *metaphors* of AI, and even on the definition of an intelligent program. As Robert Wilensky, an influential AI scholar, had mentioned in his remarkable work, *Planning and Understanding: A Computational Approach to Human Reasoning*:

Artificial Intelligence is a field renowned for its lack of consensus on fundamental issues.

Robert Wilensky

One typical example was the argument between *weak AI* and *strong AI*. Some AI scientists believed that AI should focus on the design and implementation of systems or programs that mimic and stimulate how humans *think* and *act* – the so-called weak AI. Opponents believed that AI systems should not only think and act like humans, but rather be "consciously and actually thinking" – the so-called strong AI.

It is sometimes difficult to say whether or not we humans are making decisions and choices based on *thinking*, let alone to talk about machines. For instance, in the game of chess – a human activity typically believed to heavily involve mental thinking and intelligence – we often hear that world-class chess players do not use *normal (logical) thinking* to make decisions at the most critical moments of the game, but rather use what we call *intuition* to make the choice. In another extreme case, for a computer program which plays chess simply by using *breadth-first search* to make decisions, it is rather difficult to classify whether or not the program is really "thinking."

According to the author's previous definition of intelligence and thinking, all of the above cases can also be defined as *intellectual activities*, but they are just different in the *modes* and *levels* of thinking. *Intuition* itself, of course, is a kind of thinking (intuitive thinking), and breadth-first search should also be another kind of thinking (derived thinking). Strong AI is not only a kind of intellectual activity, but also the *act* of intellectual activity, or from the ontological point of view, the *self-awareness* of thinking, which we will discuss in detail in the last chapter.

3.2.4 Searle's Chinese Room Thought Experiment

As discussed in the previous subsection, there were numerous queries and skeptics regarding the Turing Test. Searle's *Chinese Room Thought Experiment* (Boden 1990) was the most typical one. The test is very simple. Imagine in the Turing Test that the interrogator this time is a Chinese person sitting in a room with a monitor and a keyboard of Chinese characters. The subject under test is a native-English speaker who has no idea of Chinese characters or the Chinese language; the subject's room is equipped with a monitor, a keyboard (of Chinese characters), and a manual. Like all other Turing Tests, the interrogator is free to type in any question (this time in Chinese characters) and to check the responses. Suppose that the manual in the subject's room can translate every single Chinese question to an English question (or vice versa) so that the Chinese interrogator cannot differentiate whether or not these questions are from a native-Chinese speaker. Naturally, the subject will pass the test and will conclude that the subject is an *intelligent* human being. The question is: although the subject is really a human being, all the answers given did not come from the subject's own *thoughts* or *mind* (the *mental process*) (i.e., intelligence) but rather were the responses given by the manual (in fact, the subject has no idea about any of the questions given by the interrogator at all). In that case, can we claim that this *act* of performance can still be classified as *intelligent*?

Opponents of the Turing Test even added that assuming the native-English speaker is replaced or substituted by a machine with the same ability to perform that kind of *lookup table* ability, the result will be the same: that is, the interrogator will still assume that the one being tested is a human instead of a machine!

However, this paradox is valid subject to two important conditions: (1) the existence of that *universal* and *powerful* manual – that is, the existence of *universal knowledge*; and (2) the existence of the *universal* and *powerful* NLP technique for message encoding and decoding schemes – that is, the existence of the *universal thinking process*. As a whole, it means the existence of *human intelligence* (as we have defined it in Chap. 2)! In other words, Searle's Chinese Room Thought Experiment makes a basic assumption that there exists some kind of assistance from an external object with powerful human intelligence to help the subject to give answers; no matter if the subject is intelligent or not, human or machine, the test result must be the same. (In fact, this paradox is reminiscent of the famous *Twins Paradox* in special relativity. The tricky point of the paradox arises from the definition of the problem itself that the assumption of one the twins traveling in space is already outside the domain of special relativity when the twin turns around!)

3.2.5 Development of AI in the Late 1970s

After a period of "passionate" discussions and research on AI without any substantial or promising breakthroughs and achievements (especially the passion shown toward *highly intelligent* and *autonomous thinking machines* which turned out to be no more than a fantastic dream for some game playing and theorem solvers) the development of AI went into a period of hibernation for over 20 years after the Dartmouth meeting. As Lighthill pointed out in an evaluation report on AI for the Science Research Council (Lighthill 1972):

Most workers in AI research and in related fields confess to a pronounced feeling of disappointment in what has been achieved in the last 25 years. Workers entered the field around 1950, and even around 1960, with high hopes that are very far from being realized in 1972. In no part of the field have the discoveries made so far produced the major impact that was then promised.

Lighthill, 1972

Not until the late 1970s, when AI scientists began to shift their focus from building *general-purpose thinking machines* to the development of *knowledge-based systems* (KBS), did people start to regain some hope and confidence in the feasibility and applicability of building AI-based systems. Typical examples include: case-based systems (CBS), rule-based systems (RBS), frame-based systems (FBS) and expert systems (ES).

The major differences between KBS and the AI systems developed in the previous decades included: (1) the focus of the AI systems was no longer on the design and development of so-called *all-purpose intelligent machines*, but rather on the development of *expert-type intelligent machines* (and systems) with predefined knowledge (or what we called *priori knowledge*); (2) the design of these KBS used a top-down instead of a bottom-up approach compared to their predecessors; and (3) although these systems possessed learning ability (to learn new knowledge) to a certain extent, their main functions focused on problem solving and knowledge inference instead of learning or perception capabilities.

Typical examples of these KBS include the frame-based systems proposed by Minsky (1975) on active vision. Minsky extended his idea of a frame-based system and proposed the so-called *Society Theory* in 1979 (Minsky 1979). In this theory, he maintained that in a real-world system, all the intelligent tasks should not be operated and controlled by a single entity (called an *agent*), but rather these tasks should be distributed in different functional entities (*agents*) such that they could *act* as a whole to solve the daily problem – the *Society Model*. Minsky's innovative idea in 1979 had an influential impact on the development of *portable intelligence* in agent development for some decades. We will return to this topic briefly in the second part of this chapter.

Other typical KBS projects include the work done by Roger Schank and his AI research team at Yale, who focused on using KBS for NLP (Schank 1972); and the celebrated MYCIN knowledge-based expert system for medical diagnosis, which was developed in a joint effort between scientists in the Computer Science and Medical Schools at Stanford University. Owing to the extensive and thorough documentation of the project, MYCIN somehow became the *archetype* representing the years of knowledge-based expert systems in AI history (Buchanan and Shortliff 1984).

3.2.6 The "Reincarnation" of Neural Networks in the Late 1980s

Owing to the sophistication of neural networks (in terms of computational complexity) and their *black box* characteristics, there were not many promising research results (let alone breakthroughs) in the 40 years following the proposal of the first neural networks by McCulloch and Pitts (1943). Then in 1982, John Hopfield (Nobel Prize winner in physics) presented his influential paper "Neurons with graded response have collective computational properties like those of two-state neurons" (Hopfield 1982), which "reincarnated" the technology of neural networks after almost half a century.

Hopfield's major contributions to the development of neural networks injected some innovative ideas, including the integration of *adaptive learning* on neural networks; the investigation of the *memory capacity* of neural networks; the invention of *associative memory networks*; and the adoption of these networks into a number of practical problems including the well-known *Traveling Salesman Problem* (TSP).

Subsequently, feverish research on neural networks was aroused in the late 1980s. Other microscopic AI techniques (to be discussed shortly), including *fuzzy logic*, *genetic algorithms*, and *neural oscillators*, also started to join this "contest" of AI. Instead of competing with other research, the latest research started to investigate how different kinds of AI techniques could be integrated together to solve more complex problems including severe weather prediction of tropical cyclones and rainstorms, stock prediction, complex scene analysis, active vision, and so on. Typical examples for the *synergy* between different AI technologies include the research and development of *fuzzy–neuro* systems and the integration of neural oscillators with chaotic systems to produce the so-called *chaotic neural networks* (CNNs), which will also be discussed in Chap. 4.

3.2.7 The Birth of IAs in the Late 1990s

The 1990s can be called the age of *Internet technology* and *intelligent computing*. Owing to the rapid development of ICEC (Internet computing and electronic commerce) all over the world, ranging from C2C e-commerce applications such as e-auctions to sophisticated B2B e-commerce activities such as e-supply chain management (eSCM), the Internet became a common virtual marketplace for us to do business, search for information, and communicate with each other.

Owing to the ever-increasing amount of information in cyberspace, information searching, or more precisely *knowledge discovery* or W*eb mining*, is becoming the critical key for success while conducting business in the cyberworld. Moreover, with the advance of PC technology in terms of computational speed and popularity, AI scientists have started to turn their *dream* of developing intelligent and autonomous *software robots* – so-called intelligent agents (or agents for short) – to travel around this unbound "fairyland."

At the beginning of agent development, some of the implementations could only be run on propriety networks. But nowadays, most agent platforms, including the iJADK platform discussed in this book, can allow users and agent developers to implement their intelligent agents (so-called *iJADK agents*) to traverse freely over the Internet – this everlasting territory of technology.

3.3 An Overview of the Classification of AI Technologies

As an extension to the definition of AI given at the beginning of this chapter, Fig. 3.1 depicts an overview for the classification of all related AI technologies.

According to the author, AI is defined as:

An exemplification of human intellectual thoughts, acts, and behaviors for the design and implementation of intelligent systems, software objects, and robotic systems.

Raymond Lee

In terms of functionality, all AI implementations (systems and applications) can be broadly classified into two main categories: the *behavioral approach AI*, corresponding to *acts* and *behaviors*; and the *cognitive approach AI*, corresponding to *thoughts* and *mental processes*.

Behavioral approach AI can also be called *macroscopic AI*, which focuses on the design and implementation of intelligent machines (and systems) that mimic the *high-level* (meaning "appears to be seen") intellectual behaviors of humans, which are our high-level mind–body intellectual activities. It also corresponds to weak AI as discussed previously. Behavioral AI can be further divided into two subcategories: *mind–BA (mind behavioral approach) AI* corresponds to *high-level mental activities*; and *body–BA (body behavioral approach) AI* corresponds to *high-level body and control activities*.

The mind–BA AI technologies were the macroscopic AI applications during the 1950s and 1960s, including: ES (expert systems), NLP (natural language processing), LR (logical reasoning), SML (symbol machine learning), and ST (search techniques). Each category of mind–BA AI technology can be further classified. For instance, the ST can be further divided into state-space search (SSS), heuristic search (HS), and hybrid (or complex) search, but they are not described in detail within the scope of this book.

On the other hand, *cognitive approach* (CA) *AI* can also be called *microscopic AI*, which focuses on mimicking the *low-level mental activities* of humans – what cognitive scientists call the *cognitive mental activities* of humans. It also corresponds to strong AI, as discussed previously, which targets the implementation of intelligent systems (applications or agents) that can "really think."

From the technological point of view, CA AI can be further divided into four main categories:

1. the artificial neural network approach (or *neural network approach* for short)
2. the fuzzy approach
3. the EC (evolutionary computing) approach
4. the chaotic approach

Each kind of CA AI model stimulates different mental processes and activities of humans: the neural network approach models low-level *neural groupings* and operations; the fuzzy approach models low-level *fuzzy-reasoning* of mental activities; EC models the *evolutionary growth* and *self-improvement* of the human gene in the adaptation of the environment; and the *chaotic approach* models the highly nonlinear and chaotic human intellectual behaviors and decision making. These four basic microscopic AI components are also the primary technologies for the design and implementation of intelligent agents. We will discuss each of them in detail in Chap. 4.

As mentioned in the last section, since each of the microscopic AI techniques has its own characteristics and shortcomings, the latest research investigates how different AI techniques can be integrated and combined together to solve complex AI problems. In this book, we will discuss how neural networks and fuzzy systems can be integrated together (the so-called *fuzzy–neuro systems*) to implement a new generation of intelligent agents for solving realistic problems such as stock prediction, weather forecasting, active vision, dynamic product negotiation, etc.

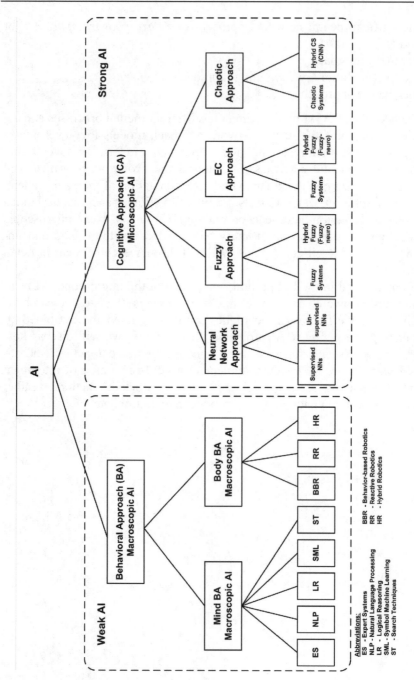

Fig. 3.1. Classification of AI technologies

3.4 AI – Where to Go?

As mentioned in Chap. 2, from the very beginning of history, philosophers, scholars and AI scientists have all investigated the same topic – *human intelligence*. The only differences between their studies and researches are the investigational perspectives, but the nature and the final objectives are the same: to understand, to explore, to model, and to stimulate human intelligence.

In view of the various setbacks in the progress of AI over the past 60 years, the author strongly believes that in order to make new breakthroughs in AI, the only way is to *ally* all the efforts from scientists and researchers in all the various disciplines involved. It is anticipated that in the near future AI will be not only a feverish topic in computer science, but also rather a *joint-discipline* topic with cooperation in various fields of research and study.

As Fig. 3.1 shows, according to the functions and the history of development of AI technologies. AI is broadly classified into two main categories: strong (microscopic) AI and weak (macroscopic) AI. Starting from the very beginning of the emergence of AI technology up to the present, there are still debates on which one should be the *correct* definition and direction of AI.

From the author's point of view, these two kinds of AI technologies should not be competing, but should rather complement each other. Although they are using totally different approaches to understand, interpret, and implement human intelligence, their sole aim is the same – to mimic human intelligence to produce *truly* and *universally* intelligent and autonomous machines (systems, software, or even robots). The author strongly believes that an integration of various kinds of AI technologies is the most appropriate (and maybe only) way to solve this *ultimate problem*. The reason is simple: recall that all the AI theories originated from the modeling of human intelligence. As we discussed in Chap. 2, human intelligence consists of both *logical* and *illogical* modes (classified into three different kinds of intellectual activities), so it is natural that the only way to "totally" model human intelligence is to integrate both the macroscopic and microscopic *modes of intelligence*. Most importantly, the time for such a "unification" is coming – the *age of IAs*.

3.5 The Coming of the Age of IAs

3.5.1 What Is an IA? A "Right" Place to Start

Before we start to discuss the topic of IAs, you may wonder why the author put their definition and introduction so far away from the beginning of the chapter. Why not just put it right at the beginning of the chapter, or even in Chap. 1 or the Preface, just like all other books on agent technology?

The answer is simple: although the definition of an IA is not complex or mysterious, basically speaking it is the *combination* of two concepts: *intelligent* and *agent*. The word *agent* is quite straightforward. In the *Oxford English Dictionary*, it has three basic meanings:

1. A person who acts for, or who manages the business affairs of, another or others.
2. A person used to achieve something, to get a result.
3. In science, "agent" means substance, natural phenomenon, which produces an effect.

The first explanation is more appropriate in our case. However, the word *intelligent* is not an easy thing to tackle. In order to understand it, we have to understand two different concepts: (1) What is intelligence? Or, more precisely, what is human intelligence? And (2) What is AI, and how is it related to human intelligence? We are just saying that an IA is the computer agent (object) that helps us to manage the business affairs of another or others *intelligently*.

In order to provide a (more or less) "better" picture for you (the author dares not say "full" because intelligence and AI cannot be fully discussed and described in just one or two chapters, but this picture is better than nothing), we have to undertake "a journey" through human intelligence and AI before we come to the "main course" of this book – namely, IAs.

Given that you have some understanding of what intelligence and AI are, let us take a look at what an IA is. In the popular AI textbook written by Stuart Russell and Peter Norvig (2003), there is a chapter on IAs, but the author could not find any *formal* definition of an IA, rather just the definition of what a *rational agent* as:

For each possible percept sequence, a rational agent should select an action that is expected to maximize its performance measure, given the evidence provided by the percept sequence and whatever built-in knowledge the agent has.

Russell and Norvig, 2003, p. 36

The book also gave a definition of an agent as: "An agent is anything that can be viewed as perceiving its environment through sensors and acting upon that environment through actuators."

Richard Murch and Tony Johnson, in their book *Intelligent Software Agents* (Murch and Johnson 1998), divided agents into four types: intelligent, learning, mobile, and believable agents. In fact they did not give any *direct* definition for intelligent agents either, and the only passage mentioning the definition of an intelligent agent is:

These (Intelligent Agents) are a very broad category of agents and can cross the definitions described before. This is the biggest area of research and has the most commercial interest shown by software developers. We shall examine the definitions and understanding of what we mean by "intelligence" later in this book

Murch and Johnson, 1998, p. 48

However, the author cannot find any other place in this book that had a formal definition of intelligence or IA.

Reference to the cognitive science "bible," *The Encyclopedia of the Cognitive Sciences* (Wilson and Keil 1999), the author surprisingly revealed that it gave a really *sound* and *concrete* definition of an IA. In the definition of the term *Intelligent Agent Architecture*, written by Stanley J. Rosschein, an IA is defined as:

An intelligent agent is a device that interacts with its environment in flexible, goal-directed ways, recognizing important states of the environment and acting to achieve desired results.

He also defined Intelligent Agent Architecture:

(An) Intelligent Agent Architecture is a model of an intelligent information-processing system defining its major sub-systems, their functional roles and the flow of information and control among them.

Wilson and Keil, 1999, p. 411

What the author would like to point out is that anything that relates to *intelligence* will be a difficult task to comprehend. From the above definitions, Rosschein's seems to be more sensible and complete; but it only explains some of the intellectual activities that IAs perform. Russell and Norvig's definition of a rational agent is quite right to a certain extent. However, as we discussed in Chap. 2, one of our most "precious assets" is that we sometimes act *illogically* (*fuzzily* or even *chaotically*, you can say), or sometimes *seem* to be *irrational*, which is also an essential part of our mental activities.

From the author's point of view, IAs can have two versions of definition (one brief and one detailed).

The *brief* definition is:

An intelligent agent (IA) is the exemplification of human intelligence as a form of device. This device (IA) can exist in the form of a system, a software program, a program object, or even a robot.

The more *in-depth* definition is:

An intelligent agent (IA) is the exemplification of human intelligence in a device. The agent's intelligence consists of possessing knowledge (with three levels: derived knowledge, stimulated knowledge, and intuitive knowledge) and the manipulation of knowledge (the "thoughts or thinking" which consists of three levels of thinking: logical thinking, lateral thinking, and intuition). This device (the IA) can exist in the form of a system, a software program, a program object, or even a robot.

As you can see, the author's definition is substantially broader and more general than other contemporary definitions. The reason is that although nowadays most IAs exist as *software agents* in the form of a software program (or software object), the author strongly believes that in the near future IAs will exist in many other forms. For instance, an IA can exist in the form of an *intelligent robot* (or robot pet) to serve (or to play with) you; or as an *intelligent refrigerator* to store food for you; or even an *intelligent PDA* (Personal Digital Assistant) to suggest a place for you to go for dinner; it can be anything *intelligent* appearing in your daily life. But there is one thing in common: all of these IAs are trying their best to mimic human intelligence to perform their daily intellectual activities. So instead of focusing on the *behavioral intelligence* of the IA, which is only the macroscopic AI part of IAs, the author includes the *overall intelligence* (i.e., both behavioral intelligence and cognitive intelligence) in the definition. As we will see shortly in this chapter, the cognitive intellectual properties of IAs are even more important than the behavioral ones.

3.5.2 The Emergence of Agent Technology – The Idea of *Portable Intelligence*

The 1990s can be described as the age of internetworking, e-commerce, and mobile computing (Chan et al. 2001). The emergence of the World Wide Web (WWW) and the Internet drove the whole community and industries onto the *information superhighway*. Previously, only people working in the fields of computer technology and engineering science used computers to perform their daily operations, but nowadays almost everyone somehow has to rely on the use of computers, the Internet, and the WWW. The Internet itself is not just a global network, but rather a *bridge* to link all of us to information and the community.

Owing to the ever-increasing number of Web sites and information that *pushes* into this global (but *uncontrollable*) network, computer scientists have started to worry about this *flood* of information which will sooner or later affect the overall efficiency and even the usability of the Internet. Take a simple example: if one tries to look for some topics on "AI" and tries to key in these topics in a search engine, one will discover that almost 90% of the search results are not what one wants. The reason is simply because of the flood of information on the WWW. The only winner (*search engine*) might be the one that really *understands* what one wants to search, rather than the search keyword itself. In other words, we have to come back to the *territory* of *intelligence*, or what we called AI from the implementation point of view.

Similar situations always happen when we are using the Internet to perform daily activities. For example, if we want to look for a book on *Intelligent Agents* on the WWW, what we will do is to check several major online bookstores. Whenever we cannot locate a book based on its title, we will broaden our search area with other *similar* (or what I call *fuzzy*) titles, such as "Agent Technology" or even "software agents," to check whether there are some other suitable choices. Wouldn't it be a good idea if we could have a *software program* (or *software object*) to do it for us? Of course, this software object should be intelligent enough to handle all fuzzy situations. It would be even better if it could do the product negotiation and bargain for us! That is why we need IAs!

"Anything that happens must have its own reason," and this may also be true for IAs. In fact, the need for *something* to help us solve problems and *make* our life more comfortable and convenient is not just limited to surfing the Internet, but to other aspects of work and daily activities as well. The adoption of IAs over the Internet is one of the hottest and most feverish topics, not only in the area of AI research, but more importantly due to the application advantages that can be obtained in various Internet-related situations, including Web-mining agents, intelligent shopping and search agents, automatic e-mail administration agents, e-banking agents, Web personalization agents, negotiation agents, weather forecasting agents, e-finance agents, etc.

However, *needs* and *demands* are not sufficient enough for the emergence and growth of any technology, including agent technology. The emergence of IAs is also favored by some other critical *environmental* requirements:

– the support of computer technology
– the provision of global networks
– the availability of agent platforms
– the availability of AI technology

Starting in the late 1980s, the emergence and rapid growth of PC technology changed both our way of living and our way of perceiving and communicating with the outside world – the Internet. The speed and memory capacity of the latest PCs are almost as fast as, or maybe even faster than, the *supercomputers* we had 20 years ago. So, in other words, almost everyone at home can possess a computing device with a speed and capacity that can operate sophisticated algorithms individually, and can in turn connect to almost any place in the world.

Actually, the idea and dream of this *portable intelligence* is not new. AI scientists already had in mind at the outset the aim of building intelligent programs that can *traverse, act*, and *react* to the environment in a highly autonomous manner. The design and implementation of IAs is just another way of building autonomous robots that focus on their intellectual activities – namely, *portable and distributed intelligence (PDI)*. From the technological point of view, all the necessary AI techniques and related technologies have *always* been there, but most of them have just stayed in the labs (in the past 10–15 years) waiting for more powerful computing machines to become available. Finally, in view of the agent platform, this is just a *chicken-and-egg* problem in the sense that once every necessary condition is ready, the emergence and growth of agent platforms is just a matter of time.

At the time of writing this book, there are already hundreds of implementations and applications of agent technology (Zhong et al. 2001). But if you want to know whether all of them are IAs or not, the answer is both *yes* and *no*. "Yes" in the sense that if one claims to be implementing an agent, that agent should also be intelligent as well, otherwise it should not be classified as an agent. "No" in the sense that there are really quite a number of agent implementations that do not focus on the AI capability of their agents; they are rather concentrated on multi-agent communication and collaboration (say) with a specified protocol and standard. Some AI scientists will classify them as *mobile agents (MA)* or *multi-agent systems (MAS)*. However, from the author's point of view, every agent should be intelligent – that is, it must contain knowledge and have some *basic mental capabilities*, or at least some simple *inference* capabilities (e.g., case-based or rule-based reasoning skills), which should be considered as a kind of *intelligent act*. The only difference is the *level of intelligence*! We will come back to this topic later in this book.

3.6 The Ten Basic Requirements of IAs

In the previous section, we discussed the general definition of an IA. For ease of implementation, in addition to the fundamental requirement of intelligence, which the author will explain in detail in the next section, there are ten basic requirements that a typical IA should (or might) possess. They are as follows:

Autonomous: An IA should be *autonomous* in the sense that it can *exist* and *survive* on its own.

Mobile: An IA should be highly *mobile* in the sense that it can traverse and navigate freely on its own for the purpose of fulfilling its task.

Reactive: An IA should be *reactive* in the sense that it can provide *rational* responses to *external stimuli* and queries.

Proactive: An IA might be *proactive* in the sense that it should possess the ability to *express* its request and/or perform *preventive actions* before the *unfavorable* event (or instance) takes place. For example, a proactive negotiation agent can provide *counter-offers* and *alternative options* during product negotiation before the other party provides further or fresh offers.

Adaptive: An IA should *adapt* itself to the *external* environment. For instance, a highly *adaptive* shopping agent can dynamically produce its clones according to the number of e-shopping malls it needs to visit. In the extreme case, it should calculate the optimal number of clones it needs to produce dynamically according to the number of shopping sites, current network traffic, loading costs, etc.

Robust: An IA should be *robust* to the *external* environment. For example, a highly robust shopping agent can still perform its tasks in various environments and platforms and it can be invoked and operated properly in both a Web environment and a wireless environment, especially when the environment has very limited resources for smooth operation.

Communicative (and Cooperative): An IA should be *sociable* in the sense that it should be *cooperative* and ready to communicate to *foreign agents*. It is also one of the major requirements and characteristics of IAs for the so-called multi-agent systems.

Learning: An IA should have the capacity to improve its *intelligence* through *learning*. In fact, it is also one of the major characteristics of IAs in the sense that an intelligent machine (or system) is claimed to be intelligent not only because of its *priori intellectual knowledge*, but, more importantly, because of its learning ability (either supervised learning or unsupervised learning). We will return to this topic in Chap. 4. For instance, a *smart* auction agent should possess the *talent to learn* the bidding pattern of an auction site such that in the future it can place its bid smartly.

Task-oriented: Normally, an IA should exist (in the world) with some predefined *missions* – what we called *tasks*. Its aim is to *try its best* to finish the tasks by using its own *intelligence*.

Goal-driven: An IA should be *goal-driven* in the sense that all its activities should be *justified* by the goal it achieved. In other words, a *good* IA should not do anything that is not related or beneficial to an increase in the chance for it to achieve the goal. For example, a goal-driven shopping agent will not (and should not) go to any non-shopping sites to search and look for products.

3.7 The Contemporary Variety of IAs

According to the above major requirements and characteristics of IAs, the majority of agent developers currently focus on one (or several) capabilities for building their agents, which leads to the existence of a variety of (what may be called) *functional agents* in the market. They include:

Multi-agents: Agents that focus on *multi-agent* communication and knowledge exchange (Ferber 1999; Shen 2001).

Internet agents: Agents that focus on the design and implementation of software agents over the *Internet* platform (Omicini et al. 2001).

Mobile agents: Agents that focus on the *mobility* of the agent over distributed networks, or possibly over the Internet or some other propriety networks (Rothermel and Popescu-Zeletin 1997; Baumann 2000).

Learning agents: Agents that focus on the *machine learning functionality* of the IAs (Furukawa et al. 1999). Typical examples are the PA (Personal Assistant) agents that target the interactive learning of the "habits" of their owners.

Adaptive agents: Agents that focus on the *adaptiveness* to the *external* environment in the sense that an adaptive agent can modify itself, in terms of its *thinking*, *knowledge*, and *action/reaction activities* according to the changes in the external environment (Alonso et al. 2003). Most adaptive agents also possess certain learning abilities as well.

Figure 3.2 shows an overview of the variety of IAs.

From the author's point of view, different kinds of agents (in the market) should also be categorized as IAs. The only difference between them is the *degree of intelligence* and the *focus* on the agent's capabilities. For instance, multi-agents are not just restricted to possessing the abilities of mobility and communicativeness, but can of course also be *intelligent enough* to be learnable and proactive as well!

Fig. 3.2. An overview of the variety of IAs

3.8 The Conceptual Model of IAs

In Sects. 3.5 to 3.7, we have discussed the following questions: What is an IA? What are the major requirements for building IAs? And what are the different types of IAs that exist in the market? Before we try to discuss how to build an IA using our iJADK (intelligent Java Agent Development Kit) in Chap. 5, let's have a look at the *conceptual model* for building IAs.

This model of agent development is divided into two parts: (1) the conceptual model for the construction of the agent's intelligence – the *BFI* agent intellectual conceptual model; and (2) the conceptual model for the construction of the *MBE* (Mind–Body–Environment) model – the *GIA* (general-purpose IA) vs. the *TIA* (task-oriented IA) structural models.

3.8.1 The BFI Agent Intellectual Conceptual Model

The BFI agent intellectual conceptual model (*BFI intellectual model* for short) conceptualizes the stage (and level) of intelligence that the IA developers should consider during the initial stage of agent development. Following the author's interpretation of human intelligence (in Chap. 2), the BFI intellectual model conceptualizes the design of IA intelligence into three main stages:
- **Behavioral** (or factual) intelligence
- **Fuzzy–neuro** (or stimulated) intelligence
- **Intuitive** intelligence

Behavioral (or Factual) Intelligence

This level of intelligence corresponds to the lowest level (entry level) of IA intelligence.

It is constructed by the integration of *derived knowledge* – as the knowledge domain – with *logical thinking* – as the thought domain for knowledge acquisition.

It is named the *behavioral level* because this level of intelligence is the mimic of behavioral intelligence as discussed in Chap. 2 and the early part of this chapter.

It is also called the *factual level* because this level of intelligence makes extensive use of logical facts and cases to mimic human intelligence.

From the AI technological point of view, it makes use of the available macroscopic mind–BA (behavioral approach) AI reasoning techniques, including rule-based reasoning (RBR), case-based reasoning (CBR), frame-based reasoning (FBR), etc.

Potential applications and IAs include: EK-IA (expert knowledge agents by adopting expert knowledge, e.g., for medical diagnosis); LT-IA (language translation agents by adopting NLP techniques); LR-IA (logical reasoning agents by adopting LR techniques, e.g., agent Chess-master), etc.

From the cognitive psychological point of view, this level of intelligence is part of the *conscious thinking* category.

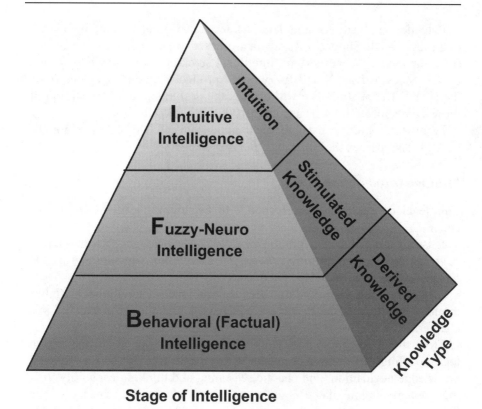

Fig. 3.3. The BFI agent intellectual conceptual model

Fuzzy–Neuro (or Stimulated) Intelligence

This level of intelligence corresponds to the middle level of IA intelligence (Fig. 3.3).

It is constructed by integration of *stimulated knowledge* – as the *knowledge domain* – with *lateral thinking* (or something called *fuzzy* or *chaotic thinking*) – as the *thought domain* for knowledge acquisition.

It is named the *stimulated level* because this level of intelligence mimics *stimulated intelligence* as discussed in Chap. 2 and the early part of this chapter.

It is also named the *fuzzy–neuro level* because this level of intelligence extensively mimics the highly fuzzy and (sometimes) chaotic features of human intelligence with neural networks as the knowledge base.

From the AI technological point of view, it makes use of the available *microscopic CA* (*Cognitive Approach*) AI reasoning techniques, including fuzzy logics, neural networks, genetic algorithms, chaos theory, etc.

Potential applications and IAs include fuzzy–neuro shopping agents (e.g., the iJADE Shopper), fuzzy–neuro-based weather forecasting agents (e.g., the iJADE WeatherMan), intelligent stock advisory agents (e.g., the iJADE Stock Advisor), and fuzzy-based product negotiating agents (e.g., the iJADE Negotiator). We will discuss the design and implementation of these agents in detail in the second part of this book.

From the cognitive psychological point of view, this level of intelligence is also part of the *conscious thinking* category.

Intuitive Intelligence

This level of intelligence corresponds to the highest level of IA intelligence.

It is constructed by integration of *intuitive knowledge* – as the *knowledge domain* – with *intuitive thinking* (or *intuition* for short) – as the *thought domain* for knowledge acquisition.

It is named the *intuitive level* because this level of intelligence mimics intuitive intelligence as discussed in Chap. 2 and the early part of this chapter.

From the AI technological point of view, it corresponds to the design and modeling of ontological agents with high degrees of self-awareness, knowledge acquisition, and chaotic reasoning and thinking capability. It is the implementation of the *cognitrons* of the "Unification Theory of the Senses and Experiences" discussed in Chap. 2. It is also one of the major research directions for the future development of agent technology. We will return to this topic in the last chapter of this book – the *Cogito iJADE Project*.

From the cognitive psychological point of view, this level of intelligence corresponds to the *subconscious thinking* process. Table 3.1 gives a summary of the BFI model in terms of various aspects, including intelligence level, knowledge type, thinking type, cognitive behavior, AI technologies, and agent applications.

In this book, we will focus on the fuzzy–neuro level of intelligence. The main reason is: in our daily lives, most of the time we have to handle activities like making choices, performing decision making, scheduling, etc., which are all highly dynamic and possess a very high degree of uncertainty – what we called *fuzzy* and even *chaotic*. In order to implement IAs to help us to perform these jobs, the most natural way to succeed is to adopt these *fuzzy decision-making* and *mental activities* into our agents as well. However, to implement agents with built-in knowledge, we also need to integrate such *portable knowledge* into this fuzzy (or even chaotic) decision making – the so-called *fuzzy–neuro agents*. In Chap. 4, we will give an overview of all the common microscopic AI techniques for implementing such fuzzy–neuro agents. Also, in Part II of this book, we will present all the related implementations of these fuzzy–neuro agents, namely the iJADE agents.

Table 3.1. Summary of BFI model

Level of Intelligence	Intuitive Intelligence	Fuzzy–Neuro (Stimulated) Intelligence	Behavioral (Factual) Intelligence
Knowledge Type	Intuitive Knowledge	Stimulated Knowledge	Derived (Factual) Knowledge
Thinking Type	Intuitive Thinking (Intuition)	Lateral (Fuzzy/Chaotic) Thinking	Logical Thinking
Cognitive Behavior	Subconscious	Conscious	Conscious
AI Technologies Adopted	Cognitron Technologies	CA Reasoning Technologies	Mind–BA Reasoning Technologies
IA Application	Cogito iJADE applications	iJADE Shopper iJADE WeatherMan iJADE Stock Advisor iJADE Negotiator, etc.	IA Chess-master LT-IA (Language Translator) EK-IA (Expert Knowledge), etc.

3.8.2 The Agent Development Conceptual Model (GIA vs. TIA)

In the previous subsection, we just discussed the conceptual model (the BFI model) for the design of the intellectual capability of IAs. In this section, we will take a closer look at how to integrate this intellectual model to develop the agent systems.

As we mentioned in Chap. 2, all our daily mental activities, conceptually speaking, are just so-called *mind–body interactions* with the *external* environment. The main concept of IAs (as we discussed at the beginning of this chapter) is the *exemplification* of human intellectual activities into certain devices. In other words, the most straightforward and appropriate way for the implementation model of IAs should be a *direct reflection* of this interaction model – the so-called *general-purpose IA (GIA)* structural model (Fig. 3.4).

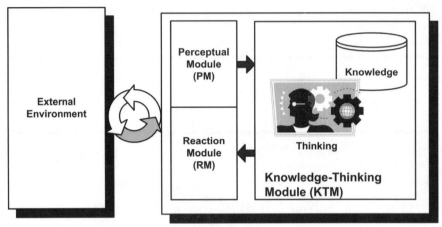

Fig. 3.4. General-purpose IA (GIA) structural model

This GIA structural model is called *general-purpose* in the sense that it is equipped with all *common sense* and *technical knowledge* for an IA to handle all daily activities – the *ideal* case. As shown in Fig. 3.4, the GIA model is just the *direct* implementation of human *mind–body–environment* mental activities into the agent systems, whereas the mind–body interaction is depicted by the interface between the *perceptual module* (PM), the *knowledge-thinking module* (KTM), and the *reaction module* (RM). The PM corresponds to the entire perceived stimulus (or queries) from the environment; the KTM corresponds to the knowledge storage and inference in the agent's "mind"; and the RM corresponds to all actions and reactions taken by the agent.

The GIA model is the ideal case in the sense that it is not an easy task to implement a general-purpose agent that can be equipped with all possible common sense and technical knowledge – at least using today's technology. In order to fix this problem, IAs can be developed in a so-called *intelligent-on-demand (IoD)* mode. That is, based on a similar architecture, the KTM is now divided into different functional modules. In other words, each submodule of the KTM will represent a different intelligent module that the agent needs to handle a particular task. So the agent will be developed as an *integrated intelligent device* according to the tasks – the *task-oriented IA* (TIA) development model. Figure 3.5 depicts a "powerful" intelligent auction agent with three different kinds of "plug-in intelligence":

active vision intelligence (e.g., for product visualization); negotiation intelligence (e.g., for product bargaining); and forecasting intelligence (e.g., for auction trend prediction).

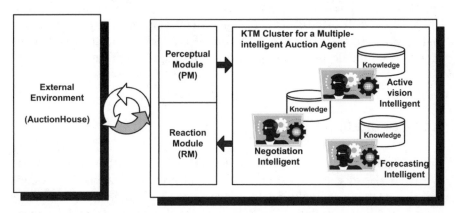

Fig. 3.5. A sample task-oriented IA (TIA) structural model for a multiple-intelligent auction agent (MAA)

Nowadays, in agent development this kind of IoD solution provides certain advantages. The most important advantage is the fact that the agent development platform can serve not only as the *common place* for the launch and implementation of IAs, but also as the "intelligent store" for the provision of these intelligent modules on demand. Actually, it is also the main feature of the iJADK compared to other agent platforms. In Chap. 5, we will discuss the design and implementation of iJADK in detail.

3.9 Major Challenges and Threats of Agent Technology

In view of the advance of technology in terms of computational speed and memory capacity, future IAs might be equipped with more powerful intelligence. It is a challenge for us to develop agents to meet these ever-increasing needs in solving more complex, fuzzy, and highly dynamic problems. Whether we can finally build general-purpose and multi-functional agents with human-like common sense and knowledge might be another challenge for us.

However, there are several risks or threats we have to handle with the increasing number of agent applications. The most critical one is the security problem, which has two aspects: (1) the risk or threat of *intruder agents*; and (2) the potential risk or threat of loss of personal (and important) information from our own agents to the outside world. In fact, an agent marketplace without any security (or housekeeping) control is just like opening your door and inviting anyone to come in; even a firewall may not fully protect your assets (your information). Standardization might be a possible solution, but it has to be reviewed from time to time. In Chap. 5, we will discuss several major agent standards, especially those that conform to the FIPA standard, one of the most popular international standards for the design and implementation of agent applications.

3.10 Concluding Remarks

In this chapter, we have presented a general overview of the history of AI. We have also discussed the emergence and growth of agent technology and presented conceptual models for the design and implementation of the agent's intelligent module – the *BFI agent intellectual model* and the agent development models – the *GIA* and *TIA structural models*. One may ask: With the launch of agent technology, does this mean the development of AI is over? In other words, does IA technology replace AI technology?

The answer is definitely "No." Owing to the rapid growth of IA technology, the needs and demands for more advanced and powerful AI techniques are even more feverish and greater than before. The author's observation is: nowadays, we are in the age of *Applied AI technology* – the so-called *AAI (Applied AI)*, in the sense that what we are working on now in the research lab might result in real commercial applications or products in the next couple of years, so we can predict that in the near future we will have even more promising AI scientific breakthroughs in terms of academic research and also industrial contributions.

During the writing of this book, a new, challenging IA topic appeared: the investigation of self-awareness and autonomous agents, the so-called OAT (Ontological Agent Technology), which is the implementation of the classical but challenging problem in philosophy, namely the problem of *ontology*. This fascinating topic will be presented in Chap. 11. The author will also present his latest research work and describe future work in the design and development of his ontological agents – the *Cogito iJADE Project*.

4 AI Techniques for Agent Construction

Most people will agree with the statement that if, in comparison with foveal vision, peripheral vision can be called "fuzzy", the same term also applies to most subjective experiences.

Wolfgang Köhler

If life were eternal all interest and anticipation would vanish. It is uncertainty which lends its satisfaction.

Kenko Hoshi

Chaos often breeds life, when order breeds habit.

Henry Brooks Adams

In a world of fuzziness, chaos, and uncertainty, what we can do in our daily lives is to find some order to sort out these *unordered problems*. To implement agents that can give *practical* help in tackling all these fuzzy daily activities, we must provide some methods and techniques to simulate and model these fuzzy matters. This chapter will discuss contemporary AI techniques for handling all these fuzzy scenarios, and also to facilitate machine learning and knowledge acquisition behaviors to produce the so-called *fuzzy–neuro agents* – to handle what happens in this highly dynamic, uncertain, and fuzzy world!

4.1 The World of Fuzziness, Chaos, and Uncertainty

In our daily lives, we have to handle numerous things all the time – solving problems, asking and answering questions, etc. At the end of the day, if you sit down and try to recall how many things you handled that day, you will find that this number is surprisingly large. If you take a "closer look" at all these things, you will find that most (or almost all) of them have the following three basic properties:
1. They are *fuzzy* and *highly uncertain* in nature.
2. We need our knowledge and/or experience to handle them.
3. The methods and/or solutions to handle them are usually highly dynamic (or sometimes *chaotic*) in nature.

In fact, you might be aware that things that happen always seem to be highly "chaotic" and "unpredictable". Does this mean that we cannot do anything to predict them, or cannot model all these phenomena to be solved and handled automatically?

As we mentioned in Chap. 3, the existence of agent technology – or more precisely *fuzzy–neuro agents* (FNA) – is used mainly to solve all these fuzzy, uncertain, and sometimes even chaotic situations by the design and implementation of the *fuzzy–neuro module* of the IA module (as discussed in Sect. 3.8).

This chapter will firstly explore all the major AI components, which include fuzzy logic, neural networks, genetic algorithms, and chaos theory. Secondly, the chapter will discuss how these AI components can be integrated to solve complex AI – the "realistic" problems – happening in our daily lives. In addition to the fuzzy–neuro agents (the *iJADE agents*), which will be discussed in the Part II of the book, this chapter will also present the author's latest work on chaotic neural networks – the "Lee-associator" – and discusses how it can be applied to visual intelligence to simulate the human progressive memory recalling scheme. This advanced hybrid AI technique will provide the foundation for the latest research of IAs – the *ontological agent technology (OAT)*.

4.2 Fuzzy Logic

4.2.1 What Is Fuzzy Logic?

The term *fuzzy* – the description of something that is *blurred* or *indistinct* (in shape or outline) as defined in the *Oxford English Dictionary* – has been used by scholars and scientists for decades. For example, Wolfgang Köhler, in his remarkable work *Gestalt Psychology* (Köhler 1947), had such a description of *fuzzy*:

> But now listen to psychologists who talk, let us say, about the *fuzziness* that is characteristic of peripheral vision. What exact meaning can be conveyed by this word so long as it has no accurate definition? Such a definition, however, seems to be impossible wherever one has to do with the ultimate data of direct experience. If the psychologist is asked for the definition of *fuzziness* he may attempt to define it negatively, for instance, as lack of clearness. But this does not help us very much because we must now ask him what he means by clearness. He may now tell us that a high degree of clearness is a normal property of the central part of an orderly visual field.

Wolfgang Köhler, Gestalt Psychology, 1947, p. 12

A more "scientific" and mathematical interpretation for the "phenomenon of fuzzy" (or one can say the "fuzzy property of matter") attracted little attention from scientists until the feverish study of the Heisenberg Uncertainty Principle of matter in the late 1920s and 1930s. In 1937, quantum theorist Max Black published his paper "Vagueness: an exercise in logical analysis" in the distinguished journal *Philosophy of Science*, which proposed to use continuous logic component-wise techniques in sets and lists of elements (Kosko 1992). However, instead of using the name *fuzzy sets* to describe these "vague sets", he referred to these structures as "vagueness". Nevertheless, he was still considered as the first person to propose and define the first *fuzzy membership function* (Black 1937).

The term *fuzzy set* was coined by Lotfi A. Zadeh in 1965 in his influential paper "Fuzzy sets" which appeared in the journal *Information & Control* (Zadeh 1965). In this paper, Zadeh proposed a modified new kind of set theory (so-called *Fuzzy Set Theory*), which was used to describe the *degree of belonging* of an individual member, which can exist as any real value between 0 and 1, instead of just either 0 or 1. Moreover, he also demonstrated how these fuzzy sets could be operated, including *fuzzy set union* and *intersection*, and also developed a consistent framework for dealing with all of these structures and operations. Zadeh believed that *fuzzy sets*, instead of *crisp sets*, should intuitively exist in our world of experience. More importantly, these kinds of existence were even more *naturally* accepted by us and *consistent* with what we understood as our world of existence (Yan et al. 1994).

In this section, we will present an overview of *fuzzy logic*, its major components, and some basic operations, which is followed by an illustration of contemporary applications using this technology.

4.2.2 Fuzzy Theory and the Uncertainty Principle

In fact, Zadeh's observations were very sensible. Most people might think that a fuzzy set tries to turn everything in our perceived world "blurry", "unclear", or "uncertain", while a crisp set is the reality. Actually, it is just the opposite situation. "Lack of crispness" should instead be the *truth* of a real-world property.

According to the Heisenberg Uncertainty Principle, we cannot exactly (100%) determine (measure) the position and momentum of an object at the same moment, as indicated in the following equation:

$$\Delta x \cdot \Delta p = \frac{h}{4\pi}$$

change in Position

Planck constant

change in Momentum

(4.1)

where x and p are the position and momentum of the object, respectively, and h is the Planck constant.

From the fuzzy theory point of view, what the Heisenberg Uncertainty Principle tells us is that all the measured qualities appearing in our world of perception are *fuzzy* in the sense that it is not the *quality* itself that is fuzzy, but rather that we cannot always measure these physical qualities with 100% certainty.

We will return to this important and interesting phenomenon in the topic of chaos theory later in this chapter.

4.2.3 Fuzzy Logic – A Structural Overview

Structurally speaking, fuzzy logic can be decomposed into four basic components – the so-called *ICMR structural framework of fuzzy logic* as shown in Fig. 4.1.

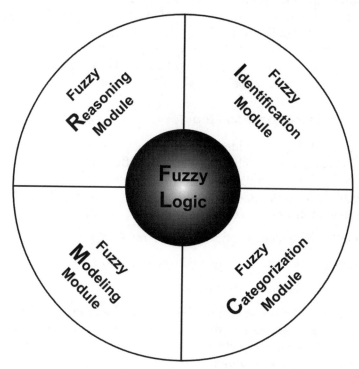

Fig. 4.1. The ICMR structural framework of fuzzy logic

(A) Fuzzy Identification Module

This module focuses on the determination and identification of the fuzzy variable(s) (FV) being used in the system. It is the first and the most important stage in the whole system design, because an incorrect (or inappropriate) identification of the FV(s) will defeat the whole purpose of system modeling. One important fact is that the same quality (variable) can play totally different roles in different scenarios for the design of fuzzy systems.

For example, if one wants to use fuzzy logic to represent the following statement:

"John is tall"

the fuzzy variable being used is the quality "height". Although this quality does not appear in the statement, conceptually speaking it is exactly what we mean by *common sense*, or what we called *priori knowledge*.

However, consider another statement:

"Most of the students in the class are tall"
In this case, if we want to represent this statement using fuzzy logic, the FV being used should not be the quality "height", but rather it should be the quality "most" – it describes the quality that describes the proportion of students that are tall in this class! In other words, we should be very careful in choosing the FV(s) being used in a fuzzy system.

(B) Fuzzy Categorization Module

Based on the FV(s) being identified in the last module, this module focuses on how to categorize the chosen FV(s) into different fuzzy sets.

By using the example discussed in the previous case, for the FV "height", the possible fuzzy sets will be "short", "average", and "tall" – in which each of them is a fuzzy set with a range of values:

"Short" – for student height below 1.55 m

"Average" – for student height between 1.5 and 1.65 m

"Tall" – for student height over 1.6 m

As shown in the above example, one major characteristic of fuzzy sets is that there exists *fuzziness* in their boundaries. In other words, there is not always a clear boundary between one fuzzy set and another, which is totally unacceptable in a traditional crisp set.

Of course, the categorization of fuzzy sets is up to the system designer in the sense that there are no strict criteria for one to decide the number, the type and nature of fuzzy sets being used. But of course, it should be *logical* and *make sense*. For instance, instead of using three fuzzy sets, one can further categorize "height" into five categories: "Very short", "Short", "Average", "Tall", and "Very tall".

(C) Fuzzy Modeling Module

For each fuzzy set, the designer has to define the *membership function* (MF) for it. The membership function is one of the most important components in fuzzy logic. It defines the *fuzzy mapping* – the *fuzzy belongings* of each element within its fuzzy set.

From the mathematical point of view, let X be a collection of objects denoted by $\{x \mid x \in X\}$, which is the so-called *universe of discourse*. A fuzzy set A in this *universe of discourse* X is characterized by a membership function $\mu_A(x)$ which takes values in the interval [0, 1]. For instance, if we define the fuzzy set A as:

$$A = \{(x, \mu_A(x) \mid x \in X)\} \tag{4.2}$$

If X is continuous, the fuzzy set A will be written as:

$$A = \int_X \mu_A(x)/x \tag{4.3}$$

Otherwise, if X is discrete, the fuzzy set A will be written as:

$$A = \sum_N \mu_A(x_i)/x_i \tag{4.4}$$

where N is the total number of possible discrete values in A.

By using the above example, one can model the fuzzy membership functions of each fuzzy element for the FV "height" as shown in Fig. 4.2.

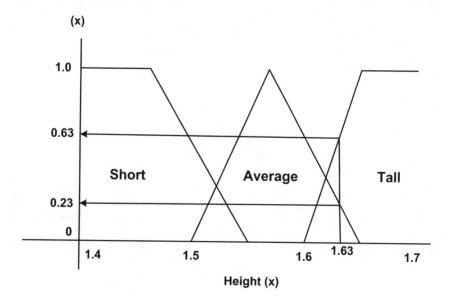

Fig. 4.2. The fuzzy membership functions of all the fuzzy elements "Short", "Average", and "Tall"

According to the fuzzy membership functions shown in Fig. 4.2, if we say "the height of a student (Jack) is 1.63", the membership functions for fuzzy sets "Average" and "Tall" will be 0.23 and 0.63, respectively. The implications for these fuzzy values are:

"Jack is tall, but he is not among the tallest ones in the class. But overall speaking, he is taller than the average students in the class."

Fuzzification vs. Defuzzification

The above example also demonstrates a very important concept in fuzzy logic – the "fuzzification" vs. "defuzzification" scheme. As discussed at the beginning of this section, the main concept of fuzzy logic is to *reflect* the *reality of our world of experience* (our *perceived world*), which is uncertain and fuzzy. In other words, the main job of fuzzy logic is to act as a bridge (or a "crystal ball" as shown in Fig. 4.3) for us to convert the "precise" values (and measurements) in the *machine world* (the so-called *digital world*) to the "imprecise" values in the real world (the so-called *perceived world*) which is full of fuzziness and uncertainty.

From the operational point of view, we denote the *forward operation*, which is the conversion of "digital measurements" in the machine world to "fuzzy values" in the real world, as the *fuzzification* scheme, while the reverse one is the *defuzzification* scheme.

From the mathematical point of view, *fuzzification* is the forward mapping of the membership function, while *defuzzification* is the reverse mapping (inverse function) of the membership function.

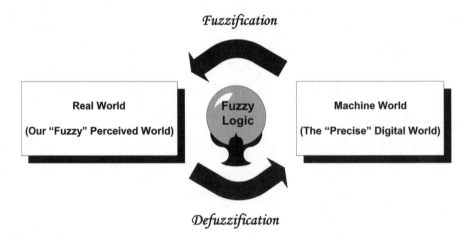

Fig. 4.3. Fuzzification vs. defuzzification

(D) Fuzzy Reasoning Module

This module is the "brain" of the whole fuzzy system in the sense that it aims at the exploration of the heuristics of the system by applying the so-called *fuzzy reasoning technique*.

This module consists of three main processes: (1) the *fuzzy rules construction process* (FRCP); (2) the *fuzzy knowledge-base construction process* (FKCP); and (3) the *fuzzy inference process* (FIP).

Fuzzy Relations (FRs) and Fuzzy Knowledge Base (FKB)

Fuzzy rules are basically sets of *fuzzy relations* (FRs), which normally appear in the form of "if–then" propositions. They are also called *fuzzy implication functions* (FIFs). Mathematically speaking, a FIF is denoted in the form:

$$\text{If } x \text{ is } A \text{ then } y \text{ is } B, \text{ where } x, A \in X, y, B \in Y \tag{4.5}$$

or written as:

$$R = A \rightarrow B \quad \text{where } R \text{ is the fuzzy rule} \tag{4.6}$$

The *fuzzy knowledge base* (FKB) is the *knowledge center* of a fuzzy system. In a typical fuzzy system, the FKB normally appears as a collection of fuzzy rules to represent a particular domain (or domains) of knowledge.

Following the above notation for the FIF used in (4.6), the FKB of a fuzzy system is denoted by a collection of fuzzy rules:

$$R_k = A_k \rightarrow B_k, \ k \in [1 \dots N] \tag{4.7}$$

where N is the total number of fuzzy rules used in the FKB.

From the implementation point of view, there are various approaches to implement the fuzzy relation operations. It is up to the system developers to choose the most suitable one for their applications. According to the comprehensive survey done by Nakanishi et al. (1993), Table 4.1 shows the four commonly used fuzzy rule implementation schemes.

Table 4.1. Commonly used fuzzy rule implementation schemes

Methods Used	Fuzzy Rule "If x is A then y is B" where $x, A \in X, y, B \in Y$
Mini Rule	$R_{\text{mini}} = A \times B = \int_{X \times Y} \mu_A(x) \wedge \mu_B(y)/(x,y)$
Product Rule	$R_{\text{product}} = A \times B = \int_{X \times Y} \mu_A(x) \cdot \mu_B(y)/(x,y)$
Max–Min Rule	$R_{\text{max-min}} = (A \times B) \cup (\text{not } A \times Y) = \int_{X \times Y} (\mu_A(x) \wedge \mu_B(y)) \vee (1 - \mu_A(x))/(x,y)$
Arithmetic Rule	$R_{\text{arith}} = (\text{not } A \times Y) \oplus (X \times B) = \int_{X \times Y} 1 \wedge (1 - \mu_A(x) + \mu_B(y))/(x,y)$

Fuzzy Inference Process (FIP)

Fuzzy inference refers to the fuzzy reasoning (heuristic) operations based on the *facets* (or fuzzy facets) and *knowledge* (the FKB) in the fuzzy systems. There are two kinds of fuzzy inference methods: (1) the *generalized modus ponens* (GMP) and (2) the *generalized modus tollens* (GMT) (Yan et al. 1994). Owing to their characteristics of inference operations, GMP and GMT are also called *direct reasoning* and *indirect reasoning*, respectively.

For example, given two groups of fuzzy sets $A, A' \in X$ while $B, B' \in Y$:

(I) GMP

For any two variables x and y, suppose we are given:

(a) Implication (the fuzzy rule):   if x is A then y is B

(b) Premise: x is A'

(c) Conclusion: y is B'

which can be denoted by:

$$B' = A' \circ R \ \text{(where } R \text{ is the relation)} \tag{4.8}$$

(II) GMT

For any two variables x and y, suppose we are given:

(a) Implication (the fuzzy rule):   if x is A then y is B

(b) Premise: y is B'

(c) Conclusion: x is A'

which can be denoted by:

$$A' = R \circ B' \ \text{(where } R \text{ is the relation)} \tag{4.9}$$

Fuzzy Compositional Rule of Fuzzy Inference

One of the most important and powerful functions of fuzzy reasoning is the *fuzzy compositional rule* (FCR) for fuzzy inference. This situation arises when there is a complex knowledge base containing a list of fuzzy rules (R_k) with the corresponding measured input signals A'_k for each fuzzy set A_k. That is:

$$x = (A'_1, A'_2, \ldots, A'_k, \ldots, A'_n)$$

$$y = B'_j, j = [1 \ldots n] \tag{4.10}$$

Based on the GMP defined in (4.8), the fuzzy variable B' can be inferred as the composition operation between the fuzzy set A_k and the fuzzy relation R:

$$B' = (A'_1, A'_2, \ldots, A'_k, \ldots, A'_n) \circ R \tag{4.11}$$

From the implementation point of view, two composition schemes are commonly adopted: (1) the *sup-min* operation and (2) the *sup-product* operation (Yan et al. 1994; Munakata 1998).

In the sup-min operation, the membership function value ($\mu_{B'}$) after the composition operations is given by:

$$\mu_{B'} = \bigcup_{k=1}^{n} \left[\sup_x \left(\wedge_{i=1}^{n} \mu_{A_i} \right) \wedge \left(\wedge_{i=1}^{n} \mu_{A_{ki}} \to \mu_{B_k} \right) \right] \tag{4.12}$$

Basically, a composite fuzzy reasoning process consists of the following four steps (Yan et al. 1994):

Step 1: Identify each fuzzy rule and determine the "connectives" for each condition in the rule base, in which an "OR" clause represents a *union* operation, and an "AND" clause represents an *intersection* operation.

Step 2: For each fuzzy rule (R_k), locate the "fire strength" α_k.

Step 3: Using either the sup-min or sup-product method, infer the overall *defuzzification control action*.

4.2.4 Fuzzy Reasoning – A Case Study on Fuzzy Air-conditioning Control Systems

In this subsection, we will make use of a simple *fuzzy air-conditioning control system* (FACS) to illustrate how fuzzy composite reasoning works.

First of all, suppose the FACS can vary its power control (Power) by two environmental factors of the surrounding air condition, namely air temperature (Temp) and relative humidity (RH), which are given by two sets of fuzzy variables:

Temp = {Very Cold, Cold, Cool, Mild, Warm, Hot, Very Hot}

RH = {Very Dry, Dry, Humid, Very Humid}

and the ranges of temperatures and relative humidity for each fuzzy variable are given by Table 4.2.

Table 4.2. Temperature and relative humidity ranges for each Temp/RH fuzzy variable

Temp Description (Fuzzy variables)	Fuzzy Temp Range (°C)	Relative Humidity (Fuzzy variables)	Fuzzy RH Range (%)
Mild	17–25	Dry	≤ 60
Warm	23–31	Moderate	55–85
Hot	25–33	Humid	65–95
Very Hot	≥ 28	Very Humid	> 75

Their corresponding fuzzy membership functions are illustrated in Fig. 4.4 and Fig. 4.5, respectively.

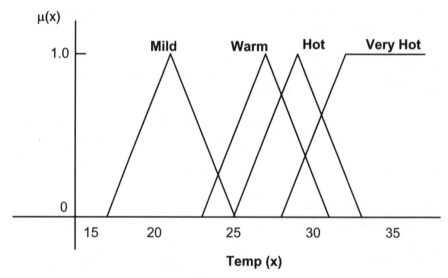

Fig. 4.4. Fuzzy membership functions for Temp

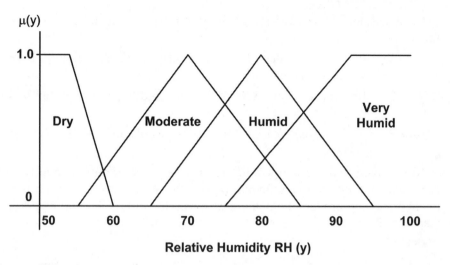

Fig. 4.5. Fuzzy membership functions for RH

Suppose that the power setting of the FACS has three different fuzzy states, given by:

Power = {Low, Medium, High}

with the membership function shown in Fig. 4.6.

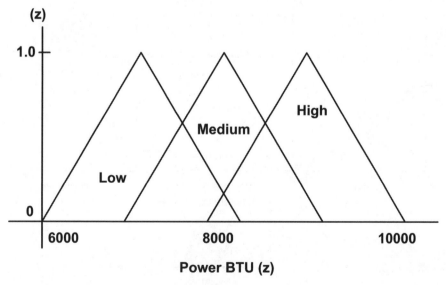

Fig. 4.6. Fuzzy membership function of Power

Now, assume this power switch is controlled by the following three fuzzy rules:

Rule 1:   If Temp is "Very Hot" **AND** RH is "Very Humid" Then switch to "High"

Rule 2:   If Temp is "Hot" **AND** RH is "Humid" Then switch to "Medium"

Rule 3:   If Temp is "Warm" **OR** RH is "Moderate" Then switch to "Low"

Now, given that the temperature is 30°C and the relative humidity is 80%, the defuzzification schemes of the Power by using the sup-min method and sup-product method are as illustrated in Fig. 4.7 and Fig. 4.8, respectively.

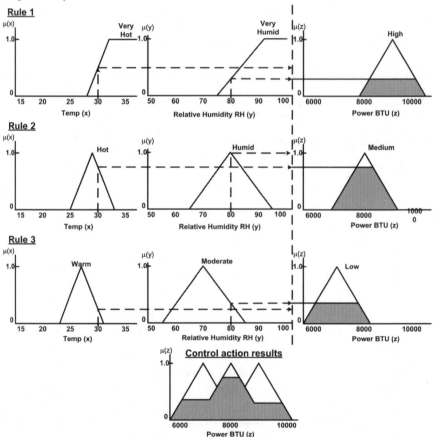

Fig. 4.7. Fuzzy reasoning of FACS (for the given conditions) by using the sup-min method

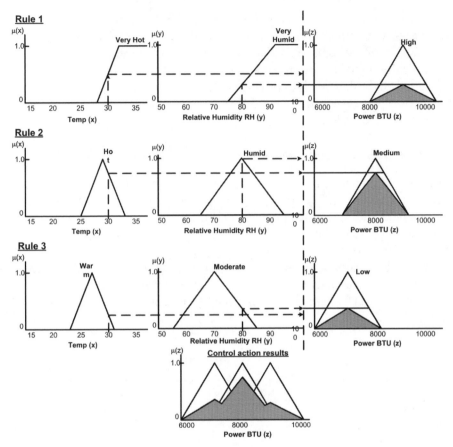

Fig. 4.8. Fuzzy reasoning of FACS (for the given conditions) by using the sup-product method

4.2.5 Applications of Fuzzy Logic

Nowadays, fuzzy logic is widely adopted in many real-world applications ranging from fuzzy electronic appliances such as fuzzy cookers, fuzzy air-conditioners, and fuzzy washing-machines, to sophisticated control systems such as fuzzy robotics and fuzzy-based ABS (automatic braking systems). In fact, many Japanese car manufacturers now incorporate fuzzy systems for antilock braking, active suspension systems, automatic transmissions, and engine emission controls into their automobiles. Fuzzy systems are easy to set up, typically require less processing power than alternative approaches, and provide robust performance.

From the implementation point of view, currently fuzzy logic are mainly integrated with other AI technologies in order to solve complex problems and produce more sophisticated and comprehensive systems.

Basically there are two major kinds of system integration techniques (or so-called "hybridization") to produce *hybrid systems*. They include:
– fuzzy expert systems (or *fuzzy-ES* for short)
– fuzzy–neuro systems

Fuzzy Expert Systems (Fuzzy-ES)

Owing to the capability of fuzzy systems that can handle imprecise concepts and values, fuzzy logic has been widely used in many practical commercial and industrial applications. Fuzzy-ES focus on the integration of fuzzy logic (e.g., fuzzification schemes) with expert knowledge in classical expert systems.

A typical schematic diagram of a fuzzy expert system, which incorporates a fuzzy knowledge base (KBS) to drive expert advice for the cold surge prediction system (CSPS) in weather forecasting, is shown in Fig. 4.9.

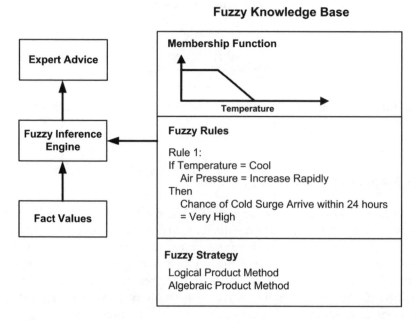

Fig. 4.9. Schematic diagram of a fuzzy expert system in the CSPS (cold surge prediction system)

Fuzzy–Neuro Systems

The major shortcoming of the fuzzy system is the lack of *learning capability*. The design of fuzzy sets and the assignment of all fuzzy relations are done by the system designers (or experts) without any way of automatically acquiring the membership functions and inference rules.

To solve this problem, *hybridization* with other AI models that provide automatic machine learning such as neural networks – the so-called *fuzzy–neuro systems* – has been developed, which is the focus of this book. Nowadays, fuzzy–neuro systems are widely adopted for solving complex problems such as stock prediction, severe weather forecasting (e.g., rainstorm prediction), adaptive tracking systems (e.g., tropical cyclone (TC) tracking systems, missile tracking systems), robot vision, etc. We will return to this topic shortly after the discussion of neural networks in the next section.

4.3 Neural Networks – The "Brain" of IAs

In Chap. 2, we presented a brief overview and the origins of neural networks. In this chapter, we will focus on the detailed functional designs and implementations of neural networks. In particular, the author will present the basic architectures of some commonly used neural networks and will also illustrate how these neural networks can be applied to problem solving and system modeling. Additionally, the author will also discuss the latest work on the development of neural networks and how they are integrated with other technologies to tackle complex AI problems.

4.3.1 Neural Networks – Background

In the early days, AI researchers aimed at modeling the function of the human brain. However, their attempts were unsuccessful until the mid-1940s, when Warren McCulloch and Walter Pitts proposed the first *artificial neural network* (ANN, or *neural network* for short) model (McCulloch and Pitts 1943), which was further explored in the late 1980s as a promising approach to deal with some classes of vital AI problems with satisfactory solutions.

Different from traditional computer systems, the main architecture of ANNs emulates the functionality of the human nervous system. This nervous system, as it is now known, consists of an extremely large number (over 10^{11}) of nerve cells, or neurons, which operate in parallel to process various types of information. Tree-like networks of nerve fiber called dendrites are connected to the cell body or soma, where the cell nucleus is located. Extending from the cell body is a single long fiber called the axon, which eventually branches into strands and substrands, and is connected to other neurons through contact points known as synapses. The transmission of signals from one neuron to another at synapses is a complex chemical process in which specific transmitter substances are released from the sending points of the junctions. The effect is to adjust the electrical potential inside the body of the receiving cell. If the potential reaches a threshold, a pulse will be generated down the axon, known as "firing" (Fig. 4.10).

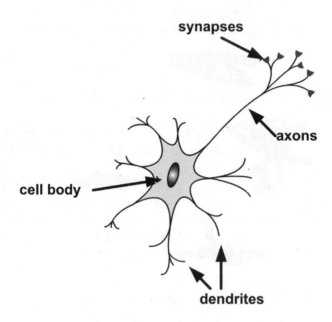

Fig. 4.10. A biological neuron

4.3.2 ANN Architecture

As an analog of the biological neuron, the schematic diagram of neuron structure in Fig. 4.11 can be interpreted as a computational model in which the synapses are represented by *weights* that modulate the effect of the associated *input signals*. The nonlinear characteristics exhibited by neurons are represented by a *transfer function* such as a binary or bipolar sigmoid function, given by:

Transfer functions (using "*S-shaped*" Sigmoid curve"):

$$f(x) = \frac{1}{1+e^{-\sigma x}} \quad \text{(binary sigmoid)} \tag{4.13}$$

$$f(x) = \frac{1-e^{-\sigma x}}{1+e^{-\sigma x}} \quad \text{(bipolar sigmoid)} \tag{4.14}$$

where σ is the steepness parameter to control the "curvature" of the sigmoid curve.

The neuron impulse (output signal) is then computed as the weighted sum of the input signals, transformed by the transfer function. The learning capability of an artificial neuron is achieved by adjusting the weights in accordance with a predefined learning algorithm, usually by $\Delta W_j = \alpha \sigma X_j$ where α is the learning rate and σ the momentum rate.

Figure 4.11 shows the schematic model of a neuron.

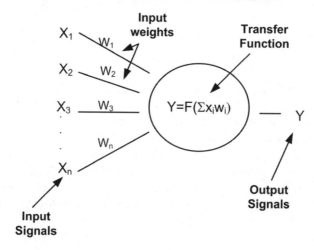

Fig. 4.11. Schematic model of a neuron

Typical ANNs often consist of intermediate layers known as *hidden layers* to facilitate the nonlinear computational capabilities of the network model. Classical ANNs, such as the feedforward neural network (FFNN) (Fig. 4.12), allow signals to flow from the input units to the output units, in a forward direction. Typical ANNs include the Kohonen self-organizing maps (SOM) and learning vector quantization (LVQ) – neural networks based on competition, and the adaptive resonance theory (ART) and feed-forward backpropagation neural network (FFBPN).

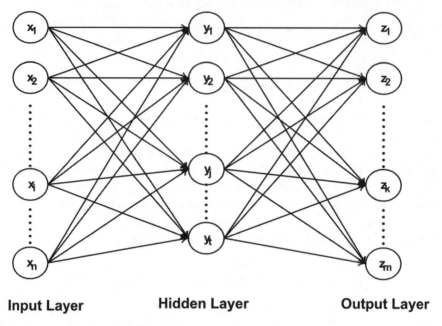

Input Layer   **Hidden Layer**   **Output Layer**

Fig. 4.12. Classical feedforward neural network model

ANNs can be regarded as multivariate nonlinear analytical tools, and are known to be superior at recognizing patterns from noisy, complex data, and estimating their nonlinear relationships. Many studies revealed that ANNs have the distinguished capability to learn the underlying mechanics of time series problems ranging from prediction of stocks and foreign exchange rates in various financial markets to the weather forecast (Fausett 1994; Munakata 1998; Patterson 1996).

4.3.3 Classification of Neural Networks

After half a century of development of neural networks, numerous neural networks have been proposed. In fact, there are over 20 different types of commonly used ANNs.

Basically, all these ANNs can be broadly classified into two groups: (1) supervised neural networks – neural networks operating with supervised learning and training strategies, which consist mainly of ANNs such as the Hopfield network, FFBPN (Feedforward Backpropagation Network), RBF

(Radial-Basis Function) network, etc.; and (2) unsupervised neural networks – neural networks that do not need any supervised learning and training strategies, including all kinds of self-organizing, self-clustering, and learning networks such as SOM, ART (Adaptive Resonant Theory), and so on.

For the ease of implementation, ANNs can also be further classified according to their system architecture and application areas (Fig. 4.13).

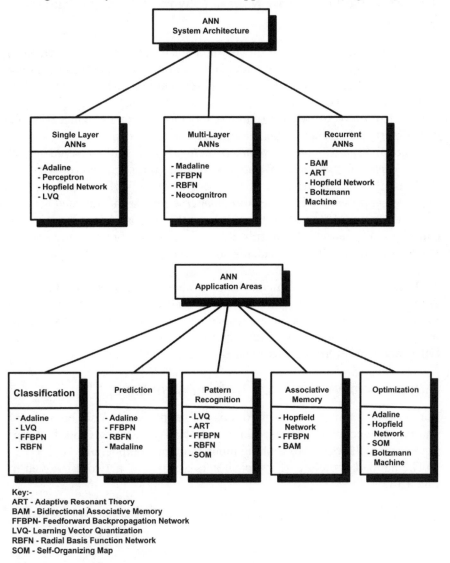

Key:-
ART - Adaptive Resonant Theory
BAM - Bidirectional Associative Memory
FFBPN- Feedforward Backpropagation Network
LVQ- Learning Vector Quantization
RBFN - Radial Basis Function Network
SOM - Self-Organizing Map

Fig. 4.13. Classifications of neural networks (Patterson 1996)

This section will deal with three commonly used neural networks and discuss their system architecture and potential applications, namely associative memory neural networks, the Hopfield network, and FFBPN. These ANNs will also be adopted for iJADE agents to be presented in Part II of this book.

4.3.4 Associative Memory Neural Networks: Auto-associative Networks

Associative learning is one of the major characteristics of human behavior, and is also widely used by humans and machines for pattern recognition such as visual pattern identification and recognition such as the *recalling* of human faces, the *recognition* of voices and music, and also including the *association* of knowledge (and memory) for problem solving. It is one of the most fundamental of human intellectual behaviors.

Generally speaking, an *associative network* is a single-layered neural network used to store a set of patterns for pattern association (or what we call "recalling"). The training of the associative network is conducted by the iterative presentation of the stored patterns for weights updated according to the training algorithm. Once the training is completed, the network can be used to associate not only the stored pattern, but also the *correct* stored pattern upon the presentation of an *incomplete* or *noisy* query pattern.

Basically, there are two major kinds of associative networks: (1) auto-associative networks, in which the input (and query) patterns are of the same type (and nature) as the associated pattern; and (2) hetero-associative networks, in which the input (and query) patterns are of totally different types (and nature) from the associated patterns.

Auto-associative Network – Training Algorithms

For network training, the *Hebb Rule* is commonly used. Also, both binary and bipolar vectors can be used in the associative networks, and the training vectors will be a set of training input and target output pairs (x', y').

The network structure of a typical auto-associative network is given in Fig. 4.14.

Input nodes   **Output nodes**

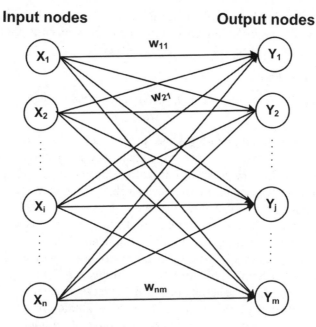

Fig. 4.14. System architecture of associative network

<u>Training Algorithm (4.1) – Associative Network (Fausett 1994; Patterson 1996)</u>

Step 1: Network weight initialization

        For all i, j *where $i \in [1 \dots n], j \in [1 \dots m]$, n, m are the total numbers of neuron input nodes and output nodes respectively.*

        Set $w_{i,j} = 0$

Step 2:   For each training pair (x', y'), perform the following operations:

    Step 2.1:   Set the activation values for the input nodes as the values of the training input

                 i.e., $x_i = x'_i$ *$i \in [1 \dots n]$*

    Step 2.2:   Set the activation values for the output nodes as the values of the target output

                 i.e., $y_j = y'_j$ *$j \in [1 \dots m]$*

    Step 2.3:   Update ALL the weights in the network

                 i.e., $w_{ij}(new) = w_{ij}(old) + x_i\, y_j$

                 $i \in [1 \dots n], j \in [1 \dots m]$

Besides the simple Hebb Rule for adjustments to weights, other methods such as the *Delta Rule* can also be adopted. In that case, the weight adjustment formula (in Step 2.3) will be replaced by:

$$w_{ij}(new) = w_{ij}(old) + \alpha(y'_j - y_j)x_i, \ i \in [1 \ldots n], j \in [1 \ldots m]$$

where α is the so-calling "learning rate" of the network.

While the architecture of the associative network is too simple to be used on complex patterns such as human face association and character recognition, it does provide an innovative means of applying neural networks for pattern association, memory storing, and recalling.

Regarding fairly recent developments of associative networks, current neuro-physiological research reveals that our memory associative mechanisms for pattern recalling are highly dynamical, oscillating, and even chaotic in nature (Freeman 2001). In fact, physiologists believe that our memory recalling scheme is acting in a highly *chaotic* manner with a *progressive recalling* scheme. Inspired by these discoveries in neuroscience and neuro-physiology, the author (Lee 2004c) proposed a chaotic neural associative network – the *Lee-associator* – to model the chaotic and progressive human memory recalling mechanisms, which will be discussed shortly in this chapter.

4.3.5 Hopfield Networks

In 1984, John Hopfield published his influential paper "Neurons with graded response have collective computational properties like those of two-state neurons" (Hopfield 1984) and described how a simple recurrent *auto-associative network* can be used for content-addressable memory systems, which can also be used for pattern recognition and to tackle complex optimization problems such as the typical Traveling Salesman Problem (TSP).

In this section, we will take a look at the original Hopfield network, the so-called *discrete Hopfield network*.

Basically, the architecture of the Hopfield network is similar to a classical auto-associative network, but with three basic differences: (1) the Hopfield network is a *recurrent network* in the sense that the *output nodes* in one time step are fed as the *input* in the next time step; (2) in the classical associative network, all the neurons will update their activations at the same time, but in the Hopfield network only one neuron will be chosen to update its activation at a time and will then "broadcast" its new state to other members of the network; and (3) each neuron will keep on receiving the "stimulus" from the external signal during the whole process. The architecture of the discrete Hopfield network is shown in Fig. 4.15.

Training Algorithm (4.2) – Discrete Hopfield Network (Fausett 1994; Patterson 1996)

Step1: Store all the (binary) patterns into the network (using the Hebb Rule). For each pattern $\mathbf{x}'_p = (x'_{p1}, x'_{p2}, \ldots, x'_{pm})$, where p is the pattern number and m is the total number of patterns to store, calculate:

$$w_{ij} = \sum_{p=1}^{m} \left[2x'_{pi} - 1 \right]\left[2x'_{pj} - 1 \right] \quad for\ i \neq j$$

otherwise $w_{ij} = 0$

Step 2: If neuron activations have not yet converged, do the following:

　　Step 2.1: Set the initial activation values for the network as the values of the external input vector $\mathbf{x}'$:
　　　　i.e., $z_i = x'_i, \quad i \in [1 .. n]$

　　Step 2.2: For each unit X, performs Steps 2.2.1–2.2.3 (update unit in random order):

　　　　Step 2.2.1: Calculate the network input:

$$z_{in_i} = x_i + \sum_{j=1}^{n} z_j w_{ji}$$

　　　　Step 2.2.2. Determine the activation value:

$$z_i = \begin{cases} 1 & if\ z_{in_i} > \theta_i \\ z_i & if\ z_{in_i} = \theta_i \\ 0 & if\ z_{in_i} < \theta_i \end{cases}$$

　　　　Step 2.2.3. "Broadcast" the new value of z_i to all neurons in the network

Step 3: Check for the convergence condition.

[Note: For a detail discussion for the algorithm of the Hopfield network, see Fausett (1994).]

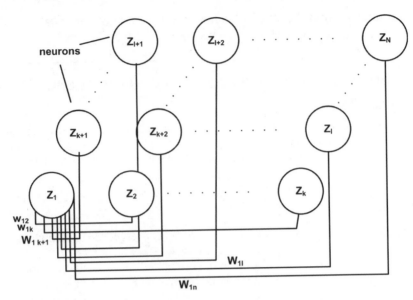

Fig. 4.15. System architecture of the discrete Hopfield network

One of the important points for the Hopfield network is that it demonstrates how a simple auto-associative network can be modified to produce a powerful *memory storage and retrieval device*. In fact, the vast application areas of Hopfield networks also triggered the rebirth of ANNs and the exploration of how neural networks can be applied to complex problems in daily operations.

4.3.6 Multi-layer Feedforward Backpropagation Networks (FFBPNs)

Different from the pervious two neural networks, FFBPNs provide a *multi-layer network architecture* (Fig. 4.16). A typical FFBPN consists of an input layer, a hidden layer, and an output layer. Although the FFBPN can consist of several hidden layers, in most of the cases one hidden layer is usually sufficient.

The network training of FFBPNs consists of three main processes: (1) the "feedforward" process of network training; (2) the "error evaluation" process to calculate the errors between the calculated output values and the target output values; and (3) the "backpropagation" process of the errors for weight adjustments. Similar to most other networks, training stops when the errors are bound within the tolerance level.

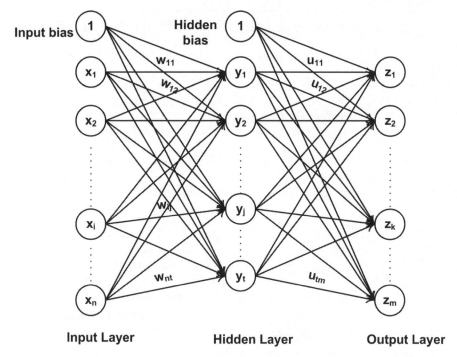

Fig. 4.16. System architecture of FFBPN

Note: Let w_{ij} denote the network weights between the input and hidden layer, and u_{jk} denote the network weights between the hidden and output layer. The total numbers of neurons in the input, hidden, and output layers are n, t, and m, respectively. For the activation functions, normally a sigmoid function is adopted.

An FFBPN can model various kinds of problems such as weather prediction and stock forecasting, pattern recognition problems such as character recognition, classification, and even optimization problems. However, the FFBPN has certain intrinsic problems and limitations such as the trapping in local minima and the difficulty in the choice of optimal parameter settings (and input vectors); the slow rate of convergence is also another major consideration.

Training Algorithm (4.3) – FFBPN (Fausett, 1994; Patterson, 1996)

Step 1:   Network weight initialization.

Set all network weights w_{ij}, u_{jk} to a small random number between 0 and 1.

Step 2:   While error $\geq$ threshold value, do the following:

Step 2.1:   For each training pair $(\mathbf{x}, \mathbf{z})$ do Steps 2.1.1 to 2.1.6.

Feedforward Procedure

Step 2.1.1 Calculate the input state of each hidden node:

$$y_{in_j} = \sum_{i=0}^{n} x_i w_{ij} \quad \text{where } x_0 \text{ is the input bias}$$

Step 2.1.2 Calculate the activation value for the hidden node:

$$y_j = f_y(y_{in_j}) \quad \text{where } f_y(\ ) \text{ is the activation function}$$

Step 2.1.3 Calculate the input state of each output node:

$$z_{in_k} = \sum_{j=0}^{t} y_j u_{jk} \quad \text{where } y_0 \text{ is the hidden bias}$$

Step 2.1.4 Calculate the activation value for the output node:

$$z_k = f_z(z_{in_k}) \quad \text{where } f_z(\ ) \text{ is the activation function}$$

Backpropagation Procedure

Step 2.1.5 For each output node:

(a) Calculate the error with the target value

$$\zeta_k = (z'_k - z_k) f'_z(z_{in_k}) \quad \text{where } f'(\ ) \text{ is } df_z/dz$$

(b) Calculate the correction errors

$$\Delta u_{jk} = \alpha \zeta_k y_j \quad \text{where } \alpha \text{ is the learning rate}$$

Step 2.1.5 For each hidden node:

(a) Calculate the accumulated errors in the hidden node

$$\lambda_{in_j} = \sum_{k=1}^{m} \zeta_k u_{jk}$$

(b) Calculate the correction errors in hidden node

$$\lambda_j = \lambda_{in_j} f'_y(y_{in_k}) \quad \text{where } f'(\ ) \text{ is } df_y/dy$$

(c) Calculate the weight adjustments

$$\Delta w_{ij} = \alpha \lambda_j x_i \quad \text{where } f'(\ ) \text{ is } df_y/dy$$

Step 2.1.6 Update all weights for the two layers (simultaneously):

$$w_{ij}(new) = w_{ij}(old) + \Box w_{ij}$$

$$u_{jk}(new) = u_{jk}(old) + \Box u_{jk}$$

Step 2.2:   Check the stopping criteria.

[Note: For a detail discussion of the algorithm for the Hopfield network see Fausett (1994).]

4.3.7 Neural Networks – Where to Go?

In this section, we have explored an overview of neural networks, their basic structure, and mechanisms. In fact, current trends in the research and development of neural networks are focused on three major areas: (1) the integration of other AI techniques to remedy some intrinsic limitations of the classical neural networks, including the integration of fuzzy logic – fuzzy–neuro systems – and the integration with GAs (genetic algorithms) to overcome the problem of parameter selection and fine tuning of networks; (2) the investigation of the neural dynamics, especially in the study of neural oscillators and neural oscillatory models; and (3) the investigation and study of the chaotic neural dynamics of chaotic neural networks to model complex AI problems.

Hybridization with Fuzzy Logic – Fuzzy–Neuro Systems

As mentioned earlier, one of the major shortcomings of fuzzy systems is the lack of learning capability. The design of fuzzy sets and the assignment of all fuzzy relations are done by system designers (or experts) without any way of automatically and dynamically acquiring the membership functions and inference rules. To address these shortcomings, *hybridization* with other models, such as neural networks, is proposed by many researchers. For instance, in the *FuzzyNet Model* proposed by Wong et al. (1991), an expert system was established by the hybridization of the neural network and the fuzzy logic in the following manner (Fig. 4.17).

The model consists of three main modules: (1) the membership function generator (MFG), to generate the membership functions which can be either provided by domain experts, or automatically generated by using some statistical methods based on historical data; (2) the fuzzy information processor (FIP), to accept three types of information from the database, namely fuzzy rules and initial weights indicating the "credibility" of the rules, historical data, and current data; (3) the backpropagation neural network (BPN), similar to the conventional backpropagation neural network except that the processing elements used are the neural gates generated by the FIP module.

Other possible hybridization schemes such as the extraction of fuzzy rules from a multi-layered neural network as proposed by Enbutsu et al. (1991) and the adaptive learning fuzzy controller using a genetic algorithm proposed by Janikow (1994) are typical examples.

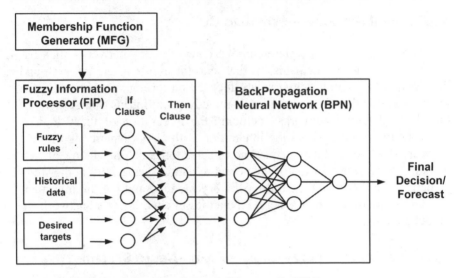

Fig. 4.17. FuzzyNet schematic diagram (Wong et al. 1991)

In the second part of this book, the author will illustrate how fuzzy–neuro systems can be integrated with agent technology to implement the iJADK agents for tackling complex problems, including: iJADE WeatherMan for active weather prediction; iJADE Negotiator for dynamic and fuzzy-based product negotiation; and iJADE WShopper for wireless fuzzy–neuro agent-based shopping.

4.4 Genetic Algorithms – The Nature of Evolution

4.4.1 Genetic Algorithms – Basic Principle

Evolution refers to the operations for the encoding of biological entities (chromosomes) rather than the living beings themselves. Natural selection is based on "survival of the fittest" – in effect, chromosomes with high fitness values will reproduce more than those with low fitness values.

In genetic algorithms (GAs) (Munakata 1998), the basic entity is the chromosome, which is a sequence of values/states. The basic algorithm resembles natural evolution, which involves the following operations (Fig. 4.18):

1. Initialization of the *population*.

2. Parent selection process.

3. Reproduction process involving *crossover* and *mutation* operations.

4. Fitness value evaluation.

5. Iterative execution on the *new population* until satisfactory performance is attained.

According to this "evolutionary theory", an offspring is normally fitter if its ancestors are better. According to this theory, chromosomes will grow better as the generations grow.

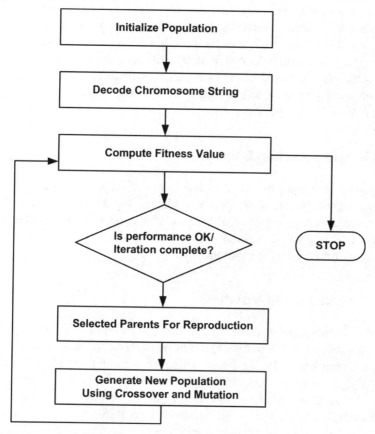

Fig. 4.18. A typical flow diagram of a GA system

4.4.2 Population Initialization

A population is a collection of chromosomes with the representation of a parameter set $\{x_1, x_2, x_3, ..., x_m\}$. This parameter set is to be encoded as a finite length string over an alphabet of finite length. It is usually encoded as a binary value of zeros and ones. To initialize the population, usually a random number generator is applied. For a chromosome of length m, the possible number of different chromosome strings is 2^m.

4.4.3 Fitness Evaluation

An evaluation function is applied to the population to compute the *fitness value* of a chromosome. It is vital that the whole GA remains in a form as it is the only selection criterion for the chromosome performance of the whole population and increases the possibility for reproduction. To justify the stopping criterion of the GA, it usually depends on whether the best chromosome in the population has attained a sufficient level or "evolution" (i.e., iteration of reproduction) has exceeded the generation limit (say a maximum of 1000 generations).

4.4.4 Parent Selection Scheme

For parent selection, a *roulette-wheel parent selection* scheme is commonly adopted. Those chromosomes selected for the possibility of reproduction are directly proportional to their fitness value, and they conform to the basic feature of natural selection that a "Fitter organism has a higher chance of survival, hence reproduction."

4.4.5 Crossover and Mutation

In the GA, there are two main operators for reproduction, namely *crossover* and *mutation*. In crossover, a pair of parent chromosomes is selected from the population. In *one-point crossover*, a random location is selected from the chromosome strings, and chromosome elements beyond this crossover point are exchanged to form a pair of new offspring according to the crossover rate. Similarly, for *two-point* and *uniform crossover*, multiple points are selected for crossover operations.

For mutation, a single chromosome is selected from the population which will be "screened" throughout the whole list. A particular element will be changed according to the *mutation rate*, which is normally much lower than the *crossover rate*.

The main purpose of crossover is to exchange information between randomly selected parent chromosomes with the aim of not losing any improvement of information. While the main objective of mutation is to introduce some genetic diversity into the population, it will remain at a slow rate in order not to disrupt the genetic characteristic of the "good genes."

4.4.6 Implementation of GAs

Based on the different parent selection criteria, reproduction scheme, crossover and mutation methods, there are numerous versions of schema for the implementation of GAs. The fundamental one is reproduction to replace all the parent population, using one-point crossover and bit mutation. For parent selection, the roulette-wheel parent selection scheme based on parent fitness value is applied.

In the *elitism scheme*, parents with the highest fitness value will be retained in the next generation in order to *guarantee* the *performance* of the population at a certain standard. For crossover operation, a two-point crossover in the other extreme to uniform crossover can be applied for other GA schemes.

For setting GA parameters, besides a fixed crossover and mutation rates throughout the whole evolutionary process, a dynamic crossover and mutation rate assignment scheme can also be used. The ratio of mutation rate will normally be set to a higher value when the number of generations increases to a higher level, such as 500 iterations. The main reason for this is to *induce* a higher diversity of the chromosomes when the whole population evolves to a more *mature stage*, whereas a higher mutation rate can bring more "freshness" to the population.

4.4.7 Hybridization of GA with Neural Networks

GAs have been widely used with neural networks in two specific areas: (1) topology optimization and (2) genetic training algorithms. In topology optimization, GAs are used to select the optimal topology for the neural network which in turn is trained using some fixed training scheme such as backpropagation. In genetic training algorithms, the learning of a neural network is formulated as a weight optimization problem, usually using the inverse mean square error as the fitness evaluation scheme. Instead of the hybridization of GA with the classical backpropagation neural net, Lee and Liu (1999) have proposed a hybrid system for the offline recognition of handwritten Chinese characters.

In their proposed model, Lee and Liu (1999) derived a new application of evolutionary computing (EC), namely the neural oscillatory elastic graph matching (NOEGM) model. This model consists of three main modules: (1) the feature extraction module using Gabor filters; (2) the character segmentation module using the neural oscillatory model; and (3) the character recognition module using the elastic graph dynamic link model (EGDLM). The GA is hybridized with the neural oscillatory model in order to enhance the accuracy and robustness of the Chinese character recognition system.

According to the schematic diagram (Fig. 4.19), the main function of the GA is to optimize the weights of the *dynamic links* within the hybrid neural oscillatory model.

Experimental results revealed that GA hybridization provides an overall 20% improvement.

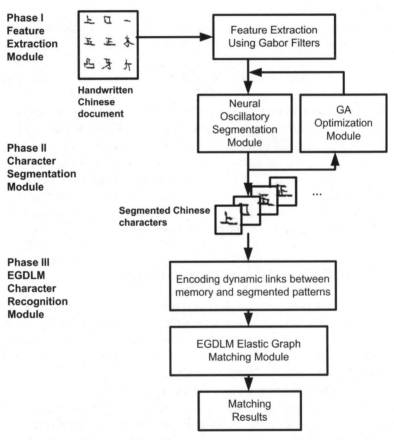

Fig. 4.19. Schematic diagram of the hybrid neural oscillatory model for handwritten Chinese character recognition

4.5 Chaos Theory – The World of Nonlinear Dynamics

4.5.1 Chaos Theory – The Study of Nonlinear Dynamics

What is the nature of our world? This problem has puzzled philosophers, scientists, poets, and scholars of various disciplines for centuries. In fact, different disciplines have their own ways and perspectives of interpreting this problem. Physicists (and most computer scientists) are concerned with the constitution of the world – with *matter* and its own *dynamics* – while most philosophers are concerned with the *nature* and the *truth* of the existence of this matter, and even the *existence of the world – ontology*. We will return to this topic at the end of the book. In the meantime, let us focus on the first question.

One might wonder: What is the importance of knowing the dynamics of all the matter in the world (and Universe)? To understand this question, let us have a look at this topic of "dynamics," which includes:

– The dynamics of *free-falling* objects – governed by Newton's Laws of Motion.

– The formation and dynamics of *black holes* – governed by Einstein's Theory of General Relativity.

– The dynamics of *subatomic particles* such as neutrinos and positrons – governed by Heisenberg's quantum mechanisms.

– The formation and dynamics of tropical cyclones, hurricanes, tornadoes, and earthquakes.

– The fluctuation of stocks …

– The chance of catching the bus this morning …

– The theory of causation …

– Your fate …

– Our future …

The fact is, this *world of dynamics* covers not only the "physical" motion of matter in the Universe, but also the "nonphysical" occurrence of events, notions, and ideas. In fact, chaos theory is the study of such "dynamics", which are believed to be highly nonlinear – *chaotic*.

In other words, if one wants to explore the *nature* of the dynamics governing matter (and notions) in the Universe, one must "enter" the world of chaos theory.

4.5.2 Battle Between Two Worlds: Deterministic Versus Probabilistic

So one might ask: As everything that happens in the world is highly dynamical (or chaotic, as we said) and uncertain, does this mean that chaos theory is the study of probability? The answer is absolutely not.

The fact is that chaos theory has a basis that is totally different from that of probability. Although chaos theory is the study of the world of dynamics, it is not a world of *uncertainty* or a matter of *chance*. Strictly speaking, chaos theory deals with the world of *determinism* rather than *probabilism*. Chaos theory maintains that all the dynamics in the world, no matter how complex they are, can be (and must be) somehow modeled deterministically by certain chaotic motions. Whether we can find these chaotic motions is another question. In fact, the *formal* name for chaos is *deterministic chaos* in order to reflect this characteristic.

From the mathematical point of view, no matter how complex a physical phenomenon is, the challenge of chaos theory is to model its dynamics by a set of equations, as follows:

(a) In discrete format:

$$x_{1,t+1} = f_1(x_{1,t}, x_{2,t}, ..., x_{n,t})$$
$$x_{2,t+1} = f_2(x_{1,t}, x_{2,t}, ..., x_{n,t})$$
$$...$$
$$x_{n,t+1} = f_n(x_{1,t}, x_{2,t}, ..., x_{n,t})$$

(4.15)

or written in vector format as:

$$\vec{x}_{t+1} = \vec{f}(\vec{x}_t)$$

(4.16)

where the **x** and **f** are variables and functions controlling the dynamics.

(b) In continuous format:

$$\dot{x}_1 = f_1(x_1, x_2, ..., x_n, t)$$
$$\dot{x}_2 = f_2(x_1, x_2, ..., x_n, t)$$
$$...$$
$$\dot{x}_n = f_n(x_1, x_2, ..., x_n, t)$$

(4.17)

or written in vector format as:

$$\dot{\vec{x}} = \vec{f}(\vec{x}, t)$$

(4.18)

The discrete chaotic motions are also called *chaotic maps*; and the continuous motions are called *chaotic flows*. From the physical point of view, the discrete maps can be regarded as taking "snapshots" (or "cross-sections") of the continuous flow on a regular (or timely) basis, as shown in Fig. 4.20.

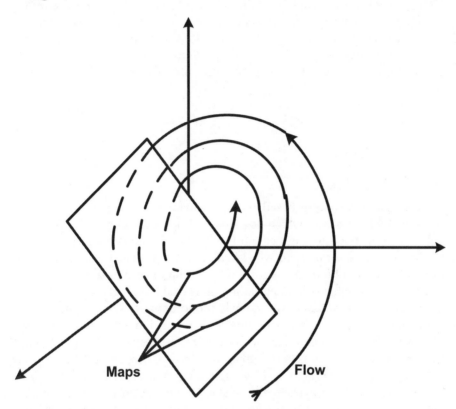

Maps   **Flow**

Fig. 4.20. Chaotic flow vs. chaotic maps in nonlinear motion

One might wonder: What is the significance of the findings of the maps and flows? The answer is: It is extremely important!

For example, if the variables under consideration are weather elements such as air temperature or rainfall, and the time step (say for a discrete map) is 5 days, then if we can find such chaotic function(s), what we have really done is to solve the weather forecasting problem! Imagine if the functions are used to model the next-day stock market or the 15-day financial pattern! So we can expect that what chaos theory is telling us is not something uncertain (or chaotic), but rather how to "identify" the *uncertain event in a chaotic way*!

4.5.3 A Snapshot of Chaos Theory

Although chaotic phenomena are not very complex and "rare" problems, the first time they were noticed by scientists was in the late nineteenth century by Henri Poincaré during his exploration of planetary motions in 1886. However, the major breakthrough in chaos theory was made by research meteorologist Edward Lorenz during his experiment on a "miniature" weather modeling system (Lorenz 1963) using three simple differential equations (the so-called *Lorenz equations*) instead of using complex statistical models (which were commonly used by meteorologists at that time).

The Lorenz equations are:

$$\dot{x} = -\sigma x + \sigma y$$
$$\dot{y} = -xz + rx - y \qquad\qquad (4.19)$$
$$\dot{z} = xy - bz$$

These equations were based on the fundamental Navier–Stokes equations of fluid dynamics, which describe weather formation as the fluid circulation of air upon distant heating by the Sun. In the Lorenz equations, x is the *fluid stream function*, whose value is proportional to the speed of motion of the fluid due to convection; y is proportional to the *temperature gradient* between the rising and falling parts of the fluid at a given height – the so-called *horizontal flow*; and z is proportional to the deviation from temperature linearity as a function of vertical position – the so-called *vertical flow*. The three parameters σ, r, and b are, respectively, the Prandtl number (a value which is based upon the physical property of the fluid involved), the Rayleigh number (a value which indicates the point at which convection starts for a particular system), and the "mystery" parameter which specifies the size of the area being represented by these equations. In Lorenz's original work, the value of b was set to 8/3.

In such a highly simplified weather model, Lorenz unexpectedly discovered two important things about this nonlinear model:

1. The nature of dynamics for the system itself can be totally changed with a change in the parameters.

    In his original work, Lorenz discovered that when the parameters σ and b are set to 10 and 8/3, respectively, the whole system will turn out to be highly chaotic without any steady states (and limit cycles) whenever the Rayleigh number (r) exceeds the critical value of 24.74. In other words, all the solutions would appear to be neither *periodic* nor *convergent* to any solution or equilibrium state.

2. The weather solution of this model, under such chaotic conditions, will be *extremely* sensitive to its *initial conditions*.

    In other words, within the *chaotic region*, only a very small deviation of initial conditions, say minor variations (or a "mistake") in inputting the initial weather conditions (of the order 10^{-5}), will result in a totally different weather situation in the following days, as shown in Fig. 4.22.

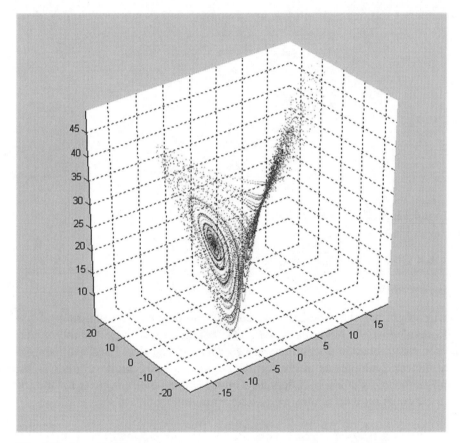

Fig. 4.21. Lorenz attractor

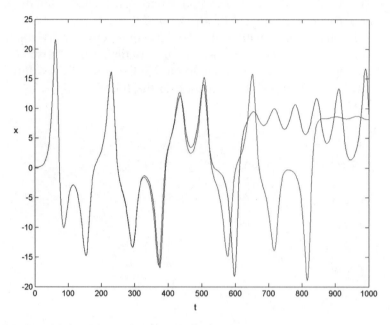

Fig. 4.22. Sensitivity of weather prediction to initial conditions

4.5.4 Characteristics of Chaotic Systems

Bifurcation

One might wonder whether only *complex* nonlinear equations such as the Lorenz equations have the *chaotic effect*. The answer is no. As mentioned previously, chaotic phenomena are so *common* and *usual* that even simple nonlinear dynamics as in the *logistic equation* (4.20) can have this chaotic phenomenon. Figure 4.23 depicts a typical *bifurcation diagram* for the logistic equation with control parameter *r* ranging from 0 to 4:

$$x_{t+1} = rx_t(1 - x_t) \tag{4.20}$$

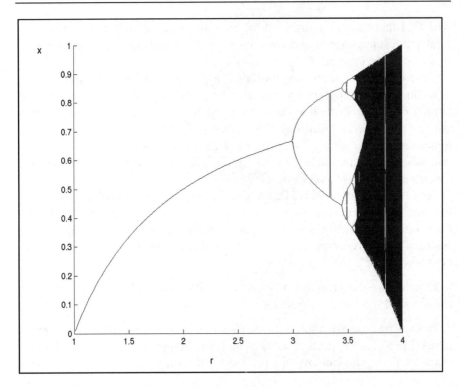

Fig. 4.23. Bifurcation diagram of the logistic equation

Bifurcation is a common phenomenon found in chaotic systems which indicates sudden, qualitative changes in the dynamics of the system under investigation either: (1) from one kind of periodic case (with limit cycle(s) and fixed point(s)) to another kind of periodic situation, such as the change in bifurcation of the logistic map from $r = 3$ (from one fixed point to two fixed points); or (2) from a periodic stage to a chaotic stage, such as the dramatic changes in the dynamics of the logistic map for r increasing from 3.5 to 4.

Fractals vs. Chaos – The Two Faces of a Coin

The bifurcation diagram of the logistic map shown in Fig. 4.23 also reveals other interesting phenomena of a typical chaotic system – namely, the existence of *self-similarity* in the chaotic dynamics. In fact, if one takes a closer look at the bifurcation pattern in the first chaotic region (i.e., $3.5 < r < 4$), one will find that similar bifurcation patterns can be found within the original pattern, but of course in a smaller or *scaled-down* size. More surprisingly, if you continue to "zoom in" to these bifurcation patterns, you will find that they contain, in turn, even more scaled-down features with totally the same shapes and patterns – what we call the *self-similarity* nature of chaotic systems.

Based on these interesting findings, a group of scientists established a new doctrine of applied mathematical geometry – *fractal geometry* (or simply *fractals*). Typical examples include the remarkable work of Koch – see the *Koch curve* (Addison 1997) shown in Fig. 4.24 – and the fractals generated by *Mandelbrot sets* in Fig. 4.25. In fact, Mandelbrot is also the one who coined the name "fractal" in his influential work *The Fractal Geometry of Nature* (Mandelbrot 1982).

As discussed previously, fractals and chaos are closely related, just like the two faces of a coin. From a geometrical point of view, all chaotic attractors are fractals; while all fractals have their bifurcations and chaotic features when presented in the form of nonlinear dynamic equations. In the author's terms:

Fractals are the graphical (visual) presentations of chaos while chaos is the physical dynamics of fractals.

In fact, fractals are applied in various real-world applications such as financial predictions, market pattern analysis, computer graphics, and landscape modeling (as one might have seen in the film *Star Wars*).

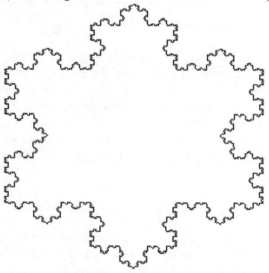

Fig. 4.24. The Koch curve

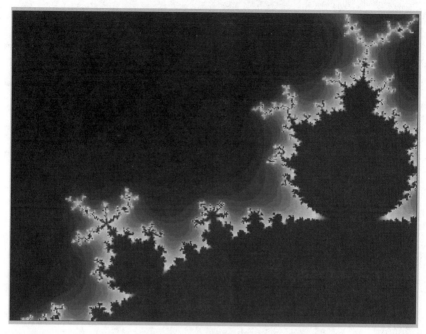

Fig. 4.25. Fractals generated from Mandelbrot sets

Major Characteristics of a Typical Chaotic System

In summary, there are several features and characteristics that can be found in a typical chaotic system:

- Sensitive to initial conditions.
- Highly nonlinear but deterministic in nature.
- The existence of bifurcation points that lead to chaos.
- The existence of self-similarity and fractals.

Applications of Chaotic Systems

Although chaos theory is rather new and its technology still emerging, there are already numerous applications in industries that have adopted this innovative technology including: consumer electronics, computer systems, health care and life sciences, engineering, and business. Table 4.3 summarizes the potential applications spun off from this fascinating technology.

Table 4.3. Potential applications of chaos theory in industry (Munakata 1998; Aihara and Katayama 1995)

Application Areas	Potential Applications
Consumer electronics	– Chaotic kerosene fan heater (Katayama et al. 1993) – Chaotic dishwasher (Nomura et al. 1994) – Chaotic air-conditioners – Chaotic mixer
Computer systems	– Lee-associator for progressive memory recalling (Lee 2004c) – Temporal pattern search (Davis 1990) – Chaotic mobile robot navigation (Tani et al. 1992) – Chaotic network design and implementation
Health care and life science	– EEG analysis of heart rhythms (Freeman 2001) – Chaos-aware defibrillator (Munakata 1998) – Chaotic brain wave analysis (Freeman 2001)
Engineering (Kapitaniak 2000)	– Circuit stability analysis – Vibration control and study – Heat combustion
Business (Mandelbrot 1997)	– Fractal market pattern analysis – Financial prediction – Market prediction (Peters 1994; Johnson 2003)

4.5.5 Chaos Theory Versus Uncertainty Principle

In the section on fuzzy logic (Sect. 4.2.2) we discussed the implication of the Heisenberg uncertainty principle on fuzzy logic. In fact, chaos theory is closely related to the Heisenberg Uncertainty Principle. As mentioned by Heisenberg in his work *Physics and Philosophy: The Revolution in Modern Science* (Heisenberg 1999), quantum mechanisms and the Uncertainty Principle should not be unusual or unique phenomena, but rather should be universal phenomena that exist in all matter (at the subatomic level). If this is the case, the subatomic phenomena somehow might be coherent with chaos theory.

Taking weather forecasts as an example, we know that most of the international weather centers use NWP (numerical weather prediction) techniques for forecasting. For every single forecast, we need to know the so-called *boundary conditions*, that is, grid-point weather observations including: wet- and dry-bulb temperatures, MSLP (mean sea-level pressure), upper-level wind speed and direction, and so on. According to chaos theory, slight differences (errors) in the measured values might result in totally different weather situations in the future. Moreover, according to the Heisenberg Uncertainty Principle, it is quite "impossible" for us to obtain 100% accuracy in measuring all the different weather conditions at the same time. Does this really mean that we can never predict our future accuracy?

The answer is "yes" and "no" – it depends on: (1) the scale of measurement; and (2) the type of weather phenomena we are going to model. As mentioned previously, the Heisenberg Uncertainty Principle is a sub-atomic-level phenomenon in the sense that from a macroscopic point of view, all the *classical* rules and relations such as Newton's Laws of Motion, the laws of thermal dynamics, and the laws of fluid dynamics are still valid. Besides, chaos theory, although common, is subject to conditions. From the meteorological point of view, the latest research has revealed that chaotic phenomena will only happen when there is an abrupt change in weather conditions, such as the formation of tropical cyclones, tornados, and severe rainstorms. In other words, under normal conditions and at the macroscopic scale, the classical NWP method for weather prediction still holds.

4.5.6 Current Work on Chaos Theory

According to what we have discussed in the previous section, one might wonder: "If we really intended to undertake the challenge to model these chaotic and highly uncertain weather situations, one possible method might be not to use the boundary conditions to perform NWP while still predicting the future. Does such a method exist?"

The answer is yes. In fact, what we have discussed in this chapter, especially on the topic of neural networks, is just this kind of problem-solving technique. For example, in using the FFBPN for weather prediction, what we need are not the current boundary conditions, but rather the past history observations (and weather records) for network training. More interestingly, for predicting the future temperature (e.g., the 3-day temperatures), we do not even need to use the historical temperature records, but rather other weather information such as MSLP, wind direction and wind speed, etc. So it is believed that these kinds of contemporary AI techniques might provide some new hope.

In order to improve system performance, current studies focus on how to integrate chaos theory into other AI techniques (as mentioned in this chapter), including: neural networks, GAs, and fuzzy systems. A typical example includes the author's latest research on *chaotic neural networks*

(CNNs) – namely, the *Lee-oscillator* (Lee 2004c) to model the human *chaotic* (and *progressive*) memory encoding and recalling scheme, which leads to the latest development in the "Unification Theory of Senses and Experiences" in OAT (ontological agent technology). The author will present this work in the next section.

Besides integration with neural networks, other hybrid systems include integration with GAs for system optimization and the development of chaotic–fuzzy systems in electronic appliances. Typical examples are the chaotic kerosene heater (produced by Sanyo Electric) (Katayama et al. 1993), which is also the first consumer product in the world to adopt chaos theory in the design of the control system. Moreover, this product is also the first commercial product to successfully integrate the technology of a fuzzy–neuro control system with chaos theory.

4.6 Chaotic Neural Networks and the Lee-Oscillator

In the past few decades, neural networks have been extensively adopted in various applications ranging from simple synaptic memory coding to sophisticated pattern recognition problems such as scene analysis. Moreover, current studies in neuroscience and physiology have reported that in a typical scene segmentation problem our major senses of perception (e.g., vision, olfaction, etc.) are greatly involved in chaotic and highly nonlinear neural dynamics and oscillations.

The chaotic neural network proposed in this section is an extension of the author's previous work on the elastic graph dynamic link model (EGDLM) (Lee and Liu 2003) of memory processing and on composite neural oscillators for scene segmentation. Moreover, it is also inspired by the work of Aihara and colleagues (Aihara 1997; Chen and Aihara 1995) and Wang (1991, 1992) on chaotic neural oscillators in pattern association.

In this section, the author proposes a new, transient, chaotic neural oscillator – namely, the *Lee-oscillator* – to provide temporal neural coding and an information processing scheme. To illustrate the capability of Lee-oscillators in pattern association, a chaotic auto-associative network, namely the *Lee-associator*, was constructed.

In contrast to classical auto-associators such as the celebrated Hopfield network, which provides *time-independent* and *static* pattern association, the Lee-associator provides a remarkably progressive memory association scheme (what the author calls the *progressive memory recalling scheme*, PMRS) during the transient chaotic memory association. This is exactly consistent with the latest research in psychiatry and perception psychology on dynamic memory recalling schemes, and this work also forms an essential component of the author's *Unification Theory of Senses and Experiences* and the design and implementation of ontological agents – the *Cogito iJADE* – which will be discussed in Chap. 11.

The section is organized as follows. Section 4.6.1 gives an overview of the latest work on chaotic neural networks, in particular on the chaotic neural oscillator proposed by Wang (1991, 1992). Section 4.6.2 presents the architecture of the Lee-oscillator, its major components and neural dynamics. Based on Lee-oscillators as the neural components, Sect. 4.6.3 presents the Lee-associator, together with the system implementation details and key experimental results. A comparison with the chaotic auto-associator proposed by Ahara and colleagues (Adachi and Aihara 1997; Aihara and Matsumoto 1986, 1987) will be discussed in Sect. 4.6.4. Section 4.6.5 discusses the *progressive memory recalling test* and the major biological and psychological implications of the proposed system, and is followed by a description of related research and the conclusion.

4.6.1 Chaotic Neural Oscillators – An Overview

Introduction

Classical ANNs are composed of the simple artificial neurons that emulate biological neural activities. The latest studies in neuroscience and neurophysiology have examined such issues as the functional properties of the hippocampus (Berger et al. 1994; Freeman 2001), the neural activities in the pyloric CPG (central pattern generator) of the lobster (Huerta et al. 2001), and other brain activities (Lehnertz et al. 2000). These kinds of neural models have been strongly criticized as being far simpler than real neural models. Studies have provided strong evidence of chaotic neural activities in these complex neural behaviors (Freeman 2000; Lehnertz et al. 2000; Yunfan et al. 1998).

Researchers have also proposed various chaotic neural models over the past decades. The latest research includes: chaotic oscillators proposed by Falcke et al. (2000) to model pyloric CPG neurons, cortical networks proposed by Hoshino et al. (2003) for recalling LTM (long-term memory), the TCNN (transient chaotic neural network) proposed by Chen and Aihara (1995) for handling combinational optimization problems, Wang-oscillators (Wang 1991, 1992) for spatio-temporal information processing, and Zhou's work (Zhou and Chen 2000) based on the chaotic annealing technique for dynamic pattern retrieval.

From the system architecture point of view, most chaotic neural network models are based on the computational neuroscience models that had been developed from the theoretical work of Hodgkin and Huxley in 1952 (Hodgkin and Huxley 1952). These computational neuroscience models focus on spiking neural dynamic behavior. The latest theoretical developments include work by Fukai et al. (2000a, 2000b) and Aihara and Matsumoto (1986, 1987; Aihara 1997). Another main stream of neuroscience has focused on the behavior of the neural populations. Celebrated models include the neural oscillatory model proposed by Wilson and Cowan (1972), which described the behavior of the neurons as interactive triggering (or what we call *oscillations*) between the excitatory and inhibitory neurons. In fact, this theory has provided a vast amount of support for work that is being conducted in various fields, including neurophysiology, neuroscience, and the latest research in brain science (Freeman 1979; 1987, 2001; Gray et al. 1989; Huerta et al. 2001; Malsburg 1985; Menon et al. 1996). This theory has also formed the basis of many subsequent studies and models in the field of *cognitive information processing* (Campbell and Wang 1996; Minai and Anand 1998), and on the synchronization and desynchronization behaviors of the *neural oscillators* (Engel et al. 1991; Gray et al. 1989; Wang and Terman 1995). The latest applications include pattern and memory associations (Adachi and Aihara 1997; Aihara 1997; Anderson 1972; Chakravarthy and Ghosh 1996), scene analysis and pattern recognition (Chen and Wang 2002; Lee 2003; Lee and Liu 2002; Malsburg and Buhmann 1992; Wang and Terman 1997; Yamaguchi and Shimizu 1994).

However, the models proposed based on these celebrated models, including the *Hodgkin–Huxley*, *FitzHugh–Nagumo*, and *Wilson–Cowan models* (and their derivatives), are either too simplified to simulate any "real" chaotic neural behaviors or too complicated to be applied as feasible ANNs (Aihara 1997; Lehnertz et al. 2000) for applications.

This study is an extension of the author's previous work on neural oscillators (Lee and Liu 2000, 2003) and on applications in various areas including face recognition (Lee 2002), scene analysis (Lee and Liu 2002), and, most recently, the implementation of an agent-based surveillance system based on a composite neural–oscillatory model (CNOM) (Lee 2003). It has also been inspired by the theoretical chaotic neural oscillator model (namely, the Wang-oscillator) proposed by X. Wang (1991, 1992). In this section, the author is proposing a new chaotic neural model, namely the *Lee-oscillator*. The *Lee-oscillator* provides a feasible solution for some critical problems encountered in the Wang-oscillator when it is adopted as a BTU (bifurcation transfer unit) (Minai and Anand 1998; Wang 1991, 1992) for *temporal information (memory) coding*.

In this section, the author will first give a brief overview of the Wang-oscillator, its architecture, chaotic neural dynamics, and the idea of BTU for temporal information coding. The author will also describe the major problems found in the Wang-oscillator, which prevent it from acting as an effective BTU for dynamic memory encoding and pattern association.

The Wang-Oscillator

Most of the contemporary neural oscillators that developed theoretically from the Wilson–Cowan model are focused on the time-continuous framework. Wang (1991, 1992) proposed a simple time-discrete neural oscillator model (namely, the *Wang-oscillator*). Unlike its continuous model counterpart, the *Wang-oscillator* provided simple but remarkable neural dynamics ranging from fixed points (through quasi-periodicity) to chaos, as revealed by its bifurcation diagram. This bifurcation diagram can be used as the computational elements (called the BTU) for temporal information processing.

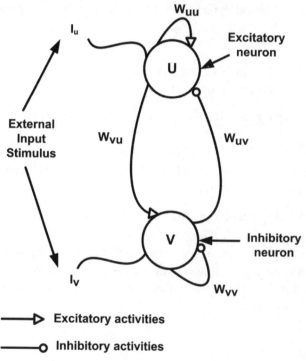

Fig. 4.26. Wang-oscillator

The Wang-oscillator is a neural oscillatory model consisting of two neurons, one excitatory and one inhibitory. The neural model is given in Fig. 4.26, and the generalized neural dynamics are given as follows:

$$u(t+1) = f(w_{uu}u(t) - w_{uv}v(t) + I_u(t) - \theta_u) \qquad (4.21)$$

$$v(t+1) = f(w_{vu}u(t) - w_{vv}v(t) + I_v(t) - \theta_v) \qquad (4.22)$$

where $u(t)$ and $v(t)$ are the state values of the *excitatory* and *inhibitory* neurons at time t, w_{ij} $(i, j = \{u, v\})$ are the weight parameters, I_u and I_v are the input stimuli, θ_u and θ_v are the thresholds corresponding to the two neurons, and $f(\ )$ is the sigmoid function given by:

$$f(p; \mu) = \tanh(\mu p) \qquad (4.23)$$

where μ is an important factor controlling the behavior of the sigmoid function.

As reported by Wang (1991, 1992), with the settings $w_{uu} = w_{vw} = a$, $w_{vu} = w_{vv} = b$, and under the condition that $a \geq 2b$, varying μ will produce a series of period-doubling bifurcations that lead to chaos.

Moreover, the neural dynamics of this discrete-time Wang-oscillator are given by:

$$z(t) = u(t) - v(t) \qquad (4.24)$$

Substituting this into (4.21–4.23), the neural dynamics of the Wang-oscillator can be described by:

$$z(t+1) = \tanh\left[\mu(a \cdot z(t) + I_u(t+1))\right] + \tanh\left[\mu(b \cdot z(t) + I_v(t+1))\right]$$
$$(4.25)$$

In the usual case of a neural oscillator with an external stimulus only to the inhibitory neuron (i.e., $I_u = I$ and $I_v = 0$), the neural dynamics of the Wang-oscillator are given by:

$$z(t+1) = \tanh\left[\mu(a \cdot z(t) + I)\right] - \tanh\left[\mu b \cdot z(t)\right] \qquad (4.26)$$

which is termed the $\mu/a/b$ *Wang-oscillator*.

One important finding of the Wang-oscillator is the bifurcation behavior of the $\mu/a/b$ Wang-oscillator with the variation of input stimulus I. Figure 4.27 depicts a typical bifurcation diagram of a 5/1/1 Wang-oscillator (Wang 1991, 1992).

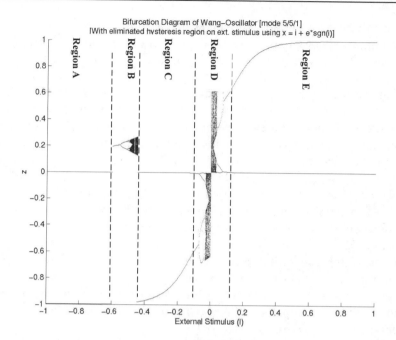

Fig. 4.27. Bifurcation diagram of a 5/1/1 Wang-oscillator (Wang 1991, 1992)

As shown in Fig. 4.27, the response of the Wang-oscillator to an external input stimulus can be categorized into five regions (starting from the negative (Region A) to the positive (Region E)). Their neural dynamics are summarized as follows. Regions A and E are the outermost regions. They depict a typical sigmoid function growth, which corresponds to a periodic response to an input stimulus, and their ends meet the tangent bifurcation regions. Region B is a bifurcation region that ends up with the reverse crisis. The bifurcation curve returns to a typical sigmoid curve in Region C, which is trapped between the crisis and reverse crisis of the attractor. Region D is the most important region in the Wang-oscillator; it denotes the region of *hysteresis* that corresponds to the chaotic behavior of the Wang-oscillator with a small input stimulus. A detailed analysis of the neural dynamics can be found in the work of Minai and Anand (1998).

Major Contributions and Limitations of Wang-Oscillators

One important finding and contribution of the Wang-oscillator is the property of the change in neural dynamics according to the input stimulus. In most classical neural network models for information encoding and association (such as the Hopfield network, SOM, etc.), the network model can be generalized as a nonlinear function operator which, based on various input stimuli, alters its internal states and "fires" the output according to the nonlinear transfer function. The Wang-oscillator, on the other hand, encodes information (i.e., the input stimulus) and gives the responses by altering the behavior of the neural dynamics (from chaotic states to sigmoid growth). This is consistent with the latest findings on how the brain processes information (Freeman 2000, 2001; Malsburg 1981). In a pattern association problem, when a stimulus is applied, and if the input stimulus is small, the network output is not only small but also chaotic, which indicates underlying complex and *aperiodic neural activities* in the neuron population. However, when the input stimulus increases to a certain level, the neural dynamics within the inhibitory and excitatory neurons become periodic, which also results in a *phase-locking behavior* in the neural population. In other words, the information processing model, using a Wang-oscillator, can be interpreted as the synchronization behavior of the neural population upon information encoding/pattern association. This is also consistent with the information processing models of the brain proposed in other contemporary studies (Campbell and Wang 1996; Engel et al. 1991; Freeman 1979).

According to this remarkable feature, the Wang-oscillator can be adopted in two ways: (1) According to its bifurcation feature, it can act as a *chaotic-growth* transfer function (namely, as a BTU) (Minai and Anand 1998; Wang 1991, 1992). Compared to a classical transfer function such as the sigmoid function, the chaotic–periodic behavior found in its bifurcation diagram can be used as a new option for the transfer function of the chaotic-to-periodic growth upon various input stimuli. (2) The neural model itself can be directly adopted as a dynamic neural unit for temporal information processing, including dynamic information encoding and pattern association.

However, the Wang-oscillator has several major limitations in the bifurcation behavior of the model, preventing it from being used as an effective BTU or temporal information processing model. As mentioned previously, for the neural dynamics of the Wang-oscillator in various regions: (1) An "undesirable" chaotic region exists in Region B which not only affects the continuity of the BTU, but also violates the original function of the BTU, namely that of stimulating the temporal information processing for the brain. In this chaotic region the chaotic dynamics only appear when the external input stimulus is small, while the neural dynamic will turn into a "stable" mode when the input stimulus becomes sufficiently strong. (2) Although there is chaotic behavior in the neural dynamics when the input stimulus is small (i.e., in Region D), the change from *periodic* to *chaotic* behavior should be gradual and continuous. (3) When the Wang-oscillator is used as a BTU, there is either a single state in the non-chaotic region or multiple states in the chaotic region. However, as shown in the bifurcation diagram, in a single Wang-oscillator, a stable rest state (i.e., $Z = 0$) exists in the bifurcation dynamics. This also prevents the oscillator from being used effectively either as a BTU or for temporal information encoding.

The next section will discuss how the Lee-oscillator works and, more importantly, how its neural dynamics allow it to eliminate the problems that appear in the Wang-oscillator.

4.6.2 The Lee-Oscillator

Different from the Wang-oscillator, the Lee-oscillator provides a *transient chaotic progressive growth* in its neural dynamics, which solves the fundamental shortcoming of the Wang-oscillator in temporal information encoding and in acting as a BTU.

The Lee-Oscillator Model and Its Bifurcation Behavior

The Lee-oscillator consists of the neural dynamics of four constitutive neural elements: u, v, w, and z.

Figure 4.28 is a depiction of the Lee-oscillator model.

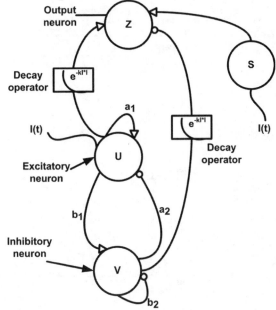

Fig. 4.28. The Lee-oscillator

The neural dynamics of each of these constituent neurons are given by:

$$u(t+1) = f\left[a_1 \cdot u(t) + a_2 \cdot v(t) + I(t) - \theta_u\right] \tag{4.27}$$

$$v(t+1) = f\left[b_1 \cdot u(t) - b_2 \cdot v(t) - \theta_v\right] \tag{4.28}$$

$$w(t+1) = f\left[I(t)\right] \tag{4.29}$$

$$z(t) = \left[u(t) - v(t)\right] \cdot e^{-kI^2(t)} + w(t) \tag{4.30}$$

where $u(t)$, $v(t)$, $w(t)$, and $z(t)$ are the state variables of the excitatory, inhibitory, input, and output neurons, respectively; $f(\ )$ is the sigmoid function given by equation (3); a_1, a_2, b_1, and b_2 are the weight parameters for these constitutive neurons; θ_u and θ_v are the thresholds for excitatory and inhibitory neurons; $I(t)$ is the external input stimulus; and k is the decay constant.

Similar to the Wang-oscillator, the most remarkable feature of this oscillator is its bifurcation behavior under different external input stimuli. Figure 4.29 shows the bifurcation diagram of a typical mode 500/5/5/1 Lee-oscillator (where "500" is the value of the decay constant k; the first "5" is the value of a_1; the second "5" the value of a_2; and "1" the value of b_1 and b_2, respectively).

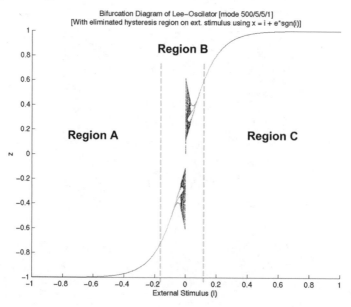

Fig. 4.29. Bifurcation diagram of a mode 500/5/5/1 Lee-oscillator

Unlike the Wang-oscillator, the bifurcation diagram of a single Lee-oscillator is composed of three main regions, Regions A, B, and C. From the neural dynamics point of view, Regions A and C denote the *sigmoid-shape* region, which corresponds to the nonchaotic neural activities in the oscillators; and Region B is the hysteresis region, which corresponds to the area of chaotic behavior that results when a weak external input stimulus is received.

In view of the major limitations of the Wang-oscillator discussed in the previous section, the bifurcation diagram of the Lee-oscillator provides clear evidence of how these problems have been solved: (1) Compared to the "undesirable" chaotic region B appearing in the Wang-oscillator, which affects the continuity of the neural dynamics and violates the information processing behavior (upon stimulus) in brain science, no "undesirable" chaotic region appears in the bifurcation diagram. (2) Where there was the problem of neural dynamic continuity between the chaotic and non-chaotic regions in the Wang-oscillator, the Lee-oscillator provides a truly gradual change from chaotic to non-chaotic dynamics due to the adoption of the decay factor appearing in output neurons. (3) Compared to the Wang-oscillator, there is no undesirable "rest" state over the whole bifurcation curve. The bifurcation upon receipt of an external stimulus is either chaotic or non-chaotic, and *sigmoid-like* with single and continuous behavior.

Potential Applications of the Lee-Oscillator

There are three main application areas for the Lee-oscillator:

1. Basic Chaotic Neural Elements for Temporal Information Processing

Basically, information processing is the overall process of encoding, recognizing, and discriminating various types of information (e.g., images, patterns, etc.). Since a single Lee-oscillator can provide a *two-state attraction* from the input space, it is suitable not just as a basic element for information processing. In addition, owing to its unique chaotic features where the neural dynamics change with variations in the input signal, the Lee-oscillator provides a good analogue for simulating chaotic and temporal information processing behavior in brain science (Freeman 2000, 2001; Malsburg 1981).

Figures 4.30 and 4.31 are bifurcation diagrams of the mode 500/5/5/1 Lee-oscillators and mode 5/5/1 Wang-oscillators with a linear gain from an external stimulus; and Figs. 4.32 and 4.33 are the bifurcation diagrams for these oscillators under a sinusoidal external stimulus. It is clear that the bifurcation behavior of the Lee-oscillator provides a better and more reasonable analogue as a chaotic BTU for information processing. For the linear gain of the external stimulus, the Lee-oscillator provides chaotic-to-periodic oscillations on the receipt of an external stimulus (rather than unrealistic multiple stable states as in the Wang-oscillator). It also provides chaotic-to-periodic sinusoidal outputs (rather than the impractical multiple stable states that appear in the Wang-oscillator). In fact, from the point of view of application, the temporal information processing of the sinusoidal inputs can be adopted to detect some periodic structures in the input, or used for signal processing problems.

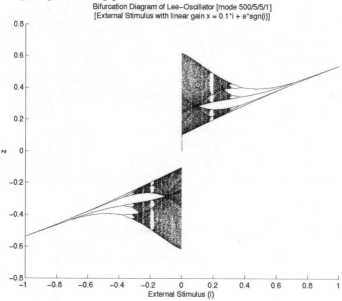

Fig. 4.30. Bifurcation diagram of a mode 500/5/5/1 Lee-oscillator under linear gain from an external stimulus

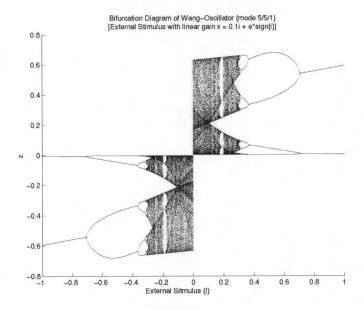

Fig. 4.31. Bifurcation diagram of a mode 5/5/1 Wang-oscillator under linear gain from an external stimulus

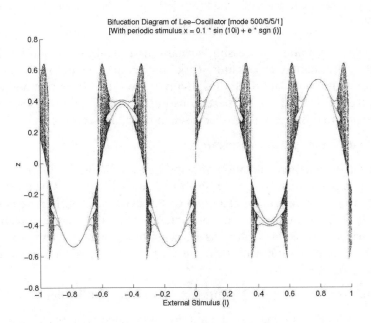

Fig. 4.32. Bifurcation diagram of a mode 500/5/5/1 Lee-oscillator under a sinusoidal external stimulus

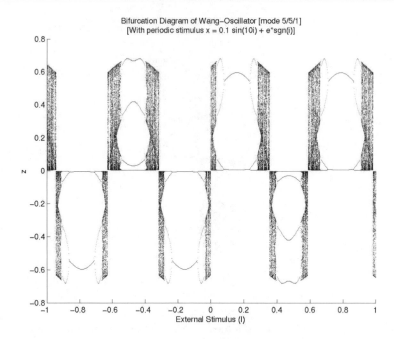

Fig. 4.33. Bifurcation diagram of a mode 5/5/1 Wang-oscillator under a sinusoidal external stimulus

A typical information processing scenario as in pattern recognition involves the information processing work of a collection of neural units (called the neural population). It also involves the synchronization and de-synchronization operations of these constituent neural units. Further research related to this area will be discussed at the end of this section.

2. Transient Chaotic Auto-associator

As an extension and generalization of using Lee-oscillators for information processing, a two-dimensional (2D) layer of Lee-oscillators can be adopted as a pattern associator. As an analogue of the classical Hopfield network (Hopfield 1982) as an auto-associator, a transient chaotic auto-associative network based on Lee-oscillators as its constituting neuron elements can be used to provide an innovative progressive memory association and recalling scheme.

3. Chaotic Neural Oscillatory Units for Advanced Applications

In fact, Lee-oscillators can be adopted and integrated with each other to form a complex chaotic neural oscillatory model to tackle problems such as scene analyses, robot vision, navigation, etc. Studies being actively carried out in these areas will be discussed at the end of this chapter.

4.6.3 The Lee-Associator

Introduction

An auto-associative network is one of the most important and fundamental applications in the fields of neural networks, information processing, and neurosciences. In fact, it is also the foundation of various complex information processing tasks such as face (pattern) recognition, figure–ground segmentation, scene segmentation, pattern classification, data mining, and so forth. Celebrated work includes the fundamental studies conducted by Hopfield (1982) and Kohonen (1988). The most recent work includes the combined evolution model of Cheng and Guan (1998), the study of associative memories and nonlinear dynamics by Bibitchkov et al. (2002), Karlholm (1993), Morita (1993), Liou and Yuan (1999), Yoshizawa et al. (1993), and studies on chaotic dynamics by Wagner and Stuck (2002).

As a direct and simple implementation of the Lee-oscillator, the author will discuss in this section how a 2D auto-associator is constructed using the *Lee-oscillator* as the neural framework. Based on its remarkable progressive pattern association mechanisms through its transient chaotic neural dynamics, this auto-associator is named the *Lee-associator.*

The Lee-oscillator will be compared to the contemporary chaotic auto-associators proposed by Aihara and colleagues (Adachi and Aihara 1997; Aihara 1997) and the Wang-oscillator (Wang 1991, 1992), and will demonstrate how it provides efficient and effective pattern association schemes. More importantly, the author will illustrate its progress pattern (memory) recalling capacity in this direct application. As a further extension, the author will also demonstrate how this characteristic can be applied in a facial pattern recalling scenario.

System Framework of the Lee-Associator

As discussed in the previous section, the direct adoption of the Lee-oscillator is based on a simple 2D single-layered neural population analogous to a classical Hopfield network. A collection of Lee-oscillators as the basic neural elements is constructed to form the Lee-associator. Figure 4.34 shows a schematic diagram of the Lee-associator.

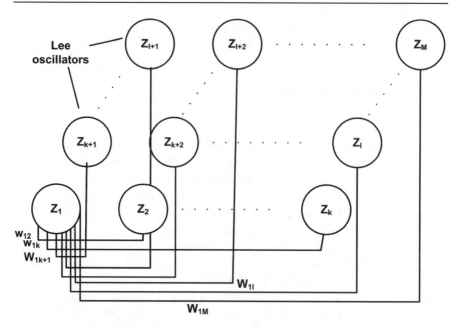

Fig. 4.34. System architecture of the Lee-associator

The neural dynamics are as follows:

$$w_{ij} = \frac{1}{N_p} \cdot \sum_p \left(2x_i^p - 1\right)\left(2x_j^p - 1\right) \tag{4.31}$$

$$z(t+1) = f_s\left[\sum_{j=1}^{M}\left(w_{ij}\, z_j(t)\right)\right] \tag{4.32}$$

Hence:

$$z(t+1) = f_s\left(w_{ij} \cdot \left(\left(u_j(t) - v(t)\right)\cdot e^{-kI^2(t)} + w_j(t)\right)\right) \tag{4.33}$$

where w_{ij} are the connection weights; N_p is the total number of patterns stored in the Lee-associator; z_j are the output neurons of the Lee-oscillator; x^p is the stored pattern in the Lee-associator; M is the total number of Lee-oscillators in the Lee-associative network; and u and v are the excitatory and inhibitory neurons found in the Lee-oscillator.

As shown in the above neural dynamic equations, the interactions among the constituent neurons of the Lee-oscillators in this network can act as an auto-associator in the presence of query patterns that are treated as external input stimuli, in analogy to classical Hopfield networks (1982) and Kohonen networks (1972, 1988). However, in contrast to these classical models, the proposed Lee-associator provides a change in neural dynamics (from a chaotic to a stable state transition) when pattern association occurs. A detailed discussion and the experimental tests of the proposed model are described in the following sections.

4.6.4 System Implementation and Experimental Results

From the point of view of implementation and system evaluation, we will compare the chaotic auto-associative behavior of the Lee-associator to the chaotic auto-associative network proposed by Aihara and colleagues (Adachi and Aihara 1997; Aihara 1997) and Wang (1991, 1992). In order to provide a fair and thorough comparison, the author adopted the same system environment and the same set of test patterns as described in Adachi and Aihara (1997) and Aihara (1997). The testing of the whole system was categorized into different sections, as discussed in the following subsections.

Chaotic Auto-association on Simple Patterns

In this test, the chaotic auto-associative performance of the Lee-associator is compared to the remarkable chaotic neural network proposed by Aihara and colleagues by using the same test patterns and system environment to evaluate the system.

The four stored grid patterns that are encoded by 10×10 binary pixel grids are shown in Fig. 4.35.

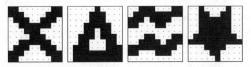

Fig. 4.35. The stored patterns (Adachi and Aihara 1997; Aihara 1997)

Parameters Selection Test

Before the Lee-associator is tested against the unseen or noisy pattern, the system is fine-tuned to its optimal transient auto-associative behavior by "training" with the stored patterns. Table 4.4 shows the list of optimal parameters used in the Lee-associator.

Table 4.4. Optimal parameter set used in the Lee-associator

System Parameter	Optimal values
a_1	5.0
a_2	5.0
b_1	1
b_2	1
k	500
θ_u	0
θ_v	0

Chaotic Pattern Association on Stored Patterns

Figures 4.36, 4.37a, and 4.37b depict the network outputs of the three models for the first 50 oscillation cycles on external stimulus (input) by the stored pattern c.

From these figures, it is clear that all these networks achieved pattern auto-association through chaotic neural oscillations. However, in the case of the Aihara model, it is clear that on the external input of a known pattern (pattern c in this case), the network did not achieve steady state; rather, it *oscillated* between different stored patterns (and their reverse patterns as well). As indicated in their previous findings (Adachi and Aihara 1997; Aihara 1997) (and confirmed in our test), the frequency of the appearance of any particular pattern is not directly correlated to the known pattern given as the test pattern. In the case of Wang-oscillators, it is even worse. As shown in Fig. 4.37b, in the presence of pattern c as the test pattern, the model cannot recall it but rather associates with a wrong stored pattern. Actually, the same cases occur when other stored patterns are used for testing. As discussed in the previous section, the main reason may be due to the discontinuity and existence of multiple stable states in the bifurcation diagram when the oscillator serves as a BTU for auto-association.

On the other hand, as revealed in Fig. 4.36, on the external "stimulus" of a known pattern (pattern c here), the Lee-associator neural oscillator, after performing chaotic neural oscillations for a short period of time (from $t = 1$ to $t = 6$ in our case), will start to *progressively reshape* (or what the author calls *progressive memory recalling*, PMR) the stored pattern after the first few time steps (from $t = 7$ to $t = 11$). Once it "recalls" the correct stored pattern, it will stabilize to a steady state, which is classical auto-associative behavior as we have seen in other similar models.

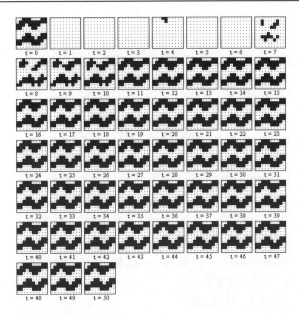

Fig. 4.36. A sample sequence of a spatio-temporal pattern association performed by the Lee-associator on the external input of pattern c

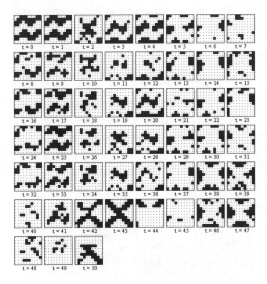

(a) Using Aihara chaotic auto-associator

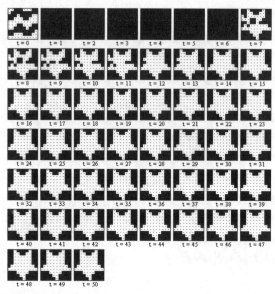

(b) Using Aihara chaotic auto-associator

Fig. 4.37. A sample sequence of a spatio-temporal pattern association performed by the Aihara chaotic auto-associator and Wang-oscillators on external inputs of pattern c

Chaotic Pattern Association on Noisy Test Patterns

In the second test, noisy stored patterns are presented as input stimuli to test how these models behave upon pattern association. The four "noisy" test patterns (with over 20% of the noise in pixels) are shown in Fig. 4.38. Since Wang-oscillators cannot recall the stored pattern, in this test we only focus on comparisons between the Lee-associator and Aihara's chaotic auto-associator. Figures 4.39 and 4.40 show the transient auto-associative dynamics of these patterns using these respective associators.

Fig. 4.38. The four "noisy" test patterns (patterns a to d from left to right)

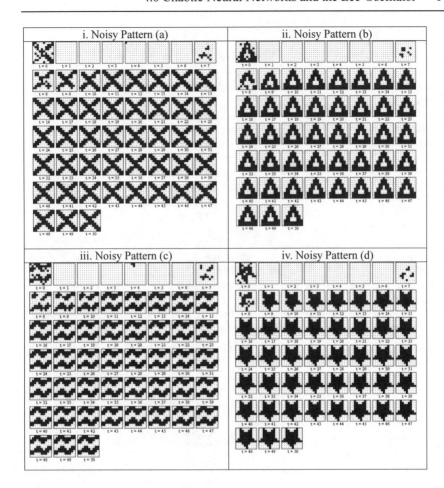

Fig. 4.39. The sample sequence of spatio-temporal pattern association performed by the Lee-associator on external inputs of four noisy stored patterns

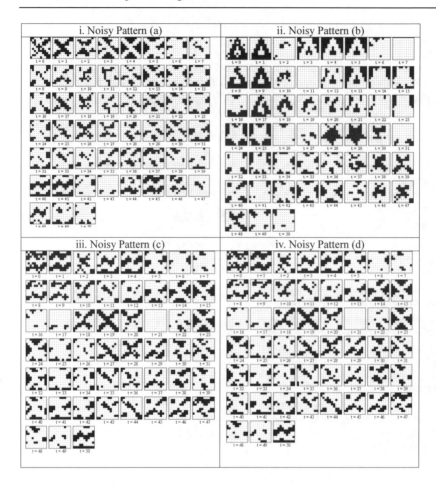

Fig. 4.40. The sample sequence of spatio-temporal pattern association performed by the Aihara chaotic auto-associator (Adachi and Aihara 1997; Aihara 1997) on external inputs of four noisy stored patterns

From these figures, it is not difficult to see that even though Aihara's auto-associator continued oscillating in various transient states of the stored patterns (and their reverse patterns) on the input of noisy stored patterns, there is no evidence to show that this chaotic oscillator associated (or recalled) any particular stored pattern. However, as shown in Fig. 4.39, on the stimulus of the four noisy test patterns, the Lee-associator successfully recalled all of the four stored patterns within ten time steps. This is less than the 1.2 seconds taken when using a Pentium IV PC for the simulation.

Also, as revealed by the above experiment, the transient auto-association process by the Lee-associator (using Lee-oscillators as constituting components) showed a *chaotic-to-stable* auto-association behavior. On the presentation of a noisy known pattern, the oscillatory network first performed a chaotic pattern association in the first few time steps. Then it began to *rebuild* (or *reshape*) the correct stored pattern in the temporal outputs until it successfully "recalled" the whole pattern. This kind of pattern recovery operation is directly analogous to the progressive memory recalling scheme (PMRS) found in brain science, as discussed in the previous section. A more detailed elaboration of this PMR behavior of the Lee-associator will be presented in the next section.

4.6.5 Progressive Memory Recalling Scheme of the Lee-Associator and Its Biological and Psychological Implications

Progressive Memory Recalling of Human Faces

This test explores how the Lee-associator performs in recognizing human faces (in gray-level photos). In the test, the author adopted a Yale University database (set A) that contains the facial images of 15 individuals from different views and with facial expressions including frontal views, side views, gimmick faces, occluded faces, etc.

This test compares the proposed system to two other models including the NOEGM system examined in the author's previous works and the enhanced DLA system proposed by Wiskott et al. (1997). Figures 4.41 and 4.42 show the sample facial patterns from the database and the PMRS of the Lee-associator on recalling facial patterns, respectively.

In terms of recognition rate, the Lee-associator provides promising recognition results on frontal face recognition. Owing to the nature of PMR, the Lee-associator also provides reasonable recognition performance on occluded and gimmick face recognition. We must remember that the proposed system is a simple, chaotic neural auto-associative network that has limited invariant recognition capability.

However, the most remarkable feature found in this experiment is the recognition speed of the proposed system. Owing to the simple network structure of the Lee-associator, the associator significantly outperforms the other two models (the NOEGM model and enhanced DLA model (Lee and Liu 2003)) in overall recognition speed by 127 and 307 times, respectively. It is able to do so mainly because of the sophisticated feature vector selection and because of the dynamic link association of these feature vectors on recognizing these models.

Fig. 4.41. Sample sequence facial database from Yale University

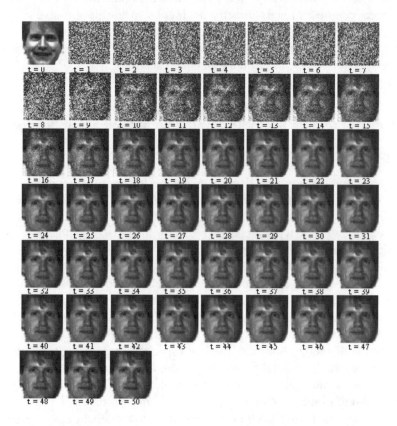

Fig. 4.42. A sample sequence of a progressive facial pattern recalling scheme performed by the Lee-associator

The Biological and Psychological Implications of the PMRS of Lee-Associators

One of the major contributions of the Lee-oscillator and associator is their biological and neuroscience implications. The latest work on visual psychology (Barry 1997) and neurosciences (Freeman 2000, 2001) has revealed that there are strong implications for chaotic dynamics in human brain activity including memory association, visual object recognition, scene segmentation, etc. Moreover, the latest research on visual psychology (Barry 1997) and psychiatry (Chey et al. 2002) has also reported that our memory association and recalling operations are not "*quantum jumps*" (either strictly *recalled* or *forgotten*) but rather a kind of *progressive memory recalling (reconstruction) scheme* which is found in memory-deficient patients. As indicated in the bifurcation diagrams and the tests of the Lee-oscillators and the Lee-associative network, it is clear that the Lee-oscillator provides an ideal framework for modeling chaotic neural activities in progressive learning, while the Lee-associator (using Lee-oscillators as constituting neural components) provides an ideal solution for modeling the progressive memory recalling (and association) scheme.

The progressive pattern association scheme is further illustrated using the Lee-associator against the *quantum jump* of the memory recalling scheme performed in a traditional auto-associative network such as the Hopfield network. In the test, three fragmented triangles (triangles (i)–(iii) in Fig. 4.43) with different degrees of fragmentation are used for the PMR test. Figures 4.44a–c illustrate the pattern association schemes using (a) the traditional Hopfield network; (b) the Lee-associator; and (c) Aihara's associator. The Hopfield network can only associate with the correct pattern when the degree of fragmentation is low (i.e., pattern (i) for the "dotted" triangle).

However, when the input pattern is highly fragmented (i.e., patterns (ii) and (iii)), the Hopfield network associates with totally incorrect patterns. For Aihara's associator, the results revealed that it will not stabilize (associate) with any particular patterns but rather "oscillates" between all the stored patterns. However, for the Lee-associator, it is clear that the associator provides a progressive pattern reconstruction scheme in all three cases, even for the highly fragmented triangle (pattern (iii)), with only the cues which show the shape of the three corners of a triangle pattern.

Concerning the pattern association dynamics, the Hopfield network "jumped" to its "goal" (a correct or incorrect pattern) in all the three tests within about four time steps, while the Lee-associator provided a progressive pattern recalling to the correct pattern in about ten time steps. This difference in association dynamics might explain why the Lee-associator (by using its transient chaotic pattern association) provides a better solution for pattern association. Or, from an *energy minimization* point of view, the Lee-associator might achieve the global minimum energy levels better than the traditional Hopfield network by using its transient chaotic neural oscillation dynamics to avoid those local minima.

From the visual psychology point of view, this experimental result provides an excellent analogue to the Gestalt theory of visual perception (Gordon 1997) which states that "perception is a constructive process capable of going beyond the information given by stimulation", or in other words, the features (the pixel images) that we use in object recognition are not only the features of the raw input, but also the features in our organized perception of all the input information. In our case, although the fragmented triangle pattern cannot provide sufficient information for "classical" auto-association, the Lee-associator can provide a somewhat constructive process to "rebuild" the correct pattern via transient chaotic oscillations. In other words, from the psychological point of view, the PMRS found in the Lee-associator provides a direct analogue of the constructive object perception in Gestalt psychology. Moreover, from the neuroscience point of view, the Lee-associator provides a new means for high-level information coding and association.

Last but not least, Jean Piaget, in his remarkable work *The Psychology of Intelligence* (Piaget 1950), stated that *Behaviour* involves a *Total Field* embracing subjects and objects, and the *dynamics* of this field constitutes *Feeling*, while its *structure* depends on perception, effector-functions and intelligence." This observation is analogous to the relationship between our transient chaotic Lee-oscillator and intelligence. If we say that intelligence (or, specifically, the "auto-association" described in this chapter) is the structure of the Lee-associator system, then the chaotic neural dynamics of the Lee-oscillator will be the anatomy of what we called *memory recalling* while the *total field* will be the memory patterns and the external input patterns. This process, as described by developmental psychology, is a progressive learning process known as *assimilation*, which is a continuous process of *adoption* and *re-adoption*.

Although the proposed Lee-oscillator (and its Lee-associator) cannot give a full interpretation of these critical psychological and neuroscience behaviors, it sheds new light on the search for an appropriate solution in computational neuroscience and visual psychology.

Fig. 4.43. Fragmented triangles (i)–(iii) used in the PMR test (the first figure is the original pattern)

(I) Using the Fragmented Triangle (i)

(a) Association using Hopfield network

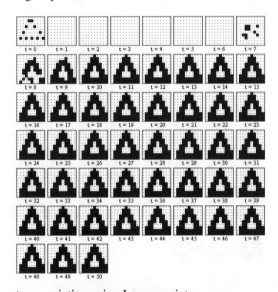

(b) Progressive auto-association using Lee-associator

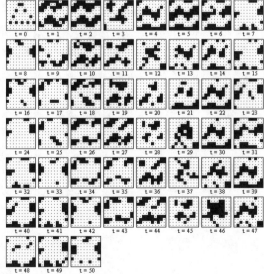

(c) Association using Aihara's associator

(II) Using the Fragmented Triangle (ii)

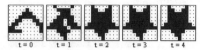

(a) Association using Hopfield network

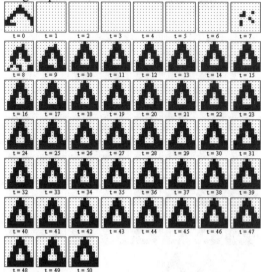

(b) Progressive auto-association using Lee-associator

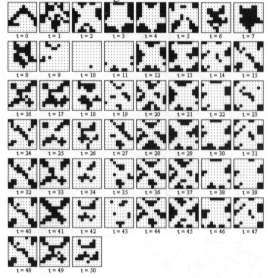

(c) Association using Aihara's associator

(III) Using the Fragmented Triangle (iii)

(a) Association using Hopfield network

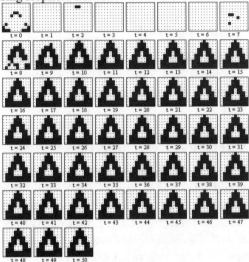

(b) Progressive auto-association using Lee-associator

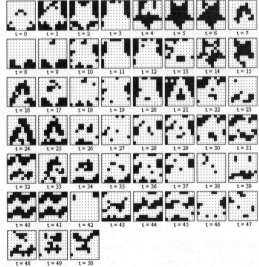

(c) Association using Aihara's associator

Fig. 4.44. Auto-association of the fragmented triangles (i)–(iii) using (a) the Hopfield network, (b) the Lee-associator, and (c) Aihara's associator

4.6.6 Related Work

The introduction of the Lee-oscillator in this chapter is one of the foundation studies of our Chaotic Neural Processing (CNP) Research Group. Current and future research related to Lee-oscillators can be summarized in
three main areas.

Chaotic Neural Modeling Study

In this fundamental study of the chaotic neural model (and its derivatives),
current research includes the study of the synchronization and de-
synchronization behavior of Lee-oscillators, stimulated annealing effects,
network hierarchy, etc.

Neuroscience Implications and Theoretical Study

This involves a study of major neuroscience effects, including the interpretation of *meaning* and *knowledge*, and a study of how these phenomena
can be modeled and simulated in the form of chaotic neural networks. Current research includes how Lee-oscillators (and derivatives) are applied to
represent, acquire, and disseminate knowledge, and the mechanisms and
interactions between working memory and LTM (long-term memory).

Chaotic Neural Application Study

This area involves all the *spin-off* applications of Lee-oscillators (and derivatives). Active research includes: (1) an extension of previous work on
scene analysis and pattern recognition (Lee 2003; Lee and Liu 2002; Lee
2002) to focus on complex scene analysis and active vision; (2) an extension of previous work on weather prediction (Lee and Liu 2000) to focus
on the prediction of severe weather such as rainstorms; (3) other "side-
track" applications such as chaotic cryptosystems and related work on
asynchronized data communication (Cuomo et al. 1993; Jakimoski and
Kosarev 2001; Parodi et al. 1993).

4.6.7 Conclusion

In this section, the author presents his latest research on the chaotic neural
oscillator (namely, the Lee-oscillator) and its chaotic dynamics. Concerning applications, a transient chaotic auto-associative network (the Lee-
associator) has been constructed to test its applicability for temporal pattern association. Compared to the chaotic auto-associative networks devel-

oped by Aihara and colleagues (Adachi and Aihara 1997; Aihara and Matsumoto 1986, 1987) and Wang (1991, 1992), the Lee-associator produces a robust progressive memory recalling scheme which is somehow analogous to the latest research on perception psychology and psychiatry on the progressive memory recalling (reconstruction) scheme.

The major aims and contributions of this new model are two-fold. Academically, instead of enhancing existing neural network models, the aim of this chapter is to introduce a totally new chaotic neural model (the Lee-oscillator) to provide a view on the neural foundation of temporal (transient) coding and information processing, and to narrow the gap between neural networks and the latest research on chaotic phenomena being conducted in the fields of brain science and neuroscience.

From the application point of view, the Lee-oscillator demonstrates how chaotic neural oscillators can be applied to the auto-associative problem – a fundamental memory encoding and information processing problem in neural networks. As discussed in the previous section, current and future studies also involve the issue of how the Lee-oscillator (and its derivatives) can be applied to various problems, such those in neuroscience, including the interpretation of knowledge and meaning, complex scene analysis, and active vision or other *side-track* applications such as chaotic cryptosystems.

Acknowledgments

The author would like to thank the Chaotic Neural Processing (CNP) Research Group of The Hong Kong Polytechnic University for providing support and facilities. The author is also grateful for the support given by The Hong Kong Polytechnic University in the form of RCG Grant PolyU 5083/02E. The author would like to acknowledge Yale University for the adoption of the face database.

4.7 Concluding Remarks

In this chapter, the author introduced contemporary AI technologies for constructing agents, including neural networks, fuzzy logic, genetic algorithms, and chaos theory, and discusses how these technologies can be successfully integrated to solve complex problems. The author also presented his latest research on chaotic neural networks – the Lee-oscillator – and its corresponding network – the Lee-associator. More importantly, the author discussed a remarkable progressive memory recalling feature and its implication for the human progressive memory recalling scheme, which forms an important basis for the latest development of the *Cognitron Theory* and the *Unification Theory of Senses and Experiences* on the design and development of future agent technologies – the ontology agent technology (OAT), which will be discussed in Chap. 11.

In view of various contemporary AI technologies, one might wonder: (1) Are there any guidelines for adopting a particular technology? and (2) Are there any "structural relationships" between these technologies?

The fact is, there are (and should be) no strict guidelines on when to adopt these technologies. However, each AI technology has its intrinsic functionality. For example, neural networks focus on the provision of a platform for the learning and training of a system (for adopting new *knowledge*); fuzzy logic focuses on the modeling of uncertain events and matters taking place, observed, or measured in the real world; genetic algorithms focus on the optimization scheme for system improvement (or what we called *evolution*); and chaos theory focuses on the modeling of highly dynamic and nonlinear systems, to study their chaotic dynamics and behavior. The relationship can be depicted as in Fig. 4.45.

As shown in this figure, one may wonder why the author has chosen chaos theory as the *core*. The reason is: if one treats a neural network as a black box model which provides network architecture and its functions but without explaining how it works, one may discover that chaos theory might be the key to unlocking this black box. In fact, what chaos theory gives us is not totally new knowledge about the systems in our world, but rather a new direction of thinking on how to "view the problem", which is the one that has been puzzling neural network scientists for years.

In addition to fuzzy logic and GA, there are some other AI technologies that provide effective tools to help with our problem solving, including rough sets, support vector machines, etc. The author believes that these technologies should not be competing, but rather should be cooperating and integrating with each other to provide a better solution for problem solving.

For various types of integration of AI techniques, the fuzzy–neuro technique – the integration of fuzzy logic and neural networks – is one of the most important and commonly adopted techniques. As we discussed at the beginning of this chapter, most of the events happening in the real world are highly uncertain and fuzzy (or sometimes even *chaotic*) in nature. For most AI applications, adaptive learning and incremental knowledge acquisition are core functions, which can be implemented by most of the neural networks. So an integration of fuzzy logic and neural networks usually provides a perfect match for most of our needs in solving complex AI problems, including of course the agents' applications discussed in this book.

In the second part of this book, we will discuss how fuzzy–neuro systems can be adopted for the design and implementation of some innovative intelligent agents including the:

– iJADE WShopper – a fuzzy–neuro intelligent shopping agent for wireless e-shopping

– iJADE WeatherMan – a fuzzy–neuro intelligent weather forecasting agent for interactive weather forecasting

– iJADE Stock Advisor – a HRBFN-based (hybrid radial basis function network) stock advisory agent for predicting stock and market trends

– iJADE Surveillant – a multi-resolution, neuro-oscillatory-based surveillance agent

– iJADE Negotiator – a fuzzy multi-agent-based negotiation system

Hopefully these agent applications will give readers more insight into how fuzzy–neuro and other integrated AI techniques can be adopted in agent technologies and be of benefit to the community.

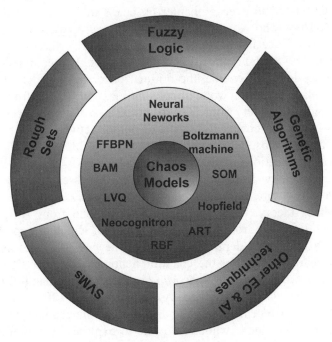

Fig. 4.45. Structural diagram for contemporary AI technologies

4.8 Further Reading

AI technology itself is in fact a very broad topic that cannot be totally covered in one or two chapters. The main aim of this chapter was to provide the reader with some fundamental knowledge and an overview of major AI technologies, which are critical for the comprehension of the iJADE agent applications that will be discussed in Part II of this book.

For a detailed understanding of each of the *component* AI technologies, the following suggestions might be a good place to start.

For neural networks, there are many good books to start with. Fausett's book on neural networks (Fausett 1994) provides extensive coverage of all the major neural networks, ranging from simple perceptrons to complex recurrent networks. The neural network books by Munakata (1998) and Patterson (1996) are also good places to begin. In particular, Munakata also covers other contemporary AI technologies, including: fuzzy logic, GA, rough sets, and even a chapter on chaos theory. For neuroscientists and researchers who would like to study the neuropsychological and cognitive neuroscience implications of neural networks, the books edited by Parks et al. (1998) and Poznanski (2001) are strongly recommended.

For fuzzy logic, of course, the original paper from Zadeh (1965) is an excellent place to start. Two textbooks on fuzzy logic, one from Yan et al. (1994) and the other from Kosko (1992), are highly recommended. Kosko's book also covers the topics of neural networks and fuzzy–neuro technology. For those who would like to explore the metaphysics and philosophical implications of fuzzy logic, Kosko's book (Kosko 1993) might give you some new insights. In fact, he also discusses how fuzzy logic is related to life, nature, philosophy, and the theory of Zen.

For chaos theory, there are two textbooks: one from Alligood et al. (2000) and the other from Moon (1992), both of which are good places to start. Both give an in-depth discussion of the basic theories and components of chaos theory. For the chaotic phenomena of brain dynamics, the book *How Brains Make up Their Mind* written by Freeman (2001) and the book *Chaos in the Brain* edited by Lehnertz et al. (2000) are excellent books that cover recent research and studies on the chaotic phenomena of brain science. For those who would like to explore the neural oscillatory behavior of brain functioning, the research monographs written by Hake (1996) and Basra (1998) are highly recommended.

For those who would like to have in-depth treatments of fuzzy–neuro systems, two books are highly recommended: *Neuro-fuzzy and Soft Computing* written by Jang et al. (1997) and *Computer Vision and Fuzzy-neural Systems* written by Ukraine (2001).

Last but not least, the author would like to introduce the excellent book written by Michalewicz and Fogel (2000), namely *How to Solve It: Modern Heuristics*. This book focuses on all the major heuristic techniques for problem solving including classical methods such as dynamic programming and gradient methods, as well as recent techniques including simulated annealing, tabu search, and EC (evolutionary computing) with neural networks, GAs, and fuzzy systems.

Part II – **Applications of Intelligent Agents Using iJADK**

5 The Design and Implementation of an Intelligent Agent-Based System Using iJADK

Intelligence is quickness to apprehend as distinct from ability, which is capacity to act wisely on the thing apprehended.

Dialogues, Alfred North Whitehead

Owing to the rapid development of e-commerce and Internet technology in recent years, many different e-commerce applications and mobile computing systems have been operating in cyberspace. Moreover, in this *sea* of information, the provision of an intelligent-based system (such as intelligent agents) seems to be a *new hope* for the future. However, contemporary agent-based developing environments such as IBM Aglet and ObjectSpace Voyager mainly focus on the mobility of agents with simple multi-agent negotiation schemes, which limit the implementation of truly intelligent agents for future needs.

In this chapter, an innovative intelligent agent-based development environment is introduced, namely iJADE (version 2.0) – *intelligent Java Agent Development Environment*. The aim of iJADE is to develop a fully integrated intelligent multi-agent-based system as the basic framework and development environment for future intelligent e-business (iEB) applications.

This chapter will describe: (1) an overview of agent technology, contemporary platforms, and standards, and their limitations for developing intelligent agent-based applications; (2) the system architecture of iJADE; (3) the current release of iJADK (intelligent Java Agent-based Development Kit) version 2.0, its major modules and its operation; and (4) examples for using iJADK to build iJADE agents.

5.1 Introduction

The exponential growth of the Internet industry in recent years has produced new challenges for businesses, especially in the field of e-commerce. Various e-commerce systems, ranging from C2C (consumer-to-consumer) e-commerce, such as e-auctions, to inter-organizational B2B (business-to-business) e-business for the international e-marketplace (Chan et al. 2001; Turban et al. 2000), have been operating in cyberspace. Currently, most of the existing systems of e-commerce over the Internet use the client-server approach. This approach is characterized by transactions that involve numerous request/response interactions. As network traffic on the Internet is difficult to control, users sometimes experience a long response time or even lose information. Therefore, we need another mechanism to control online transactions so that they can be carried out smoothly.

One of the latest solutions is to use mobile agent technology (Brenner et al. 1998). In a typical agent-based system (e.g., agent shopping), this involves sending a mobile software agent using different kinds of technologies to the remote system. The software agent can carry the user's criteria, calculation methods, filtering mechanisms, and even *intelligence* to the remote system. One of the main features of this agent-based system is that the software agents effectively act on behalf of the users, conducting all of the interactions on the remote site. By using this mechanism, an agent can go to not only one remote system, but also many systems at the same time (through agent-cloning mechanisms). Therefore, users are not required to interact manually with different remote systems. They can simply let the software agents do all of the related activities, going from one system to another, interacting with the stationary agents in the remote system, conducting negotiations, calculating results, and finally bringing useful information back to the user. It is expected that this type of agent-based system will complement the existing client-server system by providing a more advanced service and change our way of life in the near future.

Contemporary agent systems such as IBM Aglets[1] and ObjectSpace Voyager[2] focus mainly on mobility and multi-agent communications but the core functions of intelligent agents (IAs) – the AI (Artificial Intelligence) counterpart with intelligent capabilities including machine learning, forecasting, dynamic and/or real-time decision making, pattern recognition and classification functions – are not applied.

---

[1] Aglets: http://www.trl.ibm.co.jp/aglets/
[2] Voyager: http://www.objectspace.com/voyager/

In a typical e-shopping scenario, we are usually handling many kinds of *inexact* (so-called *fuzzy*) decisions. For instance, in choosing a pair of shoes, we may base our choice on factors such as the *degree of fitness* instead of the exact size, or *preferred patterns* instead of the exact pattern match. In these cases, we are dealing with different degrees of *fuzziness*, which can only be handled efficiently by using AI technologies such as fuzzy systems. Moreover, with the integration of a machine-learning technique such as neural networks, an *intelligent* product selection and advisory system can be constructed (Lee and Liu 2000b).

From a technical perspective, in order to support the mobility of agents in traveling around the heterogeneous environment over the Internet, it is necessary to provide a generic execution environment for the agents to live, work, and talk. For instance, the Object Management Group (OMG)[3], a major agent development organization, has provided a collection of definitions and interface mobile agent system interoperability facilities (MASIF) to standardize the mobile agent community and promote interoperability.

Besides mobility, communication is another critical capability that needs to be implemented in any agent-based application. In fact, a typical agent should be able to talk intelligently (in a flexible matter) and achieve a high quality of communication. Existing high-level agent-based communication languages (ACL) include FIPA (Foundation for Intelligent Physical Agents) ACL[4] and KQML[5]. FIPA ACL and KQML have similar syntaxes and structures, which provide a set of basic concepts (taxonomy) used in the message content for cooperation. ACL provides agents with the ability to exchange information and knowledge in a well-defined structure so that agents can cooperate with each other in order to achieve a complex task.

In this chapter, an integrated intelligent agent-based framework is proposed, known as iJADE, for the design, support, and implementation of truly intelligent agent-based applications. To accommodate the deficiency of contemporary agent software platforms such as IBM Aglets and ObjectSpace Voyager agents, which mainly focus on multi-agent mobility and communication, iJADE provides an ingenious layer called the *conscious (intelligent) layer*, which supports different AI functionalities, to develop *truly* intelligent and AI-based multi-agent applications.

This chapter will be organized as follows. Section 5.2 presents an overview of the iJADE framework. Section 5.3 presents the architecture of

---

[3] Object Management Group (OMG): http://www.omg.org
[4] FIPA Message Structure Specification: http://www.fipa.org/specs/fipa00061/
[5] UMBC KQML: http://www.cs.umbc.edu/kqml

iJADK (intelligent Java Agent-based Development Kit) in the current release 2.0. This section will also discuss the basic components of iJADK
and highlight some critical and fundamental agent-based operations for interactions between the iJADE server and iJADK agents. Section 5.4 provides some programming details of the internal mechanisms for implementing iJADK agents, together with some typical examples of the design
and implementation of basic iJADK agents. It will conclude with a discussion of the latest work on the iJADE project.

5.2 iJADE – System Framework

5.2.1 iJADE Architecture

The fully integrated intelligent agent model called iJADE (pronounced
"IJ") was proposed for the design and implementation of intelligent agent-
based systems. The system framework and the homepage of the iJADK official site are shown in Figs. 5.1 and 5.2 respectively.

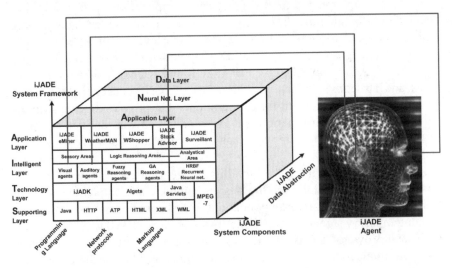

Fig. 5.1. System architecture of the iJADE (version 2.0) model

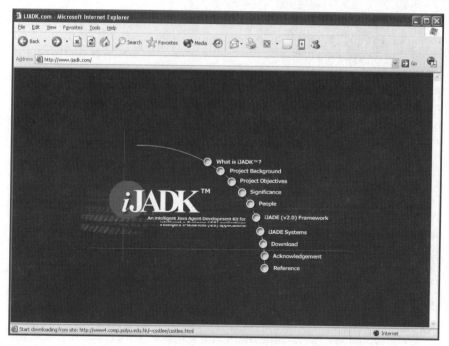

Fig. 5.2. iJADK official site (http://www.ijadk.org)

Unlike contemporary agent systems and APIs such as IBM Aglets and ObjectSpace Voyager which focus on multi-agent communication and autonomous operations, the aim of iJADE is to provide the fundamental Java-based intelligent agents construction library and, more importantly, to provide comprehensive *intelligent agent-based APIs* for the design and implementation of truly intelligent agent-based applications for future e-commerce and intelligent systems. The two-level abstraction of the iJADE system depicted in Fig. 5.1 is:

– iJADE system level – **ACTS** model
– iJADE data level – **DNA** model

The ACTS model consists of (1) the application layer, (2) the conscious (intelligent) layer, (3) the technology layer, and the (4) supporting layer. The DNA model is composed of (1) the data layer, (2) the neural network layer, and (3) the application layer.

Compared with contemporary agent systems that provide minimal and elementary data management schemes, the iJADE DNA model provides a comprehensive data manipulation framework based on neural network technology. The *data layer* corresponds to the raw data and input *stimulants* (such as the facial images captured from Web camera and product information in a cyberstore) from the environment. The *neural network layer* provides the clustering and knowledge base of different types of neural networks for the purpose of organization, interpretation, analysis, and forecasting operations based on the inputs from the data layer that are used by the iJADE applications in the *application layer*. Another innovative feature of the iJADE system is the ACTS mode, which provides a comprehensive layering architecture for the implementation of intelligent agent systems. The author will explain all of this in detail in the following sections.

5.2.2 Application Layer

This is the uppermost layer, which consists of different intelligent agent-based applications. These iJADE applications have been developed by integrating intelligent agent components from the *conscious layer* (or so-called *intelligent layer*) and data knowledge fields from the DNA model. The latest applications (iJADE version 2.0) implemented in this layer include:

- iJADE WShopper, an integrated intelligent fuzzy shopping agent with WAP technology for intelligent mobile shopping (discussed in Chap. 6).

- iJADE WeatherMAN, an intelligent weather forecasting agent which is the extension of previous research on multi-station weather forecasting using fuzzy neural networks (Chap. 7).

- iJADE Stock Advisor, an intelligent agent-based stock prediction system using a time series neuro-oscillatory prediction technique (Lee and Liu 2001b) (Chap. 8).

- iJADE eMiner, an intelligent Web-mining agent system for e-shopping (Lee and Liu 2004). It consists of the implementation of (1) FAgent, an automatic authentication system based on human face recognition (Lee and Liu 2000b), and (2) FShopper, a fuzzy agent-based Internet shopping agent (Lee and Liu 2000c).

- iJADE Surveillant, an automatic agent-based surveillance system (Lee 2003) (Chap. 9).

- iJADE Negotiator, an intelligent agent-based product negotiation agent with ingenious and dynamic negotiation strategies and negotiation protocols (Chap. 10).

5.2.3 Conscious (Intelligent) Layer

This layer provides the intelligent basis of the iJADE system, using the agent components provided by the *technology layer*. The *conscious layer* consists of the following three main intellectual functional areas:

1. Sensory area – for the recognition and interpretation of incoming stimulates. It includes (a) visual sensory agents using the EGDLM (Elastic Graph Dynamic Link Model) for invariant visual object recognition (Lee and Liu 2003); and (b) auditory sensory agents utilizing wavelet-based feature extraction and interpretation techniques (Hossain et al. 1999).

2. Logic reasoning area – a conscious area providing different AI tools for logical *thinking* and rule-based reasoning, such as GAs (genetic algorithms) and fuzzy rule-based systems.

3. Analytical area – an area consisting of various AI tools for analytical calculations, such as recurrent neural network-based analysis for real-time predictions and data mining (Lee and Liu 2000a).

5.2.4 Technology Layer

This layer provides all of the agent implementation APIs necessary for the development of intelligent agent components in the conscious layer. The technical details will be discussed in the next sections.

In this layer, server-side computing using Java servlet technology is adopted due to the fact that for certain intelligent agent-based applications, such as the WShopper, in which limited resources (in terms of memory and computational speed) are provided by wireless devices (e.g., WAP/Java phones, PDAs), all of the interactions of the iJADE agents are invoked in the *back-end* wireless gateway using Java servlet technology.

5.2.5 Supporting Layer

This layer provides all of the necessary system supports to the technology layer. It includes (1) programming language support based on Java, (2) network protocol support for HTTP, HTTPS, ATP, etc., and (3) markup language support for HTML, XML, WML, etc.

5.3 iJADK Architecture

5.3.1 Introduction to *i*JADK

The iJADK is an agent platform that implements the FIPA agent management specifications using Java 2 as the development tool. The goal of iJADK is to provide an agent platform together with a set of APIs to simplify the development of an agent system while ensuring that the system complies with FIPA standards. The basic building blocks of the platform are shown in Fig. 5.3.

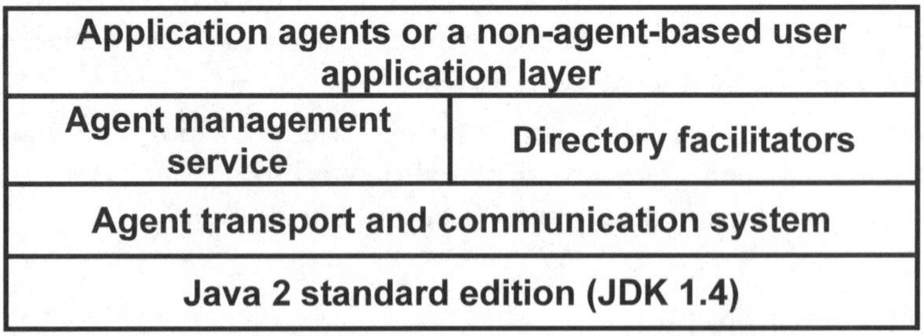

Application agents or a non-agent-based user application layer	
Agent management service	Directory facilitators
Agent transport and communication system	
Java 2 standard edition (JDK 1.4)	

Fig. 5.3. Basic building blocks of the iJADK 2.0 platform

To achieve this goal, iJADK offers the following features:

- A FIPA-compliant agent platform with an agent management system, directory facilitators, and message transporting system. All of these components are automatically started with the agent platform.

- A registration manager to act as a directory facilitator (i.e., Yellow Pages) for registering or searching for an agent inside the platform.

- A message transporting mechanism for agents to communicate with each other and dispatching agents.

- A life-cycle manager as an agent management system to control the agent's life-cycle within an agent platform.

- A GUI for users to manage, monitor, and log the agents activities.

- A typical user interface of an iJADE server process, which is depicted in Fig. 5.4.

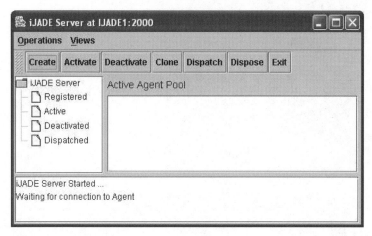

Fig. 5.4. iJADE agent server GUI

5.3.2 Basic Components of iJADK

The iJADK agent platform was developed in compliance with FIPA agent management specifications and includes all of the components that must be present in the agent platform: the agent management system, message transport service, and directory facilitator. The iJADK agent platform was developed by using the pure Java 2 standard edition (JDK 1.4). The mandatory components to start up the iJADK agent platform are LifeCycle-Manager, RegistrationManager, and CommunicationManager. The basic architecture of the iJADK agent platform is shown in Fig. 5.5. The iJADK provides the necessary mobile agent implementation APIs for the development of mobile intelligent agent systems. The basic functionalities and runtime properties of agents are defined by the Agent, LifeCycleManager, RegistrationManager, and CommunicationManager classes.

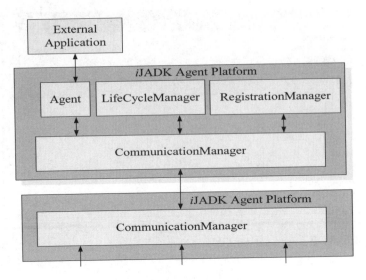

Fig. 5.5. Architecture of the iJADK agent platform

AgentPool

Basically, all iJADE agents must execute inside a virtual place within the server called the AgentPool. Thus, when an agent is created or dispatched, it must be put inside the AgentPool for execution.

LifeCycleManager

LifeCycleManager acts as the agent management system within the agent platform. It provides all of the related functionalities of controls within the agent platform including the creation, suspension, resumption, dispatch, and disposal of iJADE agents.

Agent

The Agent is the main character of the iJADE framework. It is a mobile software object that transfers its software code and status from one host to another in order to perform a specific task. The Agent has its own mechanism to broadcast or send messages to another agent for communication. When the Agent wants to ask for a specific service from another agent, it will first request the RegistrationManager for the related agent's information followed by the AgentPoolManager to get the request of the desired agent for further communication by using the message passing mechanism (Fig. 5.6).

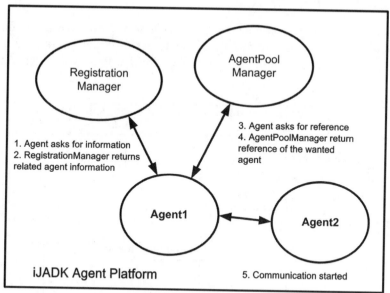

Fig. 5.6. Sequence of agent communication

RegistrationManager

The RegistrationManager maintains a list of the registered agent's information, which includes the agent's name, location of classes, and information about the service that the agent provides. It also protects the iJADE server from anonymous attacks. This is because an agent must be registered before it is allowed to execute inside the agent platform.

CommunicationManager

The message channel is maintained by the CommunicationManager. It controls all of the communicated messages passing within the agent platform. It also provides a network communication channel through which the Agent can dispatch messages from local to remote sites.

5.3.3 Internal Operations of iJADK

Registering an iJADE Agent

By using these basic components, the iJADE server can provide a number of operations that can help mobile agents to perform their tasks. The registration process of an intelligent agent over the iJADE server is depicted in Fig. 5.7.

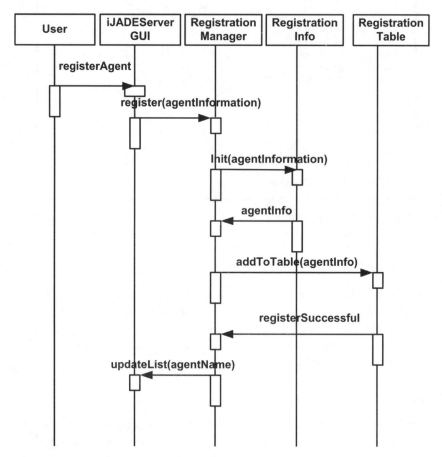

Fig. 5.7. Registering an agent in the iJADE server

Agents must be registered before they can *live* in the *i*JADE Server. Therefore, users are required to input the agent's information (e.g., the agent's name, code base and task description) by using the graphic user interface provided by the *i*JADE Server (*i*JADE Server GUI). After receiving the agent's information from the user input, the *i*JADE Server GUI will generate a request to the RegistrationManager. The RegistrationManager will then initialize an object RegistrationInfo and save it in the RegistrationTable. Then, *i*JADE Server GUI will be updated in order to inform the user after the registration has succeeded.

Creating an iJADE Agent

After registering an agent, the user can create an iJADE agent by using the *i*JADE Server GUI to choose an appropriate agent's name from the list. The *i*JADE Server GUI will ask the RegistrationManager to get the code base of the agent class file. The agent creation process over the iJADE Server is depicted in Fig. 5.8.

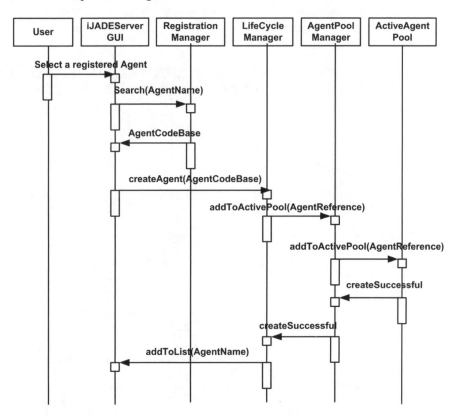

Fig. 5.8. Creating an iJADE agent in an *i*JADE Server

As shown in this figure, during the agent creation process, the iJADE server GUI will send a request to the LifeCycleManager to create an agent. After the agent file is loaded into the JVM (Java Virtual Machine), the

LifeCycleManger will send the agent's reference to the AgentPoolManager, and the AgentPoolManger will add the agent reference to the ActiveAgentPool. Then, the iJADE server GUI will be updated in order to inform the user when the creation has succeeded.

Dispatch Agent

When an agent is created within the iJADE server, the user can use the GUI provided by the iJADE platform to select and dispatch agents. When the GUI receives the user's request, it will forward it to the LifeCycleManager. The LifeCycleManager will ask the RegistrationManager for the AgentCodeBase, and then it will ask the AgentPoolManager to provide the AgentReference. After that, the LifeCycleManager will send a dispatch request to the CommunicationManager in order to dispatch the agent object and the class file if necessary.

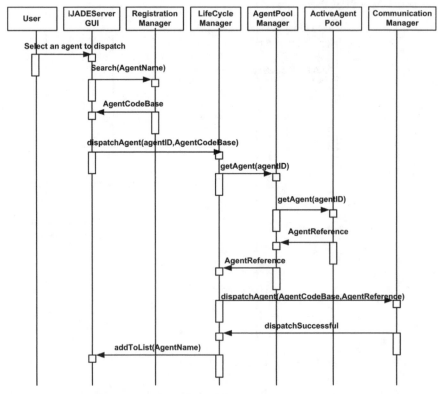

Fig. 5.9. Dispatching an agent in an *i*JADE Server (sender)

In addition, there is a server listener in a remote machine. When the listener receives the dispatch request, it will forward the request to the LifeCycleManager. The LifeCycleManager will then check with the RegistrationManager to see whether an agent is already registered in the remote server. Then the LifeCycleManager will receive the agent object and ask the AgentPoolManager to add the AgentReference to the ActiveAgentPool, and finally it will update the GUI to notify the user that an agent has come to this server. The workflows for the dispatch of an agent from and to an iJADE server are shown in Figs. 5.9 and 5.10 respectively.

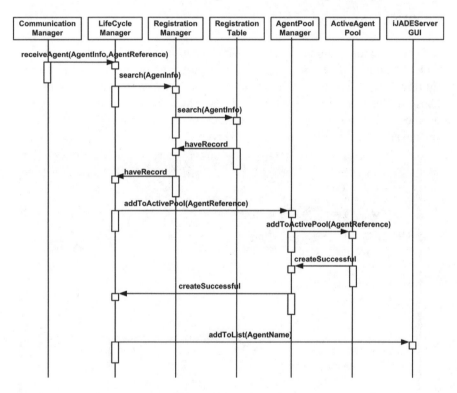

Fig. 5.10. Dispatching an agent in the *i*JADE server (receiver)

5.4 Agent Programming Over the iJADK Platform

The current release of iJADK (version 2.0) was developed under Sun Java 1.4. Java was adopted as the implementation language mainly because it is an object-oriented language and has been popularly adopted as the standard for building Internet-based applications. By using an object-oriented programming approach, program classes or interfaces can be reused or further extended such that the requirement to build every application from scratch can be avoided. Moreover, the portability of Java-compiled codes over heterogeneous platforms such as Unix, Linux and Microsoft Windows is another major reason for choosing Java as the iJADK construction language. In fact, once an iJADE agent is constructed, it can easily be migrated to different OS platforms.

5.4.1 User Interface

The four major regions on the iJADK user interface are shown in Fig. 5.11. As shown in the figure, the upper part contains a set of buttons including *Create*, *Activate*, *Deactivate*, *Clone*, *Dispatch*, *Dispose*, and *Exit*. These buttons provide a user-friendly interface to control the life-cycle of an agent. The lower part of the interface is the system log that will show the activities taking place inside the server.

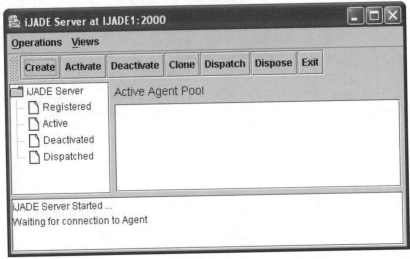

Fig. 5.11. The iJADE server user interface

The central area of the interface is divided into two parts. The left-hand side shows a list of agents that are in a different status tree style, while the right-hand side displays a message board.

Like other agent-based systems such as IBM Aglets, an iJADE agent must be registered before starting its activity. This serves to protect the agent system because such a feature can prevent anonymous agents from coming into the iJADE system and causing damage. The registration of the agent must be done by the user, by clicking the *Create* button. Then, a *Create Agent Dialogue* will appear requesting information about the mobile agent (Fig. 5.12).

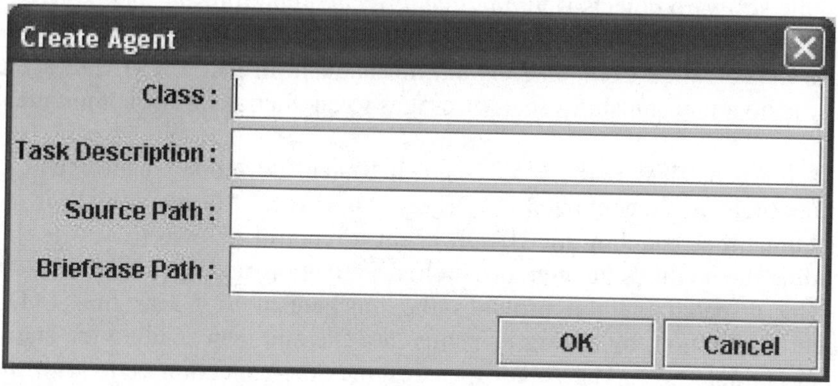

Fig. 5.12. Create iJADE agent dialogue

To create an iJADE agent, the user must first input a valid class name for the agent and a source path that contains the class files inside the iJADE file system. The task description is an optional input; it is used to register the service in the RegistrationManager. The other agent can then search for this agent by searching the registered service. After registering the agent with the task description and source path, the user can activate the agent at any time.

Moreover, the user can dispatch the iJADE agent object to another remote host at any time by clicking the *Dispatch* button. In this situation, the *Dispatch Agent Dialogue* will appear where the mobile agent should be dispatched (as in Fig. 5.13). Users are also required to input the destination host's name (or IP address) and the port number that the remote server is listening to.

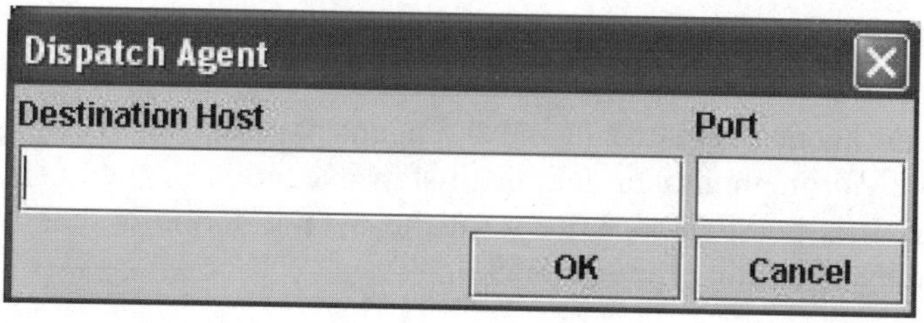

Fig. 5.13. Dispatch agent dialogue

5.4.2 Agent Class

The iJADE agent is the main spirit of the whole intelligent agent concept. It is the exemplification of this innovative idea of developing intelligent mobile software objects (the *intelligent agents*) that transfer their software code and status from one host to another in order to perform a specific task, the so-called *Code on Demand* mechanism. In fact, the iJADE agent has its own mechanism to send messages to another agent for communication.

The Agent class is the basic class that agent developers can extend to create their own customized iJADE agents. These APIs provide all of the functionalities enabling the iJADE agent to control its own life-cycle, including the methods of agent dispatch, deactivation, and disposal.

The dispatch method provides the mechanism to *freeze* the iJADE agent's operation, by saving its status in a file and then sending the status to the remote host. The Agent then resumes the execution code with the most updated status in the remote host. The deactivation method provides the mechanism to stop the Agent's operations, while the disposal method will stop the Agent's execution threads and clear its status from memory.

The Agent class also has a set of methods to obtain the attributes or the current status of the agent object: the *getAgentName* method retrieves the name of the agent inside the platform; the *getAgentID* method retrieves the agent ID number; and the *getStatus* method retrieves the current state (either active or inactive) of an agent.

An agent is programmed using the Agent class in the following manner: The ijadeserver* should be imported in order to have all the supporting libraries available for iJADE agent development. One can then define one's own iJADE agent by extending the Agent class:

```
import ijadeserver.Agent;
public class HelloAgent extends Agent {
    // implementation of the agent's method.

}
```

When an agent is created inside the agent platform, the platform must call on the *run* method as a default to start execution of the agent thread. Therefore, it is possible to write what the default action is that the agent must take by overriding the *run* method:

```
public void run() {
    // default action of the action when created.

}
```

The agent can dispatch itself to the remote host simply by using either the host name or the IP address, and the port number that the remote server is listening to:

public void dispatch(String host_name, int port_num);

When the agent arrives at the remote server, the iJADE server of the remote host will call the *arrived* method by default to resume execution of the agent thread. Therefore, the agent should be told what to do at the remote host by overriding the *arrived* method:

public void arrived() {
    // what action needs to be taken when resuming execution on the remote host.
}

When one agent wants to talk to another agent, it needs to get a reference of the other agent from the LifeCyleManager by calling the *getOtherAgent* method with the agent's name:

public Agent getOtherAgent(String agent_name);

After obtaining the reference of the other agent, these agents can communicate with each other. By using the *sendMessge* method, the user can send any message (i.e., in any object type) to the other agent:

public void sendMessage(Object msg)

On the other hand, when the iJADE agent receives a message from the other agent(s), the user can override the *handMessage* method to produce and give an appropriate response to the message:

public void handleMessage(Object msg) {
    // what action needs to be taken for the incoming message.
}

Sometimes the user may need to obtain the reference of the LifeCycleManager in order to carry out some particular action such as creating other agent(s). In that case the *getLifeCycleManager* method can be used to get the reference of the LifeCycleManager:

public LifeCycleManager getLifeCycleManager()

5.4.3 LifeCycleManager

The LifeCycleManager acts as an agent management system within the agent platform. It provides all control functions within the agent platform including creation, suspension, resumption, dispatch, and disposal of agents.

After obtaining the reference of the LifeCycleManager, the user can perform some operations to control the life-cycle of the other agent(s) inside the agent platform. The user can also create a new instance or reactivate the agent object that has already been registered in the agent platform by using the name of the agent class:

    public Agent activateAgent(String agentName, String activate)

By using the *deactivateAgent* method, the iJADE agent will cease its activity immediately and change its status to inactive:

    public void deactivateAgent(String agentName)

The *disposeAgent* method will terminate the activities of the agent immediately and remove the agent object from memory:

    public void disposeAgent(String agentName)

When the user needs to communicate to the agent through the client program, the user can use the *getOtherAgent* method of the LifeCycleManager to obtain the agent's reference, so that the user can send a message to the agent and inform the agent of what it needs to do:

    public Agent getOtherAgent(String name)

Sometimes the user may need to broadcast a message to all the agents inside the agent platform. In this situation, the user can invoke the *getAllAgent* method to obtain an enumeration of agent references in order to send the message to all these agents:

    public Enumeration getAllAgent()

5.4.4 RuntimeAgent

Sometimes the user might need to write an application that does not necessarily have to be initiated using the iJADE server interface. In this situation, the user can use a static class method from the RuntimeAgent class to create a new instance of the agent object by using the name of the server, the listening port number, and the name of the agent class as the parameters:

   public static Agent createAgent(String server, int port, String agentname)

5.5 Sample iJADE Agents

5.5.1 HelloWorldAgent

HelloWorldAgent shows the simplest way of creating an iJADE agent, which only displays the Hello World Message in an AWT frame:

```
import ijadeserver.Agent;
import java.awt.*;

public class HelloWorldAgent extends Agent {
    transient Frame my_dialog;
    // transient means that this class will not be transferred during the dispatch
    public void run() {
        message = 'Hello World! I am' + getAgentName();
            my_dialog = new MyDialog(this);
        my_dialog.pack();
            my_dialog.resize(my_dialog.preferredSize());
        my_dialog.show();
    }
}

class MyDialog extends Frame {
    private HelloAgent agent = null;
    private Label msg = null;
    MyDialog(HelloAgent agent) {
        this.agent = agent;
        layoutComponents();
    }
    private void layoutComponents() {
        msg = new Label(agent.message);
```

```
        Panel p = new Panel();
        add(p);
        p.setLayout(new FlowLayout());
        add(msg);
    }

    public boolean handleEvent(Event ev) {
        if (ev.id == Event.WINDOW_DESTROY) {
            hide();
            return true;
        }
        return super.handleEvent(ev);
    }
}
```

5.5.2 HelloWorldAgent2

HelloWorldAgent2 has a similar structure to the previous Hello-
WorldAgent example, but in this case the iJADE agent will show the Hello
World Message in an AWT frame when it arrives at the remote host:

```
public class HelloAgent2 extends Agent {
    transient Frame my_dialog;
    String message = null;

    public void run() {
        dispatch('ijade1', 4444);
    }

    public void arrived() {
        message = 'Hello World! I am ' + getAgentName();
            my_dialog = new MyDialog(this);
        my_dialog.pack();
        my_dialog.resize(my_dialog.preferredSize());
        my_dialog.show();
    }
}
```

5.5.3 TalkAgent

In this example, an agent called *TalkAgent* will be created in two iJADE servers. First of all, the user needs to click the *Connect* button to start the connection between the two chatting iJADE agents on different host machines. The users can then talk to each other using the chatting interface. These examples show how we can create a new instance of the other agent (msgAgent) by using the *getLifeCycleManager* method. This example also demonstrates how the agent sends and handles messages in agent communications.

```
import ijadeserver.Agent;
public class TalkAgent extends Agent {
    transient Frame1 frame;
    String message = null;

    public void run() {
        frame = new Frame1(this);
        // codes to show the Frame1 interface
        }

    public void setDialog(Frame1 dlg) {
                this.frame = dlg;
    }

    public void handleMessage(Object msg) {
        if
(msg.toString().substring(0,msg.toString().indexOf('@')).equals('Connect')) {

        frame.appendText('Connected from ' +
            msg.toString().substring(msg.toString().indexOf('@') + 1,
        msg.toString().length()));
        }
        else {
                frame.appendText(msg.toString().substring(msg.toString().indexOf
                ('@') + 1, msg.toString().length()));
        }
        }
    }


public class Frame1 extends JFrame {
    TalkAgent agent = null;
    msgAgent msgagent = null;
    String host = " ;
```

```
int port = 0;
String chat = '';

//Construct the frame

void btn_Connect_actionPerformed(ActionEvent e) {
  try {
    InetAddress addr = InetAddress.getLocalHost();
    host = destHost.getText();
    port = Integer.parseInt(destPort.getText());
      msgagent =
  (msgAgent)agent.getLifeCycleManager().activateAgent('msgAgent',
          'ACTIVATE');
    msgagent.setMsg('Connect@' + addr.getHostName());
    msgagent.getLifeCycleManager().dispatchAgent(msgagent, host, port);
  }
  catch (UnknownHostException ex) {

  }
}

void jbtn_Send_actionPerformed(ActionEvent e) {
  msgagent = (msgAgent)
agent.getLifeCycleManager().activateAgent('msgAgent',
          'ACTIVATE');
  msgagent.setMsg('msg@' + msg.getText());
  msgagent.getLifeCycleManager().dispatchAgent(msgagent, host, port);
  msg.setText('');
  msg.updateUI();
}

public void appendText(String _msg) {
  chat += _msg + '\n';
  text.setText(chat);
}
}

import ijadeserver.Agent;
public class msgAgent extends Agent {
  String msg = '';

  public void arrived() {
    Agent agent = getOtherAgent('TalkAgent');
    agent.sendMessage(msg);
  }

  public void run() {
```

```
    }

    public void setMsg(String _msg) {
      msg = _msg;
    }
}
```

5.6 Latest Work on iJADE

iJADE is an ongoing agent development project funded and supported by the Department of Computing of The Hong Kong Polytechnic University.

The latest developments include:

– The further development of the AI functional modules in the intelligent layer (conscious layer) of the iJADE model to support complex intelligent agent applications such as iJADE PA – an intelligent personal assistant agent that incorporates NLP (Natural Language Processing) functionality for communication with the fuzzy reasoning and decision making ability for decision making.

– The design and implementation of iJADE agents and related applications in various areas including: Internet and mobile e-business; financial forecasts and predictions; severe weather predictions; pattern recognition and knowledge discovery; etc.

– The design and development of the third generation of iJADE frameworks – the *Cogito iJADE* – a self-aware and ontologically based intelligent agent framework for future intelligent-based agent applications over heterogeneous platforms. The background and main concepts of Cogito iJADE will be discussed in Chap. 11.

5.7 Summary

In this chapter, an innovative Java-based intelligent agent development platform known as iJADE (intelligent Java Agent-based Development Environment) was introduced, and its basic framework and the main modules in the model were described. The current release of the iJADE development kit, the so-called iJADK (intelligent Java Agent-based Development Kit, version 2.0), was described, as was the agent interaction mechanisms and basic operational details. By illustrating some of the typical and basic iJADE agents, it is hoped that readers will gain a basic impression of the design and implementation of iJADE agents.

For details on current developments in iJADK, refer to the official iJADK site http://www.iJADK.org. A free version of iJADK can also be downloaded from this site and incorporated into one's own agent applications.

Acknowledgments

The author is grateful for the Departmental Grants and their partial support of the iJADE Projects, including the iJADE Framework (version 2.0) Z042, RCG Grants B-Q569 and the Central Research Grants G-T850 and A-PF74 from The Hong Kong Polytechnic University.

6 iJADE WShopper – Intelligent Mobile Shopping Based on Fuzzy–Neuro Shopping Agents

The intellect of man is forced to choose.

Perfection of the life, or of the work,

And if it take the second must refuse

A heavenly mansion, raging in the dark.

The Choice, W.B. Yeats

Owing to the increasing number of mobile e-commerce applications, applications integrated with intelligent agent-based systems are becoming a new trend in the new millennium. Traditional web-based agent systems suffer various degrees of deficiency in terms of the provision of *intelligent* software interfaces and lightweight coding to be implemented in these wireless devices. This chapter responds to this by introducing iJADE WShopper – an *intelligent fuzzy–neuro-based mobile shopping agent* based on the integration of WAP and Java servlet technology – with our iJADE API, for the development of intelligent, compact, and highly mobile shopping agents for the future intelligent e-commerce. In experiments, iJADE WShopper has provided promising results in terms of agent mobility, fuzzy–neural shopping efficiency and effectiveness.

6.1 Introduction

The exponential growth of the Internet in recent years has thrown up new opportunities for businesses, especially in the field of e-commerce. Various e-commerce systems, ranging from C2C (consumer-to-consumer) e-commerce such as e-auctions to inter-organizational B2B (business-to-business) e-business for the international e-marketplace (Chan et al. 2001; Turban et al. 2000), now operate in the cyberspace. However, in this sea of information and Internet services, web developers who wish to provide a more comprehensive service and automatic personal assistance for Internet users have been trying to integrate agent technology into their e-applications. With their ability to automatically delegate tasks and their autonomous and highly mobile characteristics in the web environment, agents will play an important role in e-commerce in the new millennium (Brenner et al. 1998).

Although some contemporary agent systems such as IBM Aglets[1] and ObjectSpace Voyager[2] focus on mobility and multi-agent communications, intelligent agents (IAs) have several core functions including machine learning and intelligent pattern recognition and classification. These functions are difficult to implement, as in most typical e-shopping scenarios we are dealing with inexact product selection criteria. For instance, when choosing a pair of shoes, we may base our choice on degree of fitness rather than exact size, or we may seek preferred patterns rather than exact ones. In such cases, we are dealing with different degrees of *fuzziness*, which can be efficiently handled by AI technologies such as fuzzy systems. Ultimately, by integrating machine-learning techniques such as neural networks, we can construct *intelligent* product selection and advisory systems.

Apart from being difficult to implement, contemporary agent-based systems require that Internet users who would like to invoke mobile agents install a dedicated agent operating system such as the Tahiti server for IBM Aglets (Lange and Oshima 1998) in both the client machine (such as an office PC) and the back-end server (the cyberstore). However, in a mobile e-commerce system such as Internet shopping via a WAP phone (mobile-shopping or m-shopping), limitations of memory capacity and communication speed in contemporary WAP phone technology make it infeasible and impractical to install such agent operating systems into WAP phones, let alone manipulate multi-agents in such environments (Vujosevic 2001).

---

[1] IBM Aglets: http://www.trl.ibm.co.jp/aglets/.
[2] Voyager: http://www.objectspace.com/voyager/.

One of the most interesting applications of iJADE in the mobile e-commerce environment is iJADE WShopper. iJADE WShopper integrates Java servlet technology (Moss 1999) into the technology layer of the iJADE model to provide an innovative intelligent agent-based solution in MEB (mobile electronic business). It integrates four different technologies: (1) *WAP technology* for mobile e-commerce (in the iJADE support layer); (2) *Intelligent agent technology* based on the iJADE framework (in the iJADE technology layer); (3) *Java servlets* for servlet-side agent dispatch in WAP servers; and (4) *AI capability* in the conscious layer using fuzzy–neuro networks as the AI backbone – an extension of the previous research on fuzzy agent-based shopping using FShopper technology (Lee and Liu 2000c).

This chapter is organized as follows. Section 6.2 provides an overview of WAP technology for MEB. Section 6.3 presents the iJADE WShopper architecture. Section 6.4 discusses system implementation followed by system analysis and the conclusion.

6.2 WAP Technology

6.2.1 WAP Technology – From Web to MEB

Owing to the advanced technology and popularity of cellular phones, together with the rapidly increasing demand for portable Internet services such as online shopping and the retrieval of real-time stock quotes, news and weather information, etc., there is a great demand for a truly portable Internet access solution that integrates cellular phone and Internet (web) technologies. This has motivated the development, or more precisely the *evolution*, of web technology to MEB using mobile computing technology (Chan et al. 2001; Mann 2000).

Most current web technologies are designed for stationary desktop computers connected to wired data networks. These technologies cannot be applied directly to hand-held mobile devices such as cellular phones and palmtop computers, because these small devices are less powerful in terms of CPU power, screen size, memory, input devices, and battery life. Moreover, wireless networks typically have many operational constraints such as limited bandwidth, higher latency, and less predictable operating conditions.[3]

Solutions that could support mobile Internet access services should be:

- reliable in order to provide consistent services

- scaleable in order to cater to different customer needs

- secure so that people can use the services with confidence

- interoperable so that different manufacturers' products can work with each other

The major goal of WAP is to provide a cost-effective solution to satisfy these requirements.

6.2.2 Constraints for Contemporary WAP Technology on MEB

Contemporary WAP devices possess limited processing power and memory space, so we cannot expect to use them to carry out similar types of sophisticated e-commerce operations as they do on PCs, let alone perform *intelligent* e-operations. It may be possible, however, to *transfer* these sophisticated operations to a *brokering machine* such as a WAP server. In an m-shopping scenario, all the WAP devices need to do is the following:

- Connect to the WAP server to get the shopping information and display it on the screen.

- Collect the customer request.

- Send the customer request to the brokering machine which will invoke the *intelligent* shopping operations and obtain the results.

- Retrieve the results and display them on the screen for further action.

In the next section, we will discuss how the iJADE model can provide an *intelligent* framework for the implementation of smart m-shopping using iJADE WShopper.

---

[3] WAP Specification: http://www.wapforum.org/new/wap2.0.pdf. During the writing of this book, the WAP Forum merged with the OMA (Open Mobile Alliance): http://www.openmobilealliance.org/.

6.3 iJADE WShopper – System Framework

6.3.1 iJADE WShopper – System Overview

iJADE WShopper provides an integrated, intelligent, agent-based solution for m-shopping via a WAP device, by extending previous work on the Fuzzy Shopper (FShopper) (Lee and Liu 2000c), a fuzzy shopping agent for Internet shopping. iJADE WShopper is based on the iJADE model and integrates the following technologies: (1) mobile agent technology based on Aglets for the agent framework (the technology layer of the iJADE model), (2) Java servlet technology for the manipulation of the server-side operations in the brokering machine (the technology layer of the iJADE model), and (3) FShopper, intelligent fuzzy neural-based shopping operations (the conscious layer of the iJADE model).

Figure 6.1 depicts the overall system framework of iJADE WShopper for m-shopping using iJADE technology in different cyberstores. Figure 6.2 demonstrates two situations of *intelligent agent shopping*: (1) fuzzy Internet shopping via a web browser, and (2) fuzzy WAP shopping (iJADE WShopper) using a WAP phone as the WAP device. In other words, any agent-based cyberstore can be operated in this framework provided that its agent servers conform to the FIPA (Foundation for Intelligent Physical Agents) standards. More importantly, under this infrastructure, both web-based e-shopping and MEB m-shopping can operate simultaneously.

6.3.2 iJADE WShopper for M-shopping – System Components

The iJADE WShopper system framework consists of the following six main modules:

1. customer requirement definition (CRD)
2. requirement fuzzification scheme (RFS)
3. fuzzy agents negotiation scheme (FANS)
4. fuzzy product selection scheme (FPSS)
5. product defuzzification scheme (PDS)
6. product evaluation scheme (PES)

Customer Requirement Definition (CRD)

As shown in Fig. 6.1, the customer uses the WAP phone (or any other WAP-enabled wireless device) to make a connection to a particular cyberstore via the WAP server as a WAP gateway. The WAP server also acts as an *Agent Brokering Center* for the dispatch, management, and collaboration of iJADE fuzzy agents. The WAP phone needs only a *channel* for the customer to input his (or her) shopping requirements; the WAP phone will then invoke the server-side program (using servlet technology, as illustrated in Sect. 3.2) in the WAP gateway to dispatch the corresponding iJADE agents.

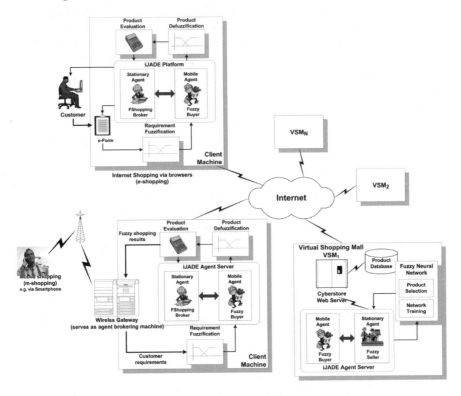

Fig. 6.1. System overview of iJADE WShopper for mobile shopping (m-shopping)

In this iJADE agent brokering center, there are two types of iJADE agents, as follows.

FShopping Broker

This is a stationary agent that acts as a buyer/broker on behalf of the customer. This autonomous iJADE agent contains all necessary information and analytical techniques (provided by the conscious layer of the model), such as the requirement for fuzzification and defuzzification, product evaluation techniques, etc.

Fuzzy Buyer

This is a mobile iJADE agent that acts as a virtual buyer in the virtual marketplace. It corresponds to all agent communications, interactions, and negotiations.

In CRD, the customer (via the WAP phone) will be provided with an FShopping Broker as a simple e-form to determine customer requirements. The FShopping Broker will also provide a set of *cues* to assist product definition.

Requirement Fuzzification Scheme (RFS)

Once the customer has input all his or her product requirements (e.g., color, size, style, fitness) into the WAP phone, FShopping Broker (in the brokering center) will convert all the fuzzy requirements into fuzzy variables by using *embedded* knowledge (i.e., the membership functions) with its knowledge base. At this point, the FShopping Broker is also responsible for the form data validation jobs as well. Sample fuzzy membership functions for selected attributes for shoes, including color and degree of fitness, are shown in Fig. 6.2.

Fuzzy Agents Negotiation Scheme (FANS)

After all the fuzzy requirements for the customer have been collected, the Fuzzy Buyer starts its buying activity in the cyberworld. To speed up the buyer process, the Fuzzy Buyer will make use of cloning operations to duplicate its identity so that parallel buying activities can be achieved.

In every virtual shopping mall (VSM), the Fuzzy Buyer will communicate and negotiate with the Fuzzy Seller, a stationary selling agent that acts as a virtual salesperson for the shopping activities.

$$Color\,(color) = \{red, yellow, blue\}$$

$$\underline{color} = \begin{cases} Light, Normal, Deep \,|\, \forall \mu_{\underline{color}}(Light), \\ \mu_{\underline{color}}(Normal), \mu_{\underline{color}}(Deep) \in [0,1] \end{cases}$$

$$\mu_{\underline{color}}(Light) = \begin{cases} 1 & if\ 0 \le x \le 64 \\ \dfrac{96-x}{32} & if\ 64 \le x \le 96 \\ 0 & otherwise \end{cases}$$

$$\mu_{\underline{color}}(Normal) = \begin{cases} \dfrac{x-64}{32} & if\ 64 \le x \le 96 \\ 1 & if\ 96 \le x \le 160 \\ \dfrac{192-x}{32} & if\ 160 \le x \le 192 \\ 0 & otherwise \end{cases}$$

$$\mu_{\underline{color}}(Deep) = \begin{cases} 1 & if\ x \ge 192 \\ \dfrac{x-160}{32} & if\ 160 \le x \le 192 \\ 0 & otherwise \end{cases}$$

$$Fitness = \begin{cases} Loose, Fit, Tight \,|\, \forall \mu_{\underline{fitness}}(Loose), \\ \mu_{\underline{fitness}}(Fit), \mu_{\underline{fitness}}(Tight) \in [0,1] \end{cases}$$

$$\mu_{\underline{fitness}}(Loose) = \begin{cases} 1 & if\ 0 \le x \le 3 \\ 4-x & if\ 3 \le x \le 4 \\ 0 & otherwise \end{cases}$$

$$\mu_{\underline{fitness}}(Fit) = \begin{cases} x-3 & if\ 3 \le x \le 4 \\ 1 & if\ 4 \le x \le 7 \\ 8-x & if\ 7 \le x \le 8 \\ 0 & otherwise \end{cases}$$

$$\mu_{\underline{fitness}}(Tight) = \begin{cases} 1 & if\ x \ge 8 \\ x-7 & if\ 7 \le x \le 8 \\ 0 & otherwise \end{cases}$$

Fig. 6.2. Sample membership functions for color and degree of fitness

Fuzzy Product Selection Scheme (FPSS)

Once the Fuzzy Seller has collected all the customer's fuzzy requirements, it will perform product selection based on a fuzzy neural network (provided by the iJADE DNA data model). Actually, the fuzzy neural network is an integration of fuzzy technology and the feedforward backpropagation neural network (FFBPN), provided by the iJADE conscious layer.

A schematic diagram of the network framework is shown in Fig. 6.3.

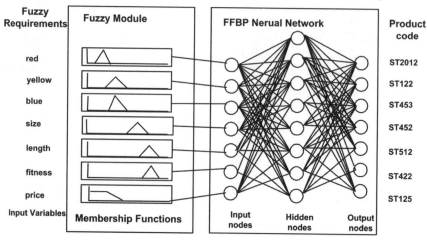

Fig. 6.3. Fuzzy neural network for product selection

The fuzzy neural network consists of two parts: the fuzzy module and the feedforward backpropagation (FFBP) neural network module. The fuzzy module provides the network with a bundle of fuzzy variables as input nodes. In the example, the fuzzy variables consist of the color components (i.e., red, yellow, and blue), size, length, degree of fitness, and price. Figure 6.3 depicts how the FPSS adopted the fuzzy neural networks in order to select a particular product (e.g., a pair of shoes).

The FFBP neural network is responsible for product selection, which is a kind of pattern classification scheme using a multi-layer neural network. The output layer is the list of items that are available in the store (under the proper product category).

In order to proceed with product classification, we need to train the fuzzy FFBP network beforehand. The next section outlines the details of network training.

Product Defuzzification and Product Evaluation Schemes

Depending on a customer's preferences, the Fuzzy Buyer will return to the client machine a number of recommended products. Before these products are displayed in the client browser, two operations are performed involving the product defuzzification scheme (PDS) and the product evaluation scheme (PES).

For the PDS, each recommended product will undergo defuzzification to return the fuzzy descriptions of all related product attributes (for ease of user understanding). According to the user's predefined ranking of the *importance* of every product attribute, an objective evaluation scheme can be performed to rank all the recommended products that could be displayed on the customer's WAP phone for the final decision.

6.4 Experimental Results

6.4.1 Introduction

From an implementation perspective, m-shopping in cyberstores was performed for simulation purposes. For the product database, over 200 items in eight categories were used to construct the e-catalog. These categories were: T-shirt, shirt, shoes, trousers, skirt, sweater, tablecloth, and napkins. The author deliberately chose soft-good items instead of hard goods like books or music media (as commonly found in most e-shopping agent systems) so that it would allow more room for the user's definition of requirements and product selection. A snapshot of intelligent wireless (WAP-based) shopping is depicted in Fig. 6.4.

For neural network training, all the e-catalog items were *pre-trained* in the sense that the author had predefined the attribute descriptions for all these items to be *fed* into the fuzzy neural network for product training (for each category). In total, eight different neural networks were constructed according to each different category of product.

From the experimental perspective, three sets of tests were conducted:

1. The round trip time (RTT) test

2. The product selection (PS) test

3. The iJADE WShopping agents selection (iWSAS) test

The RTT test aimed at an evaluation of the efficiency of the iJADE WShopper in the sense that it would calculate the whole RTT of the iJADE agents, instead of calculating the difference between the arrival and departure time to/from any particular server. The RTT test calculates all the *component* time fragments starting from collection of the user's requirements from the WAP phone, through fuzzification, to product selection and the evaluation steps in the brokering center (WAP gateway) and various cyberstores, so that a total picture of the performance efficiency can be deduced. Comparison with the fuzzy e-shopper (FShopper) can therefore be conducted.

In the PS test, since there is no definite answer as to whether a product would fit the customer's tastes or not, a sample group of 40 customers was used to judge the effectiveness of the iJADE WShopper. Details are illustrated in the following sections.

The iWSAS test focused on the evaluation of the optimal number of iJADE WShoppers being dispatched by the iJADE server, which was achieved using a cost evaluation scheme.

Fig. 6.4. Sample screens of intelligent mobile shopping using iJADE WShopper (via OpenWave WAP Simulator)

6.4.2 The RTT Test

In this test, two iJADE servers were used: the T1server and the T2server. The T1server was situated within the same LAN as the client machine, while the T2server was situated in a remote site.

Results of the mean RTT after 100 trials for each server are shown in Table 6.1.

In this table, the total RTT was dominated by the fuzzy product selection scheme (FPSS), but the time spent was within an acceptable time frame of 5 to 7 seconds. Additionally, the difference of the RTT between the server situated in the same LAN and the remote site was not significant except in the FANS, whereas the Fuzzy Buyer required a slightly longer *trip* than the other. In reality, it would depend heavily on network traffic.

Table 6.1. Mean RTT summary after 100 trials

Time (ms)	iJADE WShopper (m-shopping)		FShopper (e-shopping)	
	T1server	T2sever	T1server	T2sever
Server Location	Same LAN as client	Remote site	Same LAN as client	Remote site

A. In WAP phone and WAP gateway (iJADE WShopper)/client browser (FShopper)

CRD	–		–	
RFS	25	73	310	305

B. In the cyberstore (both iJADE WShopper and FShopper)

FANS	225	1304	320	2015
FPSS	3120	3311	4260	4133

C. In WAP phone and WAP gateway (iJADE WShopper)/client browser (FShopper)

PDS	310	335	320	330
PES	53	102	251	223
Total RTT	3733	5125	5461	7006

Compared with e-shopping using the FShopper, m-shopping using the iJADE WShopper provided a more efficient result. This happened mainly for two reasons: (1) In the iJADE WShopper scenario, all the cyberstores and WAP gateways were configured with the iJADE agent framework, better management of fuzzy shopping operations was provided, and more importantly the fuzzy agents were *lightweight* since all the related fuzzy evaluation APIs were implicitly provided by the iJADE framework. (2) As the major task of the WAP device was to collect customer requirements and display selection results, all the invoking, dispatching, and manipulation of fuzzy agents (which were originally done in the client machine) would be switched to the brokering center, as reflected by the short processing time in the RFS and PES processes.

6.4.3 The PS Test

Unlike the RTT test, in which objective figures could be easily obtained, the PS test results relied heavily on the user's preference. In order to get a more objective result, a sample group of 40 customers were invited to evaluate the system. In the test, each customer would buy one product from each category according to their own requirements. For evaluation, they browsed the e-catalog and compiled a list of the *best five choices* (*L*) which would fit their tastes. In comparison with the *top five* recommended product items (*i*) given by the Fuzzy Shopper, the fitness value (FV) was calculated as follows.

In the calculation, scores of 5 to 1 were given to *correct matches* of the candidate's first to fifth *best* choices with the Fuzzy Shopper's suggestion. For example, if out of the five best choices selected by the customer, products of rank number 1, 2, 3, and 5 appeared in the Fuzzy Shopper recommendation list, the fitness value would be 73%, which was the sum of 1, 2, 3, and 5 divided by 15.

In this experiment, four different product selection schemes were adopted:

1. Simple product selection (using product description matching, a traditional technique).

2. Product selection based on FFBP neural network training.

3. Product selection based on fuzzy product description – no network training was involved.

4. iJADE WShopper – product selection based on fuzzy neural training.

The corresponding FVs and the degree of improvement (against the *traditional* technique) for the eight different product categories are shown in Table 6.2.

In view of the iJADE WShopper PS result, it is not difficult to predict that the performance of the Fuzzy Shopper was highly dependent on the variability (or fuzziness) of the merchandise: the higher the fuzziness (which means more variety), the lower the score. As shown in Table 6.2, skirts and shoes are typical examples, in which their scores were 65% and 89% respectively. Nevertheless, the average score was over 81%. Note that these figures are for illustration purposes only, as human justification and product varieties do vary in actual scenarios.

Comparing different product selection techniques, the iJADE WShopper outperformed the FShopper by over 40%. Compared with the traditional technique, a promising improvement of 48% was attained.

Another interesting phenomenon was found in comparing the PS of the *Pure FFBP training* with the *Pure Fuzzy PS*. Although the former outperformed the latter by 5%, the latter technique produced exceptionally good results in certain product categories, such as shirts, skirts, and sweaters, which were all *fuzzy* products where the fuzzification techniques might help in product selection.

Table 6.2. Fitness values for the eight different product categories under different product selection schemes

Product Category	Fitness Value % (% improvement)			
	Simple product search	Pure FFBP neural net. training	Pure fuzzy product search	iJADE WShopper (fuzzy neural)
T-shirt	48	58 (+21)	54 (+13)	81 (+69)
Shirt	41	48 (+17)	**53 (+29)**	78 (+90)
Shoes	56	68 (+21)	58 (+4)	89 (+59)
Trousers	52	63 (+21)	56 (+8)	88 (+69)
Skirt	32	38 (+19)	**45 (+41)**	65 (+103)
Sweater	45	53 (+18)	**55 (+22)**	81 (+80)
Tablecloth	57	67 (+18)	61 (+7)	85 (+49)
Napkins	53	64 (+21)	58 (+9)	86 (+62)
Average score	**48.0**	**57.4 (+20)**	**55.0 (+15)**	**81.6 (+70)**

6.4.4 The iWSAS Test

Unlike the PS and RTT tests, which focused on the performance analysis of the proposed model, iWSAS concentrated on cost evaluation for the optimal number of iJADE WShoppers dispatched for m-shopping in different cyberstores. Suppose the price distribution of a particular item a sold in different cyberstores follows a normal distribution $N(p', \sigma)$, where p' is the mean price and σ the price variance of the product. The total cost (C_{Ta}) of purchasing item a using n_a iJADE WShopper agents is given by:

$$C_{Ta} = n_a c_a + \underset{k=1}{\overset{n_a}{Min}} \left[p_k (p', \sigma) \right] \qquad (6.1)$$

where

$$P(p_k) = \frac{1}{\sigma\sqrt{2\pi}} e^{-\frac{1}{2}\left(\frac{p_k - p'}{\sigma}\right)}$$

and c_a is the cost of dispatching a single iJADE WShopper.

Assuming that p', σ, and c_a are related by factors γ, β such that:

$$\sigma = \gamma p' \tag{6.2}$$

$$p' = \beta c_a \tag{6.3}$$

then (6.1) can be simplified to:

$$C_{Ta} = n_a c_a + \underset{k=1}{\overset{n_a}{Min}}\left[p_k(\beta c_a, \gamma \beta c_a)\right] \tag{6.4}$$

In the experiments, four types (I–IV) of products (with different price ranges) were used: (1) napkin (Type I, $\beta = 1$), (2) T-shirt (Type II, $\beta = 10$), (3) shoes (Type III, $\beta = 100$), and (4) sweater (Type IV, $\beta = 1000$). For the $\sigma : p$ ratio (γ), three different values were used, $\gamma = 0.1$, 0.3, and 0.05. The cost evaluation analysis for the number of iJADE WShoppers ranging from 1 to 100 under different scenarios is shown in Fig. 6.5.

From this figure, it is not difficult to ascertain that the performance of the total cost value (C_T) varied under different product types. Generally speaking, for *low-cost* products such as Type I and II items, for which the unit price of the product itself was comparable to the unit cost of dispatching a single iJADE WShopper, the C_T values increased monotonically with increasing numbers of iJADE WShoppers. In other words, there is no particular advantage in using more than one iJADE WShopper for m-shopping in this case. On the other hand, when the price of a shopping item was much higher than the iJADE WShopper unit dispatching cost (i.e., Type IV product with $\beta = 1000$), an increasing number of iJADE WShopper agents definitely resulted in a lower C_T. However, a significant improvement of overall cost value was found when the number of iJADE WShoppers increased from 1 to 12; above that value, a further increase in iJADE WShoppers did not give much help in lowering the total cost.

A typical situation is found for product Type III, in which there existed an *optimal* iJADE WShopper number. For ease of analysis, a special analysis of Type III products (under different β values) is given in Fig. 6.6. From this analysis, an obvious *optimal* iJADE WShopper number, $n_a = 7$, was found for $\beta = 0.3$, a similar result was found for $\beta = 0.1$, and a higher n_a value of 17 was found for $\beta = 0.05$. In fact, in a realistic shopping scenario, β normally ranged from 0.1 to 0.3. In that case, using seven iJADE WShoppers might be a wiser choice.

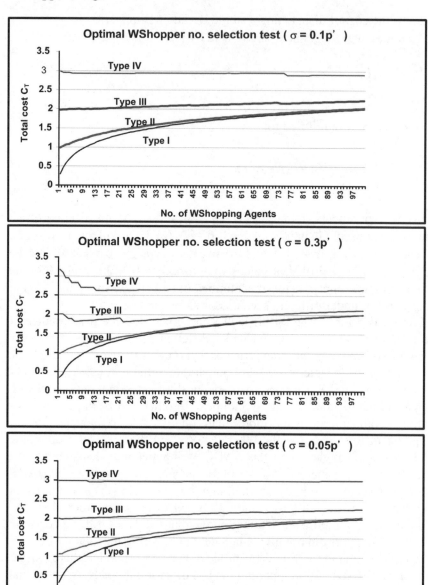

Fig. 6.5. Cost evaluation analysis of iWSAS test

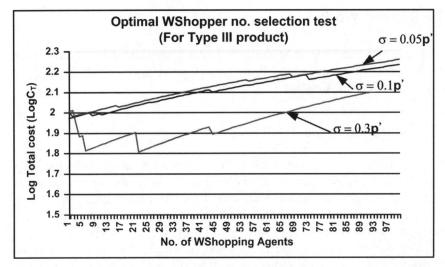

Fig. 6.6. Optimal iJADE WShopper analysis for Type III product

Three somewhat unrealistic assumptions about the results of the iWSAS test had been imposed. Firstly, the pricing strategy for any particular product sold in all the cyberstores followed a normal distribution. Secondly, the unit cost of dispatching every iJADE WShopper agent to each cyberstore was constant. Thirdly, this system assumed a *lowest-price selection* policy. The cost evaluation scheme would be much more complex if we were to take other factors into account. Nevertheless, the iWSAS test did provide a useful indicator for determining the upper bound of the number of iJADE WShopper agents that might be used in this m-shopping situation.

6.5 Conclusion

This chapter described the development of iJADE WShopper – an intelligent shopping agent for mobile shopping (via a WAP device) – on the Internet. More importantly, iJADE WShopper demonstrated how different technologies (including mobile agent technology for mobile agent framework construction, Java servlet technology for server-side programming, WAP technology for mobile computing, and AI for intelligent machine learning, classification, and selection) can be successfully integrated into the iJADE model to develop a *truly smart* agent for MEB (mobile e-business). Hopefully it will offer a new insight not only into AI technologies, but also into how these technologies can be effectively applied to contemporary e-commerce and m-business.

6.6 Related Work

With the rapid needs of and developments in wireless applications (over the Internet) in recent years, future developments of iJADE WShopper might include the following.

6.6.1 Migration to the J2ME Platform

WAP technology has some serious limitations in terms of both memory capacity and system performance (Sect. 6.2). With the launch and increasing popularity of Java J2ME technology, together with an increasing number of powerful Java phones and PDAs in recent years providing a much more promising performance, the latest work on iJADE WShopper includes the migration of the fuzzy shopping application over these Java devices using J2ME technology, as well as the support of location-aware iJADE WShopper using contemporary Java-enabled PDA devices such as HP iPAQ and Nokia communicator. For details, refer to the iJADK official site http://www.iJADK.org.

6.6.2 Incorporating Other AI Capabilities in the Shopper Agents – iJADE Negotiator

Another critical development of iJADE WShopper is to further extend the AI capabilities of the intelligent multi-agent e-shopping (and m-shopping) activities, such as in our latest development of iJADE Negotiator. iJADE Negotiator is a future development of iJADE Shopper with the implementation of a so-called INS (*intelligent negotiation system*). See Chap. 10 for details.

7 iJADE WeatherMAN – A Weather Forecasting Agent Using the Fuzzy Neural Network Model

Pale rain over the dwindling harbour
And over the sea wet church the size of a snail
With its horns through mist and the castle
Brown as owls
But all the gardens
Of spring and summer were blooming in the tall tales
Beyond the border and under the lark full cloud.
There could I marvel
My birthday
Away but the weather turned around.

Poem in October, Dylan Thomas

Weather forecasting has been one of the most challenging problems around the world for centuries, not only because of its practical value in meteorology, but also on the grounds that it is a typically *unbiased* time series forecasting problem in scientific research. This chapter introduces the iJADE WeatherMAN – a weather forecasting system using an intelligent multi-agent-based fuzzy–neuro system that automatically gathers and filters weather information, and performs time series weather prediction (done by a fuzzy–neuro network model) based on weather information provided by various weather stations.

The results are very promising compared with previous studies based on a single-point source using a similar network and with others like the radial basis function (RBF) network, learning vector quantization, and the naive Bayesian network. It is expected that this fuzzy neural-based rainfall forecasting system may be useful and may parallel the traditional forecasting of the Hong Kong Observatory.

7.1 Introduction

Traditionally, weather forecasting was based mainly on numerical models (McGregor et al. 1993). This classical approach attempted to model the fluid and thermodynamic systems for grid-point time series predictions based on boundary meteorological data. The simulation often required intensive computations involving complex differential equations and computational algorithms. Furthermore, the accuracy was bound by certain *inherent* constraints such as the adoption of incomplete boundary conditions, model assumptions, and numerical instabilities (Liu 1988). This kind of approach is more appropriate for long-term (over 24 hours) forecasting over a large area of several thousand kilometers (Chow and Cho 1993). For mesoscale and short-term weather forecasting in a relatively small region like Hong Kong, there is a need for an alternative. In addition, it is generally recognized by meteorologists that accurate rainfall forecasting is quite difficult to achieve due to the geographic and topographic features of the region. Similar studies (Li et al. 1998; Liu and Wong 1996) confirmed such difficulties, thus presenting a challenge to those who want to further investigate the problem. Moreover, with the exponential growth in Internet technology and e-commerce applications, real-time weather information gathering (from different weather stations) and weather prediction (such as temperature and rainfall forecasts) are increasingly important and demanding. Agent technology, with its automatic delegation of tasks and its autonomous and highly mobile characteristics in the web environment, is starting to play an important role in the new millennium.

However, contemporary agent systems such as IBM Aglets and Object-Space Voyager focus on mobility and multi-agent communications. The *core* functions of intelligent agents (IAs) – the AI (Artificial Intelligence) counterpart with intelligent capabilities such as machine learning, intelligent pattern recognition, and classification functions – are difficult to implement. In a typical weather forecasting scenario, most of the time we are handling *inexact* (so-called *fuzzy*) decisions and judgments. For instance, on rainfall prediction, we might be interested not in the exact amount of rainfall, but only in the degree of *rain depth*, ranging from *nil* or *trace* amounts to *heavy* rainfall. In such cases, we are dealing with different degrees of *fuzziness*, which can be efficiently handled by various AI technologies such as fuzzy systems. With the integration of machine-learning techniques like neural networks, an *intelligent* weather forecasting system can be constructed.

This chapter demonstrates how the iJADE model can be applied to real-time weather information gathering and the weather prediction process using the iJADE WeatherMAN, which integrates intelligent mobile agent technology for information gathering with a fuzzy neural network for weather prediction. For experimentation and network training, this system used eight years (from 1993 to 2000) of meteorological data collected from 11 weather stations distributed in Hong Kong to predict the rainfall situation of the following day.

The chapter is organized as follows. Section 7.2 outlines the weather forecasting model used. Section 7.3 presents the overall framework of the iJADE WeatherMAN. Section 7.4 presents the six main implementation modules of the iJADE WeatherMAN. Experimental results are discussed in Sect. 7.5, followed by a brief conclusion and a description of future work in the last section.

7.2 Weather Prediction Using a Fuzzy–Neuro Model

With the emergence of artificial neural networks (ANNs) in recent decades, extensive research has been conducted on time series forecasting. Effective tools that tackle forecasting problems can also be applied to other areas such as stock index forecasting in financial markets or fault detection in machine maintenance (Liu and Sin 1997).

The classical application of ANNs to weather forecasting appears in the work of Widrow and Smith (1963), who applied Adaline to predict the occurrence of the next day's rainfall on the basis of the fluctuations in barometric pressure over the two days preceding their calculation. More recent research (Chung and Kumar 1993; Liu 1988) using the backpropagation network (BPN) and naive Bayesian network (NBN) for rainfall prediction has achieved an average accuracy of 65%.

Among the many different meteorological parameters, such as temperature and relative humidity, rainfall is the most difficult to predict. As explained by Li et al. (1998), the low accuracy of rainfall prediction is mainly due to problems of insufficient data provision. So far, most of the weather prediction schemes using ANN models are based on meteorological data from one single weather station, with human experts (weather forecasters) using the conventional approach to correlate extra information from surrounding areas in support of this rainfall prediction.

In the proposed model structure, a neural-based model was used for multi-station weather prediction. The model included (1) genetic algorithms (GAs) (Pal and Wong 1996) for input node selection and network parameter settings; (2) fuzzy classification for rainfall parameters; and (3) neural network training using the BPN. Time series records of meteorological data (collected every six hours), such as wet- and dry-bulb temperatures, rainfall, mean sea-level pressure (MSLP), relative humidity, wind direction, and wind speed, were extracted from 11 weather stations in Hong Kong for the period between January 1993 and December 2000. This provided more than 7300 records of data, which formed the basis of the rainfall forecast.

7.3 iJADE WeatherMAN – System Overview

In this chapter, the iJADE model is used as the system framework to introduce an innovative, intelligent agent-based prediction system for extracting and analyzing weather information. This system is fed with data provided by multiple weather stations throughout Hong Kong and is known as the iJADE WeatherMAN.

This system is made up of five major components:

1. user requirement definition scheme (URDS)

2. data collection scheme (DCS)

3. variable selection and transformation scheme (VSTS)

4. fuzzy–neuro training and prediction scheme (FNTPS)

5. weather reporting scheme (WRS)

Schematic diagrams of the iJADE WeatherMAN and the agent negotiation and interaction schemes are depicted in Figs. 7.1 and 7.2 respectively.

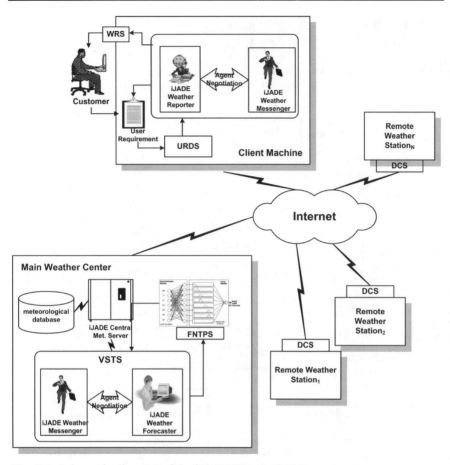

Fig. 7.1. Schematic diagram of the iJADE WeatherMAN

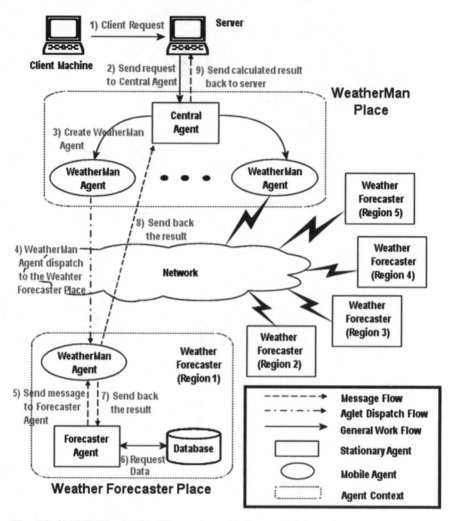

Fig. 7.2. iJADE WeatherMAN agent negotiations and interactions

7.3.1 User Requirement Definition Scheme (URDS) and Weather Reporting Scheme (WRS)

The URDS involves the collection of user requirements, including the selection of forecasting element(s) (e.g., temperature, rainfall, and humidity), forecasting range (e.g., next day or next *N*-day forecast), and other parameters such as regional/global weather reports. All this information is collected via the iJADE Weather Reporter – a stationary agent situated in the client machine for collecting user requirements, and for negotiating and dispatching mobile agents (iJADE Weather Messengers) for final weather reporting in the WRS.

7.3.2 Data Collection Scheme (DCS)

In this scheme, each iJADE Weather Messenger (a mobile agent) will "visit" different weather stations to collect weather information. This weather information will in turn be centralized within the main weather center (HKO site) for further processing.

In the implementation, meteorological data during the period between 1993 and 2000 were collected from 11 regional weather stations in Hong Kong. As shown in Fig. 7.3, these stations were located in Ta Kwu Ling (TKL), Ping Chau (EPC), Lau Fau Shan (LFS), Tai Po Kau (TPK), Sha Tin (SHA), Sha Lo Wan (SLW), Hong Kong Observatory (HKO), Junk Bay (JKB), Wong Chuk Hang (WCH), Cheung Chau (CCH), and Waglan Island (WGL). This weather information is the record of weather elements collected every six hours at 0600, 1200, 1800, and 2400.

These elements include:

– dry-bulb temperature (TT)
– dew-point temperature (DP)
– relative humidity (RH)
– hourly rainfall (RF)
– mean wind speed (FF)
– 60-min prevailing wind direction (DD)
– mean sea-level pressure (MSLP)

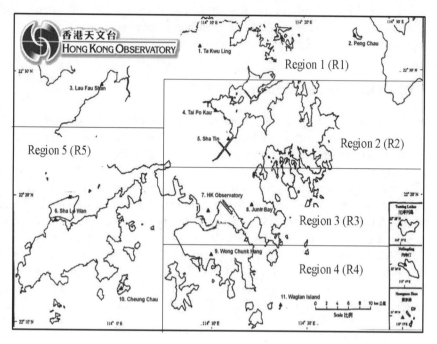

Fig. 7.3. Locations of the 11 automatic weather stations (AWS) divided into five different regions

7.3.3 Variable Selection and Transformation Scheme (VSTS)

Once all iJADE Weather Messengers are centralized in the central station, they will exchange and integrate the weather information they have collected and reorganize themselves (which involves selection, information grouping, and transformation of the weather elements) so that they can be used more efficiently for system training and testing. For instance, in the implementation stage using the weather information from the 11 stations (Fig. 7.4), there were severe losses of data from certain stations; as a result, the 11 stations were grouped to cover five regions (R1, R2, R3, R4, and R5) according to the distribution of weather records that could be collected in each region. Certain incomplete data were approximated by some regression functions interpolating nearby values of the same element within a region.

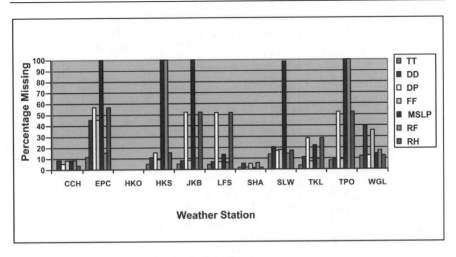

Fig. 7.4. Data distribution among 11 weather stations

In addition, the input variables are transformed from user data into formats suitable for neural network training. The transformations modify the distribution of input variables so that they better match the distribution of the dependent variables. Thus, the transform that produces the most similar distribution to the output variable will be selected accordingly. An input variable may therefore undergo several transformations like continuous transforms (e.g., linear, log, tanh, etc.), logical transforms, integer enumerated transforms, or string enumerated transforms. This means that the actual input will include the associated transformations. The GA based on the elitism model (EM) (Pal and Wong 1996) is used to optimize the selection of input nodes and the type of transformation for the networks. In our experiments, because the input variables were mainly numeric values, the first few transformations were used, and the best fit was chosen for model training.

7.3.4 Fuzzy–Neuro Training and Prediction Scheme (FNTPS)

When all the relevant weather information has been collected and preprocessed, the iJADE Weather Forecaster (a stationary computational agent situated in the central station) will start the appropriate network training and forecasting – based on a backpropagation fuzzy–neuro network (Fig. 7.5). Table 7.1 lists the five rainfall categories defined for the fuzzification of the rainfall elements.

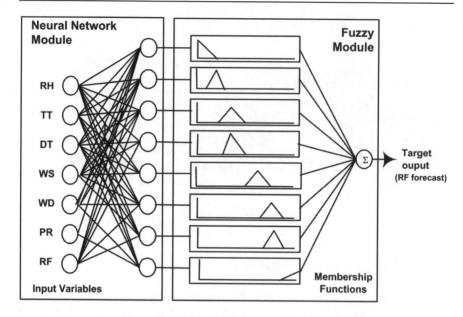

Fig. 7.5. Schematic diagram for fuzzy–neuro network on relative humidity (RH), dry-bulb temperature (TT), dew-point temperature (DT), wind speed (WS), wind direction (WD), mean sea-level pressure (PR), and rainfall (RF)

Table 7.1. Rainfall categories

Category	Nil	Trace	Light	Moderate	Heavy
Range in Depth d (mm)	$0 \leq d < 0.05$	$0.05 \leq d < 0.1$	$0.1 \leq d < 4.9$	$4.9 \leq d < 25.0$	$d > 25.0$

In the experiments, the fuzzy data for predicting the occurrence of either rain or no rain, and for the amount of precipitation, are associated with the membership functions as shown in Fig. 7.6.

$$\underline{Rain} = \begin{cases} no-rain, rain \, | \, \forall \mu_{rain}(no-rain), \\ \mu_{rain}(rain) \in \lfloor 0,1 \rfloor \end{cases}$$

$$\mu_{\underline{Rain}}(no-rain) = \begin{cases} 1 & if \ 0 \le x < 0.05 \\ \dfrac{(0.055-x)}{0.005} & if \ 0.005 \le x \le 0.055 \\ 0 & otherwise \end{cases}$$

$$\mu_{\underline{Rain}}(rain) = \begin{cases} 1 & if \ x \ge 0.005 \\ 0 & otherwise \end{cases}$$

$$\underline{Depth} = \{Nil, Trace, Light, Moderate, Heavy \, | \, \forall \mu_{Depth}(Nil),$$
$$\mu_{Depth}(Trace), \mu_{Depth}(Light),$$
$$\mu_{Depth}(Moderate), \mu_{Depth}(Heavy) \in [0,1]\}$$

$$\mu_{Depth}(Trace) = \begin{cases} 1 & if \ 0.05 \le x < 0.1 \\ \dfrac{(0.195-x)}{0.095} & if \ 0.1 \le x \le 0.195 \\ 0 & otherwise \end{cases}$$

$$\mu_{Depth}(Trace) = \begin{cases} 1 & if \ 0.05 \le x < 0.1 \\ \dfrac{(0.195-x)}{0.095} & if \ 0.1 \le x \le 0.195 \\ 0 & otherwise \end{cases}$$

$$\mu_{Depth}(Light) = \begin{cases} 1 & if \ 0.1 \le x < 4.9 \\ \dfrac{(5.38-x)}{0.48} & if \ 4.9 \le x \le 5.38 \\ 0 & otherwise \end{cases}$$

$$\mu_{Depth}(Moderate) = \begin{cases} 1 & if \ 4.9 \le x < 25.0 \\ \dfrac{(22.01-x)}{2.01} & if \ 25.0 \le x \le 22.01 \\ 0 & otherwise \end{cases}$$

$$\mu_{Depth}(Heavy) = \begin{cases} 1 & if \ x \ge 25.0 \\ 0 & otherwise \end{cases}$$

Fig. 7.6. Fuzzy membership functions for rainfall amount and rainfall depth

7.4 iJADE WeatherMAN – System Implementation

The implementation of the iJADE WeatherMAN consists of six main modules, as follows.

7.4.1 iJADE WeatherMAN Weather Site

The iJADE WeatherMAN Weather Site provides an interface for the system to accept the user's request in the HTTP get/post format. If the request is for network training, the Java servlet will create a central agent in the iJADE WeatherMAN Place. If the request is for network testing, it will create a test agent in the iJADE WeatherMAN Place. After the agent is created, the Java servlet forwards the request message to the agent for further processing.

7.4.2 Central Agent/Test Agent

The Central Agent (the administrative agent) is implemented with a fuzzy–neuro-based network algorithm. It is created by the Java servlet for network training purposes. The Test Agent is implemented with a propagation algorithm and is created by the Java servlet for network testing purposes. Figures 7.7 and 7.8 depict the network training and testing returned by the iJADE WeatherMAN.

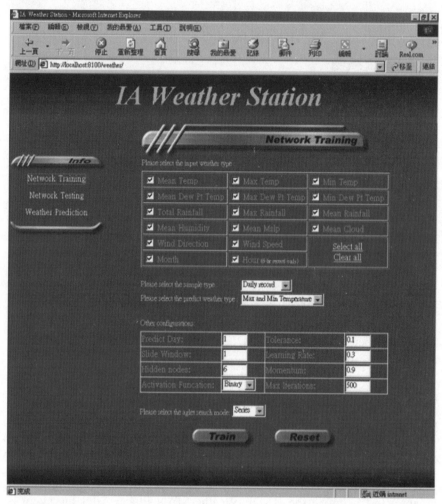

Fig. 7.7. The iJADE WeatherMAN: fuzzy–neuro network training

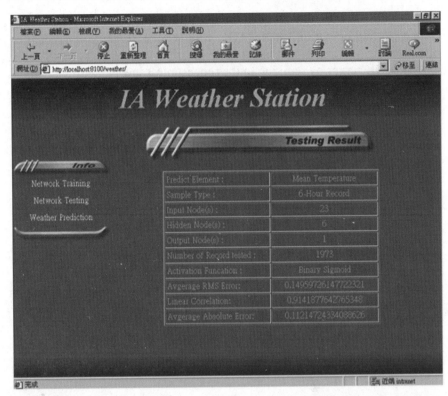

Fig. 7.8. The iJADE WeatherMAN: neural network testing results

Fig. 7.9. Message prompted by the Central Agent

After either the Central Agent or the Test Agent has been created, the iJADE WeatherMAN will create the iJADE WeatherMAN Agent and clone it into five iJADE WeatherMAN Agents for collecting the weather data from the iJADE Weather Forecasters of the five different regions. After the cloning operation, each iJADE Weather Forecaster will execute its own training/forecasting algorithm (see Fig. 7.9) and send the result back to the iJADE server by replying to the request message.

7.4.3 iJADE WeatherMAN Place

The iJADE WeatherMAN Place is where the creation of the Central Agent or the Test Agent and the cloning of the iJADE WeatherMAN Agents take place.

7.4.4 iJADE WeatherMAN Agent

After the iJADE WeatherMAN Agent is created, its creator will forward the user's request message to it. Then the iJADE WeatherMAN Agent holds the request and delivers it to the iJADE Weather Forecaster Place, where it will find the proxy of the iJADE Forecaster Agent and begin to communicate with the iJADE Forecaster Agent. Once communication is established, the iJADE WeatherMAN Agent will forward the request message to the iJADE Forecaster Agent.

7.4.5 iJADE Weather Forecaster Place

The iJADE Weather Forecaster Place is where the iJADE Forecaster Agent is on standby for the incoming agents and where the iJADE WeatherMAN Agent and iJADE Forecaster Agent interact with each other to complete the data searching process (Fig. 7.10).

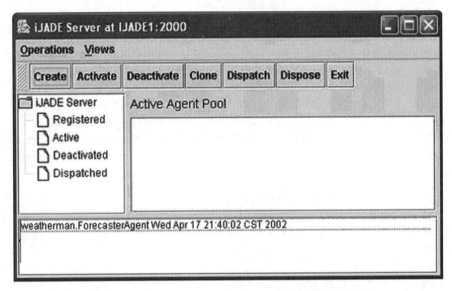

Fig. 7.10. The iJADE Weather Forecaster Place and the iJADE Forecaster Agent

7.4.6 iJADE Forecaster Agent

The iJADE Forecaster Agent is a stationary agent. Every iJADE Weather Forecaster Place has one iJADE Forecaster Agent on standby waiting for the request from other incoming agents. After receiving the request from the incoming iJADE WeatherMAN Agent, the iJADE Forecaster Agent will consider which weather elements are needed by the iJADE Weather-MAN Agent and then connect to the weather databank to find the relevant data. The information, as a reply to the request message, will be sent back to the iJADE WeatherMAN Agent. After the event, the iJADE Forecaster Agent will be on standby again for another incoming agent.

7.5 Experimental Results

Experiments were carried out using the following data sets:

Set A: Weather data from the single station at HKO

Set B: Weather data from multiple stations of HKO in Cheung Chau, Junk Bay, Sha Tin, Ta Kwu Ling, and Lau Fau Shan

Set C: Time series weather data from multiple stations

Each data record of Set A contained meteorological data that were collected every six-hour period from a single-point source (i.e., HKO); Set B contained data from multiple-point sources at 0600, 1200, 1800, and 2400 consecutive time periods; and Set C contained data also from multiple-point sources but at [0600, 1200, 1800, 2400], [1200, 1800, 2400, 0600], [1800, 2400, 0600, 1200], and [2400, 0600, 1200, 1800] consecutive time series. The aim was to find the most suitable and useful input variables for building prediction models that could minimize the training time and space complexity of the networks.

7.5.1 Evaluation Considerations

Several evaluation schemes were used for analyzing the prediction problem, as follows.

Linear Correlation (R)

This is the linear correlation between the real-world target output and real-world prediction. The analysis measured the relationship between two data sets that were scaled to be independent of the unit of measurement. The population correlation ($\rho x,y$) calculation returned the covariance ($cov(X,Y)$) of two data sets (X and Y) that were divided by the product of their standard deviations. Perfectly correlated outputs had $\rho x,y = 1.0$; anti-correlated outputs had $\rho x,y = -1.0$; and uncorrelated outputs had $\rho x,y = 0.0$.

7.5.2 Average Classification Rate

For rainfall classification, the method of average classification rate was used as a measurement criterion for best performance. Results for rain/no rain and rainfall depth classification are given in Tables 7.2 and 7.3.

Table 7.2. Classification of rain/no rain on the following day

Data Set	No. of Input Variables	Network Architecture	Accuracy (20%)	Classification Rate (%)	
	Output Evaluation Function			Average Classification Rate	
				No Rain	Rain
A	9	5–2–2	0.729238	78.10	69.77
B	96	8–6–2	0.746303	80.72	76.28
C	152	4–2–2	0.844141	93.25	82.60

Table 7.3. Classification of rainfall depth on the following day

Data Set	No. of Input Variables	Network Architecture	Accuracy (20%)	Nil	Trace	Light	Moderate	Heavy
A	9	9–13–5	0.3902	39.75	44.61	36.70	60.16	87.50
B	96	9–3–5	0.5097	61.70	28.65	37.16	57.97	84.38
C	152	486–4–5	0.6860	77.96	79.08	91.39	87.36	87.50

7.5.3 Model Performance

To summarize, the best experimental results based on different input data sets are given in Table 7.4. Generally, the performance of experiments on time series multiple stations was the best among all data sets. The results on single stations and multiple stations did not show a large difference; therefore just having multiple-station data was not sufficient to build a good model.

Table 7.4. Performance comparison

Data Set	A	B	C
Rain/No Rain Classification	73.94%	78.50%	87.93%
Rainfall Depth Classification	53.74%	53.97%	84.76%

Promising results achieved by the time series prediction method were mainly due to the availability of a large number of input data for the model to select the right variables, thus yielding a greater chance to generate better prediction results. It was observed that for all time series experiments, the accuracy was 10–28% higher than that in the single- or multiple-station experiments. It could be deduced that the correlation between data at time t and $t + 1$ is high, making it easier to build a successful model.

7.5.4 The HKO Forecast

Weather forecast information was broadcast by HKO every day. Here, a rough comparison of such information with our experimental results indicated that the overall classification rate for rainfall prediction over the five categories was around 85% (see Table 7.4). This represented an 85% and 30% improvement from that of previous studies using the RBF network, namely LVQ and the NBN in Li et al. (1998), respectively. Note that the results were based on year-round data from multiple-point sources represented by many regional stations in Hong Kong. Moreover, previous studies were done with ten years of data from HKO alone. Given that only the latest eight years of data were used, the present model achieved a better classification rate mainly due to improved preprocessing and transformation of the input data.

7.6 Conclusion

This chapter has introduced an innovative intelligent agent-based weather forecasting system known as the iJADE WeatherMAN. The chapter illustrates how this intelligent agent-based system can be efficiently integrated with a time series fuzzy–neuro prediction model to implement an online weather information retrieval, analysis, and prediction system.

From the aspect of weather prediction, it is concluded that the multiple-station model using the iJADE WeatherMAN for online information gathering by mobile agents (the iJADE Weather Messengers) is better than single-station prediction. For rainfall prediction, as shown in Fig. 7.11, the iJADE WeatherMAN shows a significant improvement over the single-station model (a three-fold increase in correlation).

To further improve rainfall forecasts, two types of techniques can be applied. Firstly, one needs to manipulate the data affecting the data distribution. Among the methods, the one that normalizes the rainfall nonlinearly and classifies it into classes gains the most significant improvement. Secondly, other algorithms can be incorporated into the neural network. However, among these methods, only fast propagation produces a positive improvement (see Fig. 7.12).

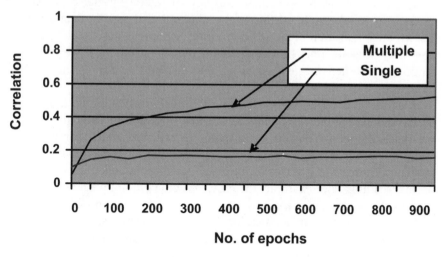

Fig. 7.11. Comparison of correlation using single- and multiple-station data

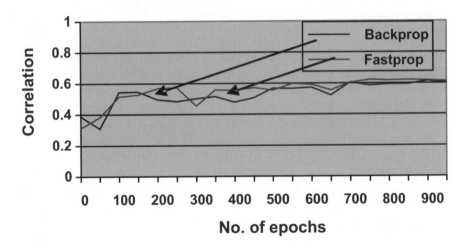

Fig. 7.12. Comparison of correlation using single- and multiple-station data

It is expected that rainfall forecast can be improved further. Originally, seasonal forecasts were expected to have a much better performance on rainfall prediction than the neural network fed with year-round data. However, the percentage improvement was not satisfactory in our experiments. In fact, the result might be due to the dramatic decrease in data quantity. As we only had eight years of data, after screening out the data for the non-rainy seasons, only half of the data could be used. So if we could obtain more weather information, say, 15 to 20 years of data, a much better improvement could be achieved.

In addition, with better-quality data the performance of the model will probably be improved. Despite the original intention to use data from 11 weather stations to forecast the weather recorded at HKO, some regions could not provide any records of certain weather elements since the data collected from several stations contained certain amounts of noise and abnormal readings. For example, the eastern region did not present its rainfall data to the neural network because the Junk Bay station did not record rainfall. This created difficulties for the model to generate better, more accurate results. For the sake of future studies, we shall continue to investigate the forecast of other severe-weather phenomena, including thunderstorms and tropical cyclones. This will require more support from multiple-point sources due to synoptic inference and a global effect on any specific domain region of interest.

7.7 Future Work

Future research on AI-based weather forecasting systems includes: (1) the *CORN* Project (*Chaotic neuro-Oscillatory Recurrent Neural network* Project), whose main objective is to model and forecast severe weather phenomena such as rainstorms and tropical cyclones and their track prediction based on a chaotic neuro-oscillatory model; (2) the design and development of an automatic tropical cyclone classification (including hurricanes and typhoons) and strength (i.e., tropical cyclone number) identification system based on a multi-resolution wavelet-based spiral snake (WBSS) model, which is an integration of the identification systems for tropical cyclone patterns of both the classical Dvorak system and the author's latest research on spiral snake technology.

In fact, the latest R&D on severe weather forecasting – namely, the classification and strength identification system of tropical cyclone patterns – can be further integrated with the iJADE WeatherMAN system to provide a comprehensive intelligent agent-based weather forecasting and severe weather prediction system.

Acknowledgments

The author is grateful to the Hong Kong Observatory for the provision of weather data and the partial support of the Departmental Grants for iJADE Projects including the iJADE Framework (version 2.0) Z042 and the CRG Project G-T850 (CORN Project) of The Hong Kong Polytechnic University.

8 iJADE Stock Advisor – An Intelligent Agent-Based Stock Prediction System Using the Hybrid RBF Recurrent Network

The best advisers, helpers, friends, always are those not who tell us how to act in special cases, but who give us, out of themselves, the ardent spirit and desire to act right, and leave us then, even through many blunders, to find out what our own form of right action is.

Visions and Tasks, Phillips Brooks

Financial prediction, such as stock forecasting, is always a popular topic for research studies and commercial applications. With the rapid growth of Internet technology in recent years, e-finance becomes a vital application of e-commerce. However, in this sea of information made available through the Internet, an intelligent financial web-mining and stock prediction system can be a key to success.

In this chapter, an innovative, intelligent, multi-agent-based stock advisory system is proposed, namely *the iJADE Stock Advisor* – a stock prediction system using our proposed hybrid radial basis function recurrent network (HRBFN) with the integration of the iJADE model. By using 10-year stock price information (1990–1999) consisting of 33 major Hong Kong stocks for testing, the iJADE Stock Advisor has achieved promising results in terms of efficiency, accuracy, and mobility compared with other contemporary stock prediction models. Also, various analyses of this stock advisory system have been performed, including round trip time (RTT) analysis, window size evaluation testing (for both long-term trends and short-term predictions), and stock prediction performance testing.

8.1 Introduction

Financial prediction (such as stock prediction) is, so far, one of the popular topics not only for research purposes but also for commercial applications. Owing to its importance, a well-established school of concepts and techniques, including *fundamental* (Ritchie 1996) and *technical* (Murphy 1986) *analysis*, has developed in recent decades. However, because these techniques or tools are based on totally different analytical approaches, they often yield contradictory results. More importantly, these analytical tools are heavily dependent on human expertise and justification in areas such as the location of reversal (or continuation) patterns, market patterns, and trend prediction. This will render them error-prone, to say the least. The second school of concepts for financial prediction, albeit less powerful, includes the *classical models* (Kamijo and Tanigawa 1990; Kaufman 1990; Liu and Tang 1996). The approach is based on the analysis of *price patterns* and *trading volume*. It relies on the detection of strong empirical regularities in the observations of the system, with the assumption that any influences on stock prices are already reflected in the price movements. The application primarily focuses on identifying patterns that can indicate *when* (the market timing) to *buy* or *sell*. Also, some other researchers believe that the adequacy of error measures such as yardsticks for neural network-based financial forecasting systems (Caldwell 1995) is more appropriate for handling financial prediction problems.

With the exponential growth of Internet technology and e-commerce applications in recent years, financial services delivered over the Internet (namely e-finance) have multiplied tremendously, mainly because the Internet provides an excellent channel to obtain an almost unlimited supply of real-time financial data. However, this leads to two major problems that remain to be solved: (1) The unlimited supply of information will finally result in a sea of information from which we have to select what is actually needed and make use of it. We, therefore, need some intelligent techniques or tools to trawl for important information – web-mining. (2) It will be very insufficient, given this sea of information, if we perform our web-mining with just a single online program. Thus, it will be advantageous to devise some mobile, autonomous, reproducible programs that can complete the web-mining task automatically and efficiently – namely, *agent technology*.

Contemporary web-mining and knowledge discovery models based on recurrent neural networks and other knowledge discovery techniques (Burrell and Folarin 1997; Funabashi et al. 1995; Nguyen 1999; Srivasan et al. 1997) typically employ a learning procedure to associate market direction with past price patterns, and other technical and fundamental inputs. They allow us, in principle, to deal with the problem of structural instability within the stock market and make up for such inadequacy. However, this requires a considerable degree of expertise in financial engineering, network engineering, and dynamical systems theory. Awareness of the complex interrelations between the model parameters and performance metrics is an essential ingredient of any successful application development.

In this chapter, an innovative, intelligent agent-based stock advisory system is proposed, namely the iJADE Stock Advisor. With the integration of the iJADE framework for the design and development of web-based intelligent agents, the iJADE Stock Advisor provides a *smart* stock prediction service for financial forecasting through the integration of agent technology with our proposed recurrent neural network, the *hybrid radial basis function network* (HRBFN). Also, this chapter will focus on how the HRBFN is effectively adopted into the stock advisory system to provide both efficient and accurate tools for stock prediction. In particular, the chapter will cover various aspects of the analysis of the proposed system, including: (1) round trip time (RTT) to evaluate the efficiency of the iJADE Stock Advisor; (2) a window-size evaluation test for both long- and short-term prediction to evaluate the optimal forecasting horizon; and (3) a stock prediction performance test to evaluate the accuracy of the system, compared with other neural network models, on next-day stock price prediction.

For experimental purposes, details of 33 major Hong Kong stocks during the period between 1990 and the end of 1999 (10-year data) have been used. Compared with other contemporary time series neural network prediction models, such as the feedforward backpropagation model from NeuroForecaster and Genetica, the iJADE Stock Advisor has achieved challenging results in terms of its efficiency, accuracy, and ability to integrate the critical techniques in technical analysis.

This chapter is organized as follows. Section 8.2 presents a general overview of contemporary work and techniques being adopted in stock advisory and prediction systems. Section 8.3 presents the system framework of the iJADE Stock Advisor, with the focus system architecture of the proposed HRBF model for stock prediction. Section 8.4 presents the experimental results and analysis of the proposed the iJADE Stock Advisor system followed by a brief summary of the proposed system.

8.2 Stock Advisory and Prediction System – A General Overview

A great deal of effort has been devoted to developing systems for analyzing, modeling, and predicting financial indicators. There are typically two stock analysis approaches, namely fundamental analysis and technical analysis (Black 1982; Murphy 1986; Refenes et al. 1993). The first and most powerful approach is based upon the study of supply and demand. It depends on exact knowledge of the laws underlying a given market phenomenon involving general economic variables, company performance statistics, prevailing business practice, political events, and many more things. Expressing this knowledge in terms of precise equations and then solving them can result in predicting the future behavior of the system once the initial conditions are completely specified. The main problem with this approach is that knowledge of the rules governing the behavior of the system is not readily available. Parameter instability and lack of nonlinearity in the models are the weaknesses of this approach (Chin 1990; Fuller et al. 1987; Pring 1985).

Secondly, albeit less powerful, the method for prediction includes the classical models (Kaufman 1990) and the adaptive models (Kamijo and Tanigawa 1990; Liu and Tang 1996; Park and Han 1995). The approach is based on analyzing price patterns and trading volumes. It relies on the discovery of strong empirical regularities in observations of the system, the assumption being that any influences on stock prices are already reflected in the price movements. The application is primarily focused on identifying patterns that can indicate *when* to buy or sell based on market timing. There are problems in that regularities are not always evident, and are often masked by noise. Many financial anomalies therefore remain unexplainable. The classical models of this approach include the study of moving averages and regression indicators. They are at best capable of picking out trends in the stock market, but have difficulty in modeling cycles that are by no means repetitive in amplitude, period, or shape.

The advancement of generalization models (Burrell and Folarin 1997; Funabashi et al. 1995), which typically employ a learning procedure to associate market direction with past price patterns and other technical and fundamental inputs, makes up for such inadequacy and allows us in principle to deal with the problem of structural instability within the stock market. This, however, requires a considerable degree of expertise in financial engineering, network engineering, and dynamical systems theory. Awareness of the complex interrelations between those model parameters and performance metrics is an essential ingredient of successful application development.

In general, most technical analysis techniques for stocks are alien to the general public and small investors are often too frightened to apply such techniques consistently and effectively to their investments. The supporters of this approach emphasize that it is a study of the action of the market and is concerned only with the identification of major turning points in the market's assessment of these factors. It is essentially a reflection of the idea that the stock market sets a trend determined by the changing attitudes of investors toward a variety of economic, monetary, political, and psychological forces.

The present study focuses on the latter approach that forms the theoretical foundation of the system. It extends the pilot system developed by Liu and Lee (1997) from which the pattern recognition of trend signals and the use of heuristics form the basis of expert knowledge.

In general, the basic strategy used for analyzing an investment is to:

– Identify the long- and short-term trends of the market.
– Identify the direction of these trends of the market.
– Identify how far the market is along these trends.
– Predict the turning points of the market.
– Predict the percentage change for different future time periods.
– Predict future tops and bottoms in the market.
– Predict points where stops should be placed.
– Develop direct buy- and sell-type signals.

The following theories are considered as part of the technical analysis for the study. More details can be obtained from John and Miller (1996), Jun et al. (1993), Lui (1990), and Plummer (1993).

8.2.1 Stochastic Indicator

This is essentially a momentum indicator, $\%K_t$, that indicates overbought and oversold conditions for time period t. Since stock prices tend to reverse their trends during a top (or bottom) period, we can anticipate reversals by detecting when a stock is at (or near) its limit. The formula is:

$$\%K_t = \frac{Current\ Close\ Price - Low\ Price\ of\ Period}{High\ Price\ of\ Period - Low\ Price\ of\ Period} \times 100 \qquad (8.1)$$

$$\%D_t = 3\text{-}Day\ Simple\ Moving\ Average$$

$$= \frac{\%K_t + \%K_{t-1} + \%K_{t-2}}{3} \tag{8.2}$$

The number calculated is between 0 and 100. It can be used as both a trending system or as an overbought/oversold oscillator when prices are consolidating. It is designed to show when prices are relatively high or low. In general, a stock is considered overbought when $\%K_t$ goes above 80%. Similarly, a stock is considered oversold when $\%K_t$ goes below 20%. A $\%K_t$ value of 100 provides an excellent entry point into the down trend. In contrast, a $\%K_t$ value of 0 provides an excellent entry point into the up trend. The time period here can be varied from 1 to 200 days.

This indicator is used to help customers buy low, sell high, or vice versa. The proper use of the stochastic indicator also requires that there will be a divergence between $\%D_t$ and price in order to generate a buy signal.

8.2.2 Relative Strength Index (RSI)

The RSI is one of the most widely used technical indicators. It is highly effective in aiding a technical analyst in chart interpretation. Some factors to consider when using the index are:

– Tops and bottoms are indicated when the RSI goes above 70 or drops below 30.

– Failure swings above 70 or below 30 on the RSI are strong indications of market reversals.

– Support and resistance often show up clearly on the RSI before becoming apparent on the chart.

– Divergence between the RSI and the price action on the chart is a very strong indicator that a market turning point is imminent.

The theoretical basis of the RSI is the momentum concept. A momentum oscillator is used to measure the velocity or rate of change of price over time. It is essentially a short-term trading indicator and also quite effective at extracting price information for a non-trending market. The RSI equation is:

$$RSI = 100 * \left(1 - \frac{1}{1 + RS}\right) \tag{8.3}$$

$$RS = \frac{Average \ of \ L \ days \ close \ UP}{Average \ of \ L \ days \ close \ DOWN} \qquad (8.4)$$

where L is a variable which can be varied from 1 to 30. If the average of L days close UP during the chosen time period is zero, the ratio RS is also assumed to be zero. However, if the average of L days close DOWN is zero, RS is assumed to be equal to the average of L days close UP. The ideal setting for RS is exactly one-half the period of the cycle.

It has been suggested that levels of 70 and 30 respectively signify tops and bottoms. The index usually leads the market and peaks before the actual top or bottom. Extreme values such as 90 or 10 signify unusual strength or weakness. Therefore, RSI can be used as an early warning signal.

8.2.3 Money Flow

It is noted that certain indicators such as the RSI place equal weight on the same difference in closing prices regardless of the number of contracts or shares traded.

Money flow may be used to measure the strength of capital entering and leaving the market. When today's average price is greater than yesterday's average price then it is an *UP* day for money flow:

$$Average \ Price = \frac{High + Low + Close}{3} \qquad (8.5)$$

A time period is chosen and positive and negative money flow are calculated as follows:

Positive Money Flow = Sum of Positive Money Flow for Time Period

Negative Money Flow = Sum of Negative Money Flow for Time Period

$$Money \ Flow = 100 * \left(1 - \frac{1}{1 + Money \ Ratio} \right) \qquad (8.6)$$

$$Money \ Ratio = \frac{Positive \ Money \ Flow}{Negative \ Money \ Flow} \qquad (8.7)$$

This ratio can be used in a fashion similar to that of the RSI.

Tops and bottoms are indicated when money flow goes above 80 or drops below 20. Failure swings above 80 or below 20 on the money flow index are strong indications of market reversals. Divergence between money flow and price action on the chart is a very strong indicator that a market turning point is imminent.

8.2.4 Moving Average

The moving average is calculated from historical price information. It represents a smoothing of actual price fluctuations. In flat or consolidating markets, moving averages would closely track the current prices. In trending markets, they can be used in buy or sell decisions. A long-term trend indicator can be obtained by comparing a short-term moving average with a longer-term average. The trend is rising when the short term is above the longer term, and vice versa. The buy signals tend to precede periods of increasing value in the stock price, while sell signals tend to precede periods of declining stock price.

The formulas for moving averages are as follows:

$$Exponential\ Moving\ Average = \sum_{K=0}^{L-1} \left[\frac{Closing\ Price}{\dfrac{\beta - \beta^K}{1 - \beta}} \right] \tag{8.8}$$

The smoothing gives a heavier weight to the most recent time periods and a lesser weight to earlier ones. If $\beta = 1.00$, then the average is a simple moving average:

$$Simple\ Moving\ Average = \frac{Sum\ of\ L\ day's\ Closing\ Price}{L} \tag{8.9}$$

Valid range for $L = 1$ to 200 (default setting $= 20$)
$\beta = 0.0$ to 1.0 (default setting $= 1$ and 0.75)

8.2.5 Support and Resistant Lines (Trendlines)

A review of stock trading will quickly reveal that prices usually move in trends. Quite often a series of ascending bottoms in a rising market can be joined together by a straight line, and so can the tops of a descending series of rally peaks. These lines, known as *trendlines*, are a simple but invaluable addition to the technical arsenal.

Significance of Trendlines

It has been established that a break in trend caused by penetration of a trendline results in either an actual trend reversal or a slowing in the pace of the trend. In general, the concept of valid up trendlines is an effective way of providing a sensitive take-profit sell signal. It is important to understand the significance of a trendline penetration; the guidelines described below provide help in evaluating this.

Length of the Line

The size or length of a trend is an important factor, as with price patterns. If a series of ascending bottoms occurs over a three- to four-week span, the resulting trendline is of only minor importance. If the trend extends over a period of one to three years, its violation marks a significant juncture point.

Number of Times the Trendline Has Been Touched or Approached

A trendline derives its authority from the number of times it has been touched or approached; that is, the larger the number, the greater the significance.

Angle of Ascent or Descent

A very sharp trend is difficult to maintain and is liable to be broken rather easily. All trends are eventually violated, but the steeper ones are likely to be ruptured more quickly. Penetration of a steep line usually results in a short corrective movement, following which the trend resumes but at a greatly reduced and more sustainable pace. Usually the penetration of a steep trendline represents a continuation rather than a reversal break.

8.2.6 Trend Generalization

Substantial parameter tuning, training, and testing (Park and Han 1995) are required for the system to adapt the market behavior and generalize prediction from historical stock data. The selection of a particular neural network architecture is based on the individual network's mean square error of predicted and actual values, the correlation, and direction symmetry performance on the data set. A typical backpropagation network gives outputs in the range [0,1] and has the following implications:

1. 0.75 or up: a trend showing that the market is expected to go up.

2. Smaller than 0.75 but larger than 0.25: a trend showing that range trading is expected.

3. 0.25 or below: a trend showing that the market is expected to go down.

8.3 iJADE Stock Advisor – System Framework

8.3.1 iJADE Stock Advisor – System Overview

In this chapter, an important iJADE application is proposed, namely the iJADE Stock Advisor, which uses the iJADE model as the system framework.

From the aspect of agent collaboration, the iJADE Stock Advisor consists of three different types of intelligent agents:

– *iJADE Stock Advisor*, an intelligent stationary agent located within the client machine. Its main role is to collect user requirements (e.g., type of financial prediction and selection of stocks). It also acts on behalf of the user to automatically disseminate user preferences, collect and analyze forecasting responses, and display the information to the client browser.

– *iJADE Stock Broker*, an intelligent mobile agent which acts as a messenger to convey user requirements to the iJADE stock analysts located at various financial sites, and *carries* the response information back to the user.

– *iJADE Stock Analyst*, an intelligent stationary agent located at a financial site. Its main duty is to perform web-based stock mining and prediction using the HRBF recurrent neural network technique.

The workflow of the iJADE Stock Advisor consists of the following five modules:

1. *Forecast requirement processing scheme* (FRPS) – done by the iJADE Stock Advisor.

2. *Stock agents negotiation scheme* (SANS) – between (1) the iJADE Stock Advisor and the iJADE Stock Brokers and (2) the iJADE Stock Brokers and the iJADE Stock Analysts.

3. *Stock prediction scheme* (SPS) using the HRBFN – performed by the iJADE Stock Analysts.

4. *Forecast information reporting scheme* (FIRS) – between the iJADE Stock Brokers and the iJADE Stock Advisor.

5. *Stock information consolidation and display scheme* (SICDS) – performed by the iJADE Stock Advisor

A schematic diagram of the iJADE Stock Prediction system is depicted in Fig. 8.1.

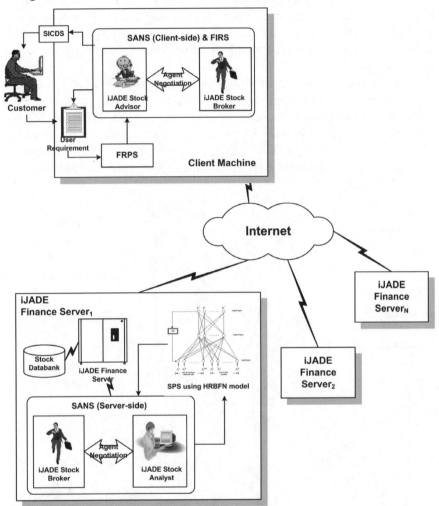

Fig. 8.1. Schematic diagram of the iJADE Stock Advisor system

8.3.2 Stock Prediction Using the HRBF Model

The *brain* of the iJADE Stock Advisor (i.e., stock prediction capability) is supported by the *analytical module* of the *intelligent layer* within the iJADE model. The current version, which has adopted the latest recurrent neural network we have developed, namely the HRBF recurrent neural network (HRBFN) (Lee and Liu 2000a), shows promising results on time series prediction, as demonstrated in weather forecast and tropical cyclone (TC) track prediction.

In short, the HRBFN incorporates into the conventional RBF network for temporal time series prediction problems two main technologies: (1) a structural learning technique that integrates the *forgetting* factor into the RBF BP algorithm (Ishikawa 1996); and (2) a *time difference with decay* (TDD) (Sutton 1983) method that is incorporated into the network to strengthen the temporal time series relation of the input data sequence for network training.

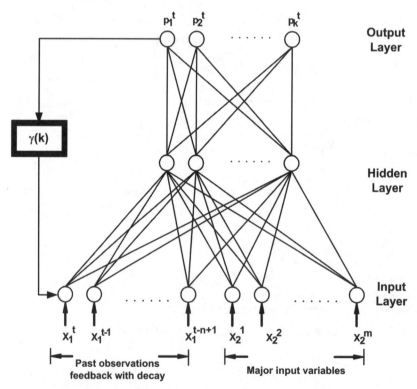

Fig. 8.2. Schematic diagram of the HRBFN for stock prediction

The HRBFN consists of three layers (Fig. 8.2). The first layer is the input layer, which is composed of two portions: (1) past network outputs that are fed back into the network; and (2) major co-related variables concerned with the prediction problem. Past network outputs are entered into the network by a time-delay unit as the first inputs. These outputs are also affected by a decay factor γ that is governed by the following equation:

$$\gamma = \alpha' e^{-\lambda k} \tag{8.10}$$

where λ is the decay constant, α' is the normalization constant, and k is the forecast horizon.

In general, the time series prediction of the proposed network is to predict the outcome of the sequence x_1^{t+k} at time $t + k$ which is based on the past observation sequence of size n, i.e., $x_1^t, x_1^{t-1}, x_1^{t-2}, x_1^{t-3}, \ldots, x_1^{t-n+1}$, and the major variables that influence the outcome of the time series at time t. For convenience, the following notation is used in the description of the network. The number of input nodes in the first and second portions is set to n and m respectively. The number of hidden nodes is set to p. The predictive steps are set to k, so the number of output nodes is k. At time t, the input will be $[x_1^t, x_1^{t-1}, x_1^{t-2}, x_1^{t-3}, \ldots, x_1^{t-n+1}]$ and $[x_2^1, x_2^2, \ldots, x_2^m]$ respectively. The output is given by x^{t+k}, denoted by p_k^t for simplicity; w_{ij} denotes the connection weight between the ith node and the jth node at time t.

HRBFN – Structural Learning Algorithms

The main idea of the RBF learning algorithm with forgetting factor is to introduce a constant decay to connected weights so as to make the redundancy weight(s) fade out quickly. The cost function of the structural learning algorithm is given by (8.11):

$$E^t = E_1^t + \varepsilon \sum_{i,j} \left| w_{ij}^t \right| \tag{8.11}$$

where E_1^t denotes the error square in traditional RBF learning, and the second term is the penalty criterion.

If the delta rule is used, the learning rule of the weights is given by:

$$\Delta w_{ij}^{t+1} = -\eta \frac{\partial E^t}{\partial w_{ij}^t} + \alpha \Delta w_{ij}^t \tag{8.12}$$

where the first term in (8.12) is the weight change obtained by the traditional RBF network, η is the learning rate, and α is the momentum. Further, ε is the forgetting factor of the connection weights.

HRBFN – TDD Method

The structural learning algorithm discussed above does provide a *dynamic* structural building of the neural network, but it cannot adapt the temporal time series relations of the input and output feedback data sequences into the model. In order to cope with this problem, a temporal difference method with decay feedback is hybridized into the learning algorithm of the proposed model. The basic concepts are presented as follows.

In a typical time series prediction problem, given a series of past observations of n time steps starting at t, i.e. $[x_1^t, x_1^{t-1}, x_1^{t-2}, x_1^{t-3}, \ldots, x_1^{t-n+1}]$, with the predictive time step of k, we obtain not only the predicted output at time $t + k$, i.e., p_k^t , but also, more importantly, the sequence of future events starting from time t, i.e., $[p_1^t, p_2^t, p_3^t, \ldots, p_k^t]$. In other words, the network can provide an overlapping and interrelated event sequence as an additional *hint* for network learning, which can be implemented by using the temporal difference technique (Sutton 1983). In addition, considering a sequence of operations on temporal difference from time $t + 1$ to $t + k$, the prediction from a *nearer* future normally has a higher level of confidence and importance than a *far* future, so a decay operator is integrated into the learning algorithm in order to reflect the situation. It is also the core idea of the HRBFN model with the incorporation of a forgetting factor component to reflect the exponential decay of the *level of importance* of past observations as input to the recurrent network. In fact, this idea is also quite sensible in terms of non-linear dynamics and even for chaotic systems in the sense that in a typical time series forecasting system (e.g., weather forecasting), the *further away* the past observations, the *lesser* the co-relation and importance to the future prediction.

With the integration of the TDD methodology, the learning algorithm discussed in (8.12) will be modified to:

$$\Delta w_{ij}^{t+1} = \eta \left\{ \sum_{h=2}^{k} \gamma(h) \cdot \left(p_{h-1}^t - p_h^t \right) \sum_{l=1}^{t} \lambda^{t-1} \frac{\partial p_h^l}{\partial w_{ij}^t} + (p_1^t - p_0^t) \sum_{l=1}^{t} \left[\gamma(l) \cdot \lambda^{t-1} \frac{\partial p_1^l}{\partial w_{ij}^t} \right] \right\}$$

$$+ \alpha \Delta w_{ij}^t - \varepsilon \text{ "sgn}(w_{ij}^t)$$

$$(8.13)$$

where ε'' is defined as:

$$\varepsilon'' = \begin{cases} \varepsilon & |w_{ij}^t| = < \theta \\ 0 & otherwise \end{cases}$$

$$(8.14)$$

Note that, from (8.13), the learning algorithm consists of three basic components. The first two terms refer to the error adjustment based on the temporal differences between the output event sequences between the two consecutive time steps, which is *weighted* by the decay functions $\gamma(1)$, $\gamma(h)$, which are governed by (8.10). The third and fourth terms refer to the structural learning operations. Also, λ denotes the exponential scale for the connection weight that determines the effective length of the history windows, and θ, is the threshold value.

In fact, instead of using the TDD method in our proposed system, some other researchers adopted other time-dependency approaches into their financial forecasting models (Refenes et al. 1993).

8.4 Experimental Results

To validate and evaluate the system, the iJADE Stock Advisor was tested under the following schemes:

– parameter selection scheme in HRBFN

– round-trip-time (RTT) test

– long- and short-term prediction, window-size evaluation test

– stock prediction performance test

For system training of the HRBFN model, time series of stock information from 33 Hong Kong major stocks in the period between 1990 and 1999 were used as the data set (in total, 3652 sets of data), in which they were randomly chosen as (1) training records (40%); (2) testing records (40%); and (3) evaluation records (20%) accordingly, with window sizes ranging from 11 to 45 days (for long-term trend prediction) and 1 to 10 days (for short-term stock prediction).

8.4.1 Parameter Selection Scheme in HRBFN

Similar to other supervising neural networks, *parameter fine-tuning* was a typical step during network training of the HRBFN in the iJADE Stock Advisor. To determine the optimal set of parameters in HRBFN, 500 cases were used for network fine-tuning. The optimal set with the best training results are given in Table 8.1. In view of the network architecture, the optimal numbers of hidden nodes used for long-term trend prediction and short-term price prediction were 34 and 22 respectively.

Table 8.1. Optimal parameter set for the HRBFN of the iJADE Stock Advisor

Parameters	Optimal Value
α	0.34
α'	0.56
ε	0.16
λ	0.2
η	0.25

Note: decay factor γ is governed by (8.10).

8.4.2 Round-Trip-Time (RTT) Test

The aim of the RTT test was to evaluate the overall operational time of the iJADE Stock Advisor starting from the collection of customer stock forecasting information, through dispatching of iJADE Brokers, and the receipt and display of stock prediction results on the user's browser.

In this test, two iJADE Finance Servers were used: the T1Server and T2Server. The T1Server was situated within the campus (i.e., within the same network cluster) while the T2Server was in a remote site. The results of the mean RTT for 100 trials are shown in Table 8.2.

The total RTT was dominated by three modules, two of which were SANS (Stock Agents Negotiation Scheme) and FIRS (Forecast Information Reporting Scheme); both involved multi-agent negotiation and, more importantly, the *traveling time* of the mobile agent iJADE Stock Broker. This could also explain why a longer time is needed in the second case. The other dominant process in the whole iJADE Stock Advisor was the SPS (Stock Prediction Scheme), which involved actual time series stock prediction operations done by the iJADE Stock Analysts. Nevertheless, the overall RTTs obtained in both cases were less than 13 seconds, which was within a reasonable level for Internet web-mining.

Table 8.2. Mean RTT summary after 100 trials

Action Module	Action located at	Time (ms)	
		T1server (within campus)	T2server (remote site)
1. FRPS	Client machine	205	221
2. SANS	iJADE servers	576	2137
3. SPS		7713	7421
4. FIRS		432	2247
5. SICDS	Client machine	236	242
Total RTT		9.2 s	12.3 s

8.4.3 Long- and Short-Term Prediction, Window-Size Evaluation Test

As the window size of the stock prediction model was a critical factor for network efficiency and accuracy, this experimental test aimed at the evaluation of the optimized window size for (1) long-term trend prediction and (2) short-term stock price prediction.

In the test, window sizes of 11 to 45 days (for long-term trend prediction) and 2 to 10 days (for short-term price prediction) were used. The predicted outputs for these two sets of predictions were as follows.

Long-Term Trend Prediction

Predicted desired value (d_i) for days between a buy and a sell signal.

Note: For long-term trend prediction, since we were interested in stock pattern variation instead of daily price fluctuation, two types of inputs (preprocessed) were used: (1) normalized daily closing stock value (x_i); and (2) normalized *desired value* for days between a buy and a sell signal (d_i) given by:

$$x_j = \frac{c_i - c_{i-j}}{c_i \kappa_j} \ , j = 1...A, -1 \le x_j \le 1 \tag{8.15}$$

where:

$$\kappa_j = \frac{2}{P-A} \sum_{i=A+1}^{P} \frac{|c_i - c_{i-j}|}{c_i} \ , j = 1...A \tag{8.16}$$

$$d_i = \frac{c_i - c_{low}}{c_{high} - c_{low}} \tag{8.17}$$

Shown in (8.15) is a predetermined scaling factor called *volatility factor* κ given by (8.16). This was based on the concept that, for most of the time, the percentage change in closing prices would be in the range of $-\kappa_j$ and $+\kappa_j$, and would provide for a good dynamic range of x_j. In fact, κ was calculated before building the input patterns and P was the number of days being analyzed.

The main purpose of this data preprocessing method given by (8.15) was to extract the difference between the current day's closing price (c_i) and the previous A closes (c_{i-j}). This difference was then normalized by dividing it by the closing price and the scaling factor κ. In order to *feed in* the critical signal for trend prediction, the normalized desired value for the days between a buy and a sell signal (d_i) was adopted. Actually, this signal was based on the concept of an oscillator-based system of the technical financial analysis discussed previously, a kind of *neural network oscillator* for stock prediction. For example, when this neural net oscillator rose above a sell threshold, it would signal an alert that the market was approaching a trend change downward. On the other hand, when the neural net indicator fell below a buy threshold, it would signal an alert that the market was approaching a trend change upward. So, these oscillatory input nodes could provide an effective indicator of trend prediction.

Short-Term Price Prediction

– Predicted next-day high (h_{i+1})
– Predicted next-day low (l_{i+1})
– Predicted next-day close (c_{i+1})

Note: Unlike long-term trend prediction, short-term stock price prediction focused on the fluctuations of the stock value on a daily basis. So, the strategy for creating input patterns was to use the daily change in price (Δ values for open, close, high, and low) in order to predict the next day's high, low, and close.

Using a similar normalization approach, for each different type of Δ values (open, close, high, and low), the volatility factor κ could be calculated as follows:

$$\kappa = \frac{2}{P}\sum_{i=1}^{P}\frac{|\Delta|}{c_i} \qquad (8.18)$$

and each normalized input value was given by:

$$x_i = \frac{\Delta}{c_i \kappa} \ , \ i = 1...A, -1 \le x_i \le 1 \qquad (8.19)$$

The desired outputs ($d_{h,i}$, $d_{l,i}$, $d_{c,i}$) for the high, low, and close values were also normalized in a similar approach, as shown below:

$$d_{h,i} = \frac{h_{i+1} - c_{i+1}}{c_i \kappa_h}, \quad d_{l,i} = \frac{c_{i+1} - l_{i+1}}{c_i \kappa_l}, \quad d_{c,i} = \frac{c_{i+1} - c_i}{c_i \kappa_c} \qquad (8.20, 8.21, 8.22)$$

Another important feature of this kind of normalization was, once the predicted outputs (o_{h+1}, o_{l+1}, o_{c+1}) were obtained, the predicted stock prices could be transformed easily based on the following equations:

$$c_{i+1} = 2 c_i \kappa_c (o_c - 0.5) + c_i \qquad (8.23)$$

$$h_{i+1} = c_{i+1} + c_i \kappa_h o_h \qquad (8.24)$$

$$l_{i+1} = c_{i+1} - c_i \kappa_l o_l \qquad (8.25)$$

Table 8.3. iJADE Stock Advisor window-size evaluation test results

Long-Term Trend Prediction			Short-Term Price Prediction		
Window Size (days)	Av. %[1] Error (%)	RMSE[2]	Window Size (days)	Av. %[1] Error (%)	RMSE[2]
10	2.345	6.45	2	2.347	12.75
15	1.075	4.37	3	1.473	9.05
20	1.073	4.31	4	1.476	9.37
25	1.238	4.63	6	1.487	9.56
30	2.487	6.71	8	2.746	13.22
40	5.347	10.06	10	3.248	14.29

Notes:

[1] The average percentage error is calculated by taking the average of the percentage errors of the prediction results for the four typical stocks, namely HSBC Holdings, Tian On China Investment, Hong Kong Telecom, and Cheung Kong Holdings Ltd. in the period 1990–1993.

[2] RMSE = Root Mean Square Error.

In the test, the 33 major stocks categorized into the four main business sectors (i.e., banking, finance and investment, public utility, and property) were used to evaluate the system. Table 8.3 shows the experimental results in terms of the average percentage error and RMSE of the iJADE Stock Advisor under different window sizes. As shown in the table, the optimal window size for long-term stock prediction was 20 days and that for the short-term 3 days; the average percentage errors achieved were 1.073% and 1.473%; and the corresponding RMSEs were 4.31 and 9.05 respectively.

8.4.4 Stock Prediction Performance Test

In this test, the 10-year (1990–1999) stock information of the 33 major Hong Kong stocks was adopted. For comparison purposes, a neural network-based forecasting aid, Neuro[TM] Forecaster, from Neuro Intelligent Business Software, was adopted in the test. Actually, Neuro Forecaster provides the following neural network models:

– A time series feedforward backpropagation model (FFBP) with different choices of transfer functions, including standard sigmoid function, hyperbolic tangent function, neuro-fuzzy function, etc.

– *Genetica Net Builder* – based on genetic algorithms (GAs) for the construction and optimization of the network model.

For ease of comparison, the 33 stock items were grouped under five critical business sectors, namely banking, finance and investment, public utility, property, and others. The experimental results for the next-day stock price predictions are shown in Table 8.4. A snapshot of the investment recommendations made by the iJADE Stock Advisor is depicted in Fig. 8.3.

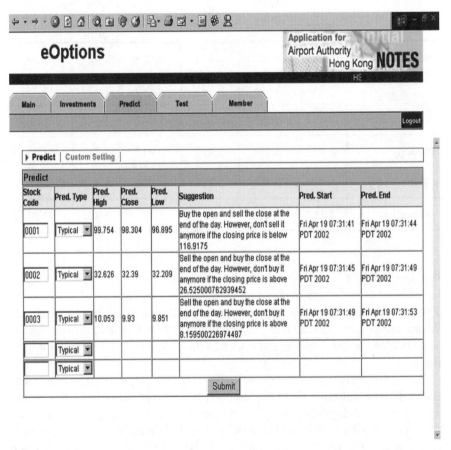

Fig. 8.3. Recommendations returned by the iJADE Stock Advisor based on stock prediction results

As shown in Table 8.3, the iJADE Stock Advisor outperformed all of the four Neuro Forecaster models for different business types. The overall average percentage error was 1.401% (the corresponding RMSE is 12.51), which was even better than Genetica, the model that attained the best results (averaging 3.417%) over the other Neuro Forecaster models, by more than 58% in terms of reduction in percentage errors.

Table 8.4. Stock prediction performance test results (for next-day stock price prediction)

Business Type	Neuro Forecaster (Av. % error)				iJADE Stock Advisor	
	Sig-moid	Hyper-bolic Tangent	Neuro-fuzzy	Genetica	Av. % error	RMSE
Banking	4.647	3.457	8.451	3.427	1.427	15.58
Finance and Investment	3.745	3.758	7.845	4.747	1.573	16.75
Public utility	3.412	4.285	10.457	2.747	1.347	9.71
Property	4.452	5.474	7.457	3.417	1.417	11.23
Others	5.124	4.789	8.982	3.746	1.379	9.27
Overall	**4.217**	**4.648**	**8.975**	**3.417**	**1.401**	**12.51**

8.5 Summary

This chapter has proposed an innovative, intelligent agent-based stock advisory application: the *iJADE Stock Advisor*. The major contributions of this chapter can be summarized under two headings: research and applications.

From the research point of view, this chapter demonstrates a feasible and efficient solution (iJADE Stock Advisor) for automatic intelligent agent-based stock prediction. With respect to the stock forecasting engine, this chapter adopts the hybrid RBF network (HRBFN) model for stock prediction. Through the integration of the iJADE framework with the HRBFN in the iJADE Stock Analyst agent, this chapter illustrates the efficiency and effectiveness of the iJADE Stock Advisor for online stock prediction. With respect to the interactive and mobile agent-based stock advisory and prediction processes, the chapter illustrates how intelligent agent technology can be successfully integrated with AI technology for online stock prediction.

From an applications point of view, this chapter demonstrates how the HRBFN model can be successfully integrated with mobile agent technology to provide a truly intelligent, mobile, and interactive stock advisory solution. Through the implementation of the iJADE Stock Advisor (with the adoption of our newly developed iJADE framework) and the adoption of the 10-year stock pricing information (1990–1999) for various system tests and evaluations, it has been demonstrated how intelligent agent technology can be successfully and fully integrated into other support technologies (such as recurrent neural networks for time series prediction, mobile agent paradigms as agent communication, etc.) to open a new era of intelligent mobile e-business (iMEB) for the development of future e-commerce.

As quoted at the beginning of the chapter, Phillips Brooks is right in saying that a good advisor should not *tell us how to act*, but rather should lead us (and leave us) to *make our own decisions*. It is anticipated that our latest and future development of Cogito advisory agents can possess this kind of caliber.

Acknowledgments

The author is grateful for the partial support of the Departmental Grants for iJADE projects including the iJADE Framework (version 2.0) Z042 and Central Research Grants (B-Q569) from The Hong Kong Polytechnic University. The author is also grateful to Dr. James Liu for the provision of technical advice and background information on the stock advisory systems.

9 iJADE Surveillant – A Multi-resolution Neuro-oscillatory Agent-Based Surveillance System

An eternal trait of men is the need for vision and the readiness to follow it; and if men are not given the right vision, they will follow wandering fires.

On Education, Sir Richard Livingstone

Recent rapid technical developments, especially in the field of Internet systems, have meant an increasing demand both for intelligent, mobile, and autonomous systems and for using and sending multimedia information over cyberspace. This chapter introduces an intelligent multimedia processing system – the *iJADE Surveillant*. It is an intelligent multi-resolution agent-based surveillance system based on the integration of three modules: an automatic coarse-to-fine, figure–ground, scene segmentation module that uses the CNOW (*Composite Neuro-Oscillatory Wavelet-based*) model; an automatic human face detection and extraction module that uses an *active contour model* (ACM) with *facial landmark vectors*; and an invariant human face identification module that uses the elastic graph dynamic link model (EGDLM). To conform to current (and future) multimedia system standards, the whole iJADE Surveillant is implemented using the MPEG-7 system framework – with a comprehensive model framework, description scheme (DS), and feature descriptor (D).

Automatic scene segmentation testing was conducted using a scene gallery of over 6000 color scene images, while the intelligent human face identification test used 100 distinct human objects (with over 1020 tested scenes). The overall correct invariant facial recognition rate is over 87%. Hopefully, the implementation of the iJADE Surveillant will provide an invariant and higher-order intelligent object (pattern) encoding, searching, and identification solution for future MPEG-7 applications.

9.1 Introduction

With advances in technology, especially in the fields of IC (Internet computing) and EC (e-commerce) systems, this area is in the process of migrating from web-based EC systems to mobile e-business (MEB) and even further to intelligence-based e-business systems (iEB) (Chan et al. 2001). However, in this new era of information overload, whether the information is raw data or sophisticated multimedia sources such as audio-visual information, two areas of technological development are of particular interest: the provision of a *smart* (*intelligent*) and *mobile* system that provides automatic information filtering, searching, and decision making (supporting) anytime and anywhere in cyberspace – an intelligent agent-based system; and the provision of a unified and standardized multi-modal platform for the encoding and decoding, interpretation and dissemination of multimedia information, so that users all over the world can make use of these intelligent multimedia applications without system incompatibility – namely, *MPEG-7 technology*.

In this chapter, the author introduces the *iJADE Surveillant* – a truly intelligent, multi-resolution, neuro-agent-based automatic surveillance system that integrates four different types of technology: automatic coarse-to-fine multi-resolution figure–ground scene segmentation using the CNOW (Composite Neuro-Oscillatory Wavelet-based) model, an extension of the latest work for color scene analysis (Lee and Liu 2002); automatic human face detection and extraction using the active contour model (ACM) with facial landmarks (Lee and Liu 1999); and an invariant human face identification scheme that uses the elastic graph dynamic link model (EGDLM) (Lee and Liu 2003) and that uses MPEG-7 as the system framework of this surveillance system. The surveillance system involves encoding (and decoding) of wavelet features, the facial template, elastic dynamic facial *graphs*, implementation of the EGDLM model as the search query engine and implementation of the CNOW subsystem as filter agents, which also provide a comprehensive standard for the modeling based on various description schemes and feature descriptors.

For system testing, the iJADE Surveillant is tested in two major ways: (1) on an automatic scene segmentation scheme, and (2) on an invariant human face matching scheme. In the first set of tests an image gallery of over 6000 color scenes (divided into eight categories) is used, while for the second set of tests, 100 human objects are used to test against 1020 surveillance scenes.

The chapter is organized as follows. Section 9.2 presents a brief overview of the surveillance system. Section 9.3 gives an overview of the major technologies for supporting the intelligent multimedia processing system. Section 9.4 provides the system details of the iJADE Surveillant. Section 9.5 evaluates the system and implementation and contains a brief conclusion.

9.2 Surveillance System – An Overview

9.2.1 Background

Surveillance systems are an attractive topic of research as they include the areas of machine vision, scene analysis, and real-time 2D to 3D object modeling and recognition, but they are also an important problem domain within the commercial and industrial sectors. Numerous research studies have been conducted in this area, including surveillance systems for traffic control (Abreu et al. 2000), automatic identification of weapons and dangerous items in customs examinations (Keller et al. 2000), and automatic surveillance systems for abandoned objects in unmanned railway operations (Sacchi and Regazzoni 2000). Of course, one of the most fundamental and vital, but also the most difficult, applications is the use of surveillance systems to identify human subjects based on their posture or face. With the advance of computer and Internet technologies in terms of computational power, popularity, and provision of worldwide distributed networks, automatic human face surveillance systems now appear to be feasible.

The implementation of such an automatic system requires that the author addresses two fundamental problem domains: the provision of an efficient automatic scene analysis and figure–ground segmentation system; and the provision of an invariant human face extraction, identification, and recognition system. In the following subsections the author presents a brief literature review of contemporary research in these areas.

9.2.2 Scene Analysis

Scene analysis refers to the task of finding and locating parts from 2D or 3D images of a scene that correspond to certain objects in the scene. According to the complexity of computation strategies discussed in Suetens et al. (1992), techniques for scene analysis can be classified into four categories:

– feature vector classification scheme – simplest strategies

- model fitting to photometry
- model fitting to symbolic structure
- hybrid scene analysis – combined strategies

Scene analysis has vast application areas, ranging from locating natural resources based on satellite images to the identification of a human face in a newspaper clipping. These are perhaps the most interesting topics in pattern recognition and machine vision.

Feature Vector Classification

Classically, objects are modeled as vectors of characteristic features, each of which corresponds to a point in the feature space. The features include gray value, color, area, perimeter, and the number of holes. Classical examples in this category are the *pixel classification approach*, such as Richards' (1986) spectral analysis, and the *object label classification approach,* such as Groen et al.'s (1989) chromosome classification.

These classical feature-space approaches work well if the problem only involves simple models that do not include constraints relating to different parts of a model, and also if we can restrict ourselves to either pixel classification or classification of labels with good photometry.

With the latest feature vector extraction and filtering technologies such as *Gabor filters* (Teuner et al. 1995), *wavelet transforms* (Chang and Kuo 1993), *wavelet frames* (Unser 1995), *optimal energy separation* (Randen and Husoy 1999), and *multiple Gabor filters* (Weldon and Higgins 1996), both the effectiveness and accuracy of object recognition using feature vector classification techniques can be greatly improved.

Model Fitting to Photometry

In simple models, the shape of the object is precisely specified but the photometric data are noisy and ambiguous. In such cases, a number of methods are used to search for features with predetermined global shapes (templates) and photometric properties. Two common approaches are the *rigid template matching approach* and the *flexible model fitting approach.*

In the rigid template matching approach, the object template of the target object is known beforehand. The model can be either rigid or parametric, depending on the set of free parameters in the problem domain. For example, Ballard (1981) made use of the *generalized Hough transform* to detect arbitrary shapes, and McLaughlin (1997) later used the *randomized Hough transform* (RHT) to improve object recognition rates.

In the flexible model fitting approach, templates are specified by a set of generic constraints on object characteristics, such as smoothness, curvature, compactness, and homogeneity. Object matching is done by minimizing an objective cost function. Typical examples include applications such as the snake model proposed by Kass and Witkin (1988) and its enhancement by Radeva and Serrat (1993) and Cootes et al. (1995).

These approaches are best adapted to situations in which an initial guess for a model shape is available and, because they impose natural limitations on the size of the search space, they also work in noisy environments with incomplete or noisy data.

Model Fitting to Symbolic Structure

In certain applications, such as face recognition, in which simple, well-defined templates are not readily available, reliable symbolic structures can be accurately inferred from the nature scenes by certain preprocessing operations (known as segmentation), yet features can often be found without shape information or contextual scene knowledge. For example, features can be extracted using filters such as *Gabor or Mallat filters*. Typical techniques under this category of recognition model include the *graph matching technique*.

In this technique, scenes are represented as relational structures whose nodes are parts of the object and whose arcs represent the relationship between the nodes they are connected to. The object matching problem is converted into that of identifying the *graph isomorphism*. Examples include Murray and Buxton's (1987) scene segmentation, the work done by Bolles and Horaud (1986), who employed a *relaxed sub-isomorphism* graph matching scheme on a 3D part orientation system, and Wiskott and Malsburg's (1995) work based on *dynamic link matching* of face recognition and scene analysis.

Hybrid Scene Analysis – Combined Strategies

When both the sample scene and image objects are complicated, for example when images are noisy, or have poor resolution or photometric anomalies (e.g., occlusions), structural and predefined sets of templates cannot be used. Scene analysis might require a combination of different strategies. For instance, Pentland (1990) employed a general-purpose *deformable parts model* to recognize 3D objects in nature scenes. In his model, objects are described in terms of the shapes of different component parts, which are modeled as deformable superquadrics.

In this chapter, a coarse-to-fine multi-resolution hybrid scene analysis scheme – namely, the CNOW model – is proposed. This model combines the Morlet wavelet filter scheme for feature extraction and the composite neuro-oscillatory model (CNOM) for scene segmentation.

9.2.3 Human Face Recognition

While a variety of techniques and models are used for human face recognition, there are three common major approaches: the *template matching approach*, the *pictorial feature approach*, and *non-model-based gray-level analysis*.

Template Versus Features

In the simplest version of template matching, a comparison is made of the query image, represented as a bi-dimensional array of intensity values. The comparison is made by using a suitable metric with a single template representing the facial features. A rather different and more complex approach uses the *parameterized model template matching technique*. In this approach, the deformable template of a facial feature model is matched to the query image, and minimization of the matching energy function is applied for facial recognition (Lanitis et al. 1997; Yuille 1991). In this model, deformable models are hand-constructed from parameterized curves that outline facial features such as the mouth, eyebrows, and facial outline. An energy function is defined as *attracting* the template model to the preprocessed query image; model fitting is evaluated by minimizing these energy functions.

In the pictorial feature approach, a pixel-based representation of facial features – this representation could be templates of major facial features or their weights in neural networks – is matched against the query image. The typical matching metric is correlated to preprocessed versions of the query image. These neural network approaches construct a network where implicit feature templates are learned from the training image set.

Unlike the previous two approaches, the non-model-based gray-level analysis does not find features with semantic content such as the eye, mouth, nose, or eyebrow detector. Instead, features are defined by the local gray-level structure of the images themselves (Rowley et al. 1998; Sung and Poggio 1998), such as corners (Azarbayejani et al. 1992), symmetry (Reisfeld and Yeshurun 1992), or the *end-inhibition* feature vectors that are extracted from a wavelet decomposition of the facial image (Manjunath et al. 1992).

Invariance Aspects

The changes and wide variation in facial appearance that are brought about under changes in pose, lighting, and expression make face recognition a highly complex problem. While existing systems do not allow much flexibility in pose, lighting, and expression, a certain amount of flexibility can be provided by using invariant representations or by performing an explicit geometrical normalization step.

Mostly, face recognition methods are not designed to handle changes in facial expression (e.g., gimmick faces). By tackling changes, pose, and lighting with the invariant representations and normalization technique as described above, most of the current systems treat face recognition mostly as a rigid 2D problem, although some exceptions do use multiple views (Akamatsu et al. 1992) and flexible matching strategies (Andreoli et al. 1997) to deal with some degree of expression and out-of-plane rotation.

Experimental Issues

The evaluation of face recognition systems is highly empirical, requiring experimental study of a set of test images. The major experimental considerations are therefore correct/false recognition rates, image gallery size, and recognition speed.

Different researchers have obtained varied recognition results. Some have achieved a high recognition rate by using a limited number of sample images. Baron (1981) achieved an impressive 100% recognition rate of 42 people and a false access rate of 0% on 108 images. Others attained an acceptable level of recognition rate on a sufficiently large image library, but then required a considerable amount of time for network learning and image preprocessing. Kruger (1997) reported challenging recognition results averaging 90% using a *FERET database* of 350 persons with 1500 library images. However, it took 12 hours to learn the weights for all the *jet* components.

9.3 Supporting Technologies

In this chapter, the author introduces an intelligent, agent-based, automatic surveillance system, the *iJADE Surveillant*. iJADE Surveillant integrates two contemporary technologies: an intelligent multi-agent that uses the iJADE model as the *kernel* of the intelligent processing framework; and MPEG-7 technology as the *backbone* of the overall system framework and the multimedia feature encoding, decoding, filtering, searching, and interpretation standards. The following subsections will provide a brief overview and discussion of contemporary work related to these core technologies.

9.3.1 MPEG-7 – System Overview

Unlike previous MPEG standards,[1] which focus on data encoding and storage standards for audio-visual information, including the storage and retrieval of moving pictures in CD-quality MPEG-1, setting the generic coding of audio–video for supporting the high-resolution digital TV standard in MPEG-2, and the provision of standardized technological elements enabling the integration of the production, distribution, and content access methods of digital TV and other multimedia applications in MPEG-4, MPEG-7 focuses on the standardization of a common interface for describing multimedia materials themselves – that is, representing information about the content, rather than the content itself (information *about* the multimedia information) (Nack and Lindsay 1999a, 1999b). In other words, MPEG-7 tries to addresses issues related to the facilitation of interoperability, the globalization of multimedia resources, and the flexibility of data management.

Under the MPEG-7 standard, every MPEG-7 multimedia application relies on three main components: a descriptor (D), description scheme (DS), and description definition language (DDL), explained as follows (Abdel-Mottaleb et al. 2000):

1. Descriptor (D) – for the representation of distinctive characteristics of the data, called *features*. It defines the syntax and the semantics of these features. Typical examples include the color histogram features, and fundamental frequencies of speech segments.

2. Description scheme (DS) – a scheme used to specify the structure and semantics of the relationships between the DS components, which may be either the Ds or other DSs. A typical DS, such as a movie, could define a temporal structure composed of different scenes, together with other Ds such as captions and audio Ds.

3. Description definition language (DDL) – a set of Ds, consisting of DSs values, is expressed using the MPEG-7 DDL, which allows for the creation, extension, and modification of existing DSs. Structurally and conceptually, the language is similar in format to the XML Schema.

---

[1] MPEG: http://www.cselt.it/mpeg/standards.htm.

9.3.2 MPEG-7 Model

Figure 9.1 depicts a typical abstract representation of a multimedia application using the MPEG-7 standard. The left side of the figure shows how data are annotated, encoded, and interpreted, while the right side of the model shows how the described data can be retrieved and manipulated. Unlike previous MPEG standards, a typical MPEG-7 application provides basic functionality such as (multimedia) information filtering and searching.

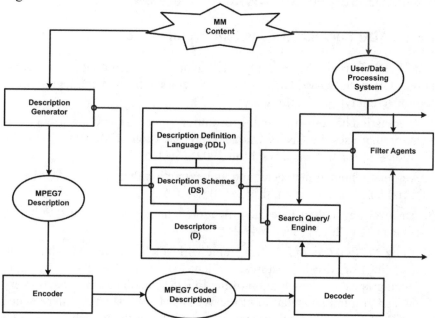

Fig. 9.1. An abstract representation of a multimedia application using the MPEG-7 standard (adapted from the MPEG homepage) (Nack and Lindsay 1999a, 1999b)

9.3.3 The Latest MPEG-7 Development Work on Visual Object Modeling

MPEG-7 standardization work began in October 1998 and was completed by November 2001. A major effort was initiated in 1999 to develop MPEG-7. The latest development done by Bober et al. (2000) involved visual object modeling, using contour shape as the object D, but the application is restricted to simple and homogeneous object patterns. Other work, such as that of Lorente and Torres (1999), used the *eigenface ap-*

proach for face recognition in video sequences; however, their work focused on automatic face recognition, for which the major visual sequence processing operation – the automatic figure–ground scene segmentation for automatic extraction of the object and hence the facial pattern – has not been implemented in the application.

9.4 iJADE Surveillant – System Overview

9.4.1 iJADE Surveillant – System Architecture

The iJADE Surveillant is a truly intelligent multi-resolution neuro-agent-based automatic surveillance system developed from the integration of four different types of technology:

1. Automatic coarse-to-fine multi-resolution figure–ground scene segmentation that uses the CNOW model – an extension of the latest work for color scene analysis (Lee and Liu 2002) (Sect. 5.2).
2. Automatic human face detection and extraction that uses the ACM with facial *landmarks* (Lee and Liu 1999) (Sect. 5.3).
3. An invariant human face identification scheme that uses the EGDLM (Lee and Liu 2003) (Sect. 5.4).
4. Using MPEG-7 as the system framework, including the encoding (and decoding) of wavelet features, the facial template, the elastic dynamic facial graphs, implementation of the EGDLM model as the search query engine, and implementation of the WCNOM subsystem as filter agents, which also provide a comprehensive standard for the modeling based on various DSs and feature Ds.

In conforming to the MPEG-7 system architecture (Fig. 9.1), the iJADE Surveillant system framework consists of the following main modules:

- The Morlet wavelet encoder, a feature-encoding module that uses a Morlet wavelet to extract coarse-to-fine and invariant image information.
- The CNOW segmentation module, which acts as the first-level filter agent, using the CNOW scheme for automatic coarse-to-fine scene segmentation.
- The ACM contour extraction module, which acts as the second-level filter agent and extracts facial features using the ACM.

- The EGDLM recognition module, which acts as the search/query engine and provides invariant face recognition using the EGDLM.

Figure 9.2 schematically depicts the iJADE Surveillant.

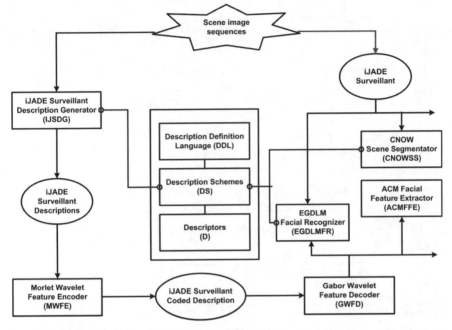

Fig. 9.2. A schematic diagram of the iJADE Surveillant

The system uses three types of iJADE agents:

1. *iJADE Surveillant Agent* – this stationary iJADE agent is situated in the client machine and acts as a surveillant, automatically capturing scene images and extracting the facial features of the human subject through the coarse-to-fine scene segmentation and ACM process (against the facial template).

2. *iJADE Messenger* – a mobile iJADE agent acting as a messenger which both *carries* the facial features to the iJADE Facial Server and *reports* the recognition result back to the client machine.

3. *iJADE Recognizer* – a stationary agent situated within the iJADE Facial Server. Its main duty is to match the invariant facial pattern of facial features (extracted from the iJADE Surveillant Agent) against the central facial database.

Figure 9.3 contains a system overview of the multi-agent interactions in the iJADE Surveillant.

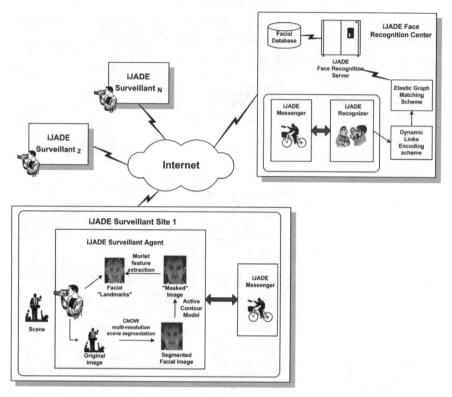

Fig. 9.3. System overview of multi-agent interaction in the iJADE Surveillant

9.4.2 Automatic Multi-resolution Scene Segmentation Scheme Using the CNOW Model

Composite Neural Oscillator – Background

Networks of interacting oscillators provide an excellent model for numerous physical processes, ranging from the behavior of magnetic materials to the activity of populations of neurons in a variety of cortical locations. Interesting results have long been reported about the cat and rabbit olfactory bulb and cortex (Gray et al. 1989), on the basis of single- and multi-unit recordings as well as EEG activity (Freeman 1978), and current study such as offline Chinese character recognition using neural oscillators for character segmentation.

As an extension to the traditional neural oscillator models (Malsburg and Buhmann 1992), the author proposes a composite neural oscillator to segment color scene images into individual objects. A composite *trinity* neuron oscillator model with common inhibitory neurons is employed to safeguard the global phase locking of composite neural oscillators. This simulates the stimulus of the visual cortex of color image perceptions. In addition, to improve the self-organization rate, a *near-neighbor* scheme is adopted for neuron oscillations.

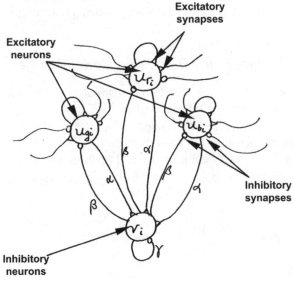

Fig. 9.4. Composite neural oscillator

As shown in Fig. 9.4, a single composite neural oscillator consists of three excitatory neurons (which represent the three primary color responses u_{ri}, u_{bi}, and u_{gi} respectively), which directly interact with a common inhibitory inter-neuron v_i. Within the composite neural oscillator, excitatory synapses (triangles) and inhibitory synapses (circles) interact together with the oscillator units according to the following kinetic equations:

$$\frac{du_{ci}}{dt} = -u_{ci} + S_\lambda (u_{ci} - \beta v_i - \theta_u + I_{ci} + O_{ci})$$ (9.1)

$$\tau \frac{dv_i}{dt} = -v_i + S_\lambda (\alpha \sum_c u_{ci} - w_i - \theta_v)$$ (9.2)

where $c = \{r, g, b\}$ denotes the neural oscillatory units for the three color components, and τ denotes the time scale of the inhibitory neurons. $S_\lambda(x)$ is a sigmoid function of the form $S_\lambda(x) = [1 + \exp(-x/\lambda)]$ with gain parameter $1/\lambda$. I_{ri}, I_{gi}, and I_{bi} denote the sensory stimulus of the nature scene, which is constant within the oscillatory time scale. The excitatory and inhibitory thresholds are given by θ_u and θ_v. The synaptic strengths of the inhibitory feedback loop that generates the activity oscillations are controlled by the weighting factors α, β, and γ respectively. O_{ci} denotes the activation from other neural oscillators in the global network, as discussed in the next section.

CNOW Model: Feature Extraction Using Morlet Wavelets

In the CNOW model, each color scene image captured by the surveillance camera is broken down into a 2D mesh of $N = N_1 \times N_2$ composite neural oscillator sites. Each site (column) consists of M layers of trinity oscillators, which denote the neural oscillation from each response of corresponding local features. To extract features, the author uses Morlet wavelets of differently oriented θ and k factors. The Morlet wavelet function is given as:

$$Morlet_{k,\theta}(x,y) = \pi^{-1/2} \, e^{\left(-\frac{x^2+y^2}{2}\right)} \cdot \left(e^{2\pi i k(xx\cos\theta + y\sin\theta)} - e^{-k^2/2}\right)$$

$$(9.3)$$

where k is the basic shape of the Morlet wavelet, which controls the width of the frequency-domain window relative to its center frequency. The first factor in the Morlet wavelet function denotes the normalized Gaussian data window. The second factor is the sinusoidal component of the wavelet. Its (x, y) term is projected in the θ direction to determine its complex exponential component.

Morlet Wavelet Descriptor (MWD)

According to the MPEG-7 standard, one of the most fundamental feature elements used in the iJADE Surveillant is the Morlet wavelet descriptor (MWD). It is given by:

```
MWD{
        orientation;
        kvalue;
        Morlet[xlocation, ylocation]
}
```

Note: The formulation of the Morlet descriptor is given by (9.3).

CNOW Model: Neural Dynamics

In addition to the local excitatory and inhibitory neurons, the neural dynamics of the composite neural oscillators are activated/deactivated by the following oscillatory units (Fig. 9.5).

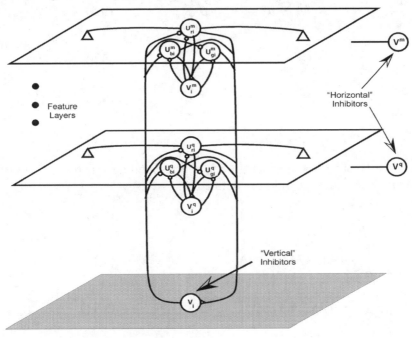

Fig. 9.5. Composite neural oscillatory network model

Vertical, horizontal and global excitatory connections: Composite neural oscillators within the same column are mutually activated with column strength $W_|$. In each feature layer, each neural oscillator is activated by the eight closest neighboring excitatory composite neurons with layer strength W_-; and the global strength is denoted by W'.

Vertical and horizontal inhibitory neurons (v_i and v^q): To control unexpected local phase locking, vertical and horizontal inhibitors are introduced, which are governed by the inhibitory strengths $T_| v_i$ and $T_- v^q$, respectively.

Global inhibitory neurons (v): A global inhibitory neuron is excited by all excitatory composite neural oscillators, and it inhibits all excitatory units with the signal T_y. The neural dynamics for the neural oscillators are given as follows:

$$\frac{du_{ci}}{dt} = -u_{ci}^q + S_\lambda(u_{ci}^q - \beta v_i^q - \theta_u + I_{ci}^q + W_{ci}^q u_{ci}^q$$

$$+ W_{ci\_}^q u_{ci}^q - T_{ci_|}^q v_i - T_{ci\_}^q v^q - T_{ci}^q v) \tag{9.4}$$

$$\tau\frac{dv_i^q}{dt} = -v_i^q + S_\lambda(\alpha\sum_c u_{ci}^q - \gamma v_i^q - \theta_v) \tag{9.5}$$

$$\tau\frac{dv_i}{dt} = -v_i + S_\lambda(W_{i_|} v_i - \theta_v) \tag{9.6}$$

$$\tau\frac{dv^q}{dt} = -v^q + S_\lambda(W_\_^q v^q - \theta_v) \tag{9.7}$$

$$\tau\frac{dv}{dt} = -v + S_\lambda(W'v - \theta_v) \tag{9.8}$$

Using a Hebbian training scheme, the corresponding synaptic strengths within the oscillatory neurons are defined as:

$$W_{ci_|}^q = \frac{1}{a}\sum_{p=1}^M \left[(u_{ci}^q - a)(u_{ci}^p - a)\right] \tag{9.9}$$

$$W_{ci\_}^q = \frac{1}{b}\sum_{j=1}^{N'} \left[(u_{ci}^q - b)(u_{cj}^q - b)\right] \tag{9.10}$$

$$T_{ci_|}^q = \frac{1}{a}(v_i - a)(u_{ci}^q - a) \tag{9.11}$$

$$T_{ci\_}^q = \frac{1}{b}(v^q - b)(u_{ci}^q - b) \tag{9.12}$$

$$T_{ci}^q = \frac{1}{c}(v - c)(u_{ci}^q - c) \tag{9.13}$$

$$W_{i_|} = \frac{1}{a}\sum_{p=1}^M \left[(v_i - a)\sum_c(u_{ci}^p - a)\right] \tag{9.14}$$

$$W_\_^q = \frac{1}{b}\sum_{j=1}^N \left[(v^q - b)\sum_c(u_{cj}^q - b)\right] \tag{9.15}$$

$$W' = \frac{1}{c}\sum_{q=1}^M\sum_{j=1}^N\sum_c \left[(v - c)(u_{ci}^q - c)\right] \tag{9.16}$$

where index $q = \{1..M\}$ represents the M feature layers of the neural oscillatory model, $c = \{r, g, b\}$ for the three primary color oscillators, and $i = \{1..N\}$ for the 2D mesh of composite oscillators in each layer.

Segmentation Criterion: Correlation Function σ_{xy}

The segmentation criterion is determined by the correlation factor, which is a measurement of the binding strength (phase relationship) between the composite neural oscillators and their nearest neighbors, given by:

$$\sigma(x,y) = \frac{<\bar{x}\bar{y}> - <\bar{x}><\bar{y}>}{\sqrt{<\bar{x}^2> - <\bar{x}>^2} \cdot \sqrt{<\bar{y}^2> - <\bar{y}>^2}}$$

(9.17)

where $\bar{x}, \bar{y}$ denote the composite oscillator vectors and $<\cdot>$ is the time average of the vector magnitude over a period of time that is shorter than the presentation of the image.

9.4.3 Automatic Human Face Detection and Contour Features Extraction Using the ACM

The ACM involves the use of a *snake* (Kass et al. 1987) to locate the face contour. The snake is a continuous curve that forms an initial state (facial template) and tries to deform itself dynamically on the image picture. This is a result of the action of external forces that attract the snake toward image features and internal forces that maintain the smoothness of the template's shape (Fig. 9.6). The sum of the membrane energy, denoting the snake stretching, and the thin-plate energy, denoting the snake bending, gives the following snake energy:

$$E_{int}(u(s)) = \alpha(s)|u_s(s)|^2 + \beta(s)|u_{ss}(s)|^2$$

(9.18)

where $u(s) = (x(s),y(s))$ is the snake curve and s is the arc-length of the curve. The parameters of elasticity α and β control the smoothness of the snake curve.

The deformation of the snake is governed by external forces. These forces are associated with a potential $P(x,y)$, which in general is defined in terms of the gradient module of the image convoluted by a Gaussian function:

$$P(x,y) = -|\nabla(G(x,y) * I(x,y))|$$

(9.19)

or as a distance map of the edge points:

$$P(s,y) = d(x,y), \quad P(x,y) = -e^{-d(x,y)^2}$$

(9.20)

where $d(x,y)$ denotes the distance between the pixel (x,y) and its closest edge point. The snake is moved by potential forces and tries to fall in a valley as if it were under the effect of gravity.

The total snake energy is given by the sum of the functional energies as:

$$E_{snake} = \int_0^1 E_{int} + E_{ext} \, ds$$

$$= \int_0^1 \alpha(s)|u_s(s)|^2 + \beta(s)|u_{ss}(s)|^2 + P(u(s))ds$$

(9.21)

The minimum of the snake energy satisfies the Euler–Lagrange equation

$$-\frac{d}{ds}(\alpha u_s(s)) + \frac{d^2}{ds^2}(\beta u_{ss}(s)) + \nabla P(u(s)) = 0$$

(9.22)

and boundary conditions.

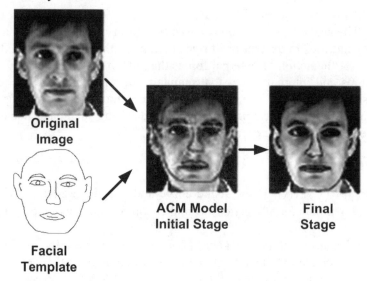

Fig. 9.6. Facial contour extraction using the ACM

Automatic Facial Landmarks Extraction Scheme

In this module, according to the 50 facial landmarks (nose, eye, eyebrow, mouth, facial contour, etc.) defined in the *deformed* facial template (Fig.

9.7), the Morlet wavelet vectors of these 50 locations will then be located and extracted automatically.

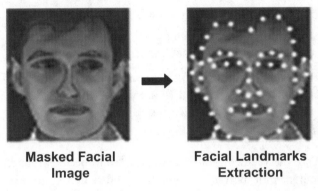

Masked Facial Image　　　　**Facial Landmarks Extraction**

Fig. 9.7. Facial features extraction scheme (on 50 facial landmarks)

Contour Mask Descriptor (CMD) and Facial Features Descriptor (FFD)

Under this scheme, two more MPEG-7 Ds are used, namely the contour mask descriptor (CMD) for the definition of the facial template (with facial landmark location) and the facial features descriptor (FFD) for the storage and manipulation of the Morlet wavelet feature vectors for an extracted facial pattern:

```
CMS{
        facial_contour();
        landmarks[number];
}

FFD{
        landmarks[location];
        morlet[location];
}
```

9.4.4 Invariant Human Face Recognition Using the EGDLM

According to the iJADE Surveillant multi-agent operation scheme depicted in Fig. 9.4, the automatic human face recognition process is carried out by the iJADE Recognizer situated in the iJADE Facial Server. This server-side subsystem basically consists of the following modules:

– the dynamic links initialization scheme;
– the elastic attribute graph matching scheme between the query image and the images from the facial database.

In the dynamic link initialization process, dynamic links ($z_{ij,kl}$) between *memory* facial attribute graphs and figure objects from the images gallery are initialized according to the following rules:

$$z_{ij,kl} = \varepsilon J_{ij} J_{kl} \ \text{ for } J_{ij} \in A, J_{kl} \in B \tag{9.23}$$

where the J are the feature vectors extracted from the facial landmarks and ε is a parameter value between 0 and 1; A and B denote the figure graph and memory graph respectively.

In the elastic graph matching module, the attribute graph of the figure is *dynamically* matched with each *memory* object attribute graph by minimizing the energy function $H(z)$:

$$H(z) = - \sum_{i,j \in B; k,l \in A} z_{ij} z_{jl} z_{ik} z_{kl} + \gamma \sum_{i \in B} \left(\sum_{k \in A} z_{ik} - 1 \right)^2 + \gamma \sum_{k \in A} \left(\sum_{i \in B} z_{ik} - 1 \right)^2 \tag{9.24}$$

within tolerance level μ

$H(z)$ is minimized using the gradient descent:

$$z_{ij}(t + 1) = \left[z_{ij}(t) - \eta \frac{\partial H(z(t))}{\partial z_{ij(t)}} \right]^w \tag{9.25}$$

where $[\ldots]^w$ denotes the value of z_{ij} confined to the interval $[0,w]$. At equilibrium (within a chosen tolerance level μ), $H(z)$ will be minimized, and the connection pattern in the memory layer represents the pattern recalled by the figure pattern.

9.5 System Implementation

In order to provide a complete evaluation of the system, testing of the iJADE Surveillant is performed under two major schemes: (1) the automatic color scene segmentation scheme; (2) the invariant human face recognition scheme. The results are as follows.

9.5.1 Automatic Color Scene Segmentation Scheme

In this test, a scene gallery of 6000 color photos from GreenStreet™ from GST Technology Ltd. was used for scenery images. An object gallery of 3000 figures was extracted from the GreenStreet software as the *memory* object database. For systematic validation of the scene analysis model and for analysis of the performance of scene analysis for different types of objects and different levels of complexity of the nature scenes, the 6000 color photos were divided into eight different categories:

1. Animals: horses, bears, camels, goats, etc.
2. People: people of different genders, nationalities, postures, and facial expressions.
3. Food: various kinds of food such as cakes, fruit, meat, vegetables.
4. Clouds: various types of clouds including cirrus, cumulus, altostratus, nimbus, cumulonimbus, and severe weather cloud formations such as topical cyclones and hurricanes.
5. Scenery: various types of natural scenery and landscapes.
6. Trees: different kinds of trees such as oak, cypress, larch, palm trees.
7. Recreation: various kinds of recreation and sporting activities such as sailing, car racing, fencing.
8. Transportation: various kinds of transportation such as trains, cars, trucks, buses.

Figure 9.8 shows the sample pictures for these eight categories of images.

Fig. 9.8. Sample images from the eight different categories

In the color scene evaluation scheme, two different tests were conducted:
– parameter selection scheme in scene segmentation
– figure–ground segmentation test

For system evaluation purposes, all color images in the photo gallery were converted into 24-bit colored pixels of resolution 320 × 192. The simulation was carried out on a Sun Sparc 20 workstation. The results are presented in the following subsections.

Parameter Selection Scheme in Scene Segmentation

To determine the optimal set of parameters in the CNOW model, a random sample of 500 images was selected from the photo gallery for figure–ground scene segmentation. Using 10000 oscillation cycles as the benchmark, the optimal set with the best segmentation result of CNOM parameters is as given in Table 9.1.

Table 9.1. Optimal parameter set of composite neural oscillators

Oscillator Parameters		Threshold Values	
α	0.3	θ_u	0.4
β	0.16	θ_v	0.6
γ	0.2	a	0.25
τ	0.8	b	0.2
λ	0.05	c	0.2

Figure–Ground Segmentation Test

To extract objects from the *memory* object gallery, 3000 images were submitted to the CNOM system for figure–ground segmentation. The results are shown in Fig. 9.9.

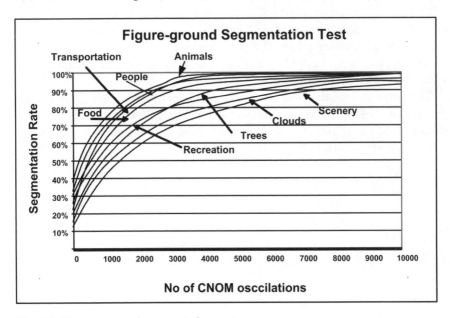

Fig. 9.9. Figure–ground segmentation test

The segmentation rate of a particular object (e.g. a car) is calculated by the *degree of coverage* (i.e. the percentage of pixels) of the segmented pattern object in the nature scene.

The experimental results shown in Fig. 9.9 reveal two important findings. Firstly, the CNOW model attains its steady state of figure–ground segmentation when the number of oscillation cycles reaches 8000; even for categories such as animals, people, and transportation, 6000 oscillation cycles are enough to achieve the steady state.

Secondly, for all eight object categories, segmentation beyond 8000 oscillation cycles was 98% correct. Some categories, such as scenery and clouds, took longer to segment, mainly because of the confusing and similar textures of objects in the same scene. Other categories, such as animals, that have a concrete texture relationship, segmented quicker.

9.5.2 Invariant Human Face Recognition Scheme

System Training

In the experiment, a portrait gallery of 100 face images was used for network training. A set of 1020 tested patterns resulting from different facial expressions, viewing perspectives, and sizes of stored templates was used for testing. The series of tested facial patterns was obtained with a CCD camera providing a standard video signal, and digitized at 512×384 pixels with 8 bits of resolution.

The computer system that was adopted to implement and measure the performance of the hybrid system was a Sun Sparc 20 workstation. Typical snapshots of the iJADE Surveillant multi-resolution facial pattern recognition screen are shown in Fig. 9.10.

Facial record not found - Stranger

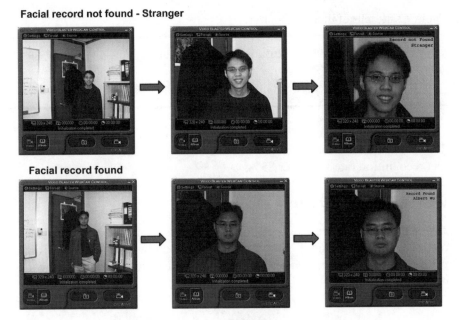

Facial record found

Fig. 9.10. Automatic multi-resolution facial pattern recognition screens

To evaluate the system, certain tests on face recognition performance were carried out, including:

– facial pattern illumination test
– viewing perspective test
– facial pattern dilation/contraction test
– facial pattern occlusion and distortion test

Facial Pattern Illumination Test

In this illumination test, 100 test patterns of various degrees of brightness were used for facial recognition, with the degree of brightness varying from +30% to −30% of the *normal* brightness level. The experimental results are given in Table 9.2.

Table 9.2. Results of illumination test

Brightness Level	+30%	+20%	+10%	Normal	−10%	−20%	−30%
Classification Rate	80%	86%	92%	95%	91%	88%	79%

The model is in fact *invariant* to the image illumination level, mainly due to the *illumination-invariant* property of the ACM. The average correct recognition rate was over 85%.

Viewing Perspective Test

This test applied a viewing perspective ranging from −30° to +30° (with reference to the horizontal and vertical axes) as shown in Fig. 9.11. Table 9.3 presents the recognition results using 100 test patterns for each viewing perspective.

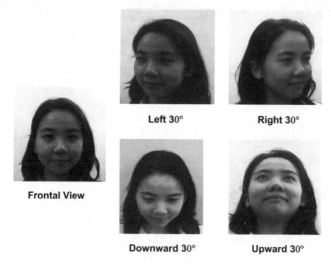

Left 30°   **Right 30°**

Frontal View

Downward 30°   **Upward 30°**

Fig. 9.11. Viewing perspective test patterns

Table 9.3. Results of viewing perspective test

Viewing Perspectives (from horiz. axis)	Correct Classification Rate	Viewing Perspectives (from vert. axis)	Correct Classification Rate
+30°	84%	+30°	86%
+20°	90%	+20°	88%
+10°	92%	+10°	91%
−10°	91%	−10°	92%
−20°	89%	−20°	87%
−30°	85%	−30°	82%

According to the *rotation-invariant* property of the dynamic link architecture (DLA) model, the EGDLM is *inherited* from the same characteristic in the *contour maps elastic graph matching* process. The overall correct recognition rate was over 86%.

Facial Pattern Dilation/Contraction Test

In this test, 300 test patterns were used, with ratios ranging from −30% (pattern contraction) to +30% (pattern dilation), i.e., partial dilation/contraction. The recognition results are given in Table 9.4.

Table 9.4. Results of facial pattern dilation/contraction test

Pattern Dilation/ Contraction	Correction Classification		
	A. Overall Dilation/ Contraction	B. Horiz. Dilation/ Contraction	C. Vertical Dilation/ Contraction
+30°	86%	80%	81%
+15°	90%	86%	88%
−15°	92%	88%	86%
−30°	87%	79%	79%

Owing to the *elastic graph matching* characteristic of the EGDLM, the system also possesses the *dilation/contraction invariant*, similar to that investigated for the *dilation invariant* of Chinese characters (Lee and Liu 2003). The overall correct recognition rate was over 85%.

9.5.3 Facial Pattern Occlusion and Distortion Test

In this last recognition test, the 120 test patterns were basically divided into three categories (Fig. 9.12):
- Wearing spectacles or other accessories.
- Partial occlusion of the face by obstacles such as cups/books (in reading and drinking processes).
- Various facial expressions (such as laughing, angry, and gimmicky faces).

The pattern recognition results are shown in Table 9.5.

| Normal View | Wearing Spectacles | Laughing | Reading | Drinking |

Fig. 9.12. Occluded face patterns

Table 9.5. Recognition results of facial occlusion/distortion tests

Pattern Occlusion/Distortion Test	Correct Classification Rate
Wearing spectacles (or other accessories)	87%
Face partially hidden by obstacles (e.g., books, cups)	72%
Facial expressions (e.g., laughing, angry, and gimmicky faces)	83%

Compared with the three different categories of facial occlusion, *wearing spectacles* had the least negative effect on facial recognition. This was because all the main facial contours are still preserved in the recognition process. Where the face is obscured by objects, the influence on the recognition rate depends on the proportion and which portion of the face is being obscured. Nevertheless, the average correct recognition rate was over 73%. Facial expressions and gimmicky faces gave the most striking results. Owing to the *elastic graph* characteristic of the model, the recognition engine *inherited* the distortion-invariant property. The overall correct recognition rate was 83%.

9.5.4 Performance Analysis

Comparison with Other Scene Analysis Models

Some contemporary studies, such as that of Triesch and Eckes (1998) on color occluded scene analysis using the enhanced elastic graph matching (EGM) model, reported that out of a scene gallery of 604 images used, their method achieved a correct recognition rate of 62.9%. In contrast, our proposed model, using a photo gallery of 6000 color images, had an overall occluded scene recognition rate of over 87%. This represents a substantial improvement of 24%. In other work, such as that done by Wiskott and Malsburg (1993) on scene analysis with only 30 scenes and 13 toy objects using the enhanced DLA model, an overall recognition rate of 80% in occluded scenes was reported. This indicates an improvement of 7% in the present study using an image database 30 times larger.

Based on the same 6000 color images used in our proposed model, recognition rate performance tests were conducted with these two competing systems.

A summary report is given in Table 9.6.

Table 9.6. Comparisons of recognition rates with other models in occluded scenes

Pattern Recognition Rate		
iJADE Surveillant	Enhanced EGM Model (Triesch and Eckes 1998)	DLA Model (Wiskott and Malsburg 1993)
87.2%	58%	65%

As shown in the table, based on the same data set (i.e., the same 6000 color photos), our proposed model outperforms the recognition rates of the other two competing models by around 30% and 23% respectively, despite the fact that the data set being used in our test is more complex in terms of the nature, varieties, and volumes of the scenes.

System Efficiency

From the system efficiency point of view, using a Sun Sparc 20 workstation as a reference, an average processing time was evaluated for the three main modules of the proposed model: (1) the feature extraction module using Morlet wavelets; (2) the figure–ground segmentation module using the CNOW model; and (3) the EGDLM object matching module.

Based on the same set of 6000 color photos from our image database, the system efficiency of our proposed model is compared with other competing systems, including (1) the EGDLM without wavelet-based multi-resolution scene segmentation (Lee and Liu 2002); and (b) the DLA model (Wiskott and Malsburg 1993). The experimental results are given in Table 9.7.

Table 9.7. Comparisons of system efficiency with other models

Module	Time Elapsed (s)		
	iJADE Surveillant *	Integrated EGDLM (Lee and Liu 2003)	DLA Model (Wiskott and Malsburg 1993)
Feature Extraction	8	50	180
Figure–Ground Segmentation	15	180	280
Object Matching	35	42	

* Time given is based on the average performance in scene analysis of a 24-bit color image of size 320 × 192 pixels matched against a photo gallery of 6000 color images. The average time lapse in the object matching process between the query image and a single color image in the photo gallery is 5.83 ms, so the total time taken for object matching with 6000 color images is approximately 35 s.

On average, the total time needed for scene interpretation and object recognition in the proposed model was 55 s using a Sun Sparc 20 workstation. Compared with that of the integrated ACM, which took 272 s for the same tasks, this is an overall improvement of 494%. In the work done by Wiskott and Malsburg (1993) using DLA, their model took 180 s and 280 s for feature extraction and scene analysis respectively.

9.6 Conclusion

In this chapter, the author has introduced a fully automatic and integrated intelligent neuro-agent based on MPEG-7 – the *iJADE Surveillant*. This integrates various contemporary technologies including intelligent multi-agent technology (iJADE model) as the *system intelligent kernel*; automatic multi-resolution scene segmentation using the composite neuro-oscillatory wavelet-based (CNOW) model; automatic facial pattern extraction using the active contour model (ACM); and invariant facial pattern recognition based on the elastic graph dynamic link model (EGDLM). Based on the latest MPEG-7 standard, the iJADE Surveillant also demonstrates how an intelligent multimedia application can be implemented using the MPEG-7 architecture as the system framework for future development in the new millennium, especially in the area of mobile e-commerce and intelligent multimedia processing applications.

10 iJADE Negotiator – An Intelligent Fuzzy Agent-Based Negotiation System for Internet Shopping

One of the things I learnt when I was negotiating was that until I changed myself I could not change others.

Nelson Mandela

Owing to the increasing demand for and requirements of Internet applications, the provision of intelligent systems using intelligent agent technology is becoming a new trend in the new millennium. Traditional web-based agent systems suffer various degrees of deficiency in terms of the provision of *intelligent* software interfaces and functions.

From the implementation perspective, this chapter aims to advance our efforts in designing and deploying an effective online negotiation agent-based system known as the *iJADE Negotiator (Intelligent Java Multi-agent-based Negotiation System)* to meet real-world requirements in bargaining settings.

This chapter (1) presents a new negotiation protocol that features trouble-free data exchange setup beforehand and supports highly dynamic and flexible changes to negotiation attributes; (2) integrates fuzzy logic to compute the utility function and apply the most appropriate strategies to maximize profits; and (3) shows the learning ability and cooperation between negotiator agents. Experimental results are performed to compare, firstly, the efficiency and effectiveness of applying the negotiation protocol; and, secondly, the level of user satisfaction in applying different negotiation strategies.

10.1 Introduction

The exponential growth of the Internet industry in recent years has brought new opportunities for business, especially in the field of e-commerce. Various e-commerce systems, ranging from C2C (consumer-to-consumer) e-commerce such as e-auctions to inter-organizational B2B (business-to-business) e-business for the international e-marketplace, have been operating in cyberspace. However, in this sea of information and Internet services, web developers have been trying to integrate agent technology into their e-applications in order to provide a more comprehensive service and automatic personal assistance for Internet users. Agent technology, with its automatic delegation of tasks, and its autonomous and highly mobile characteristics in the web environment, is starting to play an important role in e-commerce in the new millennium (Chan et al. 2001).

However, contemporary agent systems such as IBM Aglets[1] and ObjectSpace Voyager[2] focus on mobility and multi-agent communications. The core functions of intelligent agents (IAs) – the AI (Artificial Intelligence) counterpart with intelligent capabilities including machine learning, intelligent pattern recognition, and classification functions – are difficult to implement. In a typical e-shopping scenario, we often need to negotiate with the shopkeepers on the product(s) in which we are interested, in terms of different attributes such as price, quality, delivery date, etc. However, all these negotiation attributes are highly dynamic in the sense that it is very difficult to adopt a fixed algorithm to model all the changes of the negotiation attributes during bargaining. In these cases, we are dealing with different degrees of *fuzziness*, which might be efficiently handled by AI technologies such as fuzzy systems. With the integration of machine-learning techniques such as neural networks, an intelligent product selection, advisory, and negotiation system might be constructed.

This chapter will demonstrate one of the most important applications of iJADE in the mobile e-commerce environment: the *iJADE Negotiator* – an innovative intelligent multi-agent-based negotiation system which utilizes the integration of a fuzzy-based negotiation strategy with *utility function theory* to implement dynamic, adaptive, and fully automatic multi-agent-based product negotiation.

In short, this chapter will focus on two main components of the iJADE Negotiator:

---

[1] Aglets: http://ww.trl.ibm.co.jp/aglets/.
[2] Voyager URL: http://www.objectspace.com/vogyer/.

1. *iJADE Negotiation Protocol* (iJADE NP) – to provide an adaptive negotiation protocol supporting rapid changes in the content of the negotiations and carry out autoconfiguration without previous settings.

2. *iJADE Negotiation Strategy* (iJADE NS) – by applying fuzzy logics and
   utility function theory, this chapter will demonstrate how the automated
   negotiation process works, and the process of analysis. It will also show
   how the agent evaluates the fitness of an offer and generates a request
   by considering the weight of the request, the eagerness of both parties,
   and the concession rate.

This chapter is organized as follows. Section 10.2 discusses the background of negotiation systems. Section 10.3 presents the system architecture of the iJADE Negotiator. Section 10.4 discusses the system implementation and experimental results of the iJADE Negotiator, followed by
the conclusion.

10.2 Negotiation Systems – An Overview

To reach a consensus dynamically between parties with conflicting views
and perspectives is a difficult task. In real-world trading, both the buyer
and seller keep their proposal confidential and use different negotiating
strategies in order to maximize their gains. We call this kind of negotiation
strategy the *general-sum game* (GSG) (Caldwell 2001), which aims at the
achievement of an agreement that is beneficial to both parties (Guttman
and Maes 1998).

In a typical negotiation process, both parties will launch a request and
analyze the offer from their trading partner(s) using their own knowledge
and techniques. The vocabulary of business and technological terms used
to describe the demands are presented verbally (Li 2002). In such a GSG, a
great deal of information about the product is required. Thus, the difficulty
in building the computer negotiation system will be based upon the product description method, communication method, and strategies to be used.

Current e-commerce trading systems used in implementing electronic
negotiation facilities usually use predefined and non-adaptive negotiation
schemes. Actually, such systems can be simply considered as *computer-
aided* systems, rather than an *intelligent negotiation system* (Guttman and
Maes 1998). In these kinds of systems, a great many user inputs and explicit descriptions are required during the negotiation process. Even if the
user can provide a full set of product information, the user cannot be sure
that he or she will have the most suitable product because of the limitations
in communication. These e-negotiation systems employ fixed communica-

tion protocols and use fixed business terms, which will turn down user requests from the user to use alternative attributes during the negotiations. As a result, although the agent can collect all of the required information, these negotiation systems still lack dynamic negotiation strategies, which leads to a high rate of failure and unsatisfactory results (Kim and Lee 2001; Ma and Aimeur 2001; Sim and Choi 2003).

Thus far, some representative online negotiation systems that support autonomous auctions have been implemented (Alem et al. 2000; Zhang and Lesser 2002), such as FishMarket (Rodriguez-Aguilar 1998), Kasbah (Chavez and Maes 1996), and AuctionBot (Wurman et al. 1998). These systems provide certain degrees of user-friendliness to the user, as they can submit bids automatically. The user simply inputs the parameters and chooses the most appropriate strategy. The agent will then assist the user to find the solution when the situation is met. However, these kinds of systems are unable to support dynamic negotiation schemes and handle flexible decision making under different bargaining situations. Also, these systems will not learn from past experiences (Wong et al. 2000). They will only assist the user to achieve predefined targets. For the most part, they will only consider bargains in pricing, and have great difficulty coming up with a so-called *mutually beneficial* solution for both trading parties.

Tete-a-Tete did provide a cooperative approach to negotiations for retail markets (Guttman and Maes 1998). It provided a marketplace for both buyer and seller to negotiate on multiple issues, including price, delivery times, service contracts, warranties, return policies, loan options, gift services, and other value-added services. It used so-called *multi-attributes utility theory* (MAUT) to decide the fitness of offers. Several negotiation strategies are also provided for the user's selection. By sending different arguments, the shopping agents tried to compromise with the best result beneficial to both parties. This system did apply some kind of automated decision algorithms with different kinds of negotiation strategies. However, it restricted the negotiation attributes to the nine fixed items stated above. Also, the strategy being used cannot react to market changes dynamically.

Another solution proposed by Sim and Choi, called *market-driven agents* (Sim and Choi 2003), emphasizes the controlling of concession rates and adjusts the negotiating strategy by analyzing levels of eagerness and negotiation times. This design adopts the so-called *indifferent curve* economic model and the Cobb–Douglas utility function to evaluate the opportunity, competition, and remaining trading time.

Ryszard Kowalczyk and Van Bui proposed the negotiation system *FeNAs* (Kowalczyk 2000), to evaluate imprecise information, and used the concept of utility theory to analyze offers and generate requests according to fixed algorithms. They also adopted the idea of *fuzzy logic* (Kim and Lee 2001; Lee and Liu 2000c) to analyze the acceptance level, but the proposed system could not apply a dynamic negotiation strategy to react to the market situation in order to change the *bargaining strategy*.

Some other contemporary negotiation systems, including that of Li (2002), had applied the theory of *Pareto-optimal solution* to find the optimum negotiating result. Wong et al. (2000) applied a case-based reasoning technique to match negotiation episodes and generated the best negotiation strategies from past experience.

In summary, the essential features of a negotiation agent include:

Automation – This means a wide range of knowledge and *interpersonal skills*. The agent must be equipped with some knowledge to create its own perspective and directions for the decision process. Also, it should adapt to rapid changes in the negotiation contents. In order to optimize the negotiation results, it should be enabled to consider every alternative and possibility.

Dynamic and market-driven strategy – It is necessary for the agent to apply different negotiation strategies in different situations. Inefficient negotiation strategies can lead to time wastage and unsatisfactory results.

Learning ability – As the negotiation agent needs to acquire a lot of dynamic knowledge, adaptive learning through negotiation is a must in order to improve the negotiation performance.

To achieve a highly dynamic and adaptive multi-issue negotiation process, an important aspect is to provide a flexible negotiation protocol. This is essential because many alternatives will only appear during the negotiation processes, which can cause the negotiating parties either to change their minds or to make a larger concession on the offer. Also, a dynamic negotiation algorithm that can react to the market is a critical factor.

This chapter presents an innovative negotiation system that applies adaptive negotiation strategies that can be generated dynamically by analyzing the preferences of the buyer and seller. The system also applies fuzzy logic and utility function theory to analyze the *degree of eagerness* of both parties to improve the efficiency and effectiveness of the negotiation system.

10.3 iJADE Negotiator – System Architecture

10.3.1 iJADE Negotiator – System Overview

From the system architecture perspective, the proposed the iJADE Negotiator (Fig. 10.1) system consists of four main entities, as follows.

Buyer Agent (BA)

The main function of the BA is to capture the user's requirements and to search for the most suitable products for the user. Another function is to return the negotiation schema of the seller back to the Buyer Negotiator (BN). In fact, BA is a mobile agent; once it receives the order from user, it will produce a clone and dispatch itself to different remote shopping malls.

Buyer Negotiator (BN)

The main function of the BN is to capture the user's negotiation requirements, to analyze the negotiation rules, and to dispatch itself to the remote agent contest. BN is a mobile agent that contains five main modules, which will be explained shortly.

Seller Agent (SA)

The SA is the *shopkeeper* of the remote shopping mall. It is a stationary agent that stays in the seller agent's contest. The main function of the SA is to provide product and negotiation information to the buying agents.

Seller Negotiator (SN)

The SN is also a stationary agent that waits for the BN's request and negotiates with the buyer. The main function of the SN is to exchange knowledge between both parties and to optimize the results of the transaction.

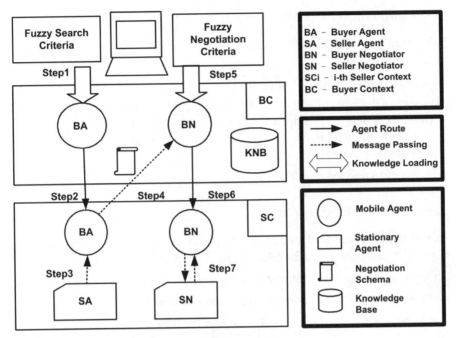

Fig. 10.1. An overview of the iJADE Negotiator

10.3.2 iJADE Negotiator – Main Functional Modules

The iJADE Negotiator consists of the following functional modules (Figs. 10.2 and 10.3).

Communication Module (CM)

This module is used to provide an interface between external parties and internal modules. Its main functions include:

– Exchanging knowledge with opponents.
– Cooperating with the *knowledge loading module* to decide the negotiation contents (attributes).
– Validating the contents of messages.
– Handling negotiation messages and passing the contents on to the Offer Analyse Module (OAM); connecting the Strategy Planning Module (SPM) and Learning Module (LM).
– Receiving the planned strategy from the SPM and formatting the negotiation messages according to the negotiation schema.

Knowledge Module (KM)

This module is used to load the relevant knowledge. Its main functions include:

- Loading the knowledge required to carry out the negotiation.
- Ensuring the ease of automation (as the iJADE Negotiator may use previous experiences to improve the performance of the negotiation performance, the KM is used to extract the relevant experience at the suitable time).
- Providing knowledge to other modules.

User Interface Module (UIM)

This module is used to consult the KM about the negotiation contents and to generate the user's selection list. It main functions include:

- Capturing the user's requirements through the browser.
- Forwarding these requirements on to the CM and SPM.
- Returning the negotiation results back to the user.

Offer Analysis Module (OAM)

This module is used to analyze the offer from the seller according to the user's requirements. It then calculates the fitness value by applying the fuzzy logics technique. Its main functions include:

- Getting details of the consolidated offer from the CM and matching them with the user's preferences.
- Passing the analyzed fitness values to the SPM in order to plan the negotiating strategy.

Strategy Planning Module (SPM)

This module is used to plan the strategy in order to optimize the negotiation result and to minimize the time cost. It main functions include:

- Getting the calculated fitness value of each negotiation issue from the OAM and then calculating the degree of consensus between both parties in the negotiation.
- Performing the gain shifting process (GSP) to reduce the conflicts between both negotiation parties.
- Adjusting the requests according to the *degree of consensus* on each issue, in order to optimize the negotiation results.

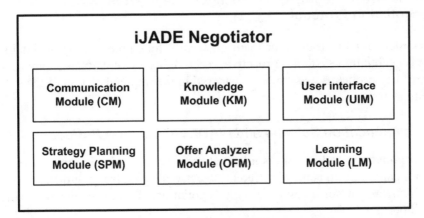

Fig. 10.2. Main functional modules of the iJADE Negotiator

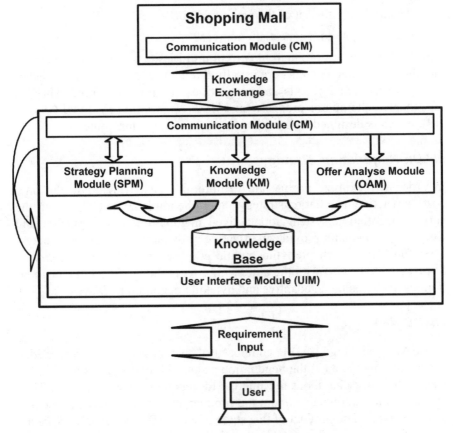

Fig. 10.3. The iJADE Negotiator – system architecture

10.3.3 iJADE Negotiator – Intelligent Negotiation Strategy and Negotiation Protocol

In order to achieve the four main objectives for implementing an intelligent negotiation system – proactive, reactive, adaptive, and autonomous – three key problems need to be considered in the implementation of the system, as follows.

Communication Scheme and iJADE Negotiation Protocol

A negotiation is a kind of complicated process of exchanging information. Both parties try to achieve different objectives by exchanging different requirements on some issues during negotiation. Therefore, the problems will be:

- What should the negotiation issues be?
- What should the format of the negotiation be?
- Can each negotiator suggest alternatives?

In fact, a common problem in current multi-issue negotiation systems is that the negotiation contents are usually fixed and predefined by the seller, and the user's requirements and suggestions are always ignored. Thus, in this chapter, the author proposes an *iJADE Negotiation Protocol* (iJADE NP), which is designed for handling dynamic negotiation contents.

iJADE Negotiation Strategy

In order to maximize profits and to minimize costs (including the time cost), a reactive negotiation strategy should be implemented. However, the current negotiation system adopts fixed negotiation strategies (Sim and Choi 2003). It cannot provide an effective or dynamic negotiation strategy. Therefore, in this chapter, the author proposes the *iJADE Negotiation Strategy* (iJADE NS) with the aim of improving the quality of the negotiation results by using an adaptive and dynamic negotiation strategy.

iJADE NP

The iJADE NP (Fig. 10.4) is composed of two stages: (1) the knowledge exchange stage; and (2) the negotiation stage. The first stage is used to exchange the message about the interest to negotiate to both parties. They exchange their knowledge about the product, and try to reach a consensus at some levels. The product of this stage is the *iJADE Negotiation Schema*. This schema shows the content, standard, and format of the negotiation message. The second stage is the negotiation stage. Both parties will send negotiation messages according to the iJADE Negotiation Schema until one of them terminates the negotiation.

(1) Knowledge Exchange Stage

Before the product negotiation, both parties should have their own preferences and expectations of the offer from their trading partner. These preferences and expectations will be stored in the knowledge base. The main objective of this stage is to exchange their expectations and preferences (Fig. 10.5). The main procedures are as follows.

First of all, the iJADE Negotiation Schema will be issued by the seller. This schema shows the format and the name of the negotiation issues (contents).

Once the buyer has received the first negotiation schema from the seller, the system will search for relevant knowledge about the trading item from the knowledge base, and will generate a selection list for the user.

If the negotiator finds out that the iJADE Negotiation Schema of the seller cannot fulfill the user's requirements, it will send another iJADE Negotiator Schema to the seller. Until the seller or buyer accepts the suggestion from the corresponding trading partner, the buyer will then send a start acknowledgment message to the seller in order to begin the negotiation process.

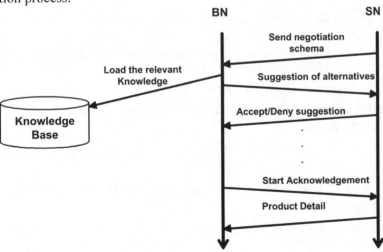

Fig. 10.4. The knowledge exchange stage of the iJADE NP

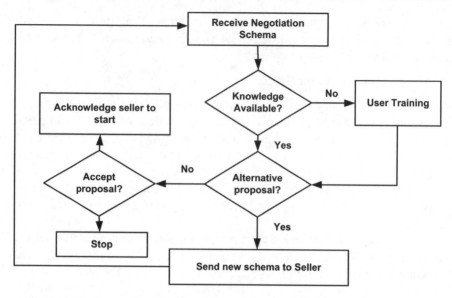

Fig. 10.5. The flow of knowledge exchange stages of the iJADE NP

(2) Negotiation Stage

After the knowledge exchange stage, both parties will agree on the same negotiation context and on the format for sending messages. They will then send messages according to the compromised iJADE Negotiation Schema. (See also Figs. 10.6 and 10.7.)

The steps in the negotiation involve:

– Receiving the offer from the seller and analyzing the offer according to the user's preferences.

– Marking the fitness value and checking whether this value is greater than the decision value.

– Deciding whether to continue the negotiations and planning the relevant negotiation strategies.

– Sending the next request.

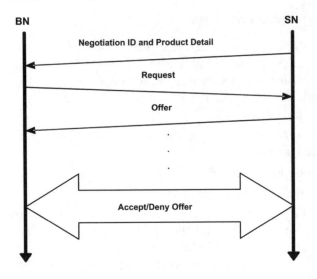

Fig. 10.6. The iJADE NP

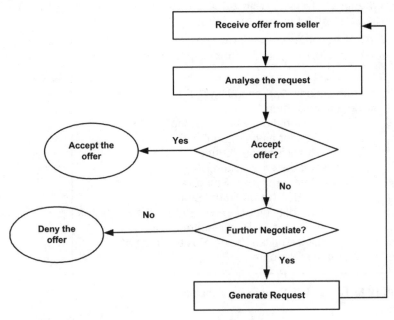

Fig. 10.7. The workflow of the negotiation in the iJADE NP

iJADE Negotiation Schema

In order to exchange knowledge about the negotiation and to initiate the negotiation, an XML-based negotiation schema (Glushko et al. 1999) was adopted to define the structure of negotiation content. The information stored in the iJADE Negotiation Schema (Fig. 10.8) includes:

- Default information.
- *NegotiationID*, a token that is assigned by the seller to record the final offer to the buyer.
- *Sender*, the name of the sender.
- *Receiver*, the name of the receiver.
- *Header*, the negotiation header to show the type of message, of which there are four types: (1) *ASK*, the first message from the buyer to ask for product details; *REQUEST*, the offer and request from the seller and the buyer; *ACCEPT*, the final message, if any party accepts the offer; and *DENY*, the final message, if any party rejects the offer.
- *Category*, the type of product.
- *ProductName*, the name of the product.
- Negotiation issue, the negotiation contents (attributes) on which both parties involved in the negotiation will compromise.
- Type of negotiation issue, the type of content of the issue under negotiation (e.g., <price type="Positive Integer">).

```xml
<?xml version="1.0" encoding="UTF-8"?>
<NegotiationContent>
        <NegotiationID type="String"/>
        <Sender type="String"/>
        <Receiver type="String"/>
        <Header type="String"/>
        <Category type="String"/>
        <ProductName type="String"/>
        <Quantity type="PositiveInteger"/>
        <Price type="PositiveInteger"/>
        <DeliveryDate type="PositiveInteger"/>
</NegotiationContent>
```

Fig. 10.8. The iJADE Negotiation Schema

iJADE NS

The core objectives for a good negotiation strategy are:

– To search for the best solution to both parties.
– To shorten the negotiation time.

These objectives seem to be quite simple, but considering how to achieve them is complex. Because different parties have different preferences, it is not possible to apply the same strategy to all types of trading partners. Therefore, a proactive negotiation strategy must be adopted.

The negotiation strategy applied in this system is known as the *iJADE Negotiation Strategy (iJADE NS)*.

The algorithm used was inspired by and has extended the concept of the indifferent curve algorithm (Alem et al. 2000; Sim and Choi 2003) by applying utility function theory, which is based on the implementation of fuzzy logic.

The following subsections will explain the algorithm from two aspects:
1. Offer analysis – analyzes the offer by applying fuzzy logics.
2. Strategy planning – generates the next request by considering the preferences of both parties.

Offer Analysis

The agent analyzes the offer from the seller by using its own fuzzy knowledge. The first step is to load the relevant knowledge and to capture the user's requirements. The offer analysis process can be described as follows.

Agent's Knowledge

Assume that there are n negotiable issues (e.g., price), $i = 1, 2, ..., n$, and the negotiable issue is N_i. Each negotiable issue includes j knowledge (e.g., cheap, expensive) where $j = 1, 2, ..., m$. The fuzzy membership function (Fig. 10.9) about knowledge j of negotiation issue i will then be $F_{Nij}(x)$:

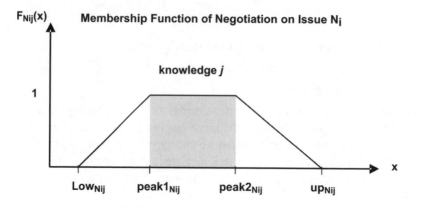

Fig. 10.9. Fuzzy membership function

$$F_{N_{ij}}(x)=\begin{cases} 1 & if\ peak1_{N_{ij}} \le x \le peak2_{N_{ij}} \\ x-low_{N_{ij}} / peak1_{N_{ij}} -low_{N_{ij}} & if\ low_{N_{ij}} \le x < peak1_{N_{ij}} \\ up_{N_{ij}} -x/up_{N_{ij}} -low_{N_{ij}} & if\ peak2_{N_{ij}} < x \le up_{N_{ij}} \\ 0 & if\ x < low_{N_{ij}}\ or\ x > up_{N_{ij}} \end{cases}$$

$$(10.1)$$

In some cases, there exists some knowledge, such as price, which tends toward either the increasing or the decreasing trend. For example, a customer may send a request such as *"as cheap as possible"*, so the agent will also ask the user how to input the preferred trend regarding this request:

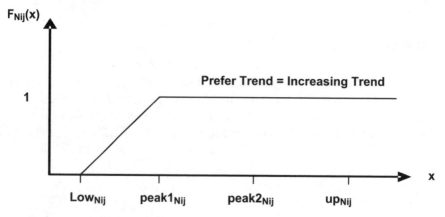

Fig. 10.10. Membership function with an increasing trend

Case 1: Preferred Trend = Increasing (Fig. 10.10):

$$F_{N_{ij}}(x) = \begin{cases} 1 & if & x \geq peak1_{N_{ij}} \\ x - low_{N_{ij}} / peak1_{N_{ij}} - low_{N_{ij}} & if & low_{N_{ij}} \leq x \leq peak1_{N_{ij}} \\ 0 & if & x < low_{N_{ij}} \end{cases}$$

$$(10.2)$$

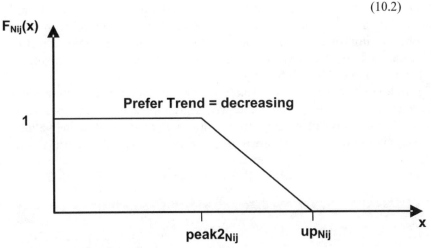

Fig. 10.11. Membership function with a decreasing trend

Case 2: Preferred Trend = Decreasing (Fig. 10.11):

$$F_{N_{ij}}(x) = \begin{cases} 1 & if & 0 \leq x \leq peak2_{N_{ij}} \\ up_{N_{ij}} - x / up_{N_{ij}} - peak2_{N_{ij}} & if & peak2_{N_{ij}} \leq x \leq up_{N_{ij}} \\ 0 & if & x \leq 0 \end{cases} \quad (10.3)$$

User's Request

The agent will generate a user query form in order to ask for the user's requirements. The query includes the following.

Requirements regarding the negotiable issues N_i – If the user requests the negotiation issue Ni that fulfils the knowledge j, it will apply the fuzzy membership function $F_{Nij}(x)$ to analyze the offer.

The request (W_{Nj}) weight – This indicates the user's weighting on each issue item in a request. That is:

$$\sum W_{Nj} = 1 \qquad , \text{where } j = 1, 2, \ldots, n \text{ and } W_{Nj} \in \{0,1\}$$

Initial decisive fuzzy value $D(t)$ – This value represents the acceptance level, which is interpreted in terms of fuzzy value. It is only the initial decisive fuzzy value, as the agent will adjust this value dynamically according to the seller's action. $t = 1, 2, .., n$ indicates the tth round of negotiation. In order to improve the negotiation performance, the agent may adjust the decision value for different issues under negotiation. The decision value of a negotiation issue N_i will be $D_N(t)_i$.

Baseline fuzzy value (B) – This is a fuzzy presentation of the baseline for the negotiation item. This value will restrict the agent to accept an offer only when all of the calculated fuzzy marks are above the baseline values.

Negotiation mode – The agent will change the negotiation strategy according to the mode of negotiation.

The user interface of the iJADE Negotiator is shown in Fig. 10.12.

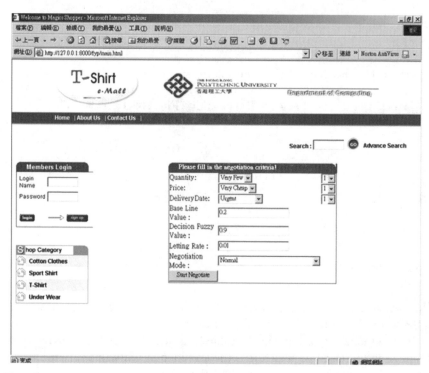

Fig. 10.12. User interface of the iJADE Negotiator

Offer Analyzer

Assume the offer of the negotiation issue N_i is $O_{Ni}(t)$ in the tth office, where $t = 1, 2, ..., n$. Therefore, according to the user's requirements, the user will use function $F_{Nij}(x)$ to calculate the fuzzy mark. The equation for calculating the fuzzy mark M_i of offer i will be:

$$M_i = F_{Nij}\left[O_{Ni}(t)\right] \tag{10.4}$$

The overall fuzzy mark M of the offer will be calculated as the weighted mean of M_i:

$$M = \frac{\sum_i M_i * W_{Ni}}{\sum_i W_{Ni}} \tag{10.5}$$

Decision Making

Recall that the user had inputted the decisive value D and the baseline value B. If M is larger than D and all of the fuzzy marks on each individual issue are higher than the baseline value, then the negotiator agent will accept the offer immediately.

Case 1: Accept the offer

The agent will accept the offer $O(t)$ if $\forall M_i \geq B \cap M \geq D(t)$.

Case 2: Negotiate further

The agent will further negotiate with the seller if $M \leq D(t)$.

Strategy Planning

The strategy applied in this chapter is called the iJADE NS, which applies fuzzy logic and the principles of utility function theory $U(x)$ to determine the optimum solution in a multi-issues (n issues) negotiation process. The utility function combines the consideration of (1) the gain and loss $G(O(t))$ and (2) the consensus ratio $K(O(t))$. Thus, both the input and output will be the n issues of offer and request.

Assume that both parties negotiated for k rounds:

$$U(O(t)) = \sum_i K(\overrightarrow{|O_{Ni}(t)|}) * S(\overrightarrow{|O_{Ni}(t)|}) \times \overrightarrow{O_{Ni}(t)} \tag{10.6}$$

where $t = 1, 2, ..., k$, $i = 1, 2, ..., n$ and the other functions are as follows.

$S(x)$ is the function of the *gain shifting process (GSP)*. The aim of this function is to eliminate the conflicts between both parties. It outputs the adjusted decision value of the negotiation issue N_i.

$K(x)$ is the function for calculating the *ratio of consensus*. This value further adjusts the decision value according to the degree of consensus.

The utility function shows that the Intelligent Negotiator tries to analyze the offer in order to reduce the conflicts between both parties. It then finds the item that is the most negotiable and further adjusts the request on that issue. Therefore, we can generalize the utility function $U(O(t))$ as the decision value of the next round $D(t + 1)$.

Gain and Loss on an Individual Issue

The concept of gain, $G(O(t))$, presented in this chapter is a relative term compared to the decision value D. To evaluate an offer $O(t)$, the agent will first calculate $G_{Ni}(O(t))$ for the individual negotiation issue N_i. The formula for the gaining function is:

$$G_{Ni}(O(t)) = F_{Nij}(x) - D_{Ni}(t) \tag{10.7}$$

As the functional terms of $F_{Nij}(x)$ and D_{Ni} are fuzzy values, the calculated gain is also a fuzzy term.

Case 1: $G_{Ni}(O(t)) > 0$

This case shows that the offer of negotiation issue N_i is beneficial to the buyer.

Case 2: $G_{Ni}(O(t)) = 0$

This case shows that the offer of negotiation issue N_i exactly fits the buyer's requirement at the moment t (because the acceptance level $D_{Ni}(t)$ varies from time to time).

Case 3: $G_{Ni}(O(t)) < 0$

This case shows that the offer of negotiation issue N_i cannot fulfill the user's requirement.

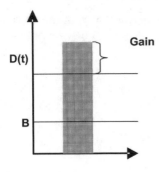 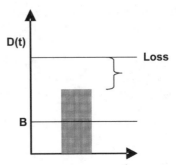

Fig. 10.13. Gain and loss of negotiation

Gain and Loss of Offer ($O(t)$)

This assumes that the negotiation is an *n-issue negotiation*, where the overall gain and loss (Fig. 10.13) will be calculated as the weighted mean of the gain on each negotiation issue:

$$G(O(t)) = \sum G_{Ni}(O(t)) * W_{Ni} \qquad (10.8)$$

where $i = 1, 2, \ldots, n$. This equation shows that the loss in some issues can be compensated by the gain in other issues. The objective of inputting the baseline value is to prevent an excessive loss in a particular negotiation issue.

Concession Ratio ($C(t)$)

The objectives of calculating the concession rate are: (1) to estimate the consensus ratio, which will be explained in the next section; (2) to decide the concession rate of the buyer's decision value; and (3) to plan the strategy. The average concession rate of the seller on negotiation issue N_i will be calculated as follows:

$$C_{Ni}(t) = \frac{O_{Ni}(1) - O_{Ni}(t)}{O_{Ni}(1)} \qquad (10.9)$$

This equation shows how to calculate the concession rate on issue N_i at the tth round of negotiation. However, the purpose of calculating this value is to find out how eager the parties are to concede on the issue under negotiation. Thus, the total concession rate of all issues should be normalized to

1. In other words, the concession ratio of negotiation N_i at the tth round of negotiation will be:

$$C_{RNi}(t) = \frac{C_{Ni}(t)}{\sum_j C_{Nj}(t)} \qquad (10.10)$$

where $i = 1, 2, \ldots, n$.

Time Factor (T)

This factor is used to adjust the request. This is because, in the real world, no seller will spend time and keep on conceding in meeting the buyer's requirements. The buyer must therefore find the best solution as soon as possible. So the iJADE Negotiator will restrict the negotiation to be completed within:

$$T = \frac{[(1 - B)/L - t]}{(1 - B)/L} \qquad (10.11)$$

where L represents the conceding rate and B represents the baseline value.

Consensus Ratio ($K_{Ni}(t)$)

The purpose of calculating the consensus ratio is to find out how much room there is to adjust the request on each negotiation issue in order to maximize the effectiveness and efficiency. The iJADE Negotiator estimates the potential for further negotiation by calculating the consensus ratio.

This includes: (1) concession ratio $C(t)$ on issue N_i; (2) weights of N_i; and (3) the time of negotiation.

This chapter presents the main ideas for calculating the degree of consensus by calculating the vector sum of the above three factors (Fig. 10.14).

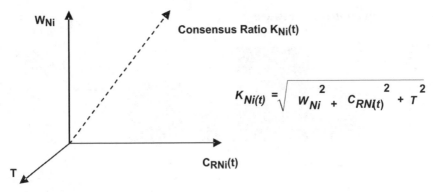

Fig. 10.14. Consensus ratio $K_{Ni}(t)$

Gain Shifting Process (GSP)

According to the information collected above, the negotiation strategy will be planned by applying the gain shifting process (GSP) (Fig. 10.15).

GSP extends the concept of the economic model indifference curve algorithm (Caldwell 2001; Sim and Choi 2003), the main idea being to balance the utility by adjusting the degree of satisfaction of different criteria. That means that, if one loses on some criteria, one must compensate the loss by requesting more on other criteria. For example, if the seller cannot deliver the product before the deadline, the seller should offer some discount on the price. The iJADE NS adopts this idea by adjusting the request according to the offers of the seller.

The main job of the iJADE Negotiator is to maximize profits and minimize costs. That is the only target a negotiator should aim for. In fact, many people interpret the term *profit* or *cost* as *money values*.

Ideally, these agents should not only bargain over the price of a product, but also take into account other aspects such as the delivery time, quality, payment methods, return policies, or specific properties of the product. In such multi-issue negotiations, the agents should negotiate so that the results are mutually beneficial for both trading parties. The complexity of that kind of bargaining problem increases rapidly, and the adoption of IAs might be needed to provide negotiation services on multiple issues at the same time.

GSP – Operational Procedures

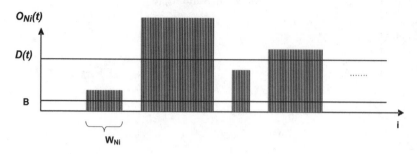

Fig. 10.15. Gain shifting process (GSP)

Step 1: Calculate the pure profit $G_P(O(t))$

This step is to find the space for concessions. If the agent discovers that the pure profit is high in some items, it can concede more on other issues during negotiation.

The equation is given by:

$$G_P(O(t)) = \sum_i G_{Ni}(O(t)) \, , \forall G_{Ni}(O(t)) > 0 \qquad (10.12)$$

Step 2: Permute the issue of loss according to the weight, and calculate the profit share ratio $P_{Ni}(O(t))$

This process is used to index the permutation of the issues of loss according to their assigned weights in inverse order (Fig. 10.16). Because a lower assigned weight means that the issue is less important to the user, the agent can compensate more for this issue by using the gain from other issues.

The equation is given by:

$$P_{Ni}(O(t)) = W_{N(n-i)} \times \frac{G_P(O(t))}{\sum_i W_{Ni}} \, , \forall G_{Ni}(O(t)) < 0$$

$$(10.13)$$

Step 3: Decide the new decisive value of N_i

As some of the losses for issue N_i have been compensated, the agent should lower the decisive value in order to reach the equilibrium point for both parties as quickly as possible (Fig. 10.17).

The equation is given by:

$$S(O_{Ni}(t)) = D_{Ni}(t+1)$$

$$= MAX\left[O_{Ni}(t), D(t) - \frac{P_{Ni}(O(t))}{W_{Ni}}, B\right] \qquad (10.14)$$

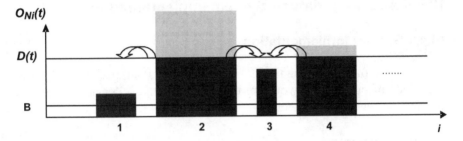

Fig. 10.16. Gain shifting process (GSP) 2

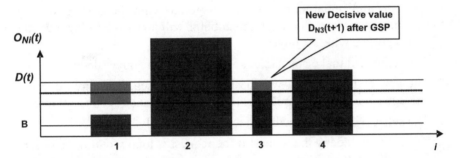

Fig. 10.17. Gain shifting process (GSP) 3

After the GSP $S(O(t))$ the negotiation issue N_i will be assigned to a new decision value $D_{Ni}(t+1)$. The agent will further adjust the request by using consensus ratio $K_{Ni}(t)$, because the iJADE Negotiator has evaluated the probability of completing a transaction by collecting different kinds of information about the transaction.

The final decision value of the next request will be given by:

$$D_{Ni}(t+1) = D_{Ni}(t+1) * K_{Ni}(t), \text{ where } j = 1, 2, \dots, n \qquad (10.15)$$

Step 4: Decide the next decision value of the offer

Because the agent had decided the decision value on each negotiation issue $D_{Ni}(t+1)$ in the previous steps, the overall decision value in the next round $D(t+1)$ should be calculated as the weighted mean of the decision value of each issue.

The equation is given by:

$$D(t+1) = \sum W_{Nj} * D_{Nj}(t+1), \quad \text{where } j = 1, 2, \ldots, n \qquad (10.16)$$

10.4 iJADE Negotiator – System Implementation

10.4.1 System Implementation

For the sake of experimental tests and system evaluations, the following two kinds of preparation work are implemented: the seller negotiator and benchmark negotiation strategies.

Seller Negotiator

As the iJADE Negotiator is designed for buyers, for experimental purposes we need to implement an opponent to negotiate with the iJADE Negotiator. In the experiment, the seller's negotiator will apply the following strategy to negotiate with the buyer:

1. The seller will make concessions if and only if the buyer does.
2. The concession strategy will be randomly chosen. The three different strategies will be: (a) increasing; (b) decreasing; and (c) constant rate.
3. The seller will choose the baseline value randomly.
4. The seller will deny the request if the request is totally out of the seller's acceptable range.

Benchmark Negotiation Strategies

In the experiment, the iJADE Negotiator will compare two kinds of benchmark negotiation strategies: (1) a strategy using fuzzy logic with a constant concession rate (FCC) and (2) a strategy using constant concession (CC) (Caldwell 2001).

FCC Strategy

This strategy uses fuzzy logic to analyze the offer and calculates the weighted sum of the fuzzy mark. If the weighted fuzzy mark is higher than the decision value, the agent will accept the offer; otherwise, it will decrease the decision value with a constant rate and generate a new request. The negotiation will terminate if the seller accepts/denies the request or if the buyer's decision value is below the baseline value.

CC Strategy

This strategy uses the user-defined ranges of negotiation criterion and will gradually decrease the degree of satisfaction until the offer fulfills the user's requirements.

10.4.2 Experimental Results

In this system, two experiments are conducted: (1) a utility test; and (2) a system performance test.

In the utility test, a particular product (*T-Shirt 078*) was first chosen (Table 10.1) in the iJADE Negotiator. The two benchmark negotiation strategies (FCC and CC) will then be applied for a comparison with the iJADE Negotiator. The experiment aims to show: (1) the differences in negotiating ability between different negotiation strategies; and (2) the comparison to the optimum utility value.

In the system performance test, 100 different products were chosen to test the performance of the iJADE Negotiator. The success rate and negotiation time will be discussed shortly.

Table 10.1. Product detail of *T-Shirt 078*

Selling Price	321
Cost	200
Minimum Delivery Day	2

Utility Test

The chosen product *T-Shirt 078* is used in the iJADE Negotiator and the result compared to the two benchmark strategies, FCC and CC, for the negotiation with the seller. By comparing the preferences of both parties, the author will first discover the maximum utility value $\hat{U}$. The preferences are shown in Fig. 10.18.

Fig. 10.18. Preferences of both parties in negotiating over product *T-Shirt 078*

The maximum utility value $\hat{U}$ is calculated by applying the following equations.

There are *n* issues during negotiation. The maximum utility value of the *j*th negotiation issue N_j is given by:

$$\hat{U}_{Nj} = Max(W_{BNj}{*}P_{BNj}(x) + W_{SNj}{*}P_{SNj}(x))/2 \quad \text{where } j = 1, 2, \ldots, n$$

$$(10.17)$$

The optimum utility value $\hat{U}$ of the negotiation is given by:

$$\hat{U} = \sum \hat{U}_{Nj} \quad \text{where } j = 1, 2, \ldots, n \text{ and } \hat{U} \in [0,1] \qquad (10.18)$$

$\hat{U}$ – *the optimum utility value*

where:

$P_{BNj}(x)$, $P_{SNj}(x)$ are the function of the buyer and the seller's preference about negotiation issue *j*; and

$W_{BNj}(x)$, $W_{SNj}(x)$ are the weighting of the buyer and the seller over the negotiation issue *j*.

Table 10.2 depicts the results of the negotiation with a maximum utility value.

Table 10.2. Negotiation results with a maximum utility value

Price	250
Quantity	13
Delivery Date	15
Maximum Utility Value	0.687

After negotiating with the seller by applying three different negotiation strategies, the results of the negotiation are shown in Fig. 10.19 and in Table 10.3.

Table 10.3. Negotiation results of applying different negotiation strategies

	iJADE Negotiator	FCC	CC
Negotiation Time	438	500	422
Negotiation Rounds	6	14	15
Buyer Satisfaction Degree	0.64	Failed	0.31
Seller Satisfaction Degree	0.53	Failed	0.57
Average Satisfaction Degree	0.59	0	0.44

The result shows that the average satisfaction degree of applying the iJADE Negotiator is 15% higher than using CC. The results of FCC cannot complete the negotiation because the strategy took too long to negotiate with the seller, and the negotiation agent would not try to do any further adjustment after a consensus had been reached on some issues. The result indicated that the iJADE Negotiator could find a solution that was closest to the optimum solution $\hat{U}$ within a short period of time. Although CC could successfully bid on the product, it did not try to estimate the seller's eagerness and kept conceding on the negotiation issues to reach a consensus. Therefore, the degree of satisfactory purchase would be very low.

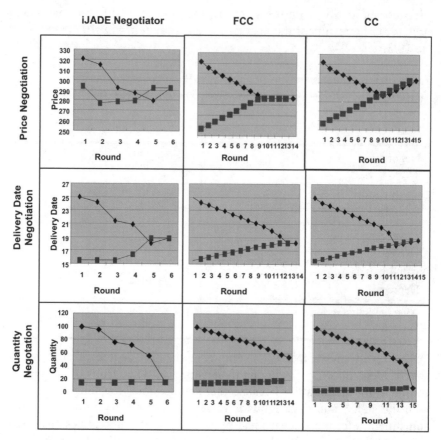

Fig. 10.19. Negotiation by using strategies iJADE Negotiator, FCC, and CC

System Performance Test

In the performance test, the author used 100 different products with different negotiation criteria to test the results of negotiation. With the same set of user requirements, the test was repeated three times and different negotiation strategies were applied. The test revealed the average degree of satisfaction, the success rate, and the negotiation time. The experimental results are shown in Tables 10.4 and 10.5.

Table 10.4. Three-issue negotiation

Negotiation Strategy	Average Negotiation Time (ms)	Average Negotiation Rounds	Success Rate	Average Degree of Satisfaction
iJADE Negotiator	432.45	8.1	48.2%	0.59
FCC	420.5	15.3	31.2%	0.31
CC	330.2	14.7	45.7%	0.41

Table 10.5. Two-issue negotiation

Negotiation Strategy	Average Negotiation Time (ms)	Average Negotiation Rounds	Success Rate	Average Degree of Satisfaction
iJADE Negotiator	150.2	7.1	46.9%	0.57
FCC	170.3	15.7	32.9%	0.38
CC	110.7	15.2	45.0%	0.42

Of the three negotiation strategies, the iJADE Negotiator achieved the best results. The success rate was about 50%. The average degree of satisfaction was around 0.6. The shortcoming was the calculation time. As the algorithm of the iJADE Negotiator was relatively complex, it took 430 ms to complete an eight-round negotiation. Although CC achieved a higher success rate, the average degree of satisfaction was only about 0.4. FCC took a longer negotiation time, but both the success rate and the degree of satisfaction were quite low. Another interesting finding in the experiment was that the degree of satisfaction was independent of the number of issues being negotiated. However, when the number of issues during negotiation was increased, the negotiation time also increased exponentially.

10.5 Conclusion

In this chapter, an intelligent multi-agent-based negotiation system called the iJADE Negotiator has been presented. This system involves the design and implementation of: (1) an iJADE Negotiation Protocol (iJADE NP);

(2) dynamic knowledge-base loading; and (3) the iJADE Negotiation Strategy (iJADE NS).

The proposed solution allows agents to negotiate autonomously and communicate in the absence of predefined communication content (Alem et al. 2000). The agents are rational and self-interested in the sense that they are concerned with achieving the best outcomes for themselves. The agents will eventually achieve their desired results (Hwang et al. 2001).

Fuzzy logic has been employed in this project. The negotiator first stored the fuzzy rules in the knowledge base and loaded the relevant knowledge to tackle the problem accordingly. The iJADE Negotiator demonstrated its intellectual negotiating behaviors through the dynamic loading and manipulation of knowledge and the implementation of a dynamic negotiation schema and GPS during the agent negotiation processes.

The experimental results further indicated that the proposed system had achieved the objective of providing effective autonomous and dynamic negotiations. The iJADE Negotiator used different knowledge and strategies under different scenarios.

To further improve the proposed system, more comprehensive tests in the real-world e-commerce environment are necessary, and a number of issues require further investigation. These include, for example, the analysis of optimality and convergence of the negotiation process; the adaptability and learning in the negotiation strategies; dynamic multi-party negotiation; and negotiation with incomplete and imprecise offers (i.e., linguistic negotiation). These are all potential subjects of future enhancements.

Acknowledgments

The author is grateful for the Departmental Grants for their partial support of the iJADE projects, including the iJADE Framework (version 2.0) Z042, the Central Research Grant G-T850, and RCG Grant B-Q569 from The Hong Kong Polytechnic University. The author is also grateful to research student William Hung for help in conducting the experiments and system evaluations.

11 Future Agent Technology – Modern Ontology and Ontological Agent Technologies (OAT)

It is a very rare matter when any of us at any time in life sees things as they are at the moment. This happens at times … that we become aware of what is going on about us and of the infinite great worlds of force, of feeling and of idea in which we live, and in the midst of which we have always been living. These worlds are really in progress all the time; and the difference between one man and another, or the difference in the same man at different times, is the difference in his *awareness* of what is happening.

Memories and Milestones, John Jay Chapman

- What exactly is the reality of the world we are living in?
- Are we living in the world as we see it?
- Are we living in the world as we think of it?
- Are we living in the world as it "used to be"?
- What is the reality of existence?
- How can we understand concepts and ideas?

The answers to abstract questions such as these are of interest not only to philosophers but also for our central considerations as we develop the latest and future AI – namely, *ontological agent technologies* (*OAT*).

In this chapter, the author will introduce a topic that is of both theoretical and practical interest – *ontology* – presenting the key issues in *modern ontology* and explaining its importance and its relevance to the thought and theory that underlie OAT.

The chapter will be organized as follows. Section 11.1 will introduce ontology, identify the major related philosophical questions, and explain why this topic is central to modern AI. Section 11.2 will discuss how ontology is related to agent technology and will explore the major ontological theory within agent technology – the *conceptualization theory*. This section will also discuss contemporary AI research in ontology. Section 11.3 contains the author's latest work on ontological agents and platforms in modern AI and OAT – the *Cogito iJADE Project*.

11.1 What Is Ontology?

The word *ontology* is derived from the ancient Greek word *ontia* meaning *the nature of existence*. It is a major doctrine in metaphysics and has had a great impact on modern sciences, especially in the arena of AI, IAs, semantic webs, and robot technology.

Grossmann defined the major roles of ontology within metaphysics as being the answers to the following three fundamental questions (Grossmann 1992):
1. What are the *categories* of the world?
2. What is the *nature* of these *categories*?
3. What *laws* define, control, and govern all these *categories*?

11.1.1 Ontology – Theories of Existence

Ancient Philosophy and Religion

Ancient philosophers such as Empedocles (1500 BC) (Kingsley 1996) believed the world to be made up of four basic elements: *earth, water, fire,* and *wind*. *Earth* represented all matter with physical shape and appearance, such as trees and stones. *Water* represented all matter without a well-defined shape and having a liquid appearance, such as water and blood. *Fire* represented all non-physical matter but the existence of such matter could be felt, such as fire and our body temperatures. *Wind* represented non-physical matter of a *windy* nature, such as wind and breath.

Ancient Tibetan Buddhism similarly interpreted the properties of matter. *The Tibetan Book of Death* (Sambhava and Thurman 1994) explained the composition of the human body in terms of these four elements, with *earth* as *flesh*, *water* as *blood*, *fire* as the *body temperature*, and *wind* as our *breath*. It also accounted for the whole process of bodily decomposition in the same terms, as a return to these four basic elements.

Plato's Theory of Two Realms

Plato (427–347 BC) in his *Phaedo* (Plato 1999) interpreted the nature of existence as a *World of Two Realms*: the realm of the *properties* of matter which is, by its nature, *immortal* (*atemporal*); and the realm of *matter* itself which is, by its nature, *changing* (*temporal*).

Plato's interpretation of the statement "This apple is green" is that the color "green" is the property of the apple, an abstract but atemporal property. When the apple later ripens from green to red, it is the apple itself which changes, not the color. An abstract quality such as the color "green" will never change!

This idea may strike us as odd and contrary to our normal habit of thinking. When the appearance of something (its color, shape, etc.) changes, we would normally say that the object's appearance has changed rather than the object itself.

Plato asked an even more puzzling question: If over time an apple ripens from green to red, can we speak of these two apples as the *same* apple?

Grossmann (1992) further extended this fundamental ontological theory and stated that not only is this abstract equality – *property* of matter – atemporal, but so too are some other abstract things (so-called *universals*) such as relations, facts, and other mathematical and topological *qualia* such as numbers, matrices, sets, vectors, and structures.

<u>Case Study 1: Are we still the same "person" we are from the past?</u>

Modern biology tells us that our body is made up of "flesh", "blood", and "bones" which in turn are collections of groups of cells. Each group of cells binds together to form different components and functional units within our body, such as the skeleton, muscles, and organs.

Every single cell in a living body will undergo the natural process of metabolism, in which the aged cells are ultimately replaced by new cells. Some neurobiologists believe that even brain cells – neurons – may undergo the same process, albeit over a longer life cycle.

If this is true, in our lifetime every single living cell in our body will be replaced, with the result that our body at middle age, for example, is quite different from our body during our youth. According to Plato's Theory of Two Realms, the body we have today should not be the same as that of the past, raising the question: "Do I remain the same person I was?" And if not, who am I?

Russell's Theory of Reality and Appearance

In *The Problems of Philosophy* (Russell 1912), Bertrand Russell provided a totally different interpretation of the *reality* and *appearance* of matter. In his theory of the *existence* and the *nature* of matter, he claimed that all the appearances of matters – such as color, shape – are *unreal*, merely sensations perceived through the interactions between our visual systems and the *sense data* that are generated by (or reflected from) matter. Russell called these features *appearance*, neither the reality of the object, nor immortal, unchanging qualia. He further concluded that our perceptual world is *unreal* and *private* to the percipient only, while the real world is *public* and *universal*.

Clearly, there is a significant divergence between Plato's and Russell's views of the nature of reality. Plato believed that physical objects are all temporal in nature while their abstract properties are immortal and atemporal. Russell believed that all the appearances and sensations that we perceive from physical objects are unreal and vary subject to different conditions and perspectives, whereas the reality (so-called *universals*) of the objects is immortal.

Case Study 2: How can our brains store visual patterns and objects?

At the beginning of *The Problems of Philosophy*, Russell asks an important question: If from different perspectives the appearance of an object, its size, shape, illumination, and color, differ completely, how can we determine the "*true*" appearance of the object?

Behind this paradox is our *perceptual idea* of the appearance of every visual object that we see; from different perspectives and in different situations they seem to be "constant" and "stable", yet we remain largely unaware of it. The visual geometry of all of these appearances constantly varies. It is not possible to speak of a "true" appearance.

How can our brains encode and store all these visual objects and patterns to become "memory?"

Lee's Cognitron and the Unification Theory of Senses and Experiences

The author addressed this critical philosophical and elementary problem in his *Unification Theory of Senses and Experiences*. By adopting both Plato's Theory of Two Realms and Russell's Theory of Universals, the author introduced a new way to interpret objects, senses and universals – the *Unification Theory of Senses and Experiences* (or *Unification Theory* in short).

Unification Theory extends Russell's theory on the appearance and reality of objects. If the senses and experiences we perceive from the physical world are neither real nor immortal, but rather are all captured, stored, and manipulated as memories, sensations, and thoughts, why can't we unify all of them as the *same nature as found in our mind*, since they are all considered and treated as *cues* (or what are called *impressions* in layman's terms)? These *cues* include:
– the representation of certain matter (physical objects);
– the association with certain concepts (universals); or
– the linkage with certain events, memories, or experience.

This view is systematized within the concept of the *cognitron* – the "universal" representation of all these: matter, concepts, events, memories, and experiences. Cognitrons provide the physical representation of concepts, ideas, universals, and impressions that constitute our interpretation of the perceptual world; they also represent all the associated memories of our experiences and our own concepts of ideas. Epistemologically, cognitrons provide the physical appearances and representations of our three levels of knowledge mentioned in Chap. 2: intuitive, stimulated, and derived knowledge.

Unification Theory not only offers simply a theory of the representation of knowledge, but also illustrates how certain critical knowledge-oriented operations are treated in the "sea" of the cognitron map (Fig. 2.5). These operations include:

- The *association* within a cognitron of abstract notions such as ideas and concepts, and physical matter such as object appearances, and memories of events, which correspond to the association and clustering of cognitrons – in lay terms, "memorizing".
- The *generation (learning)* of new knowledge, ideas, and concepts, correspond to the creation of new cognitrons – in lay terms, "learning".
- The *recall* of a particular event, memory, thought, or idea, or the recognition of a particular object or item, which corresponds to the object progressive association of cognitrons – in lay terms, "recalling".
- The *forgetting* of a particular matter, person, event, or memory, which corresponds to the *decay* and *dissociation* of cognitron links – in lay terms, "forgetting".

One interesting implication of this cognitron theory is that it provides a new way of interpreting both Plato's and Russell's theories of existence and object appearance. By using the previous statement "This apple is green" as an example, in Plato's Theory of Two Realms, the property color "green" is immortal and universal. It is only the object "apple" that changes with respect to time; while in Russell's theory, the color "green" is just the appearance of the object "apple", which is unreal and varies according to our perspectives.

So in our new cognitron theory, when we say "This apple is green", what we are doing is making a kind of association between (at least) two cognitrons – the cognitron "apple" and the cognitron "green". We can interpret "green" as a kind of property for the "apple", yet the cognitron "apple" is also an idea of notion – the sensation of green color. Ontologically speaking, the cognitron "green" is the physical representation of a particular vision sensation, while the cognitron "apple" is the physical representation of a mental idea (notion) of a particular kind of object "apple". According to Plato's theory, the color "green" can be still described as the property of a kind of object (idea) of apple, but we cannot say whether this idea (concept) is atemporal or temporal as this is only a kind of sensation and mental experience which might be subject to the mechanisms we have described above.

On the other hand, under this new theory, Russell's interpretation is still true in the sense that from the observer's point of view, the color "green" is just a particular and private appearance of the object "apple", as, according to our cognitron theory, "This apple is green" is just an *association process* between the two cognitrons "apple" and "green", which is a private and instant "experience" of the observer's perceptual world.

Ultimately, the *Unification Theory* and the concept of cognitrons are just ontological or epistemological interpretations of our world of experience, for as Kant explained in his *Critique of Pure Reason* (Kant 1934) the true existence and reality of the objects themselves are never known!

For a detailed philosophical, cognitive, and psychological overview and discussion of cognitron maps and the *Unification Theory of Senses and Experiences*, refer to Chap. 2.

11.1.2 Universals Versus Particulars

In *The Existence of the World*, Grossman (1992) claimed that *universal* is the generalized idea and concept of matter while *particular* is the individual object (matter) we perceive for that particular universal. He also extended this idea and provided an analogy of these two objects of matter as *types* and *tokens*, which have meanings similar to those of *classes* and *objects* in *object-oriented programming theory (OOP)*.

At first glance this seems to be quite similar to Russell's theory, but on closer examination we find significant differences. For Russell, *universal* is more than the generalized concept of the particular, it is the *truth* and *reality* of certain matter and objects. All perceivable matter is merely the *attributes* and *appearances* associated with that *universal*. In Grossman's theory, however, the universal is the matter itself, the "one over the many".

In cognitron theory, *cognitrons* are the physical representation of *universals*. There is neither truth nor reality in our world of experience; concepts, ideas, memories, matter, and objects are all just cognitrons – a kind of mental representation of all these types of "matter" in our mind. Nor, in cognitron theory, is there any types/tokens relationship between universals and particulars. Indeed, any object stored in our mind should be "converted" (or we can say "encoded") as a *cognitron*. For instance, upon seeing an object, our visual system will capture all the associated features and, if we believe we have seen it before, start to associate with a particular *cognitron* (*concept*). Alternatively, we will create a new cognitron and treat the perceived object as a new concept in our mind. In other words, our mind contains nothing that is "particular". On the contrary, anything we perceive will be either a "recallable" cognitron or a new concept.

Moreover, according to our *Unification Theory of Senses and Experiences*, this kind of "concept treatment" can be applicable to any sensations, experiences, ideas, and concepts.

11.1.3 Ontology – The World of Universals

Universals – The Main Doctrines of the Nature of Existence

The "Battle of the World" claimed by Grossman (1992) is in fact the argument for the *nature of existence*, and more precisely: the *reality of existence*.

Starting with Plato and Aristotle, the mainstream theories of the nature of existence include:
- idealism
- realism
- nominalism
- naturalism

Idealism

Idealists maintain that the nature of matter is not actual existence but that it is merely the mental *outcomes* and *fantasies* of the one who *senses* the existence of the world, the so-called *perceiver*. In ontological terms, no concepts or notions, not even material objects, "*physically*" exist in the world. Their *existence* depends on the existence of the perceiver. In other words, we are living in a world of fantasy and imagination!

Realism

Realism takes the position that all types of matter, even abstract ideas and concepts, truly, physically, and independently exist. In *Platonist realism*, everything in the Universe is either an individual thing which physically exists but is *temporal in nature* and *spatial in space*, or an abstract notion or idea which is *atemporal* and *immortal in time and space*.

Aristotle extended Plato's argument by saying that matter is divided into two main categories: the (physical) substances and their (abstract) accidental properties. Aristotle believed that *physical substances* further consist of *matter* and *essential properties* (or so-called *essences*). One interesting point in the Aristotelian world of existence is that matter and essence coexist like the two faces of a coin. For example, we will say that Aristotle's physical exists (i.e., substance) consisting both of "Aristotle", that particular man as a "real" existence object, and of Aristotle the "human being", with his *human-beingness* as a kind of essential property. Other properties of Aristotle, his "age", "character", even the "criticisms" of him, are all *accidental* in the sense that they vary from time to time.

But whether it is, in Plato's view, an individual thing or idea, or, in Aristotle's view, a substance or property of matter, the nature of matter is real and existent and independent of one's view or perception.

Note that, to clarify, physical existence (substance) does not mean "really exists"; similarly, an abstract idea does not mean "unreal" (or not "really exists").

Nominalism

Nominalism may be described as extreme realism.

Nominalists believe that all types of matter exist in their "distinct ways". Everything we perceive is *real* and *distinct* or is *unreal*, existing only in the imagination.

In a nominalistic view, there are no sharing *concepts* and *properties*. In other words, when we say two apples are the "same" color, say red, a nominalist would say these two "reds" are not the same. That is, not only are the two apples distinct, but so too are the two colors "red". In short, nominalists do not believe in the existence of abstract ideas and properties like color. They believe that all matter, objects, even concepts and ideas exist as "real" and "distinct". Indeed, they insist that all these types of matter and concepts can only exist spatially and temporally.

Nominalists thus deny the existence of abstract concepts and ideas, or universals, believing only in the existence of the matter and objects they see and perceive.

Nominalism was well supported in ancient and medieval philosophy but was vigorously attacked by Boethius (480–525). In his *Commentaries on the Isagoge of Prophyry – Book I*, he gave a concrete and clear refutation of the nominalists:

For anything that is common at one time to many can not be one; indeed, that which is common is of many, particularly when one and the same thing is completely in many things at one time …. Yet if there are genus and species, but they are multiplex and not one in number, there will be no last genus, but it will have some other genus superposed on it, which would include that multiplicity in the word of its single name. For as the genera of many animals are sought for the following reason, that they have something similar, yet are not the same, so too, since the genus, which is in many and is therefore multiplex, has the likeness of itself, which is the genus, but is not one, because it is in many, another genus of this genus must likewise and looked for, and when that has been found, for the reason which has been mentioned above, still a third genus is to be sought out. And so reason must proceed in infinitum since no end of the process occurs. But if any genus is one in number, it can not possibly be common to many.

McKeon, 1957

The logic of this paradox can be illustrated once again using our apple analogue. Assuming a basket of "red" apples, nominalists will regard the color of each apple as distinctly "red", say red_1, red_2, red_3, ..., red_N. Since these apples are all "red", each of these instances of "red" must have something in common, or we could not say they are all "red". So, if we are asking a nominalist whether the apples share any matter or properties, the nominalist must answer either yes or no. If the nominalist answers yes, that these "reds" have something in common, they become realists, believing in the existence of universals. Alternatively, the nominalist may answer no, that these "reds" have nothing in common and therefore that each of these "reds" has its own attribute (or property), say red_{11}, red_{22}, red_{33}, ..., red_{NM}. We might then ask how it is that they are all called "red". In other words, the same argument will come up again and again, until the nominalists finally give up their viewpoint and agree with the existence of universals.

Naturalism

Long before Plato, there were philosophers who did not believe in matter as "abstract things". These naturalists believed that all things and matter that we perceive and acquire, if they are real, must be governed and described by so-called *natural laws*, just as Newton's *Laws of Motion* govern the motion of objects in the physical world, Einstein's Laws of *General Relativity* govern the motion of celestial objects, and the *Laws of Quantum Mechanics* govern the motion of particles in the subatomic world. In other words, naturalists deny the existence of abstract ideas and properties. As described by Plato in his Theory of Two Realms (Plato 1999), naturalists believe only in the existence of the Universe, the *superset* of all the physical particles, things, and objects, and deny the existence of the world – the superset of all the abstract things and ideas – the so-called *universals*.

Contemporary naturalism is divided into two categories: *pure* and *impure*. As described by Grossmann (1992), *pure naturalism* is in fact the combination of naturalism and nominalism – so-called *traditional naturalism* – while *impure naturalism* is the combination of naturalism and realism – so-called *modern naturalism*. In summary, pure naturalists deny the existence of all *non-physical* matter – what we have referred to as the abstract properties or universals. However, this kind of nominalist belief of "distinctive behavior of object appearance", or the so-called *axiom of localization* claimed by Grossmann (1992) saying that "No entity whatsoever can exist at different places at once or at interrupted time intervals", encounters the major paradox as described in the previous section on nominalism. Contemporary naturalism, or what we called *impure naturalism*, thus tries to give up this *axiom of localization* by allowing the existence of both the *physical object*, which is distinct and localized, and the *physical property*, which is non-distinct (i.e., can be shared among different objects, such as color) and non-localized. In other words, impure naturalism differs from pure naturalism, in that it maintains that there is matter (i.e., properties) located in space (as there is actual "existence" in the naturalism perspective), and that this matter can exist in multiple locations "simultaneously".

Again taking our exemplar apples, from the perspective of pure naturalism, each of these apples has its own distinct color "red", say red_1, red_2, red_3, ..., red_N; while from the perspective of impure naturalism, although the apples are different as distinct physical objects existing in a particular time and location, they can "share" (or "own") the same "physical property" – say "red" at the same time in different locations. Figures 11.1 and 11.2 depict how the two different disciplines categorize the concept "apple".

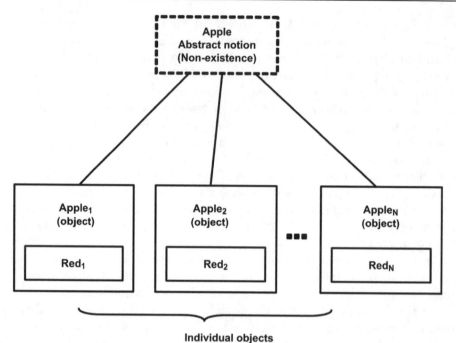

Fig. 11.1. Pure naturalism – apple case

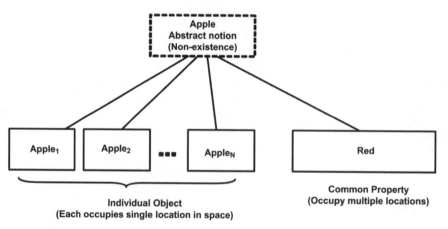

Fig. 11.2. Impure naturalism – apple case

11.1.4 Ontological View of the Nature of Existence

The ontological view is thus found within a region bounded by the doctrines of idealism, realism, and nominalism (see Fig. 11.3).

Fig. 11.3. Ontology vs. idealism, realism, and nominalism

On the one hand, ontologists agree with realists: there is actual existence which is more than our "fantasy thinking/imagination or mental creation" from other dependent matter. On the other hand, they also believe in the existence of something which is *abstract* in the universal (so-called *universals* or *concepts*), which are atemporal, non-spatial, and also exist independent of the existence of perceivers. These kinds of abstract matter are key components of the *conceptualization theory*. They include the exemplification, interpretation, classification, and categorization of the Universe of matter, concepts, and ideas.

Like nominalists, classical (pure) naturalists, and materialists, ontologists belief in the *true* existence of our physical and material world. They also believe in all the physical rules (dynamics) that govern the motion of the object (physical matter) and, in general, their causes. Yet ontologists nonetheless also believe in the true existence of non-material matter (abstract notions and ideas), whether they are properties of matter such as color and shape, ethical values such as courage or beauty, or logical concepts such as big, small, up, and down – all of which are denied by classical naturalists, nominalists, and materialists.

Ontologists are not, however, idealists. They do not conceive all matter and all objects as being made up of such abstractions. Ontologists do not focus on whether or not matters or notions are real, but on how different types of matter, objects, concepts, and notions are *linked* or *categorized* to construct our perceived world (or our world of cognitions based on *the Unification Theory*). In other words, ontologists care about the *relation of matter* rather than the *reality of matter*; they also care about the *properties of matter* rather than the *true existence of matter*. They regard an object with a view to saying what it is and in what category of the conceptual mind it should be placed, little regarding why it is being seen (or perceived) and whether it truly exists.

11.1.5 Impact of Ontology on Modern AI

Chapter 4 provided an overview of all the major modern AI technologies, including artificial neural networks, genetic algorithms, fuzzy logic and chaos theory – the so-called *microscopic AI* technology. As compared to their AI counterpart – the *macroscopic AI* technology – one might ask: What are the major differences between these two categories of AI techniques? Are they different only in their implementation or are they fundamentally different in their structure or even their nature? What impact might such differences have on our understanding of modern science and technology?

From Classical AI to Modern AI

The major technical difference between modern AI (microscopic AI) and classical AI (macroscopic AI) is the level of solving the *human intelligence* problems. In the past half-century, classical AI has dominated scientific thinking. The basic assumption is that human intelligence is rooted in its capacity for logical reasoning and inference. There are many artifacts of this viewpoint, such as logical machines (computers) and logical programs and applications (case-based and rule-based expert systems) with applications ranging from medical diagnosis to financial advisory systems.

Ranged now against this view of the essential quality of human intelligence are insights deriving from computing technology, neurobiology, neuroscience, and psychiatry, which tell us that the brain, the core of human intelligence, operates in ways that are highly nonlinear and even chaotic (Freeman 2001). Reasoning, inference, and decision making may in fact not be "orderly" and "logical" but rather "illogical", "fuzzy", and even "chaotic". AI adopts these insights in order to model our brain functions using microscopic AI techniques including: neural networks that model the highly nonlinear infrastructure of brain networks; fuzzy logics that model the highly uncertain (fuzzy) behavior of decision making; genetic algorithms that model the evolution of Intelligence; and chaos theory, modeling the highly nonlinear and chaotic behaviors of human intelligence.

The shift of focus from classical AI to modern AI not only implies a different technical implementation, but structurally and conceptually understands and interprets human intelligence differently. In the past, explanations and rationales for *intelligent human behaviors* were to be found in the investigated facts and evidence, items which are logical and predictable, but the detailed structure of the human brain appears highly illogical, unpredictable, and fuzzy. While the neural dynamics of our capacity to see and to recognize patterns are highly complex and nonlinear, recent research in neuroscience and pattern recognition has revealed that they are not unpredictable, but rather interact in a kind of deterministic chaos (Freeman 2001; Lee 2004c). If this is true, we may infer that all of our other intelligent behaviors (e.g., reasoning, thinking, decision making) can also be interpreted as dynamic chaos. In other words, these behaviors may be amenable to modeling! This leaves one particularly intriguing issue on the pinnacle of this mountain of issues, the ultimate problem of human intelligence – *ontology*.

Ontology – The Ultimate Problem of AI

In the very beginning of AI in the early 1950s, AI focused on one single question of how to design *intelligent systems*, whether software or robots, that could mimic human intellectual behaviors ranging from problem solving and perception to thinking. Yet even if we could design and model such robots or intelligent programs, the problem would remain that robots and programs could not know that problems existed to be solved, objects existed to be recognized, nor even that subjects or events existed that they might ponder.

These issues are addressed in ontology. It exists to explore and provide feasible explanations and solutions for these fundamental problems – what Russell called the "ultimate problem for the world of existence" (Russell 1912).

Certainly, this is a fundamental problem in robotics. If we wish to design a truly autonomous robot which can survive in any foreign and unvisited environment, the major challenge is: How can the robot recognize single objects in the foreign environment? Or more precisely: How can the robot segment every single vision object from its environment? (The Perception Paradox. See Case Study 3 for details.)

Or more fundamentally: How can the robot know even what things to do if it does not know in advance anything that will happen, or that it will see and experience in these foreign environments?

The next section will discuss how ontology is related to agent technology and will explore the major research and development of ontological agent technology (OAT).

Case Study 3: The Perception Paradox

One unique human intellectual behavior is vision. The latest research on human vision (Lee and Liu 2003) has revealed that the object vision of humans (and other animals as well) involves complex processes of: (1) scene capture, to capture the image of the whole scene; (2) image encoding and filtering, to perceive the 2D array of image stimuli in sensory neurons (which involves filtering and noise deduction processes); (3) figure–ground segmentation, a process of separating visual objects from their background; and (4) object recognition, a process of recognizing (recalling) objects from memory.

At first glance, the whole process seems to be quite logical and natural, but a closer look at this four-step process reveals a philosophical paradox. If we have no idea (knowledge) of what kinds of objects we can expect to see, how can we know how to segment these objects from their background? And if we know in advance the kind of objects to be segmented, why do we need to recognize them (Step 4)?

11.2 Modern Ontology and Ontological Agents

11.2.1 The Theoretical Foundation of OAT – Conceptualization Theory

In Sect. 11.1, we gave an overview of ontology and discussed how it affects the development of contemporary AI and OAT. From a philosophical point of view, ontology is the study of the nature of existence, which is the *reflection* and *modeling* of one's perceived world of experience in one's mind, such that one can *successfully* interact with the *outside environment*. However, from the OAT point of view, as described by Guarino (1998), ontology can be defined as the "specification of conceptualization", which has two levels of understanding:

1. As an *engineering artifact* – which refers to the construction, organization, and manipulation of a specific set of *vocabulary* being adopted in an agent platform and its related applications. The main concern is to define the *meaning* of all these vocabularies such that they can be shared and communicate with other *foreign agent systems* using other ontologies.

2. As a *conceptualization model* – which refers to the definition of a *hierarchy of concepts* which are related by some predefined relationships. From a mathematical point of view, it corresponds to the definition of basic axioms to define and express all the conceptual expressions used in an agent system.

It is clear that the two levels of understanding described above correspond to two distinct levels of implementation. The first level is mainly focused on the *macroscopic level* of OAT, which is strongly related to the research and development of language definition and communication between different agent systems. As a matter of fact, current research and development is focused on the adoption of NLP (Natural Language Processing) AI technology into OAT.

The second level is mainly focused on the fundamental definition, organization, and manipulation of all the basic concepts of matter and notion being used in the agent systems, which is much more fundamental, abstract, and difficult to implement. It is also the major challenge and main focus of the conceptualization theory adopted in OAT.

However, these two levels of consideration are strongly related to each other. For instance, to define an object (of matter) "table", one can focus on the linguistic point of view such that in English we called it "table" while in Chinese we called it "檯". Although they belong to totally different sets of vocabularies and languages, their intrinsic nature, properties, and meanings are the same – that is, the same "concept" in the conceptualization point of view.

In other words, the first level corresponds to more or less the *linguistic level* of ontology being used in two aspects: (1) the definition and categorization of all the matter being used in an agent system; and (2) the communication and exchange of "ideas" between one agent and another using the same set of language. The second level can be treated as a further extension of the agent's capability in the sense that not only can this agent traverse around its own ontological world, but so also can agent platforms of a totally different ontology – which is also the major challenge of OAT.

11.2.2 Characteristics of Ontological Agents

According to conceptualization theory (Guarino 1995, 1997, 1998; Gruber 1995), a conceptualization is concerned not only with the "meaning assignment", but also with the formal definition of all the matter and notions of the "structure of reality" appearing in the agent's perceived worlds, which have the following characteristics:

1. *Independence* of language.
2. *Private* to the agent's "mind".
3. *Public* for interaction and communication with other entities (agents or even human) in other foreign platforms.
4. *Consistency* over different platforms.

However, there are still debates on the notion of ontology and conceptualization theory in OAT. Guarino (1995, 1997, 1998) maintained that ontology is a "specification of a conceptualization" which is (what the author called) the "restricted" version of conceptualization. From Guarino's point of view (Guarino 1998; Guarino and Welty 2000), "ontology" in OAT adopts the so-called AI definition with the two basic understandings just mentioned, while "conceptualization" adopts the philosophical definition of ontology mentioned at the beginning of this chapter. Based on his theory, the first phase of OAT is the implementation of language and the set of vocabularies being used in agent systems, while the second phase is the implementation of the *meanings* of all the vocabularies being used (which is what he called the "conceptualization").

Genesereth and Nilsson (1987) defined conceptualization as a set of mathematical relations between the *domain space* (D), the *conceptual relations* (R), and the relevant states of affairs within the *domain space* (W) – which is also called the *possible worlds*.

From the author's point of view, ontology in OAT should be the *model* of the perceived world of experience in the agent's perspective. It is the collection of all the concepts, definitions, and categorizations of all the matter and notions in this perceived world. The ontology agents (OAs) are the specific agents which focus on the tasks of construction, maintenance, adaptive learning, and enhancement of the ontology servers (OS) and the communications and translations of ontological concepts between agents from different ontologies. Similar to the author's MIND model (discussed in Chap. 2) for the interpretation of levels of intelligence, the implementation of a *complete ontology* of the agent technology can be organized in different stages and functional modules. We will present the details of the architecture and operations of the ontological agent system when we discuss the Cogito iJADE Project in Sect. 11.4.

11.2.3 Potential Applications of OAT

With the feverish development of agent technology and the increasing number of agent systems that can be ported and integrated into the Internet environment, there might be a strong need for the implementation of agents that can traverse freely in all foreign environments, even those which are totally different in language and ontology. The potential applications of OAT include:

– ontology-based semantic webs
– ontology-based information retrieval systems
– adaptive and ontology-based expert systems and expert agents

Contemporary OAT applications include: *OntoSeek*, the ontologically based information retrieval system developed by Guarino et al. (1999); *Text-To-Onto*, a semantic web with ontology learning ability developed by Maedche and Staab (2001); *Methontology*, a chemical ontologically based KBS (Knowledge-Based System) developed by Lopez et al. (1999); the application of *core ontological technology* to enable scalable assimilation of information from diverse multimedia sources on MPEG-21, as proposed by Hunter (2003); and the ontological system of an oil refinery plant developed by Mizoguchi et al. (1999).

For agent technology, current ontology standards include *OKBC* (*Open Knowledge-Base Connectivity*) (derived from the Ontolingua[1] Frame Ontology) developed jointly by the Artificial Intelligence Center of SRI International and the Knowledge Systems Laboratory of Stanford University, and *K-Ontologies* (derived from Knowbots) developed by INM[2] of the Institute for New Media in Germany. INM also acts as an information broker, helping users to exploit the ontologies of the WWW.

11.2.4 Summary

This section introduced the theoretical basis of conceptualization theory and explored how it is related to OAT. However, OAT is still an emerging technology in which most of its theoretical and technological components are still in the process of development. Different agent developers are now doing their best to enrich this fascinating area.

The next section will introduce the author's latest work on the design and development of the third generation of iJADE technology, the Cogito iJADE Project.

---

[1] http://ontolingua.stanford.edu/okbc/
[2] http://www.inm.de/kip/kip.html

11.3 Cogito iJADE Project

11.3.1 Cogito iJADE – A New Era of Self-aware IAs

In modern AI, scientists try to build intelligent software objects (IAs) that can mimic human intellectual behavior to carry out a range of human activities such as problem solving, scheduling, and data mining. In recent years, developers have implemented agent systems such as AuctionBot for e-auctions to our own iJADE Web Miner. Most of these agents, however, are either *task-specific* or *rigidly* defined in response to specific environments. One example of this is "well-defined" negotiation protocols for shopping agents (Sim and Choi 2003) that assume all agents in different platforms share the same ontology for the domain of discourse. As yet, it has not been possible to develop agents that are *truly* adaptable to their environments and capable of autonomous learning. René Descartes' (1596–1650) dictum *"Cogito, ergo sum"* ("I think, therefore I am") drew attention to the importance of our sense of *self-awareness* and how we *sense our world of existence* (Grossmann 1992). This seemingly simple observation about our experience of being and existence not merely provided the basis for further ontological investigations and for research into the epistemology of modern science, but enunciated a basic notion of AI research, for if we would like our agents to "survive independently" and to "react autonomously" over the heterogeneous platforms, it is both fundamental and critical that they understand the ontology and the notion of matter in foreign agent platforms.

Recent work on conceptualization theory-based ontological agents such as Ontolingua or K-Ontologies mainly focuses on the categorization of logical (and linguistic) concepts and/or translation between ontologies different either in their degree of categorization or in the languages that they use. Such ontology services, however, are ineffective when the agent visits a foreign environment that uses a different language where translation is not available or a different object conceptualization method. This scenario is common in the physical world. When we travel to a foreign country in which our own language cannot be understood, we can still communicate with others through non-linguistic means such as perceptions, gestures and sensational expressions.

For instance, if one is in a foreign store and wishes to buy a lemon, one can express one's intention to the shopkeeper not only by linguistic expressions, but also by non-linguistic means such as recognizing the fruit by perception and pointing it out to the shopkeeper, without any need for linguistic or conceptual communication. In a similar way, a complete ontological system should include not only logical, linguistic, and conceptual categorizations, but also related sensations and perceptions, and even memory fragments and expressions.

The main objective of this project is to design and implement an innovative ontologically based agent platform – *Cogito iJADE* (*iJADE version. 3.0*), which will focus on the enhancement of the existing *conscious layer* of the iJADE model with the implementation of the *intelligent Java Agent-based Ontology Server (iJAOS)* with the goal of implementing truly autonomous and adaptive agents.

The iJAOS Framework integrates the author's latest research on chaotic neural oscillators, the Lee-oscillatory Network (Lee 2004c), with the author's latest ontological research (Lee 2004a, 2004b) on the cognitron map and the *Unification Theory of Senses and Experiences*. Together, these provide a solid theoretical foundation for interpreting the ontological framework by adopting both the linguistic and logical categorization of concepts (as found in traditional ontological agents) and the chaotic associations of sensations, experiences, and memory fragments for ontology construction.

From an implementation point of view, the author adopted the latest research on chaotic neural oscillatory networks (so-called Lee-associators (Lee 2004d)) to implement the cognitron maps. To ensure conformity with the international agent standard, the construction of the iJAOS and its corresponding ontology agents will adopt the latest FIPA[3] ontological standards.

The major outcomes of the Cogito iJADE Project will include the development of:

1. An intelligent iJAOS consisting of the following modules:
   - iJASC (intelligent Java Agent-based *Sensation Center*);
   - iJAMC (intelligent Java Agent-based *Memory Center);*
   - iJAKC (intelligent Java Agent-based *Knowledge Center*);
   - iJALC (intelligent Java Agent-based *Language Center*);
   - iJAEC (intelligent Java Agent-based *Ethics Center*).

2. *Cogito agents* (integrated with the previously developed task-oriented iJADE agents):
   - Cogito e-shopper, a highly proactive and adaptive iJADE shopping agent;
   - Cogito WeatherMan, a highly autonomous iJADE WeatherMan agent with forecasting capability;
   - Cogito Stock-Predictor, a highly adaptive stock advisory agent;

---

[3] http://www.FIPA.org

– Cogito Surveillant – an autonomous and adaptive iJADE surveillance
agent.

In the long term this research will provide truly intelligent, autonomous,
and adaptive agents. These agents will have widespread applications in e-
business systems as well as for domestic end-users (e.g., in intelligent
homes). The problem domain will also generate many practical, interesting, and research-oriented problems for training research students in various fields and disciplines, in AI, agent technology, and as a bridge to other
disciplines including ontology, epistemology, and behavioral and visual
psychology.

11.3.2 Cogito iJADE – A System Overview

The architectural design of the Cogito iJADE Framework will be described, which consists of the design of:
– the intelligent Java Agent-based Ontology Server (iJAOS)
– the intelligent Java Agent-based Ontology Agent (iJAOA)
– the cognitron map

Design and Construction of the iJAOS

Based on the iJADE version 2.0 Framework, the iJAOS seeks to enhance
the conscious layer with the integration of the iJAOS, which consists of
five functional modules:
1. iJASC (intelligent Java Agent-based Sensation Center)
2. iJAMC (intelligent Java Agent-based Memory Center)
3. iJAKC (intelligent Java Agent-based Knowledge Center)
4. iJALC (intelligent Java Agent-based Language Center)
5. iJAEC (intelligent Java Agent-based Ethics Center)
   Figure 11.4 depicts the system architecture of the iJAOS (embedded in
the conscious layer of the Cogito iJADE).

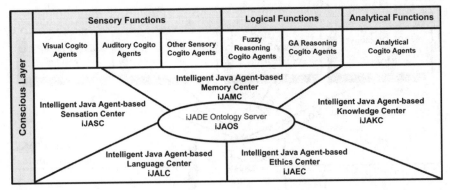

Fig. 11.4. System architecture of the iJAOS in the conscious layer of the Cogito iJADE Framework

Design of the iJAOA

In conformity with the FIPA ontology service specification (XC00086D), an ontology agent iJAOA will be designed and constructed with the following functionalities (namely, the "RATE" requirements).

Representation
To represent and discover public ontologies (especially ontologies in foreign platforms).

Administration
To maintain and administer the services and facilities provided by the iJAOS.

Translation
To communicate and translate concepts, meanings, and universals between different ontologies and/or different content languages.

Explanation
To respond to and explain all queries concerning relationships between different concepts and ontologies.

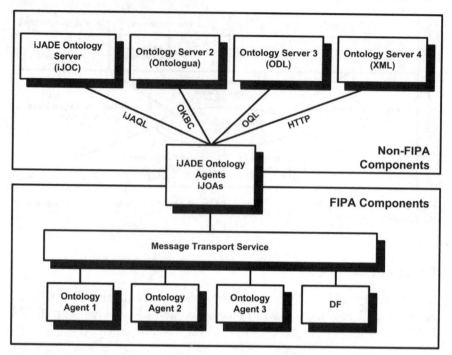

Fig. 11.5. Ontology Service Reference Model (OSRM) (conforming to the FIPA XC00086D specification)

Design of the Cognitron Map

The core of the Cogito iJADE is the construction of the ontology server iJAOS in which all five component ontological centers are constructed by cognitron maps – chaotic neural oscillatory networks which consist of the cognitrons (Lee-oscillators) (Lee 2004d) that store and dynamically connect with all the associated senses, concepts, memories, and experiences, based on the author's latest theory in terms of the philosophical, psychological, and neural dynamics.

For the theoretical details of the *Unification Theory of Senses and Experience*, the *MIND* model, and *cognitron theory* in terms of: philosophy, cognitive science, Gestalt psychology, neuroscience, and neurophysiology, refer to Chap. 2. For the implementation details of the Lee-oscillator and the "spin-off" technology – the Lee-associators for its progress memory recalling scheme (PMRS) – refer to Sect. 4.6.

11.3.3 Latest Works of Cogito Agents

From the implementation point of view, the current work of the Cogito iJADE Project involves the design and implementation of:
- system implementation of the ontology server iJAOS (with corresponding ontological centers (Fig. 11.5));
- implementation of the ontology agent iJAOA (according to the requirements designed in the analysis phase);
- system integration of the iJAOS into the iJADE Framework;
- implementation of the related Cogito iJADE agents.

The Cogito iJADE Agents

Different from the current iJADE (2.0) agents discussed in Chaps. 6–10 which focus on the design and implementation of the intelligent components in the conscious (intelligent) layer of the iJADE and adoption to different types of iJADE agents, the Cogito iJADE Project aims at the design and development of highly autonomous and intelligent agents which can traverse "freely" in foreign platforms that conform to totally different languages and ontologies.

The Cogito iJADE agents to be implemented in the project include: Cogito e-Shopper, Cogito WeatherMan, Cogito Stock-Predictor, and Cogito Surveillant.

Cogito e-Shopper

This extends the work of iJADE WShopper discussed in Chap. 6. The main focus of Cogito WShopper is to design a highly autonomous and intelligent e-shopping agent that can provide shopping facilities on foreign e-shopping sites that are using totally different languages and ontologies.

One of the major challenges of the Cogito e-Shopper Project is the integration of: (1) the adaptive negotiation skills developed in the iJADE Negotiator (discussed in Chap. 10); and (2) the Cogito linguistic capability of the Cogito technology – the iJALC functions provided by the iJAOS of the Cogito iJADE.

It is anticipated that Cogito e-Shopper will provide a new insight on proactive agent shopping in the near future.

Figure 11.6 depicts a scenario of Cogito e-Shopper in two foreign agent platforms (Grasshopper[4] and Comtec[5]).

---

[4] http://www.grasshopper.de/
[5] http://ias.comtec.co.jp/ap/

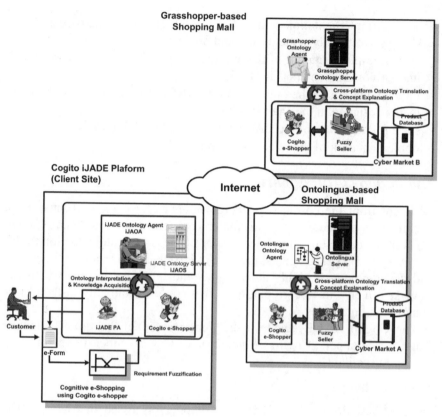

Fig. 11.6. Systematic diagram of Cogito e-Shopper for intelligent and autonomous shopping in foreign agent platforms

Cogito WeatherMan

This extends the work of iJADE WeatherMan discussed in Chap. 7. The main focus of Cogito WeatherMan is to design a highly autonomous and adaptive weather information retrieval and forecasting agent that can provide two major functions: (1) autonomously and dynamically visits various weather stations and information centers to collect all necessary weather information according to user's request; and (2) provides the Weather-FoR – the "on the spot" Weather Forecasting-on-Request service to the user.

One of the major challenges of the Cogito WeatherMan Project is to incorporate the visual intelligence capability of the Cogito technology, the iJASC functions provided by iJAOS for the visual recognition of severe weather patterns in the weather charts, and satellite pictures provided by the weather centers.

It is anticipated that Cogito WeatherMan will provide a new insight on interactive agent-based information retrieval and forecasting systems.

Cogito Stock-Predictor

This extends the work of iJADE Stock Advisor discussed in Chap. 8. The main focus of Cogito Stock-Predictor is to design a highly autonomous and proactive financial information retrieval and forecasting agent that can provide two major functions: (1) autonomously and dynamically visits various financial centers to collect all necessary financial information according to user's request and (2) provides the FinanceFoR – the "on the spot" Financial Forecasting-on-Request service to user.

One of the major challenges of the Cogito Stock-Predictor Project is to incorporate the data-mining capability of the Cogito technology with the iJAKC functions provided by iJAOS for the construction of the ontologically based finance semantic web organization and acquisition of real-time financial information.

It is anticipated that Cogito Stock-Predictor will provide a new insight into the development of interactive ontological agent-based information retrieval systems, as well as semantic web and agent systems.

Cogito Surveillant

This extends the work of iJADE Surveillant discussed in Chap. 9. The main focus of Cogito Surveillant is to design a highly autonomous and proactive surveillance system that can provide two major functions: (1) the provision of a real-time and multi-resolution-based surveillance service; and (2) the provision of an interactive semantic web for the categorization of the objects and matter appearing in the Cogito Surveillant's visual world.

One of the major challenges of the Cogito Surveillant is to explore if it is technically feasible for an ontological agent to recognize all the objects appearing in its perceived world, which involves not only complex real-time scene analysis and object segmentation skill, but also the construction and management of an efficient ontology for such a "visual world". From an implementation point of view, this project involves the implementation and integration of the iJASC and iJAKC functions of the Cogito technology, and is also one of the key applications for illustrating the author's theories mentioned above.

It is anticipated that Cogito Surveillant will provide a new insight for the development of a highly autonomous, interactive and ontological agent-based active vision and object identification system.

11.4 Agent Technology – The Future

People always ask how far we are from solving the ultimate problem of AI – mimicking human intelligence and all human intellectual activities. If you had asked me this question five years ago, I would have answered that we still at least have quite a way to go. But if you asked me the same question in spring 2004, I would tell you that we have only just started the study of the ultimate question of AI and the exploration of human intelligence. The fact is, the more you study AI, IAs, and OAT, the more you "feel" you do not know. However, the more you "feel" you do not know, the more you know what you should do.

After reading this book, readers may realize why I have to spend so much time on the elaboration and discussion of human intelligence and AI from various perspectives including classical and modern philosophy, cognitive psychology, neuroscience, and neuro-physiology before starting on the topics of agent technology and applications. The reason is, if we do not have a *full picture* and *perspective* of human intelligence, it is difficult for us to explore the core problem of AI, let alone agent technology and even OAT!

If one revisits the topic of the history of AI, one might be surprised to find that the latest research and studies of agent technology and OAT are just a "continuation" of work on the "initial motivation" for the exploration of AI – the exploration, design, modeling, and implementation of human intelligence and related intellectual activities. The only difference is that, nowadays, we even start to explore the development of highly autonomous, mobile, adaptive, linguistic, fuzzy thinking, and even self-aware agents when in fact these are all possible future trends of development!

Appendix: iJADK 2.0 API[1]

ijadeserver.Agent

public abstract class Agent extends Thread, implements Serializable, Cloneable
> *Agent is the object that clients can customize to create their own applications.*

Method Detail

public void run()
> *This method is the default method to start the agent's activities.*

Parameters:

Returns:

public String getAgentName()
> *This method will return the agent's name.*

Parameters:

Returns: the agent's name

public String getAgentID()
> *This method will return the agent's ID.*

Parameters:

Returns: the agent's ID

public String getStatus()
> *This method will return the agent's status.*

---

[1] For latest iJADK API, please refers to iJADK official site http://www.ijadk.org

Parameters:

Returns: the agent's status

public   LifeCycleManager getLifeCycleManager()

> *This method will return the LifeCycleManager that controls the agent's lifecycle.*

Parameters:

Returns: the LifeCycleManager object.

public   Agent getOtherAgent(String name)

> *This method will get the reference of an agent by using the agent's name.*

Parameters: name – the name of the agent

Returns: the agent object

public   void sendMessage(Object msg)

> *This method is used by other objects to send messages to this agent.*

Parameters: msg – an object that contains the message or other objects.

Returns:

public   void handleMessage(Object msg)

> *This method is the default method for handling messages from other agents.*

Parameters:

Returns:

public void dispatch(String host, int port)

> *This method will dispatch the agent to a specified host and the given port.*

Parameters: host – the host name of the remote server

       serverport – the listening port number of the remote server

Returns:

public void arrived()

> *This method is the default method that the agent will run when it arrives at the remote host.*

Parameters:

Returns:

ijadeserver.LifeCycleManager

public class LifeCycleManagerextends UnicastRemoteObjectimplements LifeCycleManagerInterface

LifeCycleManager is the agent management component of the iJADE-Server. It controls the activities and the lifecycle of an agent to live inside the agent platform.

Method Detail

public   Agent activateAgent(String agentName, String activate)

> *This method creates an instance or reactivates the agent object which is already registered in the iJADEServer.*

Parameters: agentName – the name of the agent.

> activate – "ACTIVATE" to create a new instance/"REACTIVATE" to reactivate a deactivated agent.

Returns: the agent object

See Also: Agent

public   void deactivateAgent(String agentName)

> *This method will deactivate an agent to stop its activity immediately.*

Parameters: agentName – the name of the agent

Returns:

public   void dispatchAgent(String agentName, String host, int port)

This method will dispatch the agent to a specified host and the given port.

Parameters: agentName – the name of the agent.

host – the host name of the remote server

port – the listening port number of the remote server

Returns:

public   void disposeAgent(String agentName)

This method will stop the activities of the agent immediately and remove the object from memory.

Parameters: agentName – the name of the agent

Returns:

public   Agent getOtherAgent(String name)

This method will get the reference of an agent by using the agent's name.

Parameters: agent – the name of the agent.

Returns: the agent object

See Also: Agent

getAllAgent public Enumeration getAllAgent()

This method will get all of the agent references within the server.

Parameters:

Returns: Enumeration of the agent object within the server.

Ijadeserver.RuntimeAgent

public class RuntimeAgent

RuntimeAgent provides the method to the client application, which is not initiated by iJADEServer, to create Agent Object.

Method Detail

createAgent public static Agent createAgent(String server, int port, String agentname)

> *This method creates an instance of an agent object which is already registered in the iJADEServer.*

Parameters: server – the hostname or IP of the agent server.

port – the port number that the agent server is listening to.

agentname – the name of the agent to be created.

Returns: the agent objectSee

Also: Agent

References

Abdel-Mottaleb M., Dimitrova N., Agnihori L., Dagtas S., Jeannin S., Krishna-machari S., McGee T., Vaithilingam G. (2000) MPEG-7: a content description standard beyond compression. In: Proc. 42nd Midwest Symp. on Circuits and Systems 2000, Vol. 2, pp. 770–777

Abreu B., Botelho L., Cavallaro A., Douxchamps D., Ebrahimi T., Figueiredo P., Macq B., Mory B., Nunes L., Orri J., Trigueiros M.J., Violante A. (2000) Video-based multi-agent traffic surveillance system. In: Proc. IEEE Intelligent Vehicles Symposium 2000, pp. 457–462

Adachi M., Aihara K. (1997) Associative dynamics in a chaotic neural network. Neural Networks 10(1):83–98

Addison P.S. (1997) Fractals and chaos: an illustrated course. Bristol, Philadelphia, Institute of Physics Publishing

Aihara K. (1997) Chaos in neural networks. In: The impact of chaos on science and society. United Nations University Press, pp. 110–126

Aihara K., Katayama R. (1995) Chaos engineering in Japan. Comm. ACM 38(11):103–107

Aihara K., Matsumoto G. (1986) Chaotic oscillations and bifurcations in squid giant axons. In: Holden A.V. (ed.) Chaos. Manchester University Press, pp. 257–269

Aihara K., Matsumoto G. (1987) Forced oscillations and route to chaos in the Hodgkin-Huxley axons and squid giant axons. In: Degn H., Holden A.V., Olsen L.F. (eds.) Chaos in biological systems. Plenum, pp. 121–131

Akamatsu S., Sasaki T., Fukamachi H., Masui N., Suenaga Y. (1992) An accurate and robust face identification scheme. In: Proc. Int. Conf. Pattern Recognition, The Hague, The Netherlands, Vol. 2, pp. 217–220

Alkon D.L., Blackwell K.T., Barbour G.S., Werness S.A., Vogl T.P. (1994) Biological plausibility of synaptic associative memory models. Neural Networks 7(6/7):1005–1017

Allard T., Clarc S.A., Jenkins W.M., Merzenich M.M. (1991) Reorganization of somato-sensory area 3b representation in adult owl monkeys after digital syndactyly. J. Neurophysiology 66:1048–1058

Alem L., Kowalczyk R., Lee M. (2000) Recent Advances in E-negotiation agents. In: Proc. in Advances in Infrastructure for Electronic Business, Science and Education on the Internet SSGRR'00, Italy, pp. 31–40

Alligood K.T., Sauer T.D., Yorke J.A. (2000) Chaos: An introduction to dynamical systems. Springer

Alonso E., Kudenko D., Kazakov D. (eds.) (2003) Adaptive agents and multi-agent systems: adaptation and multi-agent learning. Springer

Anderson J.A. (1972) A simple neural network generating interactive memory. Mathematical Biosciences 14:197–220

Andreoli J.M., Pacull F., Pareshi R. (1997) XPect: a framework for electronic commerce. IEEE Internet Computing 1(4):40–48

Audi R. (1998) Epistemology: a contemporary introduction to the theory of knowledge. Routledge

Azarbayejani A., Starner T., Horowitz B., Pentland A. (1992) Visually controlled graphs. Technical Report No. 180, MIT Media Lab., Vision Modeling Group

Ballard D.H. (1981) Generalizing the Hough transform to detect arbitrary shapes. Pattern Recognition 13:111–122

Baron R.J. (1981) Mechanisms of human facial recognition. Int. J. Man Machine Studies 15:137–178

Barry A.M.S. (1997) Visual intelligence: perception, image, and manipulation in visual communication. Albany, State University of New York Press

Basar E. (1998) Brain function and oscillations II: Integrative brain function, Neurophysiology and cognitive processes. Springer

Baumann J. (2000) Mobile agents: control algorithms. Springer

Beck J. (1966) Effect of orientation and of shape similarity on perceptual grouping, perception and psychophysics 1:300–302

Berger T.W., Chauvet G., Sclabassi R.J. (1994) A biologically based model of functional properties of the hippocampus. Neural Networks 7(6/7):1031–1064

Berkeley G. (1710) A treatise concerning the principles of human knowledge. Reprinted in 1971. Scolar Press

Bibitchkov D., Herrmann J.M., Geisel T. (2002) Effects of short-time plasticity on the associative memory. Neurocomputing 44–46:329–335

Bigus J.P. (2001) Constructing intelligent agents using Java. Wiley

Binet A., Simon T. (1916) The development of intelligence in children. Williams and Wilkins, Baltimore

Black F. (1982) The trouble with econometric models. Financial Analysis J., March/April:1361–1374

Black M. (1937) Vagueness: an exercise in logical analysis. Philosophy of Science 4:427–455

Bober M., Price W., Atkinson J. (2000) The contour shape descriptor for MPEG-7 and its applications. In: Proc. Int. Conf. Consumer Electronics 2000, pp. 286–287

Boden M.A. (ed.) (1990) The philosophy of artificial intelligence. Oxford University Press

Bolles R.C., Horaud P. (1986) 3DPO: a three-dimensional part orientation system. Int. J. Rob. Res. 5(3):3–26

Brenner W., Zarnekow R., Wittig H. (eds.) (1998) Intelligent software agents: foundations and applications. Springer

Buchanan B.G., Shortliff E.H. (eds.) (1984) Rule-based expert systems: the MYCIN experiments of the Stanford heuristic programming project. Addison-Wesley

Burrell P.R., Folarin B.O. (1997) The impact of neural networks in finance. Neural Computing and Applications 6(1):193–200

Caldwell R.B. (1995) Performance metrics for neural network-based trading system development. NeuroVest J. 3(2):22–26

Caldwell J.G. (2001) Conflict, negotiation, and general-sum game theory. Vista Research Corporation

Campbell S., Wang D. (1996) Synchronization and desynchronization in a network of locally coupled Wilson-Cowan oscillators. IEEE Trans. Neural Networks 7(3):541–554

Cassam Q. (ed.) (1994) Self-knowledge. Oxford University Press

Chakravarthy S.V., Ghosh J. (1996) A complex-valued associative memory for storing patterns as oscillatory states. Biological Cybernetics 75:229–238

Chan H.C.B., Lee R.S.T., Dillion T.S., Chang E. (2001) E-commerce: fundamentals and applications. Wiley

Chang T., Kuo C.J. (1993) Texture analysis and classification with tree-structural wavelet transform. IEEE Trans. Image Processing 2(4):429–441

Chavez A., Maes P. (1996) Kabash: an agent marketplace for buying and selling goods. In: Proc. 1st Int. Conf. Practical Application on Intelligent Agents and Multi-agent Technology, London, UK, pp. 196–203

Chen L., Aihara K. (1997) Chaos and asymptotical stability in discrete-time neural networks. Physica D 104:286–325

Chen L., Aihara K. (1995) Chaotic stimulated annealing by a neural model with transient chaos. Neural Networks 8(6):915–930

Chen K., Wang D. (2002) A dynamically coupled neural oscillator network for image segmentation. Neural Networks 15:423–439

Cheng A.C.C., Guan L. (1998) A combined evolution method for associative memory networks. Neural Networks 11:785–792

Chey J., Lee J., Kim Y.S., Kwon S.M., Shin Y.M. (2002) Spatial working memory span, delayed response and executive function in schizophrenia. Psychiatry Research 110:259–271

Chin H.T. (1990) The authoritative guide to contemporary investment theories. HK Week, April:56–63

Chow T.W., Cho S.Y. (1993) Development of a recurrent sigma-pi neural network rainfall forecasting system in Hong Kong. Neural Computation and Applications 5:66–75

Chung C.C., Kumar V.R. (1993) Knowledge acquisition using a neural network for a weather forecasting knowledge-based system. Neural Computing and Applications 1:215–223

Connor T., Robb D. (eds.) (2003) Philosophy of mind: contemporary readings. Routledge

Cootes T., Taylor C., Lanitis A., Graham J. (1995) Active shape models: their training and application. Computer Vision and Image Understanding 61(1):38–59

Cronholm B. (1951) Phantom limbs in amputees. Acta Psychiatrica Neurol. Scand. 72: 1–310

Cuomo K.M., Oppenheim A.V., Strongatz S.H. (1993) Synchronization of Lorenz-based chaotic circuits with applications to communications. IEEE Trans. Circuits and Systems II: Analog and Digital Signal Processing 40(10):626–633

Descartes R. (1968) Discourse on method and the meditations. Penguin Books, Harmondsworth

Descartes R. (1998) Meditations and other metaphysical writing. Clarke D.M. (transl.). Penguin Books

Devlin K. (1997) Goodbye Descartes: the end of logic and the search for a new cosmology of the mind. Wiley

Doren C. (1991) A history of knowledge: past, present and future, Ballantine Books

Ehrenfels C. (1890) Über Gestaltqualitaten. Vierteljährlicher fur Philosphie 14: 242–292

Elliman D., Rafael J., Pulido G. (2001) Automatic derivation of on-line document ontology. In: Proc. Int. Workshop on Mechanisms for Enterprise Integration: From Objects to Ontology, pp. 161–168

Enbutsu L., Baba K., Hara N. (1991) Fuzzy rule extraction from a multilayered neural network. In: Int. Joint Conf. Neural Networks (IJCNN 1991), Singapore, pp. 113–124

Engel A.K., Konig P., Kreiter A.K., Singer W. (1991) Synchronization of oscillatory neuronal response between striate and exstriate visual cortical areas of the cat. In: Proc. Nat. Acad. Sci. (USA) 88:6048–6052

Estes W.F. (1970) Learning theory and mental development. Academic Press, New York

Falcke M., Huerta R., Rabinovich M.I., Abarbanel H.D.I., Elson R.C., Selverston A.I. (2000) Modeling observed chaotic oscillators in bursting neurons: the role of calcium dynamics and IP3. Biological Cybernetics 82:517–527

Fausett L. (1994) Fundamentals of neural networks: architectures, algorithms and applications. Prentice Hall

Ferber J. (1999) Multi-agent systems: an introduction to distributed artificial intelligence. Addison-Wesley

Fogelin R.J. (2001) Berkeley and the principles of human knowledge. Routledge

Freeman W.J. (1978) Spatial properties of an EEG event in the olfactory bulb and cortex. Electroencephalogr. Clin. Neurophysiol. 44(5):586–605

Freeman W.J. (1979) Nonlinear dynamics of paleocortex manifested in the olfactory EEG. Biological Cybernetics 35:1177–1179

Freeman W.J. (1987) Simulation of chaotic EEG patterns with a dynamic model of the olfactory system. Biological Cybernetics 56:139–150

Freeman W.J. (1992) Tutorial on neurobiology: from single neurons to brain chaos. Int. J. Bifurcation and Chaos 2:451–482

Freeman W.J. (2000) A proposed name for aperiodic brain activity: stochastic chaos. Neural Networks 13:11–13

Freeman W.J. (2001) How brains make up their minds. Columbia University Press, New York

Freud S. (2001) The complete psychological works of Sigmund Freud (24 Volume set), Random House

Fukai H., Doi S., Nomura T., Sato S. (2000) Hopf bifurcations in multiple-parameter space of the Hodgkin-Huxley equations. I: Global organization of bistable periodic solutions. Biological Cybernetics 82:215–222

Fukai H., Nomura T., Doi S., Sato S. (2000) Hopf bifurcations in multiple-parameter space of the Hodgkin-Huxley equation. II: Singularity theoretic approach and highly degenerate bifurcations. Biological Cybernetics 82:223–229

Fuller R.J., Farrell J.L. (1987) Modern investment and security analysis. McGraw-Hill

Funabashi M., Maeda A., Morooka Y., Mori K. (1995) AI in Japan: fuzzy and neural hybrid expert systems: synergetic AI. IEEE Expert 10(4):32–40

Furukawa K., Michie D., Muggleton S. (eds.) (1999) Intelligent agents: machine intelligence. Oxford University Press

Gardner H. (1983) Frame of mind: the theory of multiple intelligence. Fontana Press

Gardner H. (1987) The mind's new science: a history of the cognitive revolution. Basic Books

Gardner H. (1993) Multiple intelligence: the theory in practice. Basic Books

Gardner S. (1999) Kant and the critique of pure reason. Routledge

Genesereth M.R., Nilsson N.J. (1987) Logical foundation of artificial intelligence. Morgan Kaufmann

Glushko R.J., Tenenbaum J.M., Meltzer B. (1999) An XML framework for agent-based e-commerce. Comm. ACM 42(3):106–114

Gordon I.E. (1997) Theories of visual perception. Wiley

Gottfredson L.S. (1997) Mainstream science on intelligence: an editorial with 52 signatures, history, and bibliography. Intelligence 24:13–23

Gray C.M., Konig P., Engel A.K., Singer W. (1989) Oscillatory responses in cat visual cortex exhibit intercolumnar synchronization which reflects global stimulus properties. Nature 338:334–337

Groen F.C., Kate T., Smeulders T., Young K. (1989) Human chromosome classification based on local band descriptors. Pattern Recognition Letters 9(9):211–222

Grossmann R. (1992) The existence of the world: an introduction to ontology. Routledge

Gruber T.R. (1995) Toward principles for the design of ontologies used for knowledge sharing. Int. J. Human-Computer Studies 43:907–928

Guarino N. (1995) Formal ontology, conceptual analysis and knowledge representation. Int. J. Human-Computer Studies 43:625–640

Guarino N. (1997) Understanding, building and using ontologies. Int. J. Human-Computer Studies 46:293–310

Guarino N. (1998) Formal ontology in information systems. In: Guarino N. (ed.) Formal ontology in information systems. Proc. FOIS 1998, Trento, Italy. IOS Press, Amsterdam, pp. 3–15

Guarino N., Welty C. (2000) A formal ontology of properties. In: Knowledge engineering and knowledge management, methods, models and tools. Dieng R., Corby O. (eds.). Springer, pp. 97–112

Guarino N., Masolo C., Vetere G. (1999) OntoSeek: content-based access to the Web. IEEE Intelligent Systems 14(3):70–80

Guttman R.H., Maes P. (1998) Agent-mediated integrative negotiation for retail electronic commerce. In: Proc. Workshop Agent Mediated Electronic Trading. Minneapolis, MN, USA, April 9, pp. 70–90

Haken H. (1996) Principles of brain functioning: a synergetic approach to brain activity, behavior and cognition. Springer

Heisenberg W. (1999) Physics and philosophy: the revolution in modern science. Prometheus Books

Hodgkin A.L., Huxley A.F. (1952) A quantitative description of membrane current and its application to conduction and excitation in the nerve. J. Physiol. (London) 117:500–544

Hopfield J.J. (1982) Neural networks and physical systems with emergent collective computation ability. In: Proc. Nat. Acad. Sci. 79:2554–2558

Hopfield J.J. (1984) Neurons with graded response have collective computational properties like those of two-state neurons. In: Proc. Nat. Acad. Sci. 81:3088–3092

Hoshino O., Zheng M., Kuroiwa K. (2003) Roles of dynamic linkage of stable attractors across cortical networks in recalling long-term memory. Biological Cybernetics 88(3):163–176

Hossain I., Liu I., Lee R. (1999) A study of multilingual speech feature: perspective scalogram based on wavelet analysis. In: Proc. IEEE Int. Conf. Systems, Man, and Cybernetics (SMC 1999), Vol. II, Tokyo, Japan, pp. 178–183

Hotho A., Madche A., Staab A. (2001) Ontology-based text clustering. In: Proc. Workshop Text Learning: Beyond Supervision, pp. 261–267

Huerta R., Varona P., Rabinovich M.I., Abarbanel H.D.I. (2001) Topology selection by chaotic neurons of a pyloric central pattern generator. Biological Cybernetics 84:L1–L8

Hume D. (1975) An enquiry concerning human understanding. Selby-Bigge L.A. (ed.). Oxford University Press

Hunter J. (2003) Enhancing the semantic interoperability of multimedia through a core ontology. IEEE Trans. Circuits and Systems for Video Technology 13(1):49–58

Hwang K., Lee K., Cho C.H. (2001) Intelligent shopping mall agent based on user's preference. In: Proc. IEEE Int. Symp. on Industrial Electronics 3:1762–1765

Ishii S., Fukumizu K., Watanabe S. (1996) A network of chaotic elements for information processing. Neural Networks 9(1):25–40

Ishikawa M. (1996) Structural learning with forgetting. Neural Networks 9(3):509–521

Jain L.C., Chen Z., Ichalkaranje N. (eds.) (2002) Intelligent agents and their applications. Springer

Jakimoski G., Kocarev L. (2001) Chaos and cryptography: block encryption ciphers based on chaotic maps. IEEE Trans. Circuits and Systems. I: Fundamental Theory and Applications 48(2):163–169

Jang J.S., Sun C.T., Mizutani E. (1997) Neuro-fuzzy soft computing: a computational approach to learning and machine intelligence. Prentice Hall

Janikow C.Z. (1994) Learning fuzzy controllers by genetic algorithms. In: Proc. 1994 ACM Symp. on Applied Computing. ACM Press, New York, pp. 181–194

Jenkins W.M., Merzenich M.M., Recanzone G. (1990) Neocortical representational dynamics in adult primates: implications for neuropsychology. Neuropsychologia 28:573–584

Jensen T.S., Rasmussen P. (1989) Phantom pain and related phenomena after amputation. In: Wall P.D. and Melzack R. (eds.), Textbook of pain. Churchill Livingstone, Edinburgh

Jeong J., Joung M.K., Kim S.Y. (1998) Quantification of emotion by nonlinear analysis of the chaotic dynamics of electroencephalograms during perception of 1/f music. Biological Cybernetics 78:217–225

John G.H., Miller P. (1996) Stock selection using rule induction. IEEE Expert 11(5):52–58

Johnson N.F. (2003) Financial market complexity. Oxford University Press

Jun W.K., Weistroffer H.R., Redmond R.T. (1993) Expert systems for bond rating: a comparative analysis of statistical, rule-based and neural network system. Expert Systems 10(3):167–171

Kamijo K., Tanigawa T. (1990) Stock price pattern recognition: a recurrent neural network approach. In: Proc. IJCNN 1990, pp. 215–221

Kanizsa G. (1979) Organization in vision: essays on gestalt perception. Praeger Publishing

Kant I. (1934) Critique of pure reason – a revised and expanded translation based on Meiklejohn. Politis V. (ed.). Everyman's Library

Kapitaniak T. (2000) Chaos for engineers: theory, applications, and control. Springer

Karlholm J.M. (1993) Associative memories with short-range, higher order couplings. Neural Networks 6:409–421

Kass M., Witkin A., Terzopoulos D. (1987) Snakes: active contour models. In: Proc. Int. Conf. Computer Vision, pp. 259–268

Kass M., Witkin A. (1988) Snakes: active contour models. Int. J. Computer Vision 2:321–331

Katayama R., Kajitani Y., Kuwata K., Nishida Y. (1993) Developing tools and methods for applications incorporating neuro, fuzzy and chaos technology. Computers and Industrial Engineering 24(4):579–592

Kaufman P. (1990) The new commodity trading systems and methods. Wiley

Keller P.E., McMakin D.L., Sheen D.M., McKinnon A.D., Summet J.W. (2000) Privacy algorithm for cylindrical holographic weapons surveillance system. IEEE Aerospace and Electronics Systems Magazine 15(2):17–24

Kim D.W., Lee K.H. (2001) A new fuzzy information retrieval system based on user preference model. In: Proc. 10th IEEE Int. Conf. Fuzzy Systems, pp. 127–130

Kingsley P. (1996) Ancient philosophy, mystery, and magic: Empedocles and Pythagorean tradition. Oxford University Press

Kohonen T. (ed.) (1988) Self-organization and associative memory. Springer

Kohonen T. (1972) Correlation matrix memories. IEEE Trans. Computers C-21:353–359

Kohler W. (1947) Gestalt psychology. Mentor Books

Kosko B. (1992) Neural networks and fuzzy systems: a dynamical systems approach to machine intelligence. Prentice Hall

Kosko B. (1993) Fuzzy thinking: the new science of fuzzy logic. Hyperion, New York

Kowalczyk R. (2000) On negotiation as a distributed fuzzy constraint satisfaction problem. In: Proc. 3rd Int. Symposium on Soft Computing for Industry of the World Automation Congress 2000, pp. 631–637

Krishnamurti J. (1973) The awakening of intelligence. HarperCollins

Kruger N. (1997) An algorithm for the learning of weights in discrimination functions using a priori constraints. IEEE Trans. Pattern Analysis and Machine Intelligence 19(7):764–768

Kulkarni A.D. (2002) Computer vision and fuzzy-neural systems. Prentice Hall

Lambridis H. (1976) Empedocles: a philosophical investigation. University of Alabama Press

Lange D.B., Oshima M. (1998) Programming and deploying Java mobile agents with aglets. Addison-Wesley

Lanitis A., Taylor C.J., Cootes T.F. (1997) Automatic interpretation and coding of face images using flexible models. IEEE Trans. Pattern Analysis and Machine Intelligence 19(7):743–756

Lee R.S.T. (2002) Elastic face recognizer: invariant face recognition based on elastic graph matching model. Int. J. Pattern Recognition and Artificial Intelligence (IJPRAI) 16(4):463–479

Lee R.S.T. (2003) iJADE Surveillant – an intelligent multi-resolution composite neuro-oscillatory agent-based surveillance system. Pattern Recognition 36:1425–1444

Lee R.S.T. (2004a) Artificial intelligence and the philosophy of human intelligence. Submitted to Int. J. Philosophy

Lee R.S.T. (2004b) Unification theory of senses and experience. Submitted to Psychological Review

Lee R.S.T. (2004c) A transient-chaotic auto-associative network (TCAN) based on Lee-oscillators. IEEE Trans. Neural Networks 15(5):1228–1243

Lee R.S.T. (2004d) Cognitron: a new interpretation of ontology framework based on chaotic neural oscillatory theory. Submitted to IEEE Knowledge and Data Engineering

Lee R.S.T., Liu J.N.K. (1999) An oscillatory elastic graph matching model for recognition of offline handwritten Chinese characters. In: Proc. 3rd Int. Conf.

Knowledge-Based Intelligent Information Engineering Systems (KES 1999), Adelaide, Australia, pp. 284–287

Lee R.S.T., Liu J.N.K. (2000a) Tropical cyclone identification and tracking system using integrated neural oscillatory elastic graph matching and hybrid RBF network track mining techniques. IEEE Trans. Neural Networks 11(3): 680–689

Lee R.S.T., Liu J.N.K. (2000b) FAgent – an innovative e-shopping authentication scheme using invariant intelligent face recognition agent. In: Proc. Int. Conf. Electronic Commerce (ICEC 2000), Seoul, Korea, pp. 47–53

Lee R.S.T., Liu J.N.K. (2000c) Fuzzy Shopper – a fuzzy network based shopping agent in e-commerce environment. In: Proc. Int. ICSC Symp. on Multi-agents and Mobile Agents in Virtual Organizations and E-Commerce (MAMA 2000), December 11–13, Wollongong, Australia

Lee R.S.T., Liu J.N.K. (2000d) Teaching and learning the AI modeling. In: Innovative teaching tools: knowledge-based paradigms. Studies in Fuzziness and Soft Computing, Vol. 36. Springer, Physica-Verlag, pp. 31–86

Lee R.S.T., Liu J.N.K. (2001a) NORN Predictor – stock prediction using a neural oscillatory-based recurrent network. Int. J. Computational Intelligence and Applications 1(4):439–451

Lee R.S.T., Liu J.N.K. (2001b) iJADE Stock Advisor – a new era of e-finance using an intelligent agent-based time series stock prediction model. In: Proc. Int. Conf. Artificial Intelligence (ICAI 2001), Las Vegas, NV, USA, pp. 43–46

Lee R.S.T., Liu J.N.K. (2002) Scene analysis using an integrated composite neural oscillatory elastic graph matching model. Pattern Recognition 35:1835–1846

Lee R.S.T., Liu J.N.K. (2003) Invariant object recognition based on elastic graph matching: theory and applications. IOS Press

Lee R.S.T., Liu J.N.K. (2004) iJADE Web-miner: an intelligent agent framework for Internet shopping. IEEE Trans. Knowledge and Data Engineering 16(4):461–473

Lee R.S.T., Liu J.N.K., You J. (1999) Face recognition: elastic relation encoding and structural matching. In Proc. IEEE Int. Conf. Systems, Man, and Cybernetics (SMC 1999), Tokyo, Japan, Vol. II, pp. 172–177

Lee R.S.T., Liu J.N.K., You J. (2001) iJADE WeatherMAN – a multiagent fuzzy-neuro network based weather prediction system. In: Intelligent Agent Technology: Research and Development, World Scientific, pp. 424–433

Lehnertz K., Arnhold J., Grassberger P., Elger C.E. (eds.) Chaos in brains. World Scientific

Leibniz G.W.F. (1982) New essays on human understanding. Remnant P., Bennett J. (transl.). Cambridge University Press

Lighthill J. (1972) A report on artificial intelligence. Science Research Council

Liou C.Y., Yuan S.K. (1999) Error tolerant associative memory. Biological Cybernetics 81:331–342

Li B., Liu J., Dai H. (1998) Forecasting from low quality data with applications in weather forecasting. Int. J. Computing and Informatics 22(3):351–358

Li H. (2002) A new category of business negotiation primitives for bilateral negotiation agents and associated algorithm to find Pareto optimal solutions. In:

Proc. 4th IEEE Int. Workshop on Advanced Issues of E-Commerce and Web-Based Information Systems 2002 (WECWIS 2002), pp. 103–109

Liu J.N.K. (1998) Computational aspects of a fine-mesh sea breeze model. M. Phil. Dissertation, Department of Mathematics, Murdoch University, Western Australia

Liu N.K., Lee K.K. (1997) An intelligent business advisor system for stock investment. Expert Systems 14(3):129–139

Liu J.N.K., Sin K.Y. (1997) Fuzzy neural networks for machine maintenance in mass transit railway system. IEEE Trans. Neural Networks 8(4):932–941

Liu J.N.K., Tang T.I. (1996) An intelligent system for financial market prediction. In: Proc. 2nd South China Int. Business Symp., Macau, pp. 199–209

Liu J., Wong L. (1996) A case study for Hong Kong weather forecasting. In: Proc. Int. Conf. Neural Information Processing, 1996, Hong Kong, pp. 787–792

Locke J. (1959) An essay concerning human understanding. Fraser A.C. (ed.). Dover Books, New York

Lopez M.F., Gomez-Perez A., Sierra J.P. (1999) Building a chemical ontology using methontology and the ontology design environment. IEEE Intelligent Systems 14(1):37–46

Lorenz E.N. (1963) Deterministic non-periodic flow. J. Atmospheric Science 20:130–141

Lorente L., Torres L. (1999) Face recognition of video sequences in a MPEG-7 context using a global eigen approach. In: Proc. Int. Conf. Image Processing (ICIP 1999), Vol. 4, pp. 187–191

Lowe E. (2000) An introduction to the philosophy of mind. Cambridge University Press

Luger G.F., Stubblefield W.A. (1993) Artificial intelligence: structures and strategies for complex problem solving. Addison-Wesley

Lui C.Y. (1990) Comprehensive explanation to financial investment graphics. Ming Cheung Publishers

Ma I., Aimeur E. (2001) Intelligent agent in electronic commerce – XMLFinder. In: Proc. 10th IEEE Int. Workshops on Enabling Technologies: Infrastructure for Collaborative Enterprises, 2001, pp. 273–278

Maass W., Markram H. (2002) Synapses as dynamic memory buffers. Neural Networks 15:155–161

Maedche A., Staab S. (2001) Ontology learning for semantic web. IEEE Intelligent Systems 16(2):72–79

Mandelbrot B.B. (1982) The fractal geometry of nature. Freeman, New York

Mandelbrot B.B. (1997) Fractals and scaling in finance: discontinuity, concentration, risk. Springer

Mann S. (2000) Programming applications with the wireless application protocol. Wiley

Malsburg C. (1981) The correlation theory of brain function. Technical Report 81-2, Max Planck Institute for Biophysical Chemistry, Göttingen, Germany

Malsburg C. (1985) Nervous structures with dynamical links. Berichte der Bunsengesellschaft for Physical Chemistry 89:703–710

Malsburg C., Buhmann J. (1992) Sensory segmentation with coupled neural oscillator. Biological Cybernetics 67:233–246

Manjunath B.S., Shekhar C., Chellappa R., Malsburg C. (1992) A robust method for detecting image features with application to face recognition and motion correspondence. In: Proc. Int. Conf. Pattern Recognition, pp. 208–212

McCorduck P. (1979) Machines who think. W.H. Freeman, San Francisco

McCulloch W.S., Pitts W. (1943) A logical calculus of the ideas immanent in nervous activity. Bulletin of Mathematical Biophysics 5:115–133

McGregor J.L., Walsh K.J., Katzfey J.J. (1993) Climate simulations for Tasmania. In: Proc. 4th Int. Conf. Southern Hemisphere Meteorological and Oceanography, American Meteorological Society, pp. 514–515

McKeon R. (ed.) (1929) Selections from medieval philosophers. Vol. 1. Charles Scribner's Sons, New York

McLaughlin R.A. (1997) Randomized Hough transform: improved ellipse detection with comparison. Tech. Report TR97-01, Dept. of Electrical and Electronic Eng., University of Western Australia, Nedlands, Australia

McInerney P.K. (1990) Introduction to philosophy. HarperCollins

Menon V., Freeman W.J., Cutillo B.A., Desmond J.E., Ward M.F., Bressler S.L., Laxer K.D., Barbaro N., Gevins A.S. (1996) Spatio-temporal correlations in human gamma band electrocorticograms. Electroencephalography and Clinical Neurophysiology 98:89–102

Merzenich M.M., Recanzone G., Jenkins W.M., Allard T.T., Nudo R.T. (1988) Cortical representational plasticity. In: Rakic P., Singer W. (eds.) Neurobiology of Neocortex. Wiley, pp. 41–67

Merzenich M.M., Sameshima K. (1993) Cortical plasticity and memory. Current Opinion in Neurology 3:187–196

Michalewicz Z., Fogel D.B. (2000) How to solve it: modern heuristics. Springer

Minai A.A., Anand T. (1998) Stimulus-induced bifurcations in discrete-time neural oscillators. Biological Cybernetics 79:87–96

Minsky M. (1975) A framework for representing knowledge. In: Winston P.H. (ed.) The psychology of computer vision. McGraw-Hill

Minsky M. (1979) The society theory. In: Winston P.H., Brown R.H. (eds.) Artificial intelligence: an MIT perspective. MIT Press, Cambridge, pp. 423–450

Minsky M., Papert S. (1969) Perceptions. Anderson J.A., Rosenfeld E. (eds.) Neurocomputing. MIT Press, Cambridge, pp. 157–169

Mizoguchi R., Sano T., Kitamura Y. (1999) An ontology-based human friendly message generation in a multiagent human media system for oil refinery plant operation. In: Proc. IEEE Int. Conf. Systems, Man and Cybernetics (SMC 1999), pp. 648–653

Moon F.C. (1992) Chaotic and fractal dynamics: an introduction for applied scientists and engineers. Wiley

Morita M. (1993) Associative memory with nonmonotone dynamics. Neural Networks 6:115–126

Moss K. (1999) Java servlets. McGraw-Hill

Munakata T. (1998) Fundamentals of the new artificial intelligence: beyond traditional paradigms. Springer

Murch R., Johnson T. (1998) Intelligent software agents. Prentice Hall

Murphy J.J. (1986) Technical analysis of the future markets. The New York Institute of Finance, Prentice Hall, New York

Murray D.W., Buxton B.F. (1987) Scene segmentation from visual motion using global optimization. IEEE Trans. Pattern Analysis and Machine Intelligence 9(2):220–228

Nack F., Lindsay A.T. (1999a) Everything you wanted to know about MPEG-7. Part 1. IEEE Multimedia 6(3):65–77

Nack F., Lindsay A.T. (1999b) Everything you wanted to know about MPEG-7. Part 2. IEEE Multimedia 6(4):64–73

Nakanishi H., Turksen I.B., Sugeno M. (1993) A review and comparison of six reasoning methods. Fuzzy Sets and Systems 57(3):257–294

Nguyen S.H. (1999) Efficient SQL-querying method for data mining in large databases. In: Proc. IJCAI 1999, pp. 281–292

Omicini A., Zambonelli F., Klusch M., Tolksdorf R. (2001) Coordination of Internet agents: models, technologies, and applications. Springer

Park J.Y., Han I.G. (1995) Predict Korea composite stock price index movement using artificial neural network. J. Expert Systems 1(2):103–121

Parks R.W., Levine D.S., Long D.L. (eds.) (1998) Fundamentals of neural network modeling: neuropsychology and cognitive neuroscience. MIT Press

Pal S.K., Wong P.P. (1996) Genetic algorithms for pattern recognition. CRC Press

Parodi G., Ridella S., Zunino R. (1993) Using chaos to generate keys for associative noise-like coding memories. Neural Networks 6:559–572

Patterson D.W. (1996) Artificial neural networks: theory and applications. Prentice Hall

Peim P., Franconi E., Paton N.W., Goble C.A. (2002) Query processing with description logic ontologies over object-wrapped database. In: Proc. 14th Int. Conf. Scientific and Statistical Database Management, pp. 27–36

Pentland A.P. (1990) Automatic extraction of deformable part models. Int. J. Computer Vision 4:107–126

Peters E.E. (1994) Fractal market analysis: applying chaos theory to investment and economics. Wiley

Piaget J. (1950) The psychology of intelligence. Taylor & Francis

Powley C., Benjamin D., Grossman D., Brodersohn E., Fadia R., Neches R., Will P., Zhu Q. (1997) DASHER: A prototype for federated e-commerce services. IEEE Internet Computing 1(6):62–71

Poznanski R.R. (ed.) (2001) Biophysical neural networks: foundations of integrative neuroscience. Mary Ann Liebert

Plato (1987) Theaetetus. Penguin Books

Plato (1999) Phaedo. Gallop D. (ed.). Oxford University Press

Plato (2003) Plato's Theory of Knowledge (transl. with commentary by Cornford F.M.). Dover Publications

Plummer T. (1993) Forecasting financial markets. Kogan Page

Pring M.J. (1985) Technical analysis explained, 2nd ed. McGraw-Hill

Prajnaparamita Hrdaya Sutra (Heart Sutra) (2000) (Translated from Sanskrit into English by Venerable Dharma Master Lok To). Sutra Translation Committee of the United States and Canada

Radeva P., Serrat J. (1993) Rubber snake: implementation on signed distance potential. In: Proc. Vision Conf. 1993, pp. 187–194

Randen T., Husoy J.H. (1999) Texture segmentation using filters with optimized energy separation. IEEE Trans. Image Processing 8(4):996–1010

Ratsch U., Richter M.M., Stamatescu I.O. (eds.) (1998) Intelligence and artificial intelligence: an interdisciplinary debate. Springer

Refenes A.N., Azema-Barac M., Chen L., Karoussos S.A. (1993) Currency exchange rate prediction and neural network design strategies. Neural Computing and Applications 1:46–58

Reisfeld D., Yeshurun Y. (1992) Robust detection of facial features by generalized symmetry. In: Proc. Int. Conf. Pattern Recognition. The Netherlands, The Hague, pp. 117–120

Restle F. (1979) Coding theory of the perception of motion configuration. Psychological Review 86:1–24

Richards J.A. (1986) Remote sensing digital image analysis. Springer

Ritchie J. (1996) Fundamental analysis: a back-to-the-basics investment guide to selecting quality stocks. Irwin Professional, Chicago

Rodriguez-Aguilar J.A. (1998) Toward a testbed for trading agents in electronic auction markets. AI Communication.: Euro. J. AI 11(1):5–19

Rothermel K., Popescu-Zeletin R. (eds.) (1997) Mobile agents: Proc. 1st Int. Workshop (MA 1997). Springer

Rowley H.A., Baluja S., Kanade T. (1998) Neural network-based face detection. IEEE Trans. Pattern Analysis and Machine Intelligence 20(1):23–38

Russell B. (1912) The problems of philosophy. Oxford University Press

Russell B. (1984) Theory of knowledge. George Allen & Unwin, London

Russell S., Norvig P. (2003) Artificial intelligence: a modern approach. Prentice Hall

Sacchi C.A., Regazzoni C.S. (2000) A distributed surveillance system for detection of abandoned objects in unmanned railway environments. IEEE Trans. Vehicular Technology 49(5):2013–2026

Sambhava P. and Thurman R.A. (transl.) (1994) The Tibetan book of death. Bantam Doubleday Dell

Sampaio E., Maris S., Bach-y-Rita P. (2001) Brain plasticity: visual acuity of blind persons via the tongue. Brain Research 908(2):204–7

Sartre J.-P. (1965) The philosophy of existentialism. Citadel Press

Schank R.C. (1972) Conceptual dependency: a theory of natural language understanding. Cognitive Psychology 3:552–631

Shen W. (2001) Multi-agent systems for concurrent intelligent design and manufacturing. Taylor & Francis

Shepard R.N. (1984) Ecological constraints on internal representation: resonant kinematics of perceiving, imaging, thinking, and dreaming. Psychological Review 91:417–447

Sim K.M., Choi C.Y. (2003) Agents that react to changing market situations. IEEE Trans. Systems, Man, and Cybernetics 33(2):188–201

Spitzer M. (1999) The mind within the net: models of learning, thinking and acting. MIT Press

Smith N., Tsimpli I.M. (1995) The mind of a savant: language, learning and modularity. Blackwell

Spearman C. (1923) The nature of intelligence and the principles of cognition. Macmillan

Srivasan A., King R., Muggleton S., Sternberg M. (1997) The predictive toxicology evaluation challenge. In: Proc. IJCAI 1997, pp. 4–9

Sternberg R.J. (1977) Intelligence, information processing, and analogical reasoning: the componential analysis of human abilities. Erlbaum

Sternberg R.J. (1985) Beyond IQ: a triarchic theory of human intelligence. Cambridge University Press

Sternberg R.J. (1990) Metaphors of mind: conceptions of the nature of intelligence. Cambridge University Press

Stevens R., Goble C., Horrocks I., Bechhofer S. (2002) Building a bioinformatics ontology using OIL. IEEE Trans. Information Technology in Biomedicine 6(2):135–141

Suetens P., Fua P., Hanson A.J. (1992) Computational strategies for object recognition. ACM Computing Surveys 24:5–61

Sung K.K., Poggio T. (1998) Example-based learning for view-based human face detection. IEEE Trans. Pattern Analysis and Machine Intelligence 20(1):39–51

Sutton R.S. (1983) Learning to predict by the methods of temporal difference. Machine Learning 3:8–44

Teuner A., Pichler O., Hosticka B.J. (1995) Unsupervised texture segmentation of image using tuned matched Gabor filters. IEEE Trans. Image Processing 4(6):863–870

Triesch J., Eckes C. (1998) Object recognition with multiple feature types. In: Proc. ICANN 1998, pp. 233–238

Triesch J., Malsburg C. (1996) Robotic gesture recognition. In: Proc. 2nd Conf. Automatic Face and Gesture Recognition 1996, pp. 170–175

Triesch J., Malsburg C. (2001) A system for person-independent hand posture recognition against complex backgrounds. IEEE Trans. Pattern Analysis and Machine Intelligence 23(12):1449–1453

Tsuda I. (1992) Dynamic link of memory: chaotic memory map in nonequilibrium neural networks. Neural Networks 5:313–326

Turban E., Lee J., King D., Chung H.M. (2000) Electronic commerce: a managerial perspective. Prentice Hall

Turing A. (1936) On computable numbers, with an application to the Entscheidungs-problem. In: Proc. London Mathematical Society, Series 2, 42:230–265

Unser M. (1995) Texture classification and segmentation using wavelet frame. IEEE Trans. Image Processing 4(11):1549–1560

Vajracchedika Prajnaparamita (Diamond Sutra) (2003) (Translated by William Gemmell). Ibis Press

Van Heijst G., Schreiber A.T., Wielinga B.J. (1997) Using explicit ontologies in KBS development. Int. J. Human-Computer Studies 46:183–292

Varona P., Torres J.J., Abarbanel H.D.I., Rabinovich M.I., Elson R.C. (2001). Dynamics of two electrically coupled chaotic neurons: experimental observations and model analysis. Biological Cybernetics 84:91–101

Vujosevic S. (2001) WAP integration: professional developer's guide. Wiley

Wagner C., Stuck J.W. (2002) Construction of an associative memory using unstable periodic orbits of a chaotic attractor. J. Theor. Biol. 215:375–384

Wang D.L., Terman D. (1997). Image segmentation based on oscillation correlation. Neural Computation 9:1623–1626

Wang D.L., Terman D. (1995) Locally excitatory globally inhibitory oscillator networks. IEEE Trans. Neural Networks 6:283–286

Wang X. (1992) Discrete-time neural networks as dynamical systems. Ph.D. Dissertation. University of Southern California

Wang X. (1991) Period-doublings to chaos in a simple neural network: an analytic proof. Complex Systems 5:425–441

Wechsler D. (1997) Manual for the Wechsler Adult Intelligence Scale-III. Psychological Corporation, New York

Weiss G. (2000) Multiagent systems: a modern approach to distributed artificial intelligence. MIT Press

Weldon T.P., Higgins W.E. (1996) Design of multiple Gabor filters for texture segmentation. In Proc. Int. Conf. Acoustic Speech Signal Processing, pp. 2243–2246

Wertheimer M. (1912) Experimental studies on the seeing of motion. Reprinted: Classics in Psychology, Shipley T. (ed.) (1961). Philosophical Library, New York

Widrow B., Smith F.W. (1963) Pattern-recognition control systems. In: Proc. Computer and Information Science Symposium, Spartan Books, Washington, DC, USA, pp. 163–172

Wilensky R. (1983) Planning and understanding: a computational approach to human reasoning. Addison-Wesley

Wilson H.R., Cowan J.D. (1972) Excitatory and inhibitory interactions in localized populations. Biophys. J. 12:1–24

Wilson R.A., Frank C.K. (eds.) (1999) The MIT encyclopedia of the cognitive sciences. MIT Press

Wiskott L., Fellous J.M., Kruger N., Malsburg C. (1997) Face recognition by elastic bunch graph matching. IEEE Trans. Pattern Analysis and Machine Intelligence 19(7):775–779

Wiskott L., Malsburg C. (1993) A neural system for the recognition of partially occluded objects in cluttered scenes. Int. J. Pattern Recognition and Artificial Intelligence 7(4):935–948

Wiskott L., Malsburg C. (1995) Recognizing faces by dynamic link matching. In: Proc. ICANN 1995, pp. 347–352

Wong F., Wang P.Z., Goh T.H. (1991) Fuzzy neural systems for decision making In: Proc. Int. Joint Conf. Neural Networks (IJCNN 1991), Singapore, pp. 216–222

Wong W.Y., Zhang D.M., Kara-Ali M. (2000) Negotiating with experience. In: Proc. AAAI Workshop Knowledge-Based Electronic Markets, Austin, pp. 85–90

Wood A.W. (2001) Basic writings of Kant. Modern Library

Wurman P., Wellman M., Walsh W. (1998) The Michigan Internet Auctionbot: a configurable auction server for human and software agents. In: Proc. 2nd Int. Conf. Autonomous Agents, Minneapolis, pp. 301–308

Yamaguchi Y., Shimizu H. (1994) Pattern recognition with figure-ground separation by generation of coherent oscillations. Neural Networks 7(1):49–63

Yan J., Ryan M., Power J. (1994) Using fuzzy logic. Prentice Hall

Yao Y., Freeman W.J. (1990) Model of biological pattern recognition with spatially chaotic dynamics. Neural Networks 3:153–170

Yoshizawa S., Morita M., Amari S. (1993) Capacity of associative memory using a nonmonotonic neuron model. Neural Networks 6:167–176

Yuille A.L. (1991) Deformable templates for face recognition. J. Cognitive Neuroscience 59–70

Yunfan G., Jianxue X., Wei R., Sanjue H., Fuzhou W. (1998) Determining the degree of chaos from analysis of ISI time series in the nervous system: a comparison between correlation dimension and nonlinear forecasting methods. Biological Cybernetics 78:159–165

Zadeh L.A. (1965) Fuzzy sets. Information and Control 8:338–353

Zhang X., Lesser V. (2002) Multi-linked negotiation in multi-agent system. In: Proc. 1st Int. Joint Conf. Autonomous Agents and Multi-agent Systems (AAMAS 2002), pp. 1207–1214

Zhong N., Liu J., Ohsuga S., Bradshaw J. (eds.) (2001) Intelligent agent technology: research and development. World Scientific

Zhou C.S., Chen T.L. (2000) Chaotic neural networks and chaotic annealing. Neurocomputing 30:293–300

Index

About the Author

Raymond S.T. Lee received his B.Sc. from Hong Kong University in 1989, in 1997 he received his M.Sc. from Hong Kong Polytechnic University, and in 2000 he was awarded his Ph.D. from that same institution.

Upon graduating from Hong Kong University, he joined the Hong Kong Government in the Hong Kong Observatory as a meteorological scientist (1989–1993) and took part in weather forecasting as well as the development of telecommunication systems for the provision of meteorological services. Between 1993 and 1998, he was employed as MIS Manager and Systems Consultant in various Hong Kong business organizations, primarily developing IS and e-commerce projects.

He now works as an Associate Professor in the Department of Computing of Hong Kong Polytechnic University.

His major research areas include artificial intelligence, ontology, intelligent e-commerce systems, intelligent agents, pattern recognition, weather simulation and forecasting, and chaotic neural networks. In 2002 he was privileged to be listed in the International Who's Who of Professional Educators.

Before publishing this book, Dr. Lee was the author of two other books, "E-Commerce: Fundamentals and Applications" published in 2001 by Wiley; and "Invariant Object Recognition Based on Elastic Graph Matching: Theory and Applications" published in 2003 by IOS Press, a comprehensive, research-oriented book which collected all the related recent research work on elastic graph dynamic link theory.

Dr. Lee has worked in the area of AI and intelligent agents for over 10 years, publishing over 70 works including books, journals, book chapters and conference papers. He was the founder of the iJADE Project dedicated to researching and developing a fully integrated intelligent Java agent-based platform and related iJADE agents. The latest developments in this include the R&D of the cognitive iJADE agents – so-called "Cogito iJADE" (iJADE ver. 3.0) – an ontologically based iJADE development environment which aims at the design and development of future cognitive agents (so-called "Cogito Agents") which are highly adaptive to environments, self-aware and truly autonomous in foreign platforms.

Springer Series in Agent Technology

M. Yokoo: **Distributed Constraint Satisfaction.** Foundations of Cooperation in Multi-agent Systems. XVII, 143 pp. 2001

M. d'Inverno, M. Luck: **Understanding Agent Systems.** 2nd edition. XIX, 240 pp. 2001, 2004

S. Bussmann, N.R. Jennings, M. Wooldridge: **Multiagent Systems for Manufacturing Control.** A Design Methodology. XIV, 288 pp. 2004

R.S.T. Lee: **Fuzzy-Neuro Approach to Agent Applications.** XVIII, 376 pp. 2006

M. Mamei, F. Zambonelli: **Field-Based Coordination for Pervasive Multiagent Systems.** XII, 241 pp. 2006

Printing: Krips bv, Meppel
Binding: Stürtz, Würzburg